D0407918

Pg 204.
hiring
employees

pg 215
St. John's 4cc

282
PURDUE

306
stem
cell

The Bill Cook Story

The

BILL COOK *Story*

READY, FIRE, AIM!

Bob Hammel

Indiana University Press
Bloomington • Indianapolis

This book is a publication of

Indiana University Press
601 North Morton Street
Bloomington, IN 47404-3797 USA

http://iupress.indiana.edu

Telephone orders   800-842-6796
Fax orders   812-855-7931
Orders by e-mail   iuporder@indiana.edu

The paper used in this publication meets the minimum
requirements of American National Standard for
Information Science—Permanence of Paper for
Printed Library Materials, ANSI Z39.48-1984.

Manufactured in the United States of America

Library of Congress Cataloging-in-Publication Data

Hammel, Bob.
  The Bill Cook story : ready, fire, aim! / Bob Hammel.
    p. cm.
  Includes bibliographical references and index.
  ISBN 978-0-253-35254-5 (cloth : alk. paper) 1. Cook,
Bill, 1931–2. Billionaires—Middle West—Biography.
3. Businessmen—Middle West—Biography. I. Title.
  HC102.5.H347 2008
  338.092—dc22
  [B]
                                        2008014308

1 2 3 4 5   13 12 11 10 09 08

Following paintings by Keith Kline

To Bill and Gayle Cook

READY
FIRE
AIM!

Ready means preparation.

Get yourself ready to do something, then do it.

If you screw up, you go back and see what happened.

What I call "aim" is hindsight—you find out where you

screwed up, and you can correct it much easier.

A lot of people would rather sit and prepare.

They can prepare all their life.

Bill Cook

contents

preface

So there we were, talking across a desk, two guys averaging about two billion each in financial worth, discussing what we had done to keep ourselves as satisfied and happy as we had these last forty years of sharing the same small hometown—forty years when we knew *of* each other far better than we *knew* each other.

I spent those years writing about sports for a newspaper. He built a company. The next billion-dollar sportswriter will be the first. The financial worth in the room was, oh, maybe 99.9998 percent his.

To the man across the desk, I mentioned a close friend of mine who started on a sports-writing plane parallel with mine, then chose to rise in our profession in a way totally different from mine. He went into administration, ultimately became an editor and publisher, and made a whole lot more money than I did. I said that at times over the years when my friend and I had talked, I almost got the feeling that he envied *me*, because I had chosen to stay in the fun part of the profession—writing, covering things, writing, meeting people, writing.

Maybe I felt that way because in truth I more often caught myself feeling sorry for him than envying him, sorry for my profession, really. He was better than me—better than anyone I ever met in the newspaper business—at running a news staff, at "using" people. That's "using" as Tiger Woods "uses" a golf club, extracting the very best there is to bring out, without a bit of abuse. My friend could have been as good a working newspaper editor as there was out there, at any level, and there was nothing in the way of talent or judgment that should have kept him from doing it at the very highest level.

But he didn't stay solely with news management. He crossed over, in newsroom scorn, to include the business side, earning increasingly bigger paychecks with his ability to make increasingly bigger profits for his newspaper—while, it must be said, continuing to insist on excellent work from his writers and editors.

But still . . .

One night when my friend and I were discussing where fate had taken us within the same profession, I know my eyes were sending out a pained message of "How . . . *could* you?" If so, it was not so much in accusation of art profaned as in puzzlement, about how he could voluntarily make such a sacrifice: the inner satisfaction of a story or column well done in trade for money-making.

"The money part . . . it's a *game*," he said.

"Yeah," billionaire Bill Cook said, nodding, totally understanding my friend. "It's not the money that you work for. It's . . . when you have an idea, and it comes to fruition, and it works!

"One of the most recent examples for me is our Triple-A stent. That generates us millions of dollars a month. It is a large part of our sales. Not that I invented it, but it's the idea that I did the things necessary to make it all happen.

"That's where I get my enjoyment. I don't even look at the P&L. The only things I look at on the Profit and Loss report for this company are the sales total and how much we made as a result of those sales. I just got a quarterly report, and I spent a grand total of probably two minutes looking at it, looking at those two numbers.

"All I could say was, 'I'm satisfied. That's okay. That's good.'

"That's all that it meant, in the form of money, to me. They're just numbers that show you you're doing okay."

And competing.

And winning.

That's the refreshing thing that familiarity with Bill Cook brought to me. His is a personal world not nearly as foreign to me as I thought going in. Like the best of the people I covered who excelled in sports, he is above all else a competitor, and that's the quality he has most admired and most sought in building from scratch his worldwide company, his winning team—his frequent world champion in its vital field.

Bill is 77. He's had heart problems. He lost a kidney. He spent some time in early 2007 at Cleveland Clinic getting fine-tuned with his medications. He didn't come back talking of feeling better, or relieved, though each was true.

"I can't tell you what it's like to go up to Cleveland Clinic and see all those boxes of our products up there—$50,000 worth of product in one box, going to one patient. And there are literally hundreds of boxes up there.

Bill Cook holds a Triple-A stent.

"Those are the things that really bring excitement—several million dollars of *your* product, and it's going to be used quickly.

"That is *excitement*. It gave me goose bumps."

Yes, my pragmatic mind interrupted, and it's saving lives.

"That is a large part," he said. "That helps.

"But I think I would get a similar excitement if I were the developer of a new door lock and saw it in use. Recently I read an anecdote about the second-generation Kohler who's running that company now, Herbert Jr. He said one of his greatest excitements was when he saw a new toilet coming out on line—what a work of art it is, how much effort it took, and to have it coming out so nice-looking. . . . So he gets the same kick that I do! He's talking about a toilet as a work of art.

"To him, it really is. We take a toilet as a toilet, a functional device that we *have* to use. He was looking at the whiteness of the porcelain, and he was so proud that that thing was going to a customer who was going to say, 'I'll buy it.' I can identify with that.

"You see, Bob, in your field there is a certain proficiency you have to acquire before you can *do* any appreciating. In the case of Kohler and myself, we can look at a product, and it's tangible. There's nothing else you have to think about.

"In yours, there are rules of construction—did it all come out explaining what you wanted to get across? In the case of Kohler and Bill Cook, we can look at our toilets and our Triple-A stents, and we really get a kick out of it.

"And we don't have to read an article, either. It takes time to read an article.

"And you also have a realization that you are so perishable. The damned newspaper ends up in the trash or at the bottom of a birdcage."

True.

"And the excitement comes again the next day."

Also true.

Each of us came through it all happy. Each of us was blessed.

But there's a lot more of a story in what he did with his blessings and his opportunities—his "ideas" that, such a very high percentage of the time, worked.

A day in a life

KIDNAPPING

I t was big news, exciting news in town that October morning in 1988. Little Bloomington had its own man in the *Forbes Magazine* list of the 400 richest people in America.

Bloomington, Indiana, is a town of 70,000 with a hefty conceit quotient. Winston Churchill said of election rival Clement Attlee that he was "a modest man with much to be modest about." Bloomington people feel they have much to be cocky about.

In 1988 it was a Bloomington of eminence in basketball, surely. Just the year before, its Indiana University Hoosiers, under 1984 U.S. Olympic coach Bob Knight, had won the school's fifth NCAA championship. The city even had a claim to its favorite sport's greatest player extant. Knight had based that '84 Olympic team in Bloomington, which that summer made a several-weeks resident of Michael Jordan, who loved the delicious "smoothies" at Peterson's Deli, town lore bragged.

Bloomington boasted, too, about several features:

- **Music**—from classical (the world-renowned artists of string, brass, and voice on the faculty of Indiana University's nonpareil School of Music) to the rock of "Small Town" and "Pink Houses" John Mellencamp and the jazz of Jazz Hall of Famer David Baker, chairman and founder of the IU Jazz Studies Department, in this, the city where hometowner Hoagy Carmichael wrote and in the 1920s first plunked out "Stardust," the mellow masterpiece voted seventy years later America's song of the twentieth century. Consider that: No. 1, out of a blue million.

- **Education**—the town's most beloved citizen was retired IU president Herman B Wells, whose tolerance and academic freedom convictions gave his university, among many things, the celebrity and notoriety of sex-studies pioneer Alfred C. Kinsey, an enduring Bloomington symbol. Herman B (no period—unlike its bearer, the B didn't stand for anything) was in his eighties in 1988 but as papal, as infallible as ever in his adoring village.

- **Architecture**—for God's gift that ran under the Bloomington area and the blessed region to its immediate south: the beds of limestone whose extractions bedecked not just the loveliest university campus imaginable but also the Empire State Building, the National Cathedral in Washington, the Pentagon, and a long list of other handsome American landmarks. The elegant, durable stone is one thing; quite another, the artists who turned that hard limestone into legendary sculptures and distinctive building fronts. A lot of those artists of stone came right out of Bloomington and southern Indiana, and others came to that limestone center of the world to be part of a rare art.

But now in Bloomington, a rich guy, home-grown?

One of the 400 richest in America?

Now that *was* new in a town much more used to getting its attention from achievers and newsmakers on its east side, where Indiana University had dominion, than on its west side and Bloomington's industrial row.

Curry Pike was a north-south road that had to be spruced up considerably—widened and resurfaced—in the late 1950s and early 1960s when some of America's industrial giants chose spots along it (just outside the western limits of Bloomington's property-tax reach) to build and thrive: Westinghouse, RCA, Otis Elevator, General Electric. Bloomington cheered the arrival of each as communities, in a perpetual fret over where their city-sustaining employment will come from, always do.

When an unknown fellow named Bill Cook moved his unheard-of manufacturing operation into a small house right in among the giant factories, not a speech was made, not a balloon popped, not a ribbon snipped.

But just as the bloom of Bloomington was fading for many of the big guys, their factories shrinking toward shutdowns and pullouts, Cook Inc. in the 1980s was growing from that house to a sprawling campus-style major manufacturing operation, the reeling community's employment bulwark.

And in 1988, twenty-five years after he and wife Gayle had been their company's entire employee list for one full takeoff year, wow! Bill Cook was on the Forbes list!

Most Bloomington people who read about him in the newspapers that morning wouldn't have known Bill Cook if they had sat in a booth next to him at the popular, folksy Big Wheel restaurant—which they might have.

Cook's name had taken on some community familiarity by then, but not so much his face, nor his financial stature, nor the persona-less personality of the fellow who did sit in Big Wheel booths, not at all as a big wheel but wearing an open-necked shirt and cardigan sweater, in the smoking section because he followed one Kent with another—common as an old shoe, the few Hoosiers who did recognize him would have said.

Bill Cook: Horatio Alger of the 1980s. From nothing to the Forbes 400. What a day that must have been for him!

What a day, indeed, the day that introduced Bill Cook to the curse of success, the dark side of the American dream . . . to the price that goes with the prize when it is great wealth. And he recognized that immediately.

"I've never seen him madder," his friend Jim Mason said.

That morning, Arthur Curry was far outside the Bloomington *Herald-Telephone*'s circulation area. But all America is *USA Today*'s universe, and that newspaper always treats the Forbes list like Moses-from-Sinai stuff—huge splash, every one of the 400 identified as to source and estimated size of fortune, as well as age, hometown, and national—even global—ranking. Maybe nobody in America dwelled longer on that day's "news" than Curry, millionaire wannabe. Story is that he clipped a part of it out and retained it. Confirmation of that isn't definite, but he clearly retained the message.

Arthur Jackson Curry had grown up in Indianapolis, son of stockbroker William G. Curry, who was with Dean Witter when Arthur was a North Central High School student. Arthur was one of six children; one of his three brothers, William Jr., died when Arthur was a teenager. His grandmother, Margaret Weymouth Jackson, lived with her husband in Spencer, an hour down State Road 67 from Indianapolis and a half-hour's drive west from Bloomington. She won acclaim as a writer, authoring six novels and more than two hundred short stories for national magazines—more than fifty for the popular *Saturday Evening Post.* When the Bloomington newspaper ran a readers' poll in 1999 to select an Area Woman of the Century, Margaret Weymouth Jackson, though dead for twenty-five years by then, was still well enough known to be the runner-up.[1] Her daughter, Ann Jackson Curry, studied in seminaries in Indianapolis and Chicago and was considered a Bible scholar.[2] She died at 71 in 1994, seven years before her husband died at 81.[3] They had lived to celebrate their golden anniversary in 1992 and to see Arthur leave Indiana University with a degree in finance and economics in 1970—and later to see him take the luster off that golden anniversary and go on to make a mark like no one before him in his distinguished family.

On December 28, 1987, Curry and wife Kristine—a polished, fluent woman, wine columnist for the *Chicago Tribune*—stood on a podium at the landmark Park Place Hotel in the northern Michigan resort town of Traverse City. Their appearance was to announce their purchase of Park Place, just as a year earlier trumpets had blared announcing Curry's purchase of the similarly historic Perry Hotel at nearby Petoskey. The nobility of each hotel was considerable but fading. Media and town leaders came out that day at Traverse City to hear Curry promise a return to glory through restoration that would link the two hotel operations and mean economic revitalization for the summer-dependent communities.

In October 1988, financial wolves were beginning to bay around silver-tongued Art Curry. Rick Coates wrote much later in the Traverse City-based *Northern Express:*

> When Curry arrived in Northern Michigan his charisma and flamboyance convinced several local investors in both communities to join him. Using the bait of funds from the Chicago-based brokerage firm he was president of, he collectively raised a couple million dollars for both hotel projects.
>
> But as bills didn't get paid and restoration projects at both properties fell behind schedule, Curry became harder to find. He was busy buying an Upper Peninsula ski resort and purchasing a hotel and restaurant in Indiana.
>
> Eventually, his brokerage firm forced him out in January 1989 and he was relieved of his role as operating partner of the hotels.[4]

Jim Mason had an odd position in the Cook empire in 1988. He was the director of the Cook-underwritten Star of Indiana drum corps, and his office was not in the Cook Inc. headquarters but in a converted school building north of Bloomington on the property where the drum corps practiced.

"I was sitting at my desk, and he was coming back from the Indianapolis airport," Mason said. "Bill had just gotten the *Forbes Magazine* naming him to the 400. I'm the first person he sees after getting the magazine. He storms into my office, he hauls off and kicks my desk, slams the magazine down on the desk, and says, '*Look* at this! My whole life's going to change now. Every nut in the book is going to be after me now.' I've seen Bill furious, but that was a rage."

They called Bill Cook a visionary as he was creating his industrial giant from nothing. Visionaries see more than the rest of us, see beyond the obvious—opportunities, yes, but also the chilling, privacy-peeling pitfalls when the usually humorous line turns ominous: "Be careful what you wish for."

Damn Forbes.

"A Forbes reporter had called Bill several months before that issue came out," Gayle said. He was told the magazine's calculation system had put his net worth at $350 million—well into the top 400. "The reporter said, 'You're going to be listed.' Bill said, 'Hey, no, don't do that. Besides, I don't think that number is accurate. *We* don't even know what the right figure is. If you don't have accurate information, don't do it.' They said, 'Under our First Amendment rights, we can say anything we want to.'"

Inveterate researchist Gayle Cook went to work on the Forbes 400. "When Malcolm Forbes started that list, he did it to compete against the Fortune 500 (a listing of the 500 top companies in America, ranked by sales volume). Forbes wanted some other kind of list people would want to read about. I've heard that his staff said at the time, 'What about kidnapping?

You're exposing all those people.'" The list was published, and its annual update became the magazine's most attention-getting issue by far.

The October 1988 issue said that William A. Cook of Bloomington, Indiana, with his $350 million net worth, was the second-wealthiest person in Indiana. When Bill showed the magazine to Gayle, she recalls, "I first thought, 'Oh, my gosh.' Because no one had ever talked about us and money before." The immediate topic between the two, she said, was: "What if one of us is ever kidnapped? We decided, 'The other one calls the FBI.'" Immediately. Period. "No delay to consider other options. Do it. Because you hear all these TV dramas where people say, 'Don't tell the FBI. I'll handle it.' And it's always a disaster," she said. "That's all we said on that subject. Probably just a couple of sentences. And we never again said anything."

The two hotel purchases in northern Michigan were classic Arthur Curry, circa 1980s. He was dealing in big numbers in those years. In August 1987, he got twenty Chicago investors together in a limited partnership that paid $4.6 million for the 149-room Sheraton University Inn in West Lafayette, Indiana, the Wabash River town that is the site of Purdue University. Just across the Wabash in Lafayette, he and Kristine leased some space and opened a restaurant, Coyote Grill.

In 1987 he had left the Bear Stearns & Co., Inc., brokerage in Chicago to be chief executive of the smaller Singer & Co. brokerage there. By fall 1988, the time of the Forbes announcement, Singer & Co. was closed because of a lack of capital, and its other officials were suing Curry for $120,000.[5]

In December 1988, the Perry hotel went into bankruptcy after a Petoskey bank sued to foreclose on a $2.4 million mortgage. The Park Place in Traverse City also was in bankruptcy.

On February 10, 1989, Purdue University—in a dubious act of selectivity—brought in Arthur Curry (accompanied by Kristine) as a Krannert Executive Forum lecturer, and tapes distributed later showed he told his listening students:

> Risk is the poor man's equity. I've found risk to be one of the strongest components of my economic value.

And:

> The first key to risk is that you have to be willing to lose everything that you are doing. You have to be willing to say, 'I've lost it. It's gone.' If you can't take that risk, don't go in the business.

And:

> Who should be on your [business] team? You need a lawyer. This is absolutely fundamental. My attitude toward a lawyer is that I would never have a lawyer that I would invite to my house.

And:

> We have bought things with no money. We have bought things with commitments to pay half a million dollars, and we didn't have one penny to pay it. And the next three weeks I'm gonna have to scramble around and find half a million dollars.[6]

In Bloomington on March 2, 1989, one day short of three weeks after the lecture, Steve Ferguson was in his office at CFC, a division of Cook Group that he heads. Arthur Curry showed up uninvited.

Ferguson was temporarily occupied, so Curry sat down to wait. Ferguson's executive assistant, Sharon Rogers, remembers, "He did do some talking—nothing about Mr. Cook, I don't think, just about how he had gone to school here, that kind of thing. I remember he came around behind my desk and looked out a window." She was glad when Ferguson was free and Curry went into his office.

Ferguson said Curry told him of his hotel background and said he was interested in building one in Bloomington. Ferguson and CFC had been working to find someone willing to go in on a downtown hotel/convention center complex in Bloomington, so he made time to talk to Curry.

Not long into the conversation, Curry changed the topic from hotels to Bill Cook. "He said he wanted to meet Bill. He said, 'I assume he lives in a big house.' I began to feel uneasy."

Curry soon left, but not without making an impression. "Sharon is very good at assessing people," Ferguson said. "After he had left, she told me, 'That guy is a real jerk.' I'd never heard her say that about anyone."

Six days later, Pizza Express deliveryman Russell Hornback, an Indiana University student, returned to the store from a delivery run at around 8 PM, went inside for about ten minutes, came back out with more pizzas in hand, and discovered he wasn't going anyplace. His light blue 1978 Toyota Corolla had been stolen.

Hornback, 20, knew what he had to do: his father was an Indiana State Police sergeant. He called campus police to report the theft and confessed to the officer who came out to investigate that he had—blush—left the keys in the ignition.[7]

Once a week, Kay Sylvester came to Bill and Gayle Cook's Wylie Street home at about 8:30 AM to do some housecleaning. Wednesday was the usual day. If Gayle was home at the time, she normally stayed in her upstairs office doing some personal work while Kay went through the rooms. On Wednesday, March 15, 1989, Gayle greeted Kay at the front door, then left about 9 to go to the home of a friend, Diana Hawes, who was collaborating with her on a book. She left the Hawes house in late morning, made a couple of unhurried stops for purchases, and, before heading home, stopped at the Jewel grocery store near the town's big eastside mall. She filled up a few sacks with twenty-four food items and six more things—e.g., a bottle of Clorox bleach, a twelve-pack of Diet Coke—that weren't food items so weren't exempt from Indiana's sales tax. At check-out, she got $3.86 taken off her bill for sale or couponed items, paid the $45.04 net bill, and loaded everything in her car. The cash register slip read 11:58 AM, and her home was five minutes away. About 12:10, she pulled up in her 1985 Buick Skylark and parked it as always on the street in front of their garageless home.

Kay Sylvester had a cleaning routine. Regularly, she worked her way through the house and at noon would be cleaning in the area of the den and breakfast table. There she'd take her lunch break and, while eating, watch the hourlong *Perry Mason* show on TV. Honoring Mrs. Sylvester's privacy while eating, this day Gayle said hello, carried the morning mail and a few things inside the house, left the grocery sacks and some other things in the car, picked up a snack for herself in the kitchen, and went upstairs. The things in the car could wait until the kitchen was clear.

At 1:55, Kay looked outside and saw her husband was waiting. They left. The house now to herself, Gayle went out to unload her car—at a little after 2, she guessed later. On her way out, she left the front door open and propped the storm door so it would stay open as she came through the door with her arms loaded.

She began to bring everything from the trunk into the house (including a framed picture she got back after loaning it to the County Museum, a movie screen left over from a talk she had given the night before, and a roll of photographs that were part of her morning session with Diana Hawes). Trip after trip, she set things down just inside the door in the foyer, intending to put everything where it belonged when the car was fully unloaded. After the last grocery sack was inside, she released the storm door prop and went back to the rear of the car to close the trunk. There, she folded up a green blanket and a white cloth used for padding in the trunk. She carried the blanket up toward the porch, returned to the car, and she had the cloth in her hands when she glanced over her shoulder and saw a small car approach from the west. Wylie is a lightly traveled street in a neighborhood of friends. She thought she might recognize the driver. "I looked inside and couldn't see a face," she testified later.

It was a long time before she ever did see that face. The driver jumped from the car, wearing a red ski mask, and rushed at her, brandishing a gun and yelling, "Get in the car! Get in the car!"—*his* car, a light blue Toyota Corolla. It took her an instant to realize what was happening. Frequently since, in her mind she has gone over and over and analyzed the whole ordeal that followed. Especially those first few seconds.

"I have read since that when it comes down to your life, suddenly your mind starts working like a computer. It's strange—and this is the way I've read it described by other people—suddenly you don't hear anything else, you don't see anything else, you're in a zone: 'Okay, what do I do next?'

"At first, I thought, 'It's a robbery. He wants my purse.' My mind is saying, 'Don't make a sound. When someone has a gun, you give them your money or jewelry or whatever.'

"Then as soon as he said, 'Get in the car! Get in the car!' everything changed. I thought, 'Now the odds are better if I do scream. People who get into cars often meet a bad end. I will resist, and I'll scream.'

"I tried to resist—so there was enough time for someone to help me. I screamed as loud as I could. I was hoping a neighbor would hear me and at least see the car." But no one was around on the quiet, pleasant street—to help or even, inside the neighborhood homes, to hear her screams.

"That's how it started."

Maybe no one else heard those screams, but the man in the ski mask did and became hostile, shouting obscenities at her. "At that point, he slammed me against the car," Gayle said. Her face hit the car—probably just above the open door—with force that cut her forehead and raised a bump. "He put me in that car [on the floor of the front seat]. He had the gun and a knife in the car, and he said, 'If you don't want to be hurt, do what I say.'" Holding the knife in front of her face, he ordered her to lie on the front-seat floor, her eyes still uncovered.

He got back in the driver's seat and drove forward, still wearing the ski mask. After about a block, he pulled over again. "He had prepared strips of duct tape which he slapped over my face and he tied my hands. Then at some place—I don't know where—he moved me (from the small car) to his own brand-new luxury van. I was blindfolded, gagged, feet tied, hands tied, tied to the back seat [a captain's chair behind the passenger-side front seat], and tied with duct tape 'round and 'round." The tape on her mouth was not so tight that she couldn't converse.

Arthur Curry hadn't driven far at all in the car, just around the block, before pulling in behind the van, which he had parked on Wylie. He made the transfer of Gayle, then sat in the van waiting to see if the scream had brought police. It hadn't. He got out and walked over to the car. He didn't want to leave it so close to the abduction scene, but after waiting back in the van for a while, he drove off.

They went for a long, long ride. There was no building involved, no hiding place. She never left the van. For almost twenty-six hours.[8]

Sometime before 4 PM, the telephone rang on the direct line to Bill Cook's office. Cook's administrative assistant, Linda Stines, answered, and the caller asked to speak to Cook.

"I said, 'May I ask who is calling?' He said, 'Jeff Clark.' I said, 'What does this concern?' He said, 'His wife.'"

Linda Stines was Indiana University basketball coach Bob Knight's secretary for his first six years in Bloomington, and she was in her eighth year with Bill Cook, two positions that guaranteed she was world-class as a call screener and sensitive to the extraordinary. "Linda had handled numerous crank calls," Cook Inc. security chief Dennis Troy says. This time, she said, "My instincts came alive. I knew he wasn't calling from an office. I could hear cars in the background. So I said, 'Has Mrs. Cook been in an accident?' He said, 'No.' I said, 'Is she okay?' He said, 'She won't be if you don't get Bill Cook right away.'

"I went right in to Mr. Cook's office [he was on the phone talking to Steve Ferguson] and told him I had a phone call for him. He took the call. And I left.

"A few minutes later, I heard him hang up. Then he called out, 'Linda, get Dennis Troy.' I knew something was wrong. But I didn't know anything about a kidnapping until Dennis had met with him and come out with a notebook and some notes. Dennis told me, 'I've got to have these copied right away for some people who are coming.' I took the notes to the copier, and while I was working there I looked down and saw the word *kidnapped*. I was in shock."

What she copied were the notes Cook scribbled down while talking with the man who called himself Jeff Clark. "He said he had Gayle," Bill remembers. He told Cook he would find her car in front of the house with the trunk lid and the front door of the house open, told him about the groceries in the foyer, the purse and car keys on the kitchen table, and other quick details.

With a measured voice that Cook said "sounded like he was reading from a script," the caller laid out the ransom demand: $1.2 million in unmarked, nonsequential $100 bills without bank wrappers, and $500,000 in gold bullion. He said he would call Cook at home at 1 o'clock the next afternoon to give him time to get the ransom together and make plans for the exchange. He told Cook to be ready then to take down several messages and to use several cars. Then he hung up.

"My heart was in my mouth when he was talking and all during the instructions," Cook said. "It was unusual for me that my voice was steady. I seemed to be thinking quite clearly even though my heart was racing and I was having a little angina at the time, I remember that."

Troy came in, responding to Stines's call, and was told what had just happened. "I asked Bill who he trusted the most to keep his mouth shut, who knew where Bill lived and could go see if the trunk lid was up and the front door was open. He said, 'Get Ross Jennings.' I got Ross and told him what was happening, and told him to go down there, see if the trunk lid was up and the door was open, but don't stop—drive by and see, and call us as soon as possible so we can decide if this is a crank or the real thing."

"As I was driving toward the house," Jennings recalls, "I was praying, 'Please, let there be no car there.' But there it was, just as they said it would be—trunk open, front door open." Jennings called Bill Cook's office with his confirmation, and Troy immediately called the FBI.

The call went to the Bloomington office, to the special agent in charge there, Thad Drost. Within minutes, Drost and two other agents from Bloomington were in Cook's office. Following FBI procedures, Drost had immediately notified the agent in charge of the Indianapolis bureau office, Bill Ervin, that he had reports of a possible kidnapping that he needed to verify. From Cook's office, Drost and Cook drove to the house and went inside. Drost recalls noticing what appeared to be footprints on the nap of the freshly cleaned carpeted steps leading upstairs. He drew his gun and went cautiously up the stairs. He found no one, returned downstairs, made notes on what he saw—the purse, the keys in the kitchen, the grocery bags and items in the foyer—and got back to Ervin reporting, "It's a go."

Troy said, "I got a call from Bill Blacketter, who was the supervisor of the kidnapping squad out of Indianapolis. He said, 'I'll be there in fifty minutes.' Then Bill Ervin arrived a short time later. We set up a command post right there in Bill's office." Ervin headed it up.

Cook's permission was asked for installation of traps and tracers on his telephone conversations. "I'll give you consent to do anything that is necessary," he told Ervin. He would be advised what steps to take as things developed. "I'll do anything you people want me to do," he said. Later, Ross Jennings said, "It was one time Bill didn't even try to take over. He just listened."

"Jeff Clark" had Bill Cook's direct office number because Gayle Cook gave it to her abductor, along with details about what was on the kitchen table, the sacks in the foyer, and instructions on what he had to say to get through Linda Stines to her husband. She volunteered the information to hasten the contact—she had been in Arthur Curry's van for almost two hours by the time the call was made. "I was very anxious for him to make the phone call," she testified later, "because I knew until he made the call, no one would be looking for me. It seemed like a long time between the time I knew he was going to call with a ransom demand and the call was actually made."

In her mind throughout the ordeal was the agreement they made the night the Forbes list came out: the one not kidnapped would go straight to the FBI. "That was so comforting, because Bill knew that I knew he would call the FBI. Regardless of how it turned out, that's what I wanted him to do. Arthur Curry said, 'You don't think your husband is calling the FBI, do you?' I assured him, 'Oh, no, he won't call anyone. He'll handle it himself.' But I knew that he would. Just that exchange [the night of the *Forbes* article] made everything so much better for both of us.

"Bill was under a lot of pressure. If you're told, 'If you don't do this, your wife is going to be killed'—that's a lot of pressure. People don't always think of what *he* went through."

Six men were involved in the abduction, "Clark" had told Bill Cook—two were holding her somewhere, one of those a "hit man." And in the early minutes of abduction, according to a signed confession that became public record after the trial, he said he told Gayle that he was out of his league and needed the advice of more sophisticated criminal minds, so he was being assisted by what his statement called "a fictional gang of x-cons."

Fictional, indeed. Arthur Curry was operating alone, and he never planned a hideaway place. The van was it, and he kept it on the move. After the call he drove to Terre Haute (about sixty miles west of Bloomington via State Road 46). On the way, along a roadside he discarded every bit of evidence he could—the ski mask, the knife he had pulled on her in the car to stop her screaming, and the coat, shirt, and pants he had worn when the abduction was made. In his signed confession, Curry said the gun was a toy, claiming he pointed the barrel toward himself when he ran toward Gayle to hide its red plastic tip. The victim's memory was starkly different: "What I saw looked like a real, black gun, and he was waving it at his car as he was telling me to 'Get in! Get in!'" Curry could say whatever he wanted. Whatever it was had been thrown out of the car window along a highway at 40 mph, he said in front of police later.

The knife certainly was real. Its empty sheath was found later in the van.

He had no problem finding replacements for the clothes he shed. When apprehended, he had in the van eighteen shirts, two pairs of pants, seven suits, a tan jacket, twenty-one ties, and two boxes with new size-10½ D Florsheim shoes.[9]

Spencer, Indiana, the home of Arthur Curry's literary grandmother, was along Highway 46, halfway between Bloomington and Terre Haute. In the hours Curry had Gayle in his van, he drove to and past Spencer several times, making notes of possible points for the ransom exchange. West of Spencer, he found a church that appeared perfect, and he noted all details: driveway, a spot behind the church that would be out of highway view and perfect for the exchange, etc.

KIDNAPPING

"He drove almost constantly," Gayle said, "except once in a while he would get out of the car." He stopped at gas stations to fill up a few times, times when Gayle heard voices outside and—though terrified and unsure exactly where Curry was—she tried to move around enough to, maybe, attract attention. But the van's windows were "smoked," making outside–in viewing impossible.

Curry got occasional coffee at fast-food places. He made stops around Bloomington to note numbers of outdoor pay telephones. When he needed to stop for a brief nap or longer sleep at night, he pulled into motel parking lots, where the van looked natural.

"He did sleep in the car some," she said. "I could hear the breathing."

She'll never forget hearing something else: her captor singing while driving along from time to time, maybe to keep himself awake, singing one song in particular, along with artist Kenny Rogers, over and over again:

> You picked a fine time to leave me, Lucille,
> With four hungry children and crops in the field
> I've had some bad times,
> Lived through some sad times,
> But this time your hurting won't heal
> You picked a fine time to leave me, Lucille![10]

"That was a haunting thing to me, to think that I was back there miserable, and sick, and bleeding. And this guy was singing, 'You picked a fine time to leave me, Lucille.'"

Within Cook Inc., only a few knew of the kidnapping. Steve Ferguson, whose phone conversation with Bill Cook was interrupted by the "Jeff Clark" call, was brought into the office. "Bill called and said, 'Come out here.' By that time, the FBI was on the way." Besides Ferguson, Dennis Troy knew. Linda Stines knew. Ross Jennings knew. That was it. Even company president Phyllis McCullough, on family vacation in Mexico, didn't know for a full day, and she was angry about that later, because of the incident's potential impact on company operations. "We weren't telling *anybody*," Ferguson said. The priority was on a complete news blackout, which is why Bloomington went to bed that night and woke up the next morning without news—on TV, in the newspaper, anywhere—about the biggest crime in the city's recent history.

"My lips were sealed," Linda Stines said. "People began to show up, cars came into the parking lot, even our managers came up and asked me, 'What's going on?' I didn't say a word."

Bill Cook wanted his 26-year-old son, Carl, home in Bloomington, back from Leechburg, Pennsylvania, where he was working. When the subject of kidnapping had first come up, Carl was the one both parents had feared for the most. "Bill kept saying, 'Nobody's going to mess with two old people,'" Jim Mason said. But now it had happened, and Bill wanted Carl to know, but he also wanted to make sure the plot wasn't more widespread than he thought.

"Dad called me that night," Carl said. "He had been calling and calling and calling. I had been at a friend's house, then I went running." It was about 9 PM in Pennsylvania, 8 PM in Indiana, when the phone connection finally was made. "Dad just said, 'Mom's been kidnapped. We got this call. We've got the FBI here. There's a plane coming out to pick you up. Don't talk to anybody about anything.'

"That's not something they teach you how to deal with in high school health class. I packed a bag very hurriedly, went to the airport, got on the plane, and flew back to Bloomington.

"The pilot had been told that something had happened, but he didn't know what, and he also had been told not to ask me. He got a direct routing—the thing you ask for if you're carrying a transplanted heart or something—and ran the thing full-power all the way. I was back in Bloomington by 11."

Ferguson was there, along with Dennis Troy and a growing group of FBI agents. "I went home from the office with Bill," Ferguson said. "I was there until everybody went to bed. Then I came back the next morning. They wanted me on-site in case Bill, because of his physical condition, couldn't handle something. Then I would step up and talk to the guy."

He didn't think that would be a problem, and it wasn't. "Bill handles crisis really well," Ferguson said. "In high crisis, he really homes in. He gets really good concentration."

First questioning by the FBI within the Cook home was more a matter of brainstorming to find if there was a logical suspect. "Obviously, it was somebody who knew something," Ferguson said. "But who was it? An employee? Somebody outside?"

A few names surfaced, one in particular—a former company executive who had been fired, arrested, and sent to prison but now was out. His location in New York was pinpointed quickly, and FBI agents there questioned him that night. His sheer presence there left no reason for the agents to go farther with him. No other name prompted follow-up action.

"A profiler from the northern part of the state arrived about 9 PM," Cook said, "with a profile of the guy, based on the facts that the FBI gave." What the profile said to expect in the kidnapper's makeup and background turned out to be "on the money," Cook said. "The profiler was a special agent. He stayed all night. The other people in the house that night were four FBI men, and two women [also FBI agents]. The women rotated shifts that night walking around on the street, just looking. They were very young, looked like students walking around the neighborhood, which was pretty common."

Carl arrived to find "a bunch of FBI agents there. And they were bringing in another agent from Washington who was a negotiations specialist."

Around midnight, Ferguson went home and the Cooks went to bed. "Surprisingly, I slept very well," Bill said. "I was dead tired. I woke up at about 4 AM and got up between 4 and 4:30." That's his normal wake-up and get-up time, as abnormal as this day was.

"I knew I was going to get a telephone call from this guy at 1. I was scared and yet steady; I seemed to have a presence of mind, a focus . . . able to remember things a lot better than normal. It was very unusual."

Carl also surprised himself with the rest he got. "You'd think you'd just toss and turn. But Dad and I talked about it. We both actually got a pretty good night's sleep."

As the morning passed, Carl found the more time he spent talking with the FBI agents in the house, the better he felt. "They were great. None of them had handled a kidnapping case, but they'd all studied it and they knew the dynamics of it. They told me there are only about four true ransom kidnappings a year in the United States, and they generally end well. The kidnapper always has to make contact, and that gives him away. I felt a little bit better when they told me that."

All of that driving gave Arthur Curry endless time to go over plans in his head. The Spencer trips had been not just to look for an exchange site but also to be as precise as possible about driving time needed for Cook to carry out what Curry was going to demand. Weariness was a constant problem. His day had started a long time before.

He had driven down from Chicago the night before the kidnapping, slept a while in his car after getting to the Cooks' neighborhood, then awakened about 6 AM and begun to implement his abduction plans. He knew the neighborhood well. He had visited it repeatedly in the two weeks since settling on his rough plan to get money from the Cooks. His plan was continually revised: he'd talk with Bill and get him to back his hotel-building plans. No, forget it, that would never work. He'd get it by robbery, his evolving "plan" ultimately worked out. He'd rob Gayle. Yes, Gayle. *She'd be alone, and she'd have a big stock and bond portfolio she could get to easily—they're the wealthiest people in town, they'd do all their business with brokers in New York or Chicago assuming no one in Bloomington was skilled enough—but they'd have small-town paranoia and keep their stock and bond certificates in their possession—the very rich do that. They'd be easy to convert, if you know the system. I know the system and have a million friends. . . .* He'd watch Bill leave for work in early morning and, at the right time during the day, strike. Which he did.

But this wasn't robbery, this was kidnapping, a much bigger crime, a federal crime since the Charles Lindbergh baby case in the 1930s. He had to make it complicated now, he felt, with too many steps for the FBI—by now he knew they had to be at work—to anticipate or follow. *If she just hadn't screamed. . . .*

Twelve hours into the abduction, at about 2 AM on the day he planned to collect the $1.7 million in ransom, he went to the Big Wheel for breakfast. Gayle was secure behind the van's smoked windows in a dark area of the parking lot. He came out fed and with time for more thinking and a little rest before, about 6 AM, he stopped at the Bloomington Holiday Inn and went over telephone numbers and addresses of local car rental companies. He made a final trip to Spencer to check out timing details. Back in Bloomington about 8, he had coffee at Burger King on the city's east side and went to the restroom.

Back in the van, using the red ink pen he carried, he put on paper the exchange plan he had worked out in his mind, the plan he would read off to Cook when it was time to go for the payoff: *bring the money and gold . . . the delivery process will take several hours . . . you will need your wallet and driver's license . . . drive to the Checker gas station in Spencer and wait for a call at pay phone there . . . do not speed . . . should take thirty minutes . . . you are being watched at all times . . . from the station, go nine miles west to Garrard Chapel church . . . get out, leave the car, walk back to Spencer . . . no hitchhiking, no calls. We will release your wife in twelve hours after you leave the car. . . .*

Bill Cook had said in the initial call Curry sounded like he was reading from a script. He was.

Stores in and around the eastside College Mall opened at 10 AM, and one of the early Kmart shoppers was Arthur Jackson Curry. He looked in the store for luggage that would be big enough to handle the payoff, and when he found it he took down notes: *two Vintage Deluxe brown plastic bags with both a zipper and straps.* Then he was driving again and tired, and he found a park that he remembered from his college days. He stopped there for a peaceful thirty-minute retreat from reality.[11]

Time was advancing toward that 1 o'clock phone call.

Shortly after noon, Curry was at a northside McDonald's, across the street from the Budget Car Rental agency, so close he could see it while on the phone.

Office manager Shirley Buehler told investigators she remembered getting a call around noon from a man telling her Bill Cook would be in shortly to rent a car and asking what she had available. A maroon Chevrolet Celebrity and a white Oldsmobile Cutlass Ciera, she told him. She remembered the man saying the maroon car was "too much like his wife's car" and—never asking the rate—choosing the Ciera. Buehler asked about a credit card and was told Cook has "several." She asked the caller for his phone number or where he could be reached, and he "hesitated, then said, 'I'll be on the road.'"[12]

That morning, Dennis Troy said, "We met in Bill's office about 6 AM. I was there, Ervin, Blacketter, I think Steve Ferguson. Bill was told what we could do and what we couldn't. He was very cool throughout the whole ordeal. At his best . . . doing everything he could to get Gayle back *and* get the guy."

By 1 PM, a full FBI team was at work—about fifteen agents, four from Bloomington and others from around the state, including one in the air above Bloomington in radio contact with the ground operation. In Indianapolis, the telephone company and FBI had a sophisticated joint telephone-monitoring facility that had been put in for the 1987 Pan American Games there. Quickly it was tied into the Bloomington goings-on. And, in Bloomington, agents in the hours since the first call had put tracking devices in pay phones all around the city—in by no means all, but many.

Local authorities—Sheriff's Department and state and city police—also were on alert, but of those groups only Sheriff Jimmy Young, Police Chief Steve Sharp, and State Police Lieutenant Ken Fowler knew why. Others in their departments were on stand-by, to look—when the time came—for a vehicle or vehicles as yet unknown, for reasons to them unknown.

The "1 o'clock call" rang in at the Cook home at about 1:20. Bill answered and was told, "Drive your wife's car to the Big Wheel. There's a pay phone in front of the Big Wheel, and I will call you there." The phone-tapping device in Indianapolis pinpointed where the call to Cook was coming from: a pay phone at Arby's Roast Beef, two blocks up College Avenue from the Big Wheel. A police unit hurried to the scene, but by the time they arrived the caller was gone. An FBI unit bugged the pay phone inside the Big Wheel. When the call came, it wasn't to that phone but to a pay phone outside the restaurant that wasn't being tapped.

Cook and Ferguson left the house immediately in Gayle's red Buick to go to the Big Wheel. FBI Special Agent Donna Wech went with them.

Ferguson said, "When they set up the plan the day before and said this young gal was going to be with us—she looked like a college kid—I took Bill Ervin aside and said, 'Hey, are you sending the right person?' He said, 'She has the highest marksmanship of anybody we have.' So when we went out there, she sat in the back seat with this big baggy coat on, and this big .357. She was loaded for bear.

"We were standing outside the Big Wheel waiting on the phone call. Bill and I are known by a lot of people, so I'm making light of things with people as they go by us to go in to eat. She's standing out there behind us. I said, 'It seems to me, if you're with the FBI, and we don't know where these guys are and what's going on here, you ought to be standing in *front* of us.' She said, 'Well, think about it this way: If I get shot, who's going to shoot them?'"

At 1:41, the unbugged pay telephone rang and Cook picked it up. Curry read from his script: east side Kmart . . . two Vintage bags, $90 . . . Budget Car Rental . . . place the two bags in a white Ciera . . . go back to Big Wheel for further instructions. Cook, following FBI instructions, asked to speak to Gayle. Couldn't be done, Curry said, because she was forty-five minutes away from where the call was being placed. He hung up.

Bloomington has two Kmarts, east and west. While FBI agents moved in to put a trap on the phone that had been used and presumably would be again, Cook, Ferguson, and Agent Wech went to the Kmart on Bloomington's west side. Carl, listening from home to radio transmissions, shouted out immediately, "They're going to the wrong Kmart." But there they found and bought tan Vintage luggage. They then went to Budget as directed, and Cook went through all the paperwork it takes to fill out the rental contract ($38 a day . . . yes, include insurance, $7.99 . . . with tax $52.88 total . . . sign here, initial here, sign here) and get the Ciera. Budget employee Shirley Sublette, who handled the deal, said she recognized both Cook and Ferguson but not the young blonde woman with them. She said they had arrived in a Buick Skylark and left in it after she heard Cook in the parking lot tell Ferguson to be sure to leave the rear door of the Ciera unlocked. The empty luggage was in the Ciera's back seat.

At 2:41, back at the Big Wheel phone, Cook got the promised call. Curry told him to drive the Ciera with the ransom to a shopping center parking lot on the west side. Cook said he would not go any farther and would not pay the ransom without hearing Gayle's voice, proving she was alive. Curry had anticipated that, and before the call he had repositioned her on the floor so he could pull the phone cord into the van far enough for her to talk into it.

"He had given me a very short speech to memorize—'I'm okay. Get the money right away.'" Gayle said. "He held the phone to me and told me to say my speech. I did. He got back on the phone, and Bill said, 'That doesn't sound like my wife.' Curry said, 'That's because she has a gag on.' Bill said, 'No, I've got to ask her a question only she can answer.' So I got the phone back, and Bill asked me to give the itinerary of a trip we had taken. I did. And this is taking time—and allowing the FBI time to trace the call.

"Curry was about to hang up, and Bill said, 'Wait a minute, I can't pay the ransom until I know where the key is for the safe-deposit box.' This is made up, too. But he puts me back on again, and I tell him where the key is: in an envelope in a purse. . . . Bill managed to keep it going a little more than four minutes."

"And by that time," Bill said, "they were on him."

Almost instantaneously the tracking unit in Indianapolis had pinpointed the source of the call Cook was answering—the parking lot at the Travelodge motel on the city's east side. Blacketter informed all surveillance units by radio that Cook was on the phone with the kidnapper and where the call was coming from. FBI Special Agent Jeffery Smith was driving in a car at the intersection closest to the Travelodge. He arrived in time to see "a black and silver customized van pulled alongside a pay telephone . . . one occupant in the front seat . . . the telephone receiver and cord from the pay telephone extending into the van through the front seat passenger window." That's all he was to do at that point: spot the vehicle, keep it in his sight, but make no move to apprehend. It made sense: What if the caller had accomplices? What if Gayle was somewhere else, in considerably more jeopardy if the plan was blowing up? One step at a time.

When the call ended and the van pulled out of the lot onto Third Street headed west toward downtown, Smith and Special Agent Philip Goodwin stayed close enough in separate cars that they never lost sight of it. An armada of other unmarked surveillance units—federal, state, and local—converged toward the area. En route, Smith got close enough to take down the van's Indiana license plate: 79R5289, quickly traced to ownership by Coyote Grill at Lafayette.[13]

The van moved at normal speed through downtown Bloomington and on west. Watching an intersection on the west side, Bloomington Special Agent Thad Drost had noted the van's description and looked up to see a match approaching him. He pulled out and followed the van west on Third into the Kmart parking lot, near the far end of the lot in front of a Hook's Drug Store. The lot was busy with afternoon shoppers. When the van stopped and parked amid the rows of shoppers' vehicles, Drost pulled in one row away and watched. Other units also closed in. Drost saw the driver get out for a few minutes, then saw the van start to move. An "idiot in a pickup truck" got in Drost's way as the van moved out of his sight, onto a west-side drive that took it behind the building, he surmised. A car carrying Special Agents Dick Bryan and Jack Osborne drove around the building from its east side. Another unit saw the van stop at a dumpster to allow the driver to get out and throw some objects in it, then get back in.

Carl Cook was listening to everything on radio with the agents assigned to the Cook home. "When it went behind the Kmart, they were positive that was the van," he said. "The lead agent gave the order to take them." The lead agent on the scene was Bill Blacketter, and Cook Inc. security director Dennis Troy was in a car with him. Troy says, "I'll never forget the way Bill said it: 'It's the ninth inning and there's two outs. What do you think we ought to do?' I said, 'Let's take the van down.' He said, 'I agree. Let's do it.' They just surrounded the van and took him down."

Bryan and Osborne drove straight up into the front of the van, blocking it, as other cars pulled in behind. Bryan and Osborne leaped out, guns drawn, shouting at the driver, "Hands up, FBI!" They pulled the unresisting Curry from the van. Drost said when he arrived at the scene Curry was already spread-eagled on the concrete drive with Bryan and Osborne over him, applying handcuffs. It was 3:25 PM.

The ending was Gayle Cook's dream. "I had imagined, okay, how can this end? I would like to hear someone say, 'Hands up!' I hadn't added, 'FBI,' but that's exactly what I heard—'Hands up, FBI!' Then the next voice I heard was, 'Hands up, everyone in the van.'"

From the pavement, Curry spoke up. "I'm all alone. It's just me. She's the only one in the van. I would never have hurt her."[14]

Cook, in the Ciera, and Ferguson and Wech, in Gayle's Buick, had driven to the Cook home. They were back together in a car just a few blocks from Cook's home, headed for the designated contact point, when the news crackled on Wech's receiver: "We've got him, and she's okay."

"I can remember just where we were," Ferguson said, "going down First Street headed west, at the bottom of the hill at Washington, when we heard that she was all right. I can remember that scene, the joy—Bill and I are hugging each other, I'm beating on the dashboard."

In minutes they were at the scene, and Bill was hugging Gayle. Carl arrived in a car of FBI agents a few minutes behind them and did his own hugging.

Ferguson watched those final steps in taking Curry into custody, and to this day—especially during Curry's trial he has had one regret:

"I wish they had killed him there."

I'm 77 years old, and I can't believe that
I'm here thinking about what is past.
I like to think of what's next.

Bill Cook, 2008

the young Bill Cook

Playing in Peoria

Billy Cook spent first grade in nine schools, in nine towns. He averaged entering a new town and a new school every month in and around his family's uprootings and moves.

That explains it all, of course. No wonder the William Alfred Cook who survived that year is so . . .

> Unbridled?
> Self-reliant?
> Eternally curious?
> Stubborn? Temperamental, even?
> Adaptable?

Is there room in there for . . .

> Successful?

If that sputtering scholastic start really was what made Indiana businessman Bill Cook a billionaire, and the word got around, there'd be peripatetic parents botching up school enrollment patterns all over the country.

A Widow at Twenty-three

The Great Depression was tightening its chokehold on America when Cook was born in Mattoon, Illinois, on Tuesday, January 27, 1931, the first and only child of George and Cleo Cook. He arrived on what his mother remembered as an unusually warm day for January. She also remembered the sound of an Illinois Central Railroad train whistle blowing somewhere close at the very moment of her son's birth, 6:10 PM. His dad couldn't be there; he was in Wisconsin making rural sales calls on his $10-a-day Depression job.

In not just Mattoon but all across the globe, January 27 was a newsy day involving historic figures. The front page of the New York *Herald-Tribune* that morning had items on FDR (not yet a president), Winston Churchill (a supplanted national leader at his political nadir, booed in the House of Commons that very day), Mahatma Gandhi (after a victory by hunger strike), Pierre Laval (on the day he went into office as premier of France, which fourteen years later hanged him as a Nazi collaborator), Haile Selassie, Calvin Coolidge, and even a Hoosier—author Booth Tarkington (he had cataract surgery that day). It was an impressive alignment of historic figures involved in newsworthy things on that one January day, and Cleo Cook kept that paper around as a treasure, the kind of things mothers have tended to do since at least as far back as Luke 2:19 ("Mary kept all these things, and pondered them in her heart").

On that day in 1931, there surely was no happier new mother anywhere on the globe than baby Bill's. Cleophus Javay DeLong Orndorff Cook was 38, a strikingly attractive woman for whom life had taken a devastating turn almost two decades earlier. She was born to Charles and Ada South DeLong on August 9, 1892, at Neoga, Illinois. At 21, she married a young man from a prosperous Mattoon family who was already on the rise in his own career as an employee in the thriving railroad business. "I understand he was a very nice guy," Bill Cook says. Just two years after the marriage, Harry Orndorff collapsed at work and died of what today probably would be called a congenital heart condition. At 23 Cleo Orndorff was a widow, her apparently settled world and promisingly comfortable financial future abruptly altered.

"She was very young, and he was from a family with more money than hers—they owned properties and businesses," Gayle Cook says. "But he died, and there she was. She had a lot of gumption."

Her decision: "She went to secretarial school to acquire a skill so she could work," Bill said. "Then she went to Chicago by herself to find a job, and she lived in an Eleanor Club. They were residential clubs, founded in 1898, to provide safe residence for genteel young working women. They were protected at night, and there was camaraderie—she had friends there she kept in touch with all her life. Those clubs existed until 2001. One that she lived in was next-door to what now is the Playboy Mansion."

She did well as a secretary, working her way to a job in the brand-new, glistening white Wrigley Building downtown, where she worked directly for chewing gum magnate William Wrigley (not yet involved with the Cubs, hence his name not yet on the landmark ballpark that still bears it).

Cleo DeLong Orndorff didn't rush into a second marriage. "It took me a long time to get over Harry," she told Gayle Cook.

"She often said to me she was glad she hadn't had a child," Bill Cook said. "It would have been difficult for her to earn a living in Mattoon. She said it was far better that she went to Chicago and made a life for herself."

George Cook—George Alfred Cook, son of Alfred Cook, the one who brought the family name to the United States from England (his own first name perpetuated as middle names of not just son George but also grandson William and great-grandson Carl)—was born March 13, 1894, in New York State, but he grew up in Peoria.

One day, young George was clinging to a wire on the back of a trolley when he fell off and broke both wrists. "From then on, his wrists were locked," Bill said. It didn't cost him any strength. "It was unreal how hard he could throw a bowling ball. And it never really bothered him in doing his job. My dad was strong-willed, a very good-looking guy."

George Cook served in the army for two and a half years during World War I. One letter he sent home to his mother was published in the Peoria Star because of his candid humor. He was Corporal George Cook then, of Company D, Second Balloon Squadron, and he wrote of his sports experiences in the army:

> The village we are billeted in is full of French soldiers and we have great times together. One night we played duck on a rock and we were all right except for a few broken fingers. We have to play their games as they are positively no good at our game, baseball. They just can't seem to learn.

"Dad played baseball in the good Peoria leagues when he was growing up," Bill said. "In those years, before World War I, Peoria had terrific baseball."

George Cook was a sergeant when he was in an artillery battalion commanded by First Lieutenant Everett Dirksen. It was a relationship George cherished through the years as Dirksen ascended in national government and Republican politics—an eight-term Illinois congressman, then four-term senator and ten-year Senate minority leader, renowned for balance, leadership, good humor, and one undying quip about governmental life: "A billion here, a billion there, pretty soon it adds up to real money."

"I never met Dirksen, but they were friends," Bill said. "He was born and

George Cook and Cleo DeLong Orndorff were married June 29, 1923, at Warren Avenue Congregational Church in Chicago.

raised in Pekin (just south of Peoria), and that group of men he commanded was out of Peoria.

"One of the last things Dad did in his life was go to Akron, Ohio, for a reunion of his battalion. When he came back, he said he had met with Dirksen. I'll never forget that. Dad was so content that he got to see him and all the buddies he had been in the war with. It was the first time I ever saw my Dad really proud of doing something that very few people did.

"Dad got hurt very badly in the war. He was gassed, and he also had a head wound. There was some question in his mind whether they ever put a plate in his head. He said, 'Sometimes I can feel something up there, but I don't know if they put a plate in or not.'"

After the war, he became a buyer of men's apparel at Marshall Field's in Chicago. He was working for Western Electric when he met Cleo, and on June 29, 1923, in the Warren Avenue Congregational Church in Chicago, the chaplain of the Eleanor Club where Cleo was living officiated at their wedding.

Baby Makes Three

Almost eight years after the marriage, son Bill was born.

"He was their only child, born when his mother was pretty close to 39," Gayle Cook said. "She was wrapped up in that child. That figures."

"I was a mother's boy," Bill said. "My father was a disciplinarian—he was very proud of me as I grew up, being an athlete, my grades, just in general how I behaved."

His mother was the bigger influence on what the son became. "My mother taught me religion and to try to be a good person. My dad was a very good person as well, hard to get to know, in some respects. He was somewhat reserved, had a temper. He was a big man, very strong. I was afraid of him, because of his size. He could take a 100-pound bag of seed and throw it twenty feet—it was just incredible what his bulk could do.

"He weighed about 265 pounds, and it was good weight. He could hit golf balls farther than you could believe. He was an excellent bowler. In golf he would shill people now and then. He'd hit a few duffer shots and then say to a person, 'Would you like to play for ten bucks?' Dad had a good sense of humor, but he really hated phony people. If guys just struck him the wrong way, he took 'em. I saw him do it."

Young Bill's first years were in the Great Depression. George paid the family bills with the job that forced all those first-grade moves. He went farm to farm, knocking on doors, meeting farmers and convincing them the product he had was worth the hard-earned dollars they had to pay him.

Radio station WLS—50,000 watts, clear channel—boomed out of Chicago as the hub to a wide area of farmers in Indiana, Illinois, Iowa, and Wisconsin. That was the place most of them got their vital farm information, on grain prices and other rural economic necessities—including weather. When tornadoes or storms approached, during emergencies and catastrophic events, WLS was the place farmers went. That's why it was governmentally designated as a clear-channel station, no one else allowed to operate on its dial number.

The station also published a magazine for farmers, *Prairie Farmer*. Dozens of times a day its announcers used the on-air identification: "This is WLS, the Prairie Farmer station." A subscription to the magazine, its information as vital for farmers as the radio station's, was what George Cook sold—that, and a related insurance policy against a rampant threat of the day, rural theft, covering homes, crops, and outbuildings. Coverage came with membership in the Prairie Farmers Protective Association.

Bill Cook keeps in his office one of the association's membership placards that his father gave to his customers. "You put it on your barn door, or you put it on your car, and for $10 a year, if somebody stole something—up to $1,000—you were covered by insurance. Plus, the 'protective' part was they would send somebody out to see if they could track down the bad guys."

Even in the Depression, George Cook found a market for what he was selling. But what he was selling covered a full year, and it didn't take him long to go through a new area. He'd work a territory, then move on, taking his wife and son with him. "He'd set up in a community, go out and sell the community, and have to move on," Bill Cook remembers. That's why, in the academic year of 1937–38, son Bill was a first-grader in

Plymouth, Indiana
Logansport, Indiana
LaSalle, Illinois
Peru, Illinois
Prairie du Chien, Wisconsin
Cassville, Wisconsin
Hazel Green, Wisconsin
Princeton, Illinois, and
Metamora, Illinois

Hazel Green—so green, so small, so pretty—lives on in Bill's memory as his favorite, a town with a population barely over 1,000 just north of the Wisconsin-Illinois border and within ten miles of Iowa. "That was such a nice place. I loved it. Leaving there was kind of traumatic because I really enjoyed the town and the kids there."

They lived mostly in the cheapest hotels they could find, in one room. There was not a lot to pack up when moving time came, no lease to break.

"Those were tough times. My dad and mother were big people, and it was hot. I don't know why they didn't get a cot or put me on the floor. We slept three in a bed."

A twinkle, a start of a smile:

"That's probably why I don't have any brothers or sisters."

In each of those nine towns, he entered a new teaching system and made new acquaintances. "I'd meet these friends, and they wouldn't be friends very long. Pretty soon we'd be taking off."

One more move with Prairie Farmer took the Cooks to Peoria, Illinois, where the vagabonding ended. Peoria, Bill remembers, is where "Mom finally said, 'George, that's enough! We can't do this anymore.'"

The family of three moved back into the Peoria home of George Cook's parents, who several years earlier had taken George and Cleo in for a while when Chicago proved too expensive for them during the worst days of the Great Depression.

No Bullying Problem

George Cook remained with Prairie Farmer for two more years. "I went to second and third grade in Peoria," Bill remembers.

Somehow all those moves didn't take an expectable educational toll. Cleo Cook was meticulous in preserving pictures, clippings, and other memorabilia from Bill's childhood. Included is a note she got early in their first school year in Peoria, from his second-grade teacher:

> Mrs. Cook,
>
> I've been thinking about placing Billy in ending-second. He seems more advanced than his class and I believe he would get along in the work very well. In a reading test that I gave him today, he showed 3rd grade reading ability. He seems so eager to work and finished everything so quickly that perhaps he would be more satisfied in the ending-second class. You can let me know what you think about doing this. I haven't said anything about it to Billy, yet.

Cleo and George Cook said no, thank you, preferring to keep him with his classmates, though they must have been happy and almost relieved that all the moving if anything might have actually helped in their son's education. "It wasn't inhibiting, obviously," Cook says. "But a lot of other people caught me later." There wasn't a social toll, either. "I was somewhat outgoing. I wanted to have friendships. One way of doing it was just by being friendly. I never had any problem with anybody bullying me, because I was usually bigger than most kids in the class."

The summer after his third-grade year was epochal for both Bill and his parents. His mother would give him eight cents every Saturday to ride a trolley downtown to the YMCA and back. There he learned to swim and, in the process, how to respond to pressure. He was just plain bigger than most boys in the swimming class, but he also carried extra weight. "My friends teased me about being fat. I was embarrassed." On the last day of the class, the "final exam" was to swim the full length of the pool. He wasn't first up. "Four or five of my friends tried and failed to make it. Nothing was going to stop *me*." He swam the length of the pool and was the first to get his certificate signifying course completion. Eventually, everyone made it, "but I was the first. And my friends stopped teasing me."

That was the summer George Cook left Prairie Farmer and went into business for himself. "My dad had a friendship with a banker in Trivoli, Illinois [between Peoria and Canton]. In 1939 Dad got a $2,500 loan from him so he could buy three grain elevators." Almost immediately, George had to tear down one of the three, keeping a 30,000-bushel elevator at Norris and a 40,000-bushel elevator at Fiatt—each about five miles from Canton. The family moved twenty-five miles southwest from Peoria to Canton almost as soon as the deal for the grain elevators went through. That business sustained the Cooks for the rest of young Bill's educational years, up through high school at Canton—population under 15,000 and the community Bill Cook has always cherished as his real home town.

It was an introductory time for George Cook with Depression-pinched Canton area farmers. "Dad was very careful with his money. And I always admired him as a businessman—always very fair with everything he did. He played the market [the grain market, by radio, WLS]. He'd try to sell at exactly the right time—by phone, with the Chicago Board of Trade. He'd deal with a broker. Whenever Dad had a good day, we'd go out and eat."

Nine-year-old Bill had his own self-introducing to do. In the fall of 1940, he had a whole new group of classmates to meet and get to know at Central Elementary School in Canton.

"Bill was a very good student," remembers Gloria Saurbaugh—Gloria Pschirrer now but still "Glo" to friends, as she was from childhood. "He more or less took over the class. There was some resentment—'the new kid on the block.' But that didn't bother Bill. He wasn't bashful." Didn't bother Gloria, either. "In fact, I was pretty impressed."

There was no Little League baseball then, but young Bill found plenty of playground competition in Canton—neighborhood things: touch football, softball, basketball. And there were new impressions to make.

Confidence from his swimming conquest in Peoria helped. In fourth-grade gym class the challenge was to climb a rope from the gym floor to a beam high overhead. "It must have been forty feet up. Same thing—several guys went ahead of me and failed. Couldn't make it." Halfway up, his own arms aching and breath short, "I thought about giving up and coming down." Instead, he held his place for a few breath-catching seconds, then started to climb again and made it all the way up. Same result as Peoria: newfound respect. "My acquaintances became friends—lifelong friends I still see frequently, guys who have been a part of my life since way back then in childhood."

A Basketball Town

In Canton, a couple of pets came into his life—a dog he called Spot (the name straight out of the elementary reading books about Dick and Jane) and a cat named Susie. One day Susie ran out in the street and was run over by a car. "That was very traumatic. That was the first thing I ever had die." Spot, a wirehaired fox terrier with a cut-off tail, stayed on, through grade school and junior high, then high school, then lived at home when Bill went off to Northwestern.

"When I was 21—I was getting ready to go back to school, so it would have been August—I went to the filling station one night, and Spot got out of the car. That's what he would do: get out, go do his business, and get right back up on the seat." That night, he didn't come back. "He went back behind the filling station and I never saw him again. We looked for him. I doubt if anybody picked him up. I think he was sick enough that he went back there and found a place where he could just lie down and die.

"I've never had another dog. I didn't want to get that close to a dog again."

Bill Cook found Canton "a pretty little town—wonderful people. Most everyone then owned their own home.

"It was a basketball town. For years, Canton held the record for going to the state tournament the most times. They won the state in 1928, and there weren't two classes then the way there is now." The basketball aura continued into Bill Cook's high school days in the 1940s. "Ingersoll Gym held 3,500 people, and it was sold out every game."

It didn't take long before "basketball town" Canton had noticed him a little. He was the center on the Central team that reached the finals of the Canton sixth-grade tournament before losing, 20–18. Canton *Ledger* sports columnist Jimmie Murphy covered the tournament and listed him among sixth-graders "worth keeping an eye on . . . awkward now but showing much promise."

Two years later he captained an unbeaten eighth-grade team that reached something Illinois had then that even basketball-crazy Indiana never had: a state tournament for eighth-grade teams. "We played probably fifteen games my eighth-grade year. We went to Lewistown, Pekin, Peoria, one time to Streator, which was a long way away. Then we went to the state tournament at Washington—and lost our first game."

He was showing promise in another field, too. Almost as soon as the family moved to Canton, he began taking piano lessons from Canton's leading teacher, Alice Klingman.

"I just enjoyed playing the piano. I'd get up at 5:30 to 6 in the morning to practice, and I enjoyed it. I played and practiced piano until I was 14. When I was a freshman football player, I racked up my finger and that was sort of the end of my piano days. I had a stiff finger—it's still stiff.

"Classical music was my favorite. I dearly loved playing 'Warsaw Concerto' because it was something I could handle—not that difficult but something that was stirring; you could make it emotional."

History and a memory for details blend for him from those pre–high school days.

He heard about Pearl Harbor when he and his mother returned home from a Sunday afternoon at the movies—at the Capitol Theater, where they saw *Blood and Sand*, starring Tyrone Power as a bullfighter. The movie won that year's Oscar.

He was 14 when the two wars ended in 1945, with "V-E Day" (Victory in Europe, with Germany's surrender) in April and "V-J Day" (Victory in Japan) in August. "I was already driving [under wartime laws]. V-E Day and V-J Day we all drove around the square—just delightful, thousands of people up on the square both times."

In between the two celebrations he remembers April 12, 1945. He competed in a piano solo contest about ten miles away at Smithfield—not a banner day, got a B rating. Afterward he heard the news that had stunned the world: President Franklin D. Roosevelt—America's Depression president, wartime president, the only president young Bill had ever known of—had died.

Meanwhile in Evansville . . .

Evansville, in the state's southwestern tip, is Indiana's southernmost major city. The Ohio River, which is Indiana's southern border, is Evansville's as well. And it was the southern border, too, of the farm on which sat the home of Arthur and Thelma Karch when Gayle was born March 1, 1934.

The majestic Ohio provided Gayle years of the pleasant, almost mysterious relaxation that vast rivers, lakes, and oceans bring to most people. Shortly before Gayle's third birthday, the beautiful and serene Ohio River turned brutal and savage. It is moderately deep where it goes past her girlhood farm and then Evansville. Flood stage is a water depth exceeding thirty-five feet. For a Noah-like forty days in January and February of 1937,

Evansville had above-flood-stage readings—way above, much of the time. For two weeks in the middle of that stretch, the relentless river's Evansville depth was fifteen feet above flood level.

"The '37 Flood was the demarcation in Evansville—'so-and-so was born before the flood' or 'married after the flood,'" Gayle says. "There were lives lost, there were epidemics, there was livestock lost. It was so widespread, so hard to get away from. Our house was a long way from the river, but pictures show the water over the windowsills."

The Karch farm was a good one, but the family home on it wasn't luxurious. "I grew up without running water and indoor plumbing," Gayle says. That translates to outhouses: unpleasant trips to an unpleasant place, whatever the time or the weather, for unpleasant necessities. "I thought I was the last person in the world to live like that, and I just about was. None of my friends did."

Almost next door to the Karch farm was Angel Mounds State Historic Site. There, archaeologists have concluded, Native Americans of the Middle Mississippian culture had a town almost 1,000 years ago—from AD 1100 to 1450. Renowned archaeologist Glenn A. Black of Indiana University sees strong evidence that Angel Mounds is precisely the area that Spanish explorer Hernando de Soto wrote about visiting in the early 1500s. A life of interest in historic preservation had an early start for Gayle Karch.

Purple Ribbons and State Fair

Gayle went through the eighth grade at a rural school, Caze, where she was repeatedly mentioned in newspaper clippings for academic excellence that gave her No. 1 ranking in her class. When she reached 10 and became eligible, she joined a 4-H Club and began an eight-year run of competing—and excelling—at the Vanderburgh County 4-H Fair. Her first year, she won a blue first-place ribbon in clothing. Every year, she had excellent results with her exhibits, extending into baking and the fair's Dress Revue. A purple "Grand Champion" ribbon on anything qualified her to take that exhibit to the State Fair in Indianapolis.

"Going to the State Fair was a big deal. And the County Fair was really a big occasion, too." So was 4-H Camp, which she attended each of those eight years. She was among 2,000 teenagers who attended a 4-H Round-up at Purdue University, where her older brother, Glenn, already was on his way to a degree in agriculture. In his 4-H days, he had shown the reserve grand champion (second-place finisher) in the Tri-State hog show and sold it at auction for $123.75.

The kids' dad, Arthur Karch, had his own 4-H Fair background. When Gayle and Glenn were winning ribbons, Arthur got the big newspaper ink, recognition of his victory in the fair's hog-calling contest—his picture five inches high and two columns wide, mostly of his mouth, so wide open his interior teeth were on display. It was prominence that might have embarrassed a young girl, except it was fair time, and fun time, and she knew her dad was outgoing and a leader among farmers and in farm organizations. Also, the winning bellow wasn't one Daddy ever used on Darling Daughter. "Not that one," she says.

Gayle was also studying piano. At twelve she played Mozart's "Minuet" and the French folk tune "Bon Voyage" in the Evansville College preparatory school recital.

She was eighth-grade class president at Caze, and she was growing up in an active and fascinating family.

Born Republican

Gayle Karch's maternal grandfather, John Weinsheimer, was born in the early days of the Civil War and lived into his nineties. Among the passed-down Evansville newspaper clippings she treasures is one applauding his 1902 purchase of a farm in Warrick County (adjacent to Vanderburgh on the east):

> It is gratifying to learn that real estate is somewhat advancing in this community. Last Saturday, Mr. John Weinsh[e]imer became the owner of 160 acres of land near Stephenson, paying $7,000 cash ($43.75 per acre). This is as fine a piece of land as can be found in Warrick County, and Mr. Weinsh[e]imer can be congratulated upon his purchase.

Evansville and Vanderburgh County are two of the strongest Democrat sections of mostly Republican Indiana, but Weinsheimer—the Republican candidate for township trustee in 1898—was typical of Gayle's upbringing, in Republican hands right from the start. The doctor who delivered her, H. G. Weiss, was the Republican candidate for state representative from Vanderburgh County.[1]

When she was 14, her father was a Republican precinct committeeman in the presidential election that incumbent Democrat Harry Truman won over Thomas E. Dewey. Twelve years later, Arthur Karch was in Chicago with a seat in the eighth row of the mezzanine at the 1960 Republican convention, which nominated Richard Nixon to run against John F. Kennedy.[2]

2

The Canton High Years

It was fourth-and-goal, in the last minute of the last football game Bill Cook ever played. Canton trailed unbeaten Farmington, 7–6. The ball was inside the Farmington two-yard-line, but it had been there a while, and Farmington wasn't yielding. "We were having a hell of a time—we ate up three downs and couldn't get the ball across," Cook remembers. He was the center, a good one, an experienced senior responsible for getting the football to quarterback Dick Fouts and helping to clear an opening for an on-charging back. It wasn't happening.

Junior end Bob Heppenstall, whose recovery of a fumbled punt gave Canton its late chance to win, recalls, "We called a fourth-down play, and the next thing I knew Bill was lying in the end zone on top of the football. I didn't have any idea what happened."

Cook had spotted something. Farmington's goal-line defense put linemen in the gaps on both sides of him, but no one head-on. "Usually they have somebody over the top of the center. They didn't have anybody there. On the way to the line, I whispered to Fouts, 'Look like you fumbled.' We all lined up for the snap, he called the signals, the play started, I got the ball up to my crotch, then instead of snapping it back to Dick just heaved it forward over the goal line underhanded, and jumped on it like I was trying to recover a fumble. Dick made a good act. He dived down like he was going for the ball." Officials, blocked out by bodies from seeing what really had happened, bought it as a fumble. When they found the football, with Cook on top of it, the referee's arms shot up: "Touchdown!" And Canton won, 12–7.

It was a trick play more resourceful than legal. Rules don't allow the center to advance the football. After the game, Cook recalls, "The coach [A. L. Buckner, new to Canton] wasn't too happy. He said, 'Don't you say another word about this.'" And he didn't, for nearly sixty years. "I really don't know what the ruling would be. The ball was on the ground, and it was not in my control."

It was the only touchdown he ever scored, so confusing a play that the newspaper the next day credited the touchdown to a running back, then corrected it a day later. With no details.

All Heppenstall knew then and remembers today is that "Bill had it in his mind that he was going to take over, and he did. That's the kind of player he was. He took charge."

Desperate times do call for desperate measures, but on the football field Bill Cook wasn't desperate very often. He made the varsity as a freshman and grew to play at around 230 good football pounds.

The last-minute last-game victory made the "Little Giants" 5–4 his senior year, and the team voted him their Most Valuable Player. Pekin coach Jim Lewis, a member of the All-State board, called him "a tower of strength as a defensive linebacker."

Fullback Jim Van Sickle doesn't limit him to defense: "He was equal on both sides of the ball, an exceptional blocker as a center as well as an excellent linebacker." Van Sickle, a career lawyer who is one of the gang of friends Cook ran with then and has been close to ever since, has special reasons to remember how good Bill Cook was on offense. "He would come back to the huddle and say, '4-0 is ready.' That was me over center, and there was always an opening there when he said there was. It was exciting. It was an advantage to me like nobody else because he liked that play.

"He was just an excellent football player. I always thought he could play college ball. He was tough."

Bill also won three high school letters in basketball. The team his junior year added to the legacy of the "basketball town." The Little Giants finished 22–8, sweeping through the Regional and Sectional tournament rounds to, one more time, put Canton in the eight-team state tournament at Champaign. There, they got by Quincy, 41–37, but lost to a tall La Grange team in the semifinals, 43–41. "We should have won the state tournament," Cook said. "We had a great team. We were No. 1 most of the season. I think we might have peaked a little too soon." The team his senior year tailed off to 11–14, eliminated from the tournament in its second game.

Bill left basketball-conscious Canton one unforgotten moment. He ended a one-sided victory over Galesburg his junior year with a long at-the-buzzer heave that went through—so long it made the newspaper the next day even though it was ruled too late to count. The story said forty-six feet, which would be four feet back of the centerline. His high school buddy, John Myers, says, "I always said they should have driven a spike in the floor to mark where it was." Gayle said at a business event "a man came up to me and said he was from Canton and as a little kid he saw Bill hit 'that shot—the longest shot ever made in a game there—didn't you know?' He said Bill took a rebound and threw it the length of the court at the buzzer."

Double-Trucking Days

Bob Heppenstall and Jim Van Sickle were in a group with Bill that was pretty well formed by his junior year. It was mostly boys, with some girls, and it formed around Bill Cook and Bill Carper because they were the ones who had "wheels."

"My dad was a plumbing contractor, and I had a truck," Carper said. "Bill had a truck from his dad's elevator." The Carpers' truck was a gray Studebaker, emblazoned "Carper Heating and Plumbing." Cook's was an orange 1946 International pickup, with "Norris Elevator Co." on the side.

Night after night, pretty much the same group piled into the trucks and "had a lot of fun," said Carper, who became a career family-practice physician in Canton. "We did a lot of crazy things—nothing that was really harmful, except to some of his father's vehicles."

Memories vary on how—and how often—Bill blew the transmission out in his dad's vehicles. "I think he went through a couple," Carper said. "One time we were out in the country. He decided to turn around, so he whipped into a driveway, threw the thing in reverse while it was still going forward at about 30 mph, and he just tore the heck out of the transmission. His classic quote was 'Ohhh, George is gonna shit.' George, of course, was his father."

Len Kuchen remembers situations that brought the comment more than once. "I think George shit several times, actually," he said.

Summer evenings, Carper said, "We'd line up a bunch of guys and gals—not really dates—and go to the drive-in theater. Bill would drive his truck in backward, then everybody would get in the back end of the truck and we could all see the movie."

Bill Cook dated Gloria Saurbaugh all through high school. Bill Carper and future wife Eleanor Webb had their first date on her sixteenth birthday and stayed with it. John Myers, another of the group, also dated his future wife, Harriet Hill. "We double-dated a lot with Bill and Ellie, or Bill and Glo," Myers said. Ellie Carper corrects that: "We didn't double-date. We double-trucked."

Ronnie Casson, voted the class's best athlete, was in the group. So was Gus Elliott. And there were more, most of them class leaders. Kuchen (who rose in later life to treasurer of the giant Caterpillar Corporation of Peoria, where Myers also became an executive) was president of the Senior Honor Society. Carper was Senior Class president. "Those boys were the popular group in school, no doubt about it," Gloria Saurbaugh Pschirrer said. "We all ran around together, it was such a close relationship. There were times I could have wrung Bill's neck because we always had to be with someone."

A clique? "I never got the sense that we turned anybody off," Kuchen said. "We did all manner of things together, including a lot of mischief. But everybody was involved with other kids. I think we interacted pretty broadly."

Clique wasn't the name that American history and civics teacher Connie Harrison had for the boys in the group. "She called them the OWGs—Old Women Gossipers," Gloria said. "She loved those boys. Most of them were good students, and they were good kids. But they could be mischievous." John Myers said Miss Harrison "thought we couldn't do anything wrong. The fact was we did. Quite a bit."

In the mischief, too, a leader was Bill Cook. Most of the group was in chemistry class with him under teacher Terry Ziegler, who wore a large early-edition hearing aid, a "big thing, hung on his chest," Bill Carper said. "Bill came along, took that hearing aid in his hand, and said right into it, 'Hey, Terry, are you on the air?' Nearly blew him away."

Gene Taylor was in that class. "Everybody laughed and the teacher laughed. It was just, 'Oh, well, that's Bill.'"

Taylor, a career lawyer who retired as a Canton judge, has his own Bill Cook driving story. After graduation in spring 1949, both enrolled in summer school at the University of Illinois at Champaign-Urbana. When that session ended, the two were headed home to Canton on an afternoon in August, in George Cook's four-door Ford, Taylor recalls. "We were on Route 136, about twenty minutes from home, and Bill said, 'Man, I'd like to get home.' I said, 'Boy, I would, too. I can hardly wait.' Bill just pushed the accelerator to the floor, and we were flying. I said, 'Goddamn it, Cook, I do want to *get* home!' I thought this was my last day on earth. All of a sudden—ka-bam! A piston went through the side of the motor. I just wanted to reach over and kill him. We didn't get home till 10 o'clock that night."

Canton High School friends and graduates, 1948. *Bottom row, from left:* Allen "Gus" Elliott, John Myers, Pete Laken, Bob Lindbloom. *Upper row, from left:* Ron Casson, Bill Carper, Fred Mercer, Bill Cook, Len Kuchen, Jim Van Sickle.

A Driver, in Many Ways

Under war-loosened laws, driving began early for Bill. Speeding tickets did, too. An entry among his mother's scrapbook collections shows he was ticketed for speeding (and fined $10) in Peoria on November 23, 1946—two months before his sixteenth birthday.

"In junior high I worked summers at my dad's grain elevator. I was driving a semi when I was in the eighth grade. It was during the war, and I was big for my age. I'd drive 275 miles up to Janesville, Wisconsin, spend the night there, and drive back. I made that trip eight or nine times."

In high school, he was a lifeguard at the Canton pool. That made it a regular, and cheap, social spot in evenings for the gang. "He was night watchman," John Myers recalls. "We'd sneak in out there and swim. Frequently."

Coke Grove was a place Canton kids went to dance. Gloria Pschirrer remembers going there to a dance with Bill—"my first date, and I'm pretty sure it was his." That place went out of business, and the teen social scene shifted to the YMCA, right downtown, on the corner of Main and Walnut. "That's where everybody just congregated, and we had dances after every athletic event," Gloria said. It was a good teen gathering place, but it wasn't enough, Bill decided. So—at an age when the average high school junior or senior blushes and stammers through a speech class assignment in front of a class of peers—he got a group together and took on City Hall.

The Canton *Ledger* told of the results in a page 1 story:

YOUTH CENTER IS URGED BY CANTON TEENAGE GROUP

An overflow crowd heard an impetuous and enthusiastic group of high school students press its claim for a youth center at last evening's informal meeting of school officials, park board members, and others, held in the city council chambers.

Following a lengthy discussion of the desirability, availability, and cost of a proposal to transform the Wallace Park pumping station building into a modern teen age center, committees were named and directed to report next Monday evening at 7 o'clock in the council chambers.

William Cook was selected as secretary of the committee. . . .

Mayor Gus Chambers, who presided, was named chairman of a permanent committee charged with the responsibility of providing a youth center somewhere in the city should the Wallace park project be abandoned.

A Peoria newspaper's story on the meeting said:

Bill Cook was the first young person to speak. He told how he believes such a project could be financed, saying the building could be rented to organizations for concerts or meetings of various kinds and he believed it could in time be self-supporting.

It turned out to be an idea whose time had not come, quite. Gene Taylor was one of the group Cook talked into going with him into the council chambers. Taylor's memory of that evening differs from the tone of the newspaper accounts. "They practically laughed us out of the room. But Bill was a visionary. He could see this would be a good thing. And a few years later they ultimately had a teen center. That's the way he was, always thinking."

During that time, he regularly attended Sunday morning services at First Methodist Church with his mother. "He was pretty involved in church," Bill Carper said. He sang in the church choir. Gloria also was in that choir. "He was musical," she said. His finger injury had caused him to give up serious piano practice. But, Gloria said, "Sunday afternoons he would play for his mother. I loved to hear Bill play, particularly 'Malaguena' and 'Rhapsody in Blue.'"

Bill sang in the Canton High mixed chorus all four of his high school years. He, Bob Heppenstall, Ron Casson, and Jim Campbell also sang together as the Varsity Four, performing at school programs or in barbershop quartet competition. His natural voice was closer to baritone, but Heppenstall says, "Bill was our tenor. We'd come to a song that had some high notes, and we'd say, 'We can't sing that one.' Cookie would say, 'I'll sing falsetto.' He'd warble away, and we'd do it. We just had a lot of fun."

Crackpot, Full of baloney, Risk-taker

And now it's three generations later. Canton has a handsome new high school, gym attached, football stadium adjacent—with a Memorial Wall and a plaque that lists Bill and Gayle Cook among contributors to an all-weather track around the field. "Bill's name is up on top," says Gloria Pschirrer, a primary fund-raiser in the drive. "He gave a nice contribution. We're really proud of it."

The nucleus from the "OWGs" and some spouses get together with Bill and Gayle Cook at least a couple of times a year, every year—sometimes in Canton, frequently in Bloomington, transported by a Cook airplane.

It's never the whole group anymore. Ronnie Casson, the handsome athlete who became a career computer analyst, was the first to die. Cancer. Then Fred Mercer (whose wife Raelene was part of the high school group, and remains in the bunch). Then Harriet Myers.

"Harriet was a year ahead of us in school," John Myers said, "but I went with her all through high school. She died of Lou Gehrig's disease [amyotrophic lateral sclerosis] in September 2004.

"Bill and Gayle were in town for our fifty-fifth class reunion when she died. The reunion was on Saturday night, and she died on Friday. I couldn't go to the reunion, of course. Sunday morning, I was in the shower. The doorbell rang, my son opened the door, and I heard a loud voice: 'I don't care if he is in the shower. Tell him to get his ass out here.'"

It was perfect therapy, Myers feels—the shout and the follow-up warm conversation between friends. Perfect and typical. "He's been over here with Gayle for every one of those funerals. That's a measure of the man."

In the early 1950s, after the Canton High Class of '49's tight core of friends spread out for college and other post–high school pursuits, the Four Aces had a hit record, "Those Wedding Bells Are Breaking Up That Old Gang of Mine." It's an eternal truth. Almost every high school in every town in every year has groups similar to the Canton gang, up through high school. Rare is one that, more than half a century later, maintains such a tight bond.

Myers has a theory on why that particular group has stayed together. "We were Depression babies, and several of us were 'only' children—Bill,

Bill Carper, Jim Van Sickle, myself. Better than half of us didn't have any brothers or sisters. Our relationship was close to sibling. That's probably why we have maintained such a close relationship over time."

Bill Cook, the one who moved two hundred miles away, "has made so many efforts to keep that relationship going," Ellie Carper said. "Before he had the airplane we would drive over to Bloomington. And he always made us feel so welcome . . . that it was important to him. You can tell that Canton people mean a lot to him."

They're the people who marvel most at what this man from their midst has accomplished. Separately, they remember what they were seeing in him then, in those high school days.

Gene Taylor thought for a minute, trying to put himself back in Canton High, senior year, looking at Bill Cook. "Oh, I would have thought he might end up not amounting to much . . . or where he is today. I wouldn't have given you two cents either way. He just seemed like he was about half-cracked. But looking back on it, when he made up his mind that he was going to do something, he was fearless. He didn't know the meaning of the word no."

"He had lots of ideas—a lot of them," Bill Carper said. "Really, we thought he was full of baloney. He'd say, 'I think what we need to do is . . .' or 'What I'm going to do is . . .' and we'd say, 'OK, Bill.' But he did everything he said he was going to do. He kinda blew us away, to be honest. He was a leader. He did OK in class gradewise (graduated twenty-fourth in a class of 129)—not at the top of the heap, but he was right up there."

"He *could* have excelled in everything," Gloria Pschirrer says. "It just wasn't his priority then. Back then I thought he'd go into medicine and probably be a doctor now."

John Myers concedes that Bill Cook "wasn't a super-great student, but when he put his mind to something, he accomplished it. And even as a senior in high school, Bill was beginning to be bigger than life-size. I just always thought he would succeed big-time, or go down the tubes."

Len Kuchen looked for a word to describe the high school Bill Cook he saw. He settled for risk-taker. "I think he liked to be innovative—on the edge. Sometimes I sensed a danger in Bill that made me uncomfortable. Principally driving. I would avoid being in a car with Bill, if I could. The last thing I wanted was to be in the front seat.

"I knew at the time he wanted to be a doctor. There never was a doubt that he was smart enough. But did I ever sit down and say, 'By golly, I think Bill is really going to amount to something big'? Probably not.

"Now, knowing what Bill has done with his life, and the philanthropist he has become, all of the medical innovations that he has brought into being—I guess when you look back, it's not surprising."

These are people who knew him as Bill but also as "Duck"—"because he *ran* like a duck, with his feet in and his chest out," Bill Carper said, smiling at the memory. "And we also called him 'Chesty'"—because the high school Bill Cook was a robust, big-chested football player and a robust basketball player, too, who fouled out a time or two.

Gayle Cook smiles as she thinks of the gang she met as her husband's friends and long ago counted among her own. "It's a group of people he can be himself with. You feel at ease with people who know who you really are."

She feels a part of the Canton group, and she should. "I think most of us have said Bill has done a lot of wonderful things, but the best thing he ever did was marry Gayle," Bill Carper said. "She's a sweetheart."

"You can call it dumb luck or discernment," Gene Taylor said, "but he could not have met a better woman to keep him in balance. Gayle had the stability and common sense to make Bill the man he finally became."

That "man he finally became" is the Bill Cook who says: "My best friends, people I will remember when I die, are my friends in Canton."

Twenty-six years after the Class of '49 had graduated, Canton was ravaged by a tornado. It was Bill Cook, long since transplanted to Bloomington, who—the Canton *Daily Ledger* later reported—"was appalled at finding the large elm trees which once lined the city streets were gone. He then donated funds to purchase trees which were given to homeowners for planting in the terraces along city streets."

Hundreds of trees. "My friends took them out—gave them to people," Cook said.

"He saw to it that anybody who wanted a tree had one," Bill Carper said.

That was 1975. "Those trees are now tall and beautiful," Ellie Carper said in 2007.

Bill Cook's fondness for his hometown that hadn't begun to dim by 1975 still hasn't. "It's a pretty place, a cute little town," he says. "It had the bad luck of being in the Rust Belt and losing its only industry, International Harvester. Slowly but surely it's coming back."

So many friends there, so much feeling for the town . . .

"So why didn't I go back to Canton and start the business?

"Because you never go home to fail.

"I wanted someplace to hide. Just in case."

Meanwhile in Evansville . . .

A career in nursing was in the back of Gayle Karch's mind as she put together a superb academic record at Bosse High School, on Evansville's southeast side.

Her older brother, Glenn, started at Bosse but switched to Reitz High to get agriculture classes that Bosse didn't offer. Glenn went on to graduate at Purdue, return to Evansville, marry and raise his family, and turn his background and degree into a successful career. He also turned a lifelong fascination into an area of expertise. "He's a nationally known collector of one-cylinder gasoline engines and author of two books about engines," his proud sister says.

Gayle's extracurricular high school interests brought out her talent as an artist. Bosse's arts department was outstanding. The school put on full-scale Broadway theatrical productions. As a senior, Gayle painted the scenery for the Bosse production of the Lerner and Loewe musical *Brigadoon.* The 1952 Bosse yearbook portrayed its thirteen faculty advisors not with pictures but with sketches by student Gayle Karch.

With a curriculum that included science courses that cultivated another special interest for her, she graduated as salutatorian in her class. Her 96.97 grade point average, a strong A, placed her second in the class of 365 students, just below the valedictorian's 97.17. Foreign languages were another special interest area—and skill—for her. She received state honors for "superior merit" in Latin, and in French tests she ranked thirteenth in the state.

She was one of the two seniors in Vanderburgh County to receive a state scholarship from Indiana University, paying 60 percent of tuition. At the time, it was more honorary than lucrative. For a normal fifteen-hour class load, that paid $36 a semester.

3

A Wide Gold Band

Bill Cook came out of graduation ceremonies at Canton High School in 1949 sure that he was going to go to college but not at all sure where. Maybe Illinois, maybe Northwestern. Maybe he would go out for football, wherever it was, hoping to earn a scholarship. And maybe he wouldn't. Probably, almost surely, he would major in some premed field, aiming for medical school and a career as a doctor. Of such are billion dollar business careers forged.

A Champaign Start

Bill's college career had started early with those summer classes at the University of Illinois in Champaign. "I was planning to be a football player." He took four hours of German and four of English, and worked with other University of Illinois football candidates in daily conditioning drills during summer heat. The football didn't include much acquaintance with a football—"a lot of running, and working in rubber suits, that was about it." He went into it with no more than a vague promise, what he called "the typical thing coaches do today: 'Come to the University of Illinois and maybe you'll be a football player.'" By the end of the summer, he had been told that if he practiced for a year with the freshmen (who were ineligible for varsity play in major colleges then), he would have a scholarship.

He went back to Canton at the end of the summer session uninterested in either the football scholarship or returning to Illinois. "I just felt Illinois was too big for me. I knew I would feel more comfortable at Northwestern."

He was familiar with the Northwestern University campus and the Evanston area. His uncle, Joseph Fucilla, was a professor of romance languages at Northwestern. Bill had visited in summers with cousin Ivan "Van" Fucilla there.

Northwestern today is one of the most difficult universities for freshmen to enter. His less than all-out academic performance in high school didn't make his entrance application glitter, but he knew he probably could get in. "There was *some* entrance pressure at Northwestern academically. Even in those years, you had to be accepted, and there were a lot of turndowns, but nothing compared to today. Northwestern gave what was called a 'College Entrance Exam' to all prospective students. That's how they did their weeding. I can't even remember getting my score, but I think I was in the upper 25 percent." And, besides, "Having an uncle on the faculty didn't hurt. I probably could have gotten in with his influence."

He arrived at Northwestern still considering giving Big Ten football a try. Northwestern had made a surprise trip to the Rose Bowl in the 1948 season, the year before he reported to school, but football teams there usually didn't have depth in manpower to match most other Big Ten schools.

"I really do think I could have played in the Big Ten there. I was big, I could have played at 236, and it was carried well. I was a linebacker and center. We had some football players in the fraternity house—Art Murakowski, an All-American fullback, Ray Evans, Ed 'Hunky' Nemeth—they all played on the Rose Bowl team. The rest of us played intramural football, and some of the football guys in off-season, particularly before they started playing, came out and helped as much as they could with our fraternity team." They also got in the mix and played some, and that bolstered his feeling that he could have been a varsity player if he had chosen to try. "I could hold my own with the football guys. But Northwestern was so much tougher academically than I expected. I thought, 'I'd just like to get through school.' I was able to pay for a part of my cost, but for the most part my mom and dad were paying. I was not on scholarship, and I had to get through."

A Neat Freak

The fraternity was Beta Theta Pi, Northwestern's Rho chapter. "I went through rush, like anyone else. I didn't know one fraternity from another. I visited two houses, Acacia and Beta. Beta made an offer to me, and I accepted. I really didn't know what I joined. Up to that time, I had never met anybody from the house except the ones who were rushing me."

In four years there, he acquired lifelong friends. One was the freshman roommate his junior year, Dan Sterner, fresh in from South Side High School in Fort Wayne, Indiana. Years later, Sterner was the Indianapolis-based attorney who during the company's rise was in on every major dealing involving Cook Inc. Even after retirement, he regularly came down from Indianapolis for board meetings.

When Sterner was a pledge, upperclassman Cook wasn't a lenient roommate. "He was a neat freak," Sterner said. "Everything had to be in its place. He said, 'If it isn't, I'm going to throw it out the window.' We were on the fourth floor. And sure enough one day when he didn't like the way I kept my stuff, he threw it all out the window—my clothing, everything, even my typewriter. I had to go down in the snow and pick it all up and haul it back up."

Northwestern's Beta house was small—about eighty residents at a time, twenty per pledge class. The eighty in Bill's years included two named William Cook, so within the house one was called "Clean Bill," and he was "Dirty Bill," an odd name for a "neat freak," Dan Sterner agreed. "He always had a mischievous side to him, I suppose that's why he got it." Language could be another possibility.

Sterner was the link that brought Cook and John Mutz together for what has become a close lifetime friendship, although their Northwestern-Beta years did not overlap. Cook graduated in 1953 and Mutz entered school the next fall, on his way first to a career in business ("We leased our first computer from John's company," Cook says), then in politics. He served fourteen years in the Indiana legislature, then two terms as Indiana's lieutenant governor before an unsuccessful run as the Republican candidate for governor against young Evan Bayh in 1988. Cook was to become a Bayh friend, confidant, and strong supporter, but in that election everything he gave, including his time in hosting fund-raising events, was for Mutz. "He's a man I'm proud to know," Cook said.

He and Mutz met when Cook came back to campus on army leave. "Dan Sterner was my pledge father," Mutz said. "And, oh yes, he did have some stories about Bill—I heard about that time he threw Dan's stuff out. Around the house, I'd say Bill was known as a promoter. That's the reputation I heard, and I can see that in the entrepreneur he became. He has always been a man of candor and great character. When we had a family tragedy, he was the one I called first, and he was tremendously supportive."

Among what Cook calls the "bunch of interesting people" who were in that Beta house during his school years were Fred Pearson, "a Big Ten champion wrestler—he handled our insurance for many years, Lloyd's of London," and the man who was to be Bill's first business partner, Brian Baldwin, who was in Northwestern's engineering tech school, a five-year program.

College life and even the fraternity provided Bill with a continuing link with music. He sang with the 150-member Northwestern Chorus, highlighted by what he called "a real thrill" when the group sang the Brahms *Requiem* in a program with the Chicago Symphony Orchestra in the Chicago Music Hall. He directed the Beta Theta Pi choir to victory in Northwestern's prestigious "Men's Sing" in 1953, his senior year.

You'd Just Sit There and Listen

Along the way at Northwestern, Bill Cook learned to study. "It didn't come easy for me in college, because I had never done anything like that in high school. I was in a tough college." He was taking a hard road: courses that would prepare him for acceptance into medical school. He majored in biology, with a minor in chemistry. He had his favorite courses and favorite professors, not all of them in his primary area of study.

"I liked English, mainly because we had great English professors. One was Bergen Evans." Even before he enrolled at Northwestern he knew about Evans, who was nationally renowned as a newspaper and magazine writer, a panelist on some hit radio and TV shows, and an author of several books, including a dictionary he wrote with his sister. In every role, his wit made people laugh.

As a lecturing professor, there was more to Evans than a quick wit, Cook found. "Gosh, what a speaker. I took two years with him. He had a squeaky, high-pitched voice, but his lectures just made literature come alive.

"I really enjoyed my comparative anatomy courses, and my biology courses, because two of the professors, Albert Wolfson and Ray Watterson, were just phenomenal—wonderful, wonderful teachers. I enjoyed going to class and taking notes, because the notes from both of them were so great. They always spoke with such emotion. It was something real. And they both drew gorgeous pictures on the blackboard. Then I had Orlando Parks, who played around with bugs. He was an exceptional professor.

"These guys all impacted me. You'd just sit there and listen to them, with your mouth hanging open. How could they know so much?"

What his curriculum at Northwestern didn't include much of was business classes.

"I took one business course—in salesmanship, two hours credit, and that was just to fill out my senior year. I already had my degree made. I wanted a light course, because my last quarter I was taking German after two years' layoff and I was scared to death of it."

That one business course he did take "taught play-acting, and how to think on your feet. It became indelible in my mind that you have to be effervescent—you have to believe in what you are selling. The guys in that course who were most animated got the best grades. It was one of the few A's I got."

The schedule during most of the previous semesters was heavy.

"In the afternoon, Tuesdays and Thursdays I had three hours of lab. Then there were Monday, Wednesday, and Friday lectures in four courses. The rest of the time, I had to figure out what to do. As a freshman and sophomore, I always figured I had to study. By my junior year, I figured out I didn't always have to."

In January of that junior year, he turned 21. That opened up a whole new adventure for him.

Cindy, Mindy, and Robert A. Taft

All along he had taken occasional part-time jobs, to pick up some spending money and help toward his bills. At 21, he was old enough to get a chauffeur's license to drive taxicabs in nearby Chicago. "I did it the rest of my junior year and my senior year, and all summer between those two years. When I first started, I got 42 percent of the billing, plus tips. It was 45 percent when I finished. I'd take the elevated subway to the Broadway Garage, get my cab at about 2 PM, and off I'd go. The guys who had been on since midnight would be coming in about then. I'd get off at 11. It was a good way to make very good money—sometimes $150 a shift. I had to do some hustling to do that, but I could make $10 on a tip, even up to $50. I had one fare to Madison, Wisconsin, and another to Streator, Illinois—guys who flew in to Midway Airport or O'Hare. Fares like those were terrific.

"I *worked* for tips. I tried to get people where they wanted to go as fast as I possibly could. If they got obnoxious, a little short and curt, or they were giving me a rough time, I'd see to it I put a couple of extra miles on, to pay me for my trouble."

He found it a perfect job for a college student. "If I had tests, I'd bring my books along, pull off at a cab stand at a hotel or airport, and get in a long line. Then I'd study while I worked my way up the line. I could get an hour, maybe even two hours of study in."

Cabbies have a reputation for being chatty. "I could be, to the extent that they wanted to talk—or if they wanted to know something about the town."

Standing out among all those conversations was one he had in July 1952, his first year as a taxi driver.

That summer Robert A. Taft—a third-term Ohio senator and son of President William Howard Taft—was running for president. The 1952 Republican convention was in Chicago, and on Sunday, July 6, the convention's opening day, with the nation looking in at the first televised convention, 532 delegates pledged to support Taft on the first ballot—just 72 short of what he needed to win the nomination—walked with arms linked into the Stockyards International Amphitheatre singing "Onward Christian Soldiers." It was showy stuff for the reserved conservative they called "Mr. Republican," and the speeches and placard-waving demonstrations hadn't even begun.

It turned out to be his high-water mark. In first-ballot voting, Taft lost thirty-two of his pledged votes. He still was the leader, but before the ballot was declared closed, shift after shift came—away from Taft, for the hot new political name with all the momentum, retired five-star army general Dwight D. Eisenhower. There was no second ballot. Less than a year later, Eisenhower was in the White House, and Robert A. Taft, majority leader in the Senate, was dead, victim of a fast-spreading cancer.

Taxi driver Bill Cook doesn't remember what day of the convention it was: day 1, with all the exuberance, or later, with the growing apprehension, then the swift and crushing defeat. What he does remember is pulling up in front of the Stevens Hotel and realizing that the man who was getting into his cab was Robert Taft. "He just came down the steps from the hotel, got into the cab, and said, 'I'd like to go to the Stockyards.'

"Then he started asking *me* questions: 'Where are you from?' I told him southern Illinois. 'How old are you?' I told him I was 21 and a junior at Northwestern. 'Are you a Republican or a Democrat?' I told him both my mom and dad are registered Republicans but my mother does go for Franklin Roosevelt. He got a big charge out of that and said, 'They all do.'

"That was a thrill. I know what they always said about him being aloof and cold, but he was very personable that day, just like a common, ordinary guy. And he was by himself. *Nobody* with him. Weird."

Early in his cabbie career Cook learned some Chicago rules. "You kept a $2 bill under your driver's license, so you always had that when a cop pulled you over. You knew you'd be stopped at least once a day for a multitude of reasons: double-parking when a fare was getting out or getting in, or your rear end was out in traffic, or you made a left-hand turn or right-hand turn a little too quickly. You'd get out your $2 bill, hand it over, and you'd be on your way."

There were other "rules."

"When I drove nights, I had to know where the, uh, places were. The whorehouses. I got paid good money for that. Every guy I brought out there was ten bucks.

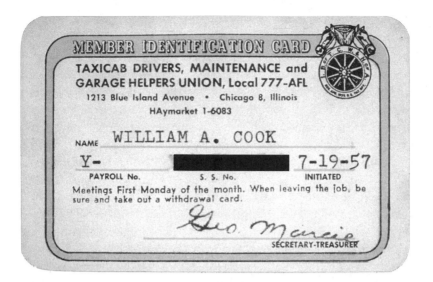

Bill Cook's taxicab driver's union identification card, Chicago, 1957

"There were twins, Cindy and Mindy, black girls, gorgeous. Whenever I'd find a guy, or guys, who said they really wanted to have a good time and didn't mind spending a hundred bucks each, I'd take them down to Cindy and Mindy. They got taken care of. Then I'd come back and pick 'em up.

"I had to know where they were, because they were always moving. These were floating whorehouses—they'd last about a week in one place and move. Sometimes they'd be on Fortieth Street, sometimes around White Sox Park (Thirty-fifth), sometimes clear down to Sixty-third—they always had the same telephone number, so I'd find out where they were by phone before I took off.

"Guys would say, 'How long will it take?' And I'd say, 'How strong are you?'

"I'd give them a certain time I'd be back to pick them up and 'If you're not ready, I'll wait for you.' When they did come out, most of them had a smile on their face.

"If you're a cab driver, those are the kinds of things where you make your best money. I liked to work weekends, because that's when I'd hit these guys. I could work two or three loads. Weekends I'd start at 5 and stay on until 3. On weeknights, I'd drive until about 10. After 10, I couldn't take guys to the South Side and get back at a decent hour."

There are tales of the dangers of Chicago taxi driving—cab drivers robbed, mugged, even killed. Bill got by with no incidents—"nothing that caused any problems. I was big, and I knew where not to go. I knew the city of Chicago very well."

Meanwhile, Elsewhere

Maybe if she had come along in a future era, Gayle Karch would have gone to Indiana University with the same career plan Bill carried to Northwestern: to be a doctor. She had taken the high school science courses that would have prepared her for pre-medicine studies. But she was in the high school Class of '52, and bright young women interested in the medical field then weren't disciplined to think of a career as a doctor. "I spent one semester as a nursing major, but that Art Department was always over there and I thought that was really where I wanted to be. So my freshman year I switched to art, without really planning what I could do with it."

She continued to take science courses at Indiana University—biology, zoology, and botany among her favorites. She thought there might be a career niche out there for someone with her dual interests—perhaps "illustrations for textbooks and publications."

As a freshman, she pledged Alpha Omicron Pi sorority, which became a lifelong interest for her. Her academic achievements got her elected to Alpha Lambda Delta, the national honorary for freshmen. And on IU's Founders Day in May of her senior year, she was inducted into the ultimate Arts and Sciences honorary, Phi Beta Kappa.

London and Leonardo

Late in her junior year at IU, her parents got a letter from Sam Braden, associate dean of arts and sciences:

> Your daughter Gayle is one of three girls who have been recommended by professor Alma Eikerman of our Department of Fine Arts as being qualified for the program of summer study to England. The trip will last from June 10 to September 3 and will permit the group to do some sightseeing as well as complete the study project. The cost will be about $800, which is several hundred dollars less than the ordinary trip of shorter duration.

Federal statistics say the 1955 dollar would be equivalent to a little more than $7.50 today, so that cost estimate was about $6,000 in 2008 money. It was a bargain price for all that it covered, and it offered an invaluable lifetime experience, but as an unplanned cost it wasn't a trivial amount for Arthur and Thelma Karch. Braden recognized that and closed his note with a semi-pleading tone: "Because she has been so highly recommended for this, I hope that she will find it possible to go." She went, with the two other IU girls who had been similarly recommended.

Their trip in the summer of 1955 was the first overseas study project for an official IU group after World War II. "That seems strange because it was ten years after the end of the war," Gayle says—sixteen years after the Nazis' London blitz that ravaged the proud and historic city. "Even in 1955, there were still bombed-out buildings and a lot hadn't changed. We saw it before the rebuilding. There were no high-rises yet."

The twelve-week tour was loosely constructed to allow the three students to do some trip-improvising of their own. The only requirement was that six weeks be spent at work in London. "We had a supervisor [Dean E. Mowbray Tate of Hanover], and we each had study projects previously approved by our instructors," Gayle says. "Mine was approved by Professor Eikerman, to study the Windsor Castle's collection of drawings by Leonardo da Vinci. So every work day for six weeks I went to Windsor Castle and studied the Leonardo drawings."

The access she was granted left a lifelong thrill. "I asked to see the Leonardo drawings and they brought them to my desk. I actually held one of his drawings in my hands. They didn't have all the security they have now. The only requirement was that you not have any ink with you."

The one she chose to copy, with a pencil sketch, was an untitled bust of a woman. The sketch was harder for her to do than it might have been. "Because he was left-handed and I'm right-handed, I found it was very difficult to make the kind of delicate shading that he did."

She still has the sketch she made, her Leonardo link.

The rest of the summer, the three students traveled together. "We did a loop through Holland, France, Germany, and Italy. All three of us were art majors, so in every town we hit every museum, every architectural attraction that was there. When we came back, we each wrote a paper for six hours' credit."

The Art of Adapting

After graduation from IU in June 1956, she faced the new degree holder's usual challenge: how to put a college education to work in the job market. "I did have a back-up of teaching, but I didn't really want to do that. I went to Chicago to get an art job. I was looking for anything—illustration, fashion design, commercial art studios, advertising agencies, whatever."

Instead, she found that "beginning artists made exactly one-half of what people made clerking in Loop stores—$50 a week clerking, $25 to start in an art department somewhere. I couldn't live on that.

"Each day between interviews in the Loop, I went to Kroch's and Brentano's [Chicago's leading downtown bookstore] just to kill time, looking at books. I finally applied for a job there." Nothing available fit her training.

"Their art work was done out of house. However, the interviewer said, 'How is your English?' English and writing were other interests of mine in college, so I said, 'Well, I think okay.' He said, 'We need someone to proofread every written item that leaves this building. Because we deal in the printed word, we want the grammar and the usage to be better than it is now.' People were writing their own letters—clerks in each department, and someone in art books, music books, technical books, fiction, all these people were writing letters, and executives were writing letters. "We're going to have every letter read by you and rewritten by you," her new employer told her.

"Actually, it *was* a good way to get into the store's business. Kroch's and Brentano's listed itself as the largest bookstore in the world. All I had to do was rewrite the letters and get them back on time. In the meantime, I was allowed to check out any book I wanted to and read it, as long as I protected it cover to cover. I heard about all the latest books, read descriptions and criticisms of them—I enjoyed that."

She was sharing a South Side apartment—"a four and a half–story walk-up"—with Rita Dalke, whom she had met when both were in the Alpha Omicron Pi sorority house at IU. Mornings she would ride downtown on the "El," the city's sometimes-elevated subway train, returning on it in late afternoon. No personal automobile was needed or wanted.

When a car did come into her life, it had a future husband attached.

Death of a Doctor Dream

Medical school still was on Bill Cook's mind when he graduated from Northwestern, but so was military duty. The Korean War had just ended, but the draft was still on. Awaiting his call-up, he took a job with the arsenal in Joliet, Illinois. "They were glad to have me. They needed someone to do inspections on accidents. But they didn't know I was going to be called into service so soon. They thought it would be December." He received an almost immediate commendation, a promotion, and a glowing letter— "rather unusual to consider a person as young as you for this position . . . recommendations from your immediate superior commended the manner in which you conducted yourself in Tetryl gravity line investigation of July 6–8 and the procedures you used in establishing your program."[1] That came on July 16, 1953. Three weeks later, on August 6, he went into the army and came out May 5, 1955.

"I took my six weeks of basic training at Camp Pickett, Virginia, and Camp Crowder, Missouri. From there I went to Fort Sam Houston, Texas, and I was an operating-room technician for two months, doing debriding." Debriding is removing burnt tissue, and virtually all patients treated there were military men burned in Korea. "Napalm was one of the main instruments of death. It didn't take much to misfire and get our own guys, or a truck would blow up and the gas tanks would spew all over them. There were so many bad injuries in that war, particularly from napalm, I didn't think we'd ever use napalm again. Too many got hurt." A decade later, it again was a "main instrument of death" in Vietnam.

Operating-room technician Cook's job in debriding burn victims was to "take antiseptic soap and rub that burn until it bled real well, and then put antibiotics on it and wrap it up." It was day-in, day-out duty, and yet individual cases stayed in his mind. "You would identify with a guy," he said, recalling a particular patient. "We spent a lot of time trying to keep him alive. He could talk, even though he was dying. We did everything we could to keep him comfortable while he was alive. It was just one of those experiences. . . .

"I was pre-med when I went *into* the military."

But not when he came out. "I identified with the burn patients, and that really got to me. I got involved with those kids. I knew then that I didn't want to become a doctor. I had an interest in medicine, but more in the mechanical parts of medicine."

Most of his army time came after the hospital stint. "The people at Fort Sam Houston found out I had a little bit of physics—at least I told them I had. And while I was there that first year, I did take some courses in physics and organic chemistry at Trinity University. They said, 'Can you prepare a course outline? We don't have any doctors with your background.' So I wrote an outline, and the rest of my time there I taught doctors and nurses the physics of anesthesia.

"They gave me a white coat and $110 a month to live off post. Every morning I'd get in the '53 Ford that my Mom and Dad gave me, head up the hill to Fort Sam, and park my car in the officers' section. I had my little coat, and I saluted everybody. I had my hat off, so they didn't see I was a private. I never made Pfc."

He became the doctors' friend, his Chicago taxi background coming into play. "Those doctors didn't have cars. During the week, I'd take them down to Laredo, Texas. On weekends I'd pick them up on Friday night and head down past Laredo into Monterrey, Mexico. I'd show them where they could buy booze and where they could have a good time. Then I'd pick them up on Sundays and take them home.

"I only lost one doctor during all those trips. He was AWOL for two days—he met and married a Mexican girl."

Bridge to Godot

The year that Gayle Karch spent as a senior at IU, Bill Cook was back in civilian life trying to get a career going. He returned to Chicago and took a job with Martin Aircraft as a recruiter. That lasted six months. "Then I went with American Hospital Supply [in Chicago], as a salesman first. Then they had me prepare the first Scientific Products Division catalog they ever did. The writing was secondary to assembling all the material and literature on the manufacturing. Putting that catalog together was a lot of fun."

His life circle began to tighten when he left American Hospital Supply to take a sales job with Nelson Instrument Company, "a small company I had heard about. They made several things—the very first treadmills . . . an electrical control box for a drill press or a lathe, quite a nice little gadget. The problem was that the company owner liked to invent something and then move on to something else. I found out very quickly that commission sales there wasn't going to be the best thing in the world."

The owner-inventor was Lloyd Nelson, a second-cousin of Gayle Karch. "Bill could sell a product, but Lloyd lost interest after making the first one," Gayle said. "Lloyd was a child prodigy, according to his mother, especially with electronics.

"His job was to do custom-made instruments. Bill's job was to sell those to other labs, and the company's money was to be made from volume, because the big expense was in the first one. The problem was Lloyd was a scientist, and he always wanted to go right on to something else."

The short-lived link-up with Nelson paid off big for Bill Cook in other ways. "Through Lloyd I met Gayle," he said. It happened in a bridge game, and Lloyd Nelson didn't play bridge. "I brought a date with me to the Nelsons' house that night. The foursome was Lloyd's wife, Editha, my date, myself, and Gayle. Editha invited Gayle to come up.

"I knew the first night I met her that I would marry her."

She smiles at the comment: "Well, he had been looking around a long time, and he might think about something like that. I went with no expectation of even meeting somebody. I enjoyed him, but I had no reason to evaluate him, because he was there with someone else. I wasn't really rating him as a prospect, although he was certainly pleasant."

Bill expanded on his quick impression. "Even though I had another date with me, I knew that night Gayle probably was going to be the one. She was quiet, and witty—a very unusual sense of humor, she said some really funny things—bright, very attractive, she had an hourglass figure. She was a person I felt immediately relaxed with. Also, I could sense that she was in with the program, really the very first time."

Neither Bill nor Gayle, even now, suspects the Nelsons of matchmaking. "I went to visit my second-cousin," Gayle said. It was a major trip, from 7200 South to 7400 North, without a car. "I planned to spend the night. I took the train, and I was picked up at the train stop by Lloyd and Bill. Bill didn't say much. He was there with his date. The four of us played cards."

Nothing happened right away. "Three weeks later, I asked Lloyd if he would call Gayle and see if she would be interested in going to a play," Bill said.

Three *weeks*? "I didn't have any money."

Asked *Lloyd* to call? Why? "Just bashfulness, I think."

"She told him that would be great. I went down, picked her up, and we saw the play *Waiting for Godot*."

"We've always said we got married in spite of *Waiting for Godot*," Gayle said. The Samuel Beckett play to some is a classic, but not to the young couple on their first date.

"Oh, was that gross!" Bill said. "We went with Betty and Brian Baldwin. The free tickets were from Betty. It was in the Roosevelt Theater, which was rather unusual, for a play to be there—but with *Waiting for Godot* you don't need any stage sets, you just need a garbage can and light post and that's about it. But we had a good time."

This time, Gayle *was* doing some evaluating. "Many of the young employees at the bookstore were like me, people who had college majors that didn't really translate into careers. I was an art major, and there were music, philosophy, political science, literature majors—it was a nice group of young people. We had evening get-togethers where people talked, and talked, and discussed books. At first I thought that was really good, very stimulating. But after about a year I realized that people weren't actually doing anything. There was a lot of talk and theory.

"That's when I met Bill. He was like a blast of fresh air. He was doing things, and getting things started. Even with Nelson Instrument Co., he was working with concrete things that advanced science. He was much more grounded than the atmosphere I had been in at work. Suddenly I saw what sounded like a better idea."

"We were married in four and a half months," Bill said.

Nelson's company had a storefront at 607 Howard Avenue in Chicago. "The little plant had a cot in it, and that's where Bill slept," Gayle said. "It didn't have a shower or bath in it, so he took his showers at Lloyd's house, in Wilmette, a northern suburb. Bill didn't have any furniture. He didn't have anything there except the cot."

The eyes of Gayle the Artist twinkle as she paints that verbal picture, then delivers the plaintive, factual punch line: "I married a homeless man."

Cheesecake and Conversation

In those intervening weeks of courtship, up and down Lake Shore Drive Bill's Packard went. "I'd be at home, with nothing to do that night, maybe 4 or 5 o'clock, might even be a weeknight, and she'd call me or I'd call her and she'd say, 'Why don't you come on down?' Which always meant to me, 'That sounds like a lot of fun. I've got enough gas. I'll just get in the car and do that.'

"We'd go out. I'd drink coffee, and she'd drink Coke. Gayle and I got off on cheesecake, which in those days was brand-new. We'd see it advertised in the paper—'Special, 89 cents a slice'—and off we'd go. We'd go a long way for cheesecake."

By then, Bill and Northwestern fraternity brother Brian Baldwin had talked of starting their own business, manufacturing hypodermic needles. That was "the program" that he sensed early Gayle could envision right along with him. "He asked me before he proposed what I thought of starting a business—the hypodermic needle business," Gayle said. "I said I thought that sounded like a good idea and was exciting."

"She always was very positive, interested in what I was doing at the plant, in my background," Bill said. "That's always a male ego trip, when somebody asks you about yourself. And then she started telling me about herself.

"She could see a lot more in me than I could see in myself. She knew I was hard-working and aggressive. She always felt, I think, that I would do everything to take care of her—of us might be a better way to say it.

"We met the latter part of April. By July 1 we were talking about marriage. There was no doubt in her mind. I knew that, and she knew it."

And he knew when the time had come to wed.

"My Packard broke down. I thought, 'Boy, I don't want to be doing this through the winter and now I don't know how I'm going to get down there.' I thought it was best to just go ahead and get married. She had the money."

A Flight, a Fright, a Hike

Bill had been a licensed pilot since his college days. He didn't have household items, but he had made a good buy on an airplane, an "Air Coupe." Gayle's first flight ever was with Bill in that plane. On a July flight to Canton they had their first kiss.

"One day in August, we got in that Air Coupe and flew down to Evansville. I asked her dad if I could marry her. Actually, I proposed to her on the riverbank of the Ohio the night we got down there. Then the next day, I asked her father and mother."

Picture the romance of that moment: a summer evening riverside proposal . . .

"It was awful," Bill said. "Grim. Hot. I swatted mosquitoes the whole time, and within five minutes we got out of there."

"There *were* lots of mosquitoes," Gayle said. "And heat. It was Evansville, and it was summer. Our house wasn't air-conditioned. Bill told my dad, 'You really have to get air-conditioning.'"

Already by then, the Karches had grown fond of their brash-but-bright prospective son-in-law. "Oh, yes, they liked him. Bill could talk to a farmer, because he had that experience with the grain elevator in a small town. They got along well."

There definitely was no ring exchange, down by the riverside.

"No," Gayle said, "I didn't expect a ring."

Parental permission granted, the two got back in the plane and headed for Chicago. "The airplane's canopy blew off in the air," Gayle remembers. "It had a windshield, but without the canopy, we couldn't talk in the plane because it was very noisy. I began to see oil streaming back over the windshield. I pointed to it with a kind of 'What is that?' look. He looked back, indicating it was nothing to worry about.

"We flew on a little farther and he said, 'Look for an airport.' He was always testing me when we were up in the plane. I would have the map and he'd tell me to try to figure out where we were. I thought he was just challenging me to do that, find out where we were. But I looked down and did see a little airport, and I pointed down at it. That's where we landed, right away. And then I found out it was urgent. I didn't know until we got down."

"A little misfortune," the pilot calls it. "The engine froze. It was getting dark. She pointed down—there was a silo, and a barn, and I saw the airport with just a little grass strip. I landed and stopped the airplane. I didn't stop it, it stopped itself. The engine just quit."

They had almost made it back. Their emergency landing was at Matteson, about twenty miles south of Gayle's apartment. "We hitchhiked back," she says. "Bill's car was at the little airport where we had taken off. It was late at night by the time we got back.

"He slept on the couch in my apartment. Which my roommate has never let me forget. Shocking! Then he took off in the morning. She has always remembered that."

Reverend Eugene Durham married Bill Cook and Gayle Karch in a single-ring ceremony, Saturday evening, September 21, 1957, at First Methodist Church in Evanston, Illinois.

A Very Pretty Gold Band

Roommate Rita Dalke was Gayle's maid of honor. Her own wedding came not long after. "We used to say we married the only two guys who would climb four and a half flights of stairs and not complain," Gayle said.

Lloyd Nelson was Bill's best man at the wedding, which came in the chapel of the Evanston Methodist Church, before about fifty guests. Ronnie Casson sang. It was September 21, 1957, at 6 o'clock on a cold, crisp Saturday night. "Our wedding was quite beautiful, even though it was small," Bill says.

"Because we were older and out of school, we planned the wedding ourselves and paid for it," Gayle said. "We were watching our money. We were watching the same amount of money." Essentially, hers.

After the ceremony, bride and groom headed out to family receptions, first to Gayle's side at Lloyd and Editha Nelson's house, then to Bill's side, which had a reception at his aunt's house, just off Peterson Avenue. Then they headed out on a weeklong honeymoon that took them into Wisconsin and up to Minnesota, until the money ran out.

The marriage was a single-ring ceremony. "I don't wear a ring because I broke my ring finger," Bill said. "Gayle had no hesitation about a single-ring ceremony. We bought a $25 wedding ring that she still wears today—a very pretty gold ring."

It was exactly what she hoped for, Gayle said. "We looked for it together. I wanted just a wide gold band.

"I think it was $19.95."

Road to Bloomington

The experience of working for Lloyd Nelson, coming after other similarly unsatisfying jobs, was the final convincer for Bill Cook that "it was very difficult for me to work for somebody else." He jokes about it: "At American Hospital Supply, I always knew more than my boss. The boss didn't like it. He never quite terminated me, but sometimes he got really nasty. I decided very early that it would be best if I went out on my own."

In his first venture like that—as a married man who had just left employment by his best man—Cook discovered that the entrepreneurial instinct within him was not fool-proof.

Cook and Brian Baldwin put their minds and names together and formed Balco, to manufacture and distribute shot glasses. "Unusual ones. But there was a problem with these shot glasses. It seems the filter we used to hold the film to the bottom of the glass didn't hold too well, and the film began to curl. Pretty soon we found out there were 50,000 shot glasses out all over the United States with the film curled at the bottom. The glasses had a 35-millimeter art picture on the bottom, with a filter atop. In the middle

LITTLE BEAUTY SHOT GLASS

- GIFT
- NOVELTY
- BAR ACCESSORY

Hold Bottom of Glass
Toward Light and
P E E P

of the glass a lens magnified the picture. They were called 'art photos,' but they were just nudes. We got the pictures from California—800 of them. Gayle and I and her cousin sat in her cousin's living room going over all 800 pictures, evaluating them, to pick out four. It took us quite a long time one evening. We repeated several times to view them for their art. We had a good time."[1]

Brian Baldwin scraped up a $15,000 investment that got them a mold and 800 sets of picture equipped glasses. "We sold them through a place called Black Bar Accessories, out of the Merchandise Mart in Chicago." Black Bar got the glasses into department stores throughout the country. When the curling problem developed, Cook said, "We got out of that business, closed the doors of that shop, and discontinued our mailbox. We just had to write off the $15,000 investment."

They tried another business together, a little more orthodox. Baldwin, an engineer, also had worked for American Hospital Supply. Their experience there made them aware of a market for disposable hypodermic needles, which were just beginning to gain acceptance over reusable needles. A company out of Deland, Florida, was the only competition when the two decided, "We ought to go into business."

They found a building at 4620 Ravenswood on Chicago's North side. Bill painted the walls inside and lined up some equipment—designed some, bought some, helped bring some in—and Manufacturing Process Laboratories (MPL), Inc., was ready to go.

"It was a successful company. We turned out about two million stainless steel hypodermic needles a day—a lot more needles than I ever wanted to see again." American Hospital Supply was one of its leading customers. He stayed with MPL five years. "My last year there we were doing $2 million a year. Quite profitable."

A Good Dad, a Strong Disciplinarian

During his MPL years, he lost his father. The Peoria newspaper account says George A. Cook, 66, "died at 11 AM Saturday [October 1, 1960] at the Veterans Administration Research Hospital, Chicago, after an illness of about a week."

"It was a cerebral vascular accident—a cerebral hemorrhage," Bill says. "It came very suddenly."

George had been out of the grain elevator business for several years by then. He had kept his elevators going through some good and some tough years. "During World War II it was a successful and profitable business," Bill said. "After the war, it was successful and profitable up until about 1950. Then more and more farmers were buying their own mills and storing their own grain. Rather than making money off the storage of grain and feed, his function became buying the grain from them and selling it at a profit."

The Fiatt elevator sat pretty much out in the open in a rural area. A lot of trust was involved in its operation. In off-hours, when owner Cook was about five miles away at his home in Canton, Bill said, "People loaded and unloaded grain at night all the time—that's what you do if you have an elevator that's miles away from anything, and there's nothing around it."

One night there was activity at the elevator. "Some of the farmers around there noticed something was going on, but they just thought it was an honest dealing. It turned out to be crooks." Big trucks with Mississippi license plates loaded up and drove off into the night with George Cook's livelihood. "The FBI came in because this was government-stored corn. They were able to trace the trucks going to Staley's in Decatur." (That's about eighty miles away, and the Staley Grain Co. has a place in history. In the 1920s, George Halas bought its company-sponsored pro-football team, the Decatur Staleys. Halas moved the franchise to Chicago, where he renamed the team the Bears.)

The investigators' work produced little more than the issuing state of the license plates. The thieves got away. George Cook's business was never the same, Bill says. "Basically it was destroyed, financially. The investigation was hard on him. The FBI guys said, 'You should have been more careful.' That definitely hurt him for a while. He went through a mental depression. Then he and Mom bought a Dari-Delite ice cream store, and they were very happy about it. They had a store in a little town south of Joliet, sold it, and made a profit. They bought one in Fox Lake, Illinois, sold it, and had a nice profit. Then they had one in Evanston that just did very, very well. After I came out of the army, I worked three months there.

"They enjoyed living in hotels for the summer. At the end of the year, they'd go back to Mattoon and spend their winter. Or they might go down to Florida. They had a good life. But they were always a little bit edgy until

George Cook's 1940 Ford beside his grain elevator in Norris, Illinois

May came around and they could go back to work. It's just a darned shame that Dad died early and they couldn't enjoy it a little longer. They were making good money, they enjoyed what they were doing, and they enjoyed the public. They were having a ball."

The Evanston store was the site of George Cook's hemorrhage. "I had taken Mom out to supper. We got back to the store, went in, and he was on the floor. The people working with him that night were attending to him. A doctor came with an ambulance, and they took him away. We moved him immediately to the V.A. Hospital in Chicago. That had always been an expressed wish of his. We got the news there that he would never recover. He died a week later."

The week had an agonizing climax. "At the end, Mom and I had to make up our minds whether to remove life support. It's tough. But we did know enough about it—even if he had come out of it, he would not have been the same person. The doctor said there was no hope because he was flat-lined. Mom didn't want to see him suffer.

"He was a good dad, a strong disciplinarian. He was really proud of my accomplishments, as was Mom."

Cleo Cook lived twenty-five years after her husband's death. She ran the Dari-Delite store for a few seasons before selling it. She was 92 when she died at Meadowood Retirement Community in Bloomington, where she lived her last three years.

A Time for Self-Study

In MPL's fourth year, Carl Alfred Cook was born in Evanston Hospital to Gayle and Bill. "We were living in an apartment in Chicago—not in a suburb," Gayle said. "Bill was always going to the office at odd hours and needing to be close to where he worked. A long commute would not have fit into the way he worked."

Those were not exactly years of carefree big-city social life. "We did not have a lot of money, and we didn't have many friends," Bill said. "Our college friends and high school friends were like us, trying to get a family going and trying to make some money. Brian and Betty Baldwin were the only people we associated with quite a bit."

"We realized we didn't want to live in Chicago forever," Gayle said. "We wanted a smaller town. Bill was determined to see MPL successful. Five years later it was. So we began to look around."

And so, at 32 years of age, Bill Cook decided it was time to do some self-assessing.

"I had to figure out what I wanted to do with my life. I sat down one time for a day and a half. I made a list of things I liked to do, and things I didn't like to do—things I was good at and things I wasn't good at. I'm not particularly precise with my hands, but I can build things with my hands. I can conceptualize. I can think sometimes in three dimensions, but not always. I like to talk to people, enjoy being around people. I like to learn about what they do. I'm inquisitive.

"The other side of the sheet said I wasn't as precise as I should be. I didn't like a lot of procedure. I loved the process, but the devil in the detail was not my bag. That's how I learned to think modular. Whenever I have a problem, I don't think of the big picture. I think of one particular aspect of that problem. When I think I've got that, I take the next step. If you look at this company, a lot of that was involved. Modular thinking."

Gayle was involved in the assessment, Bill said. "I'd put down 'too quick to judge,' or 'I'd rather organize than carry out detail.' She'd say, 'I think you're a little hard on yourself here' or 'I think you ought to put a little more emphasis on this.' I thought I might even have a little attention-deficit disorder. If there's a problem to solve, I can focus on it. But in conversation, in many cases I lose interest.

"I knew I wanted to manufacture something mechanical. And that I liked medicine but didn't want to be a doctor.

"The list would get longer, then shorter. At the end it was two pages long. I think I had myself pretty well analyzed. Then I said, 'That's it. That's what I'm going to be shooting for.'"

That notebook—spiral, with a tan cover—lists twenty potential areas of interest for him under the heading of Manufacturing, including purchasing agent, salesman, personnel, public relations, sales promotion, sales representative, wage evaluation, "troubleshooter," college relations, technical writer, and comptroller.

Under personal strengths, interests, or preferences he listed:

Travel
Farming and farm problems
Driving
Working with hospitals
Meeting customers
Honesty
Working with my hands on mechanical things
Drawings of scenery
Furniture and redecorating
Trotters and pacers

He touched on his interest in airplanes and flying, allowing possibilities for utilizing that interest in:

Sales
Crop dusting
Manufacturing an airplane
Mining

The most prescient list broke down what he wanted most to find, or to be, in a career in "general manufacturing," one of his few lists in which each item was given a numerical priority:

The boss (sole owner)
1. Small town, city, near large city, central Indiana
2. 100 employees max
3. Small product (patented or secret)
4. Useful or humanitarian
5. Provide income for family
6. Provide free time or occupy free time
7. Profit potential, profits do not necessarily have to be large to expand, growth can come from debt on corporation

When the self-assessment was over, he and Gayle were still in Chicago. Grimy, winter-gripped Chicago.

This Is No Way to Become

"That last winter in Chicago, 1962–63, was really bad," Gayle said. "Snow piled up and stayed on the streets and got blacker and blacker for weeks and weeks, and parking got harder. We were in an apartment neighborhood, and all the parking was on the streets."

"I'd spend all day Sunday shoveling out the snow for my car," Bill said. "I'd pull out, and in five minutes somebody had pulled into my space and I had no place when I came home." Street parking had other hazards. "A guy tried to steal the seats out of my Corvair. He had all the bolts out. I got in the car and fell flat on my back."

Even mild-mannered Gayle felt tense. "People in a big city look out for themselves. You get treated very rudely. I remember saying, 'I know it's time to get out of Chicago because in the supermarket I'm beginning to hit people back with my shopping cart.' Which was true. I'd go to the checkout lane, and people would actually push my cart out of the way.

"Carl was an infant. I got on a bus one time carrying him, and no one gave me a seat. The bus was lurching around, and I was hanging on and holding a baby. People were taking care of themselves, and I found myself getting that way, too. I said, 'This is no way to become.'"

So in those dismal winter months of early 1963, Bill said, "I thought, 'Man, I've got to get out of here.'"

When MPL was formed, Bill recalled, "Brian Baldwin put up some money, I put up what little I could, Brian's parents put up some, and his in-laws put up a lot of money. Brian was the majority shareholder, and his ties were to Chicago. But not mine."

At the end of five years of working to build the company to its profitable status, he said, "I really didn't have a whole lot of stock. What little I had, I sold to Brian for $15,000." He put $1,500 aside for start-up money and designated the rest to live on until income began from the company that was only a vague dream at the time.

A depressing time for the wannabe entrepreneur? "No," Gayle said. "Sobering. It was a very sobering experience when he realized he was going to have just a small amount of stock after all the dedication he put into it, and his skills—none of that made any difference, because the money was on the other side. My impression was he knew from that moment that he was not going to let this happen again—and that a fraternity brother's friendship was not the deciding factor, input and skills would not be the deciding factor, it was money.

"He stayed there five years because he wanted to stay until he knew that what he had done was a success—to finish the job, so to speak. After it was going, he felt he could leave honorably and be proud of what he did. No one could resent his leaving, because he had done the job he agreed to do. He left vowing that he would never make that mistake again. That, in the future, he would own the company. And that it would be ideal if he could start with a small investment."

Settling on Bloomington

First there were steps to take, beginning with escaping Chicago to a place where ideas could be tried out.

Together, Bill and Gayle went to work on their relocation. They began with a broad scope. "We looked at Palo Alto, California, because that's where my cousin Van Fucilla ended up," Bill said. "We looked at Los Angeles as a possible place to live, looked at the San Francisco Bay area."

Gayle said, "Bill had always liked San Antonio, because he had been stationed there and was familiar with that area. But in the end we decided we wanted to stay close to our families.

"We drew circles on a map around Bill's family in Illinois and my family in Evansville, and we looked at what towns were within reasonable distance of both families." They were determined to relocate outside what they considered the "snow belt"—the northern third of Indiana and Illinois. "We picked out all the cities that seemed to be big enough to have some goods and services but within driving distance, an easy day trip, of a major city," she said.

Bloomington was one, located about fifty miles south of Indianapolis and its major airport—a good hundred miles south of Indiana's "snow belt." Bloomington's weather usually comes east from St. Louis on its way toward Cincinnati, unlinked with the snow-producing Great Lakes that reach down as far south as Indiana's northern tier—more than a three-hour drive north of the town the Cooks chose.

Bloomington was familiar to Gayle because of her college days, but they hadn't left her predisposed toward eventually living there. "I always was sure I would go to a big city, as I did to Chicago for my first job." So much for that factor. Experience had made "big city" a negative, not a positive.

So in their kitchen-table research, she said, "We also looked in Indiana at Columbus, at Seymour. We preferred Bloomington just because of the university. We looked at Lafayette—that's in the snow belt. Too much snow. And Indianapolis, that's a big city. We looked at Columbus, Ohio—that seemed just a little foreign, too far away. We looked at Cincinnati."

She subscribed to some newspapers, including the Bloomington *Herald-Telephone*. She wrote to the Chambers of Commerce "in ten or twelve towns, and got information on what was going on in the town—if there were labor problems or other big things. Then we decided to make a trip to however many towns we still had on that list." The preserved notebook shows Gayle had sketched Indiana and penciled in dots where the cities under consideration were, then three optional three-day routes connecting those dots—loops taking them through some of the towns on the way down and others on the swing back up north toward their Chicago home.

The one chosen broke down distances and overnight stops:

> Day 1: Shelbyville (225 miles from Chicago, 41 from
>   Indianapolis), Franklin (16—first-night stopover);
> Day 2: Columbus (20 from Franklin), Seymour (18),
>   Bedford (35, then starting the swing back),
>   Bloomington (23), Spencer (18—second-night stopover);
> Day 3: Martinsville (27), Greencastle (38),
>   Crawfordsville (29), and home to Chicago (152).

The itinerary "budgeted" 601 miles.

"In Bloomington, we called on the Chamber of Commerce," Gayle said. "The director there was Bob Distelhorst, and he treated us that day like we were bringing Westinghouse to Bloomington. That made a big impression, because we had nothing at the time—no business at all. Bill just wanted to see what the climate was. They were very helpful, spent time with us.

"Bill had been to Bloomington with me and sort of liked the town. I had never thought of living here because as a student I hardly got off campus. I'd go from campus down Kirkwood to a movie, and that was about it. But when we looked around the town, it did have an appeal. After we had seen all the towns, Bloomington was the one we thought was pretty good. Columbus, Indiana, was the runner-up."

Bill recalls, "We thought, 'This town has so many things—the university and all of this culture.' We thought we would enjoy the students. And we do."

Bloomington came out perfectly on another consideration. "In Bloomington, we both would be 128 miles from our parents," Bill said. "It worked out very well."

Now it was a matter of timing and affordability.

If It's Not Snowing . . .

As one of his last acts with MPL, Bill represented the company in replacing some faulty needles. That's how, in the dead of that brutal winter of 1962–63, he found himself in the town of Cadillac in Michigan's frigid Upper Peninsula.

He got his business done there just as a snowstorm blew in. "It was a blizzard. I couldn't see my hand in front of my face. I couldn't leave. I was one of the lucky ones who got a hotel room real quick so I was able to wait it out. But sitting there two days in a hotel room, actually three days because it was 5 o'clock on the third afternoon before I could get out—God!"

When he and his car were free at last, he started driving toward Chicago. "When I saw the Fort Wayne turnoff, I thought to myself, if I go to Bloomington maybe it's not snowing, and if it's not snowing, maybe I won't go back to Chicago.

"So instead of making the right-hand turn on the tollway, I kept on going south and got to Bloomington. There was no snow on the ground. I called Gayle up that night and said, 'How would you like to move to Bloomington right now?' She said, 'Would you tell me why first?' I said, 'It's not snowing in Bloomington.' She said, 'Well, I'm ready to move.' In a few weeks we got our plans together and moved."

Cook Inc. was founded in July 1963 in the Cooks' three-bedroom apartment in Bart Villa, a new apartment complex on Bloomington's east side.

Bedroom Beginning

*For me to make my product, all I needed was a
blowtorch, a soldering iron, and a few little tools
and fixtures I could make myself.*

—*Bill Cook*

Within Bloomington, Indiana, within the worldwide medical devices industry, within the no-pikers Forbes 400 "family," the most familiar part of the billionaire Bill Cook story is how everything started with a $1,500 investment and a small apartment's spare bedroom.

In any bible about Bill Cook, that always will be Genesis 1:1. "In the beginning . . ." It is legend without much myth. That really is the beginning for everything that Cook Inc. grew to include.

Bill closed his days at MPL and even arrived in Bloomington with not one but two thoughts about how he might get going with a new, solely owned Cook Company.

One would have put him at least temporarily in the disintegration business. He came in contact with a man in Minneapolis–St. Paul who had bought from the U.S. military about four hundred "disintegrator" machines. Originally built for use on ships, the machines "would grind up anything—metal, food," Cook said. His plan was to buy the four hundred machines for $400 each, upgrade them, and sell them for $5,000 to hospitals, so they could readily handle a fast-developing number of disposable items—MPL's needles, for example. That would turn $160,000 into $2 million, in loose terms. Very loose. "Each sale would have meant maintenance, and I wanted to stay out of the maintenance business if I possibly could. It also meant installation. I'd probably have had to transport them, one way or another. Each of them weighed about a ton.

"But I thought it was a pretty good idea, and the guy in Minnesota was looking forward to doing business, too. But before I could do it, I got a telephone call, and the fellow said, 'Mr. Cook, I'm sorry I can't sell you these disintegrators. My plant burned down.' He lost a whole warehouse full of those machines and a lot of other things."

Divining Intervention

The second idea was more of an inside tip from a close cousin—Northwestern medical school resident Van Fucilla, born eleven days after Bill and his adventuresome comrade in boyhood fun and mischief every time the two got together.

In Bill's MPL years, Van and his wife, Judy, frequently spent evenings playing bridge with Bill and Gayle. During one of those bridge evenings Van mentioned something new that was being taught in radiology, "the Seldinger technique."

In the book *Pioneers in Angiography,* Dr. Sven-Ivar Seldinger describes how—in 1952, as a radiology student in his native Sweden—he found himself stymied in his attempts to find a better method of catheterization (inserting a catheter into the bloodstream). He called his light bulb moment "a severe attack of common sense. . . . I found myself, disappointed and sad, with three objects in my hand—a needle, a wire, and a catheter—and . . . in a split second I realized in what sequence I should use them: Needle in, wire in, needle off, catheter on wire, catheter in, catheter advance, wire off."[1]

Seldinger's discovery opened a new way to use the bloodstream to navigate detection devices into previously unreachable areas. It started with percutaneous entry—going through the skin by needle penetration. Of course, there had been shots injected into the bloodstream long before that, and there had been use of catheters in the blood before, implanted by cutting through skin, tissue, and muscles if necessary to the artery. Seldinger employed a needle, a catheter (a tiny tube), and a wire guide as a steering device that—together, in skilled hands—was what he called "the better way of catheterization." Those eventually were the cornerstones of the Bill Cook empire.

By late in the 1950s, the Seldinger method was in routine use in radiology departments all over the world. Northwestern University Hospital was one of those, and Van Fucilla was one of the early students learning the technique.

In layman's language, the Seldinger method meant one of medicine's common terms, and practices, was about to become obsolete. Instead of what was called "cut-down entry"—cutting through flesh and muscles into an artery wall to see if a problem within the body could be cured—percutaneous entry sought and found those answers with only a needle hole as an entryway. And exploratory surgery was a casualty, about to become obsolete.

An early interventional friend of Cook, Dr. Charles Dotter, in 1973 at a Bloomington dinner honoring Cook, said that because of the doors Seldinger opened, "There is now no need for surgery in many cases that ten years ago would have had to have major abdominal surgery. Surgery should never be used to find out something; it should be used to fix something."[2]

Years later, Cook told a Jasper, Indiana, Chamber of Commerce banquet group, "You may remember exploratory surgery. You don't hear much about exploratory surgery anymore. Intervention took its place. With intervention, you are first diagnosed with a catheter going into your body. Then after you're diagnosed, you're treated, usually through the same catheter. Intervention has another definition. It's minimally invasive surgery, or surgery through a needle hole. We like to say it separates the surgeon from his pocketbook."[3]

Fucilla and Cook could see the possibilities of that bright new world and its openings for manufacturers who could get there early with good ideas. For Bill Cook, 1963 was the time and Bart Villa was the place.

A Short Trip to the Office

Bart Villa is an apartment complex on Bloomington's east side. It's at 2305 East Second Street. A block north is Third Street, the big IU campus's southern border.

It was high-ticket for 1960s Bloomington. "Bart Villa was rather new at that time, and we really splurged," Gayle says. "It was more rent [$165 a month] than we were paying in Chicago [$130]. But we wanted to be in a place where we could stay and not move again. We decided it was better to step up a little bit."

The apartment the Cooks moved into on May 19, 1963, was No. 10, on the first floor. "It went from front to back, three bedrooms with a long hall in the middle," Gayle remembers. There was a small, windowless kitchen, and a living room–dining room that also served as an office work area for Gayle. One bedroom became the unlikely launching site for what was to grow into a medical-devices giant.

The product niche Bill had picked involved making and selling Seldinger-method kits to hospitals, who up to that time had to fashion their own needle, catheter, and wire guide sets. The birth of Cook Inc. was announced in the July 5, 1963, issue of the *Indiana Investor,* under New Indiana Corporations Formed Week Ending Friday, June 28:

Cook, Inc., 2305 E. 2nd St., Bloomington, 1,000 shares
(Resident Agent) William A. Cook Incorporated,
(Purpose) Merchandising

The bedroom beginning was only part of the future global marketing operation's simple "Mom and Pop" start. For a year, Cook Inc. was Bill and Gayle Cook. Period.

The MPL experience was put to work: they kept the initial investment down, to avoid starting with high debt, and the business was solely owned, without stockholders. "That lesson was applied in starting the company very small," Gayle said. "At first we bought components for the catheters and the wire guides, then we started by making some from scratch, then a few more, and a few more—inexpensive small items that we put together. We didn't need investors.

"That was the key to ending up owning the company. A lot of people start out, 'Oh, boy, I'm going to get into this.' And the machine to make their product costs $100,000. So they have to go get outside money, and right away they're in debt, and if their product fails, they're *really* in debt. We didn't think about being private or not, just being able to get through the start-up without giving the company away."

One at a time, working in that spare bedroom, Bill built the products. "I took care of Carl, who was an infant," Gayle said. "Bill was scrambling to get products." After dinner, Carl was put to bed, and Gayle started on her "shift"—7 to 1. Bill had some sleep hours logged by the time she joined him.

Each morning, Gayle said, "we tried to be very businesslike. He went in the 'office,' closed the door, and stayed there. We had seen friends who worked at home, or were working on PhDs at home or something, and discipline kind of falls apart. Pretty soon you're running around in a bathrobe and the baby's crawling over the desk. We said no, we will treat that room as if he has gone to work. I didn't interrupt in any way during the day. If he was on the phone, I was always sure that Carl was out of earshot, so they couldn't hear a baby in the background."

That was every day's schedule, everything done in the apartment, including breakfast, lunch, and dinner. Bill says he "didn't want to go out to have lunch with Gayle and play with Carl—that kind of thing. I would go in there at 8 o'clock in the morning, have lunch at home, and come out about 4:30." Then morning came, and everything started over.

Today Bill Cook never wears a tie to work. He did then, every day. "I wore a coat and a tie simply because I wanted to keep formality in the office. It was just a way for me to have an understanding that my business was manufacturing wire guides, catheters, and needles."

Same with the corporation's other employee. "I was dressed and ready every morning, too," Gayle said. "We just kept up the routine that we knew eventually we would have to have if things were successful."

A Tough Inspector

Bill did his production work on a small wooden table, which had its own history. The construction company of brothers Richard and Charlie Pritchett was building the second and third buildings on the expanding Bart Villa compound when, Cook recalls, "I came out one afternoon and asked them to build a work table for me. They did, and when they handed it to me and I asked them what I owed them, Charlie just said, 'Cook, you can't afford us.' And walked away."

Cook never forgot. "I had liked their craft, and I was indebted to them for that table. So we just stuck with them." As Cook Inc. grew, the building projects that went to the Pritchetts without competitive bidding ultimately soared into nine figures. Maybe ten.

"I still have the table in my basement at home," Cook says.

On that table, in that apartment bedroom, the onetime pre-medical student began a career that called into play his classroom learning and some personal skills. "It was two-pronged—having a knowledge of how to attack the problem, with my background in biology, and learning techniques and methods to join metals, mechanical bonds, or with solder or welding materials. That was fascinating. I was always so proud when I could get a real weld that just looked great. And finding a cleaning material that wouldn't stay on your product, being able to rinse that and get it out of there—that was a real challenge. When you hit it, when you got the right mixes, boy, what a wonderful feeling that was."

The personal-manufacturing experience had long-range payoffs. "Learning how to make a needle, how to make a catheter, how to make a wire guide helped me conceptualize other products. It was easier for me after actually producing these things or having other people produce them with me supervising."

The last step was Gayle's. For every product Bill turned out, she was the inspector. "Inspection always has to be done by a second person. You can't inspect your own work," she said.

She wasn't easy on him. "When we moved out of Bart Villa, I found some wire guides that she had hidden from me, because I would have shipped them," he said. "She found flaws in them and hid them down in the basement. The coil would be just a little bit upset, or the tip would be bent, or there would be too much solder on the tip. Sometimes the wire would break; she would test for that. Sometimes the bond would break when she would give it a little tug. There were lots of wires in those things."

Gayle says, "Bill would say, 'I *know* these are good enough to ship,' but I would say, 'You gave me these standards, and something is wrong here.' I had to hide them to force him to make some more."

Two months after the incorporation papers were filed, Cook Inc. received its first purchase order: from Illinois Masonic Hospital, for two "Seldinger Wire Guides," at $3.50 each. The invoice from that order is a framed treasure piece for the Cooks. And when that order was filled and the first payment check came in, a tradition began. "Every time we got paid on an invoice from a shipment, we'd go out to have a hamburger at McDonald's," Bill said.

In the next few months when sales became more frequent, "I started doing the bookwork, the correspondence, the invoicing," Gayle said.

Word of the product was getting around. And there was almost no competition. "United States Catheter Instrument, a division of the C. R. Bard health care corporation, was a competitor," Cook says. "We had two distinctly different thoughts. They did not believe that percutaneous entry was going to be the method of choice for putting in catheters. They thought that was just too simple, and there might be more predisposition with the wire guide for clotting. They thought the cutdown catheter—which you put into a nick in the vessel—was going to be the method of choice and that cardiologists would continue to do that. It didn't take long for doctors to discover that this percutaneous-Seldinger method was easy. I was always awed by the number of doctors who began to take it up who had never done it before."

A Key Sales Trip

To have some income during those dry start-up months, Bill contracted with Hypo, a dental needle company from Biloxi, Mississippi, to be Hypo's liaison with unhappy customers, most of whom had received some dull needles. "They paid me $800 a month plus transportation, and I used that as a consulting fee," he said. His job involved visiting and placating Hypo's unhappy customers and replacing their faulty needles.

He also was sales director as well as chief manufacturer for Cook Inc. In the sales role one day he drove to Indianapolis to see if he could generate any interest at the Indiana University Medical Center. He tried the Department of Radiology, "but they were not doing any catheter work," Ross Jennings said. "They said, 'Go over to Dr. Walter Judson's lab.' That's where he met me."

Jennings ultimately was to join Cook Inc. for a long executive career, but at the time the Texas native was a research assistant in cardiology under Dr. Judson at the Medical Center. "In about 1959, we began using the Seldinger method, on which Cook's first products were based," Jennings said. "When Bill came up in 1963, he told us what he was doing. He began to send us the things that he would make—especially his catheters—for us to evaluate. We had a lot of contact with him, and we were impressed because there was no company doing what he was. Like everybody else who was using percutaneous entry, we'd had to make our own catheters. And the wire guides we used we ordered from a company in Chicago, which in turn ordered them from a manufacturer in Sweden." That sometimes meant a delay of several weeks, and there was no guarantee the guide that arrived would be the one requested. "Whatever they had, that was it. Maybe the diameter was okay, but you wanted a different length. They were not very attuned to that.

"So we were happy to see Bill Cook making them. He was a very sincere person. He was looking to products for what they could do, how they would work. We were delighted to have that kind of association [as a customer as well as testing agent for Cook]. We were evaluating what he did. We used them in patients, of course, and we'd give him ideas back on things like the design—is the taper too blunt?

"One of the things we showed him was how we made catheters. We had been taught some years before by Folke Brahme, a visiting radiologist from Sweden. Folke went home, and Bill eventually paid his way back to the United States to be on the faculty at IU Medical School on a visiting professorship. He wound up at the University of California, San Diego. When UCSD got ready to hire him, Bill—in the early days of the company—paid for his flight. Folke never forgot that. It's just another characteristic of Bill Cook in supporting things that he thought would be good, not necessarily for Cook Inc. but for medicine."

At the time, Jennings says, IU's radiology people "were not doing anything with the Seldinger technique. Dr. Judson, a cardiologist, was using it to put in catheters to get up into the coronary arteries. Before Dr. Judson, there was no adult cardiac catheter lab in Indiana.

"Across the hall [in IU's famed Riley Hospital for children], a pediatric cardiologist, Paul Lurie, was using this technique in children with congenital heart defects. Dr. Lurie was really a pioneer in this. Although we worked with adults, our catheter lab was in the research wing off Riley Hospital." Lurie also was an early Cook Inc. customer and field-tester, with suggestions that were invaluable in leading to innovations and product improvements.

The First "Outside" Employees

There's some question as to who was the first outside employee added to Cook Inc.'s starting twosome—either Miles Kanne or Tom Osborne, depending on what constitutes hiring. Both became pillars of the company.

Kanne (pronounced Connie) was the first to come across Bill Cook. At the time, he was a Chicago area sales representative for a borderline-rival firm to Cook Inc.—Cordis Corp., based out of Florida. Kanne grew up in Minnesota and graduated with electrical engineering and communications degrees from the University of Minnesota, in and around two military stints. His route to Cordis took him through several states and two companies. Cordis, he says, at the time was "an equipment manufacturer in the medical business aligned toward cardiovascular devices. The device I was selling was called a power injector—it would force contrast media into a catheter and then into the body. I sold to doctors, basically radiologists, who controlled the purchasing of equipment and supplies for what they were doing in percutaneous-entry catheterization, what Bill built his business on.

"In 1963, only centers like Los Angeles, Chicago, New York, and Miami had people who were trained enough to do the Seldinger procedure. Major teaching institutions were starting to train physicians to go out to other hospitals—institutions like UCLA, Cal-Berkeley, University of Chicago Medical School, and Indiana University at Indianapolis. Ross Jennings was a customer of mine. On one of my trips, Ross told me, 'Miles, there's a guy in Bloomington that we're doing some testing for. He's in the catheter business. You told me you were interested in that area.'

"He gave me Bill's name, and I wrote him a letter: 'I'm interested in your area of business. I'm wondering if you're looking for a sales representative.' And I talked a little bit about my philosophy of sales.

"He wrote back and said, 'We're on the same page, but I can't afford you.'

"I responded, 'Let's get together and talk.'

"I came down, we had lunch together, and we agreed that, while I was making my rounds for Cordis, I would pass out his literature, because it was compatible with what I was trying to sell." What sounds like a possible ethical breach wasn't, Kanne says. "No, no. In fact, I told my boss what I was doing, and he said, 'That's great.' It actually helped me on several Cordis sales."

While Kanne was still with Cordis, he and the Cooks "went to dinner one night, and Bill said, 'Miles, I have an idea how I might be able to take you on. I've got a consulting contract with a needle company down in Biloxi, Mississippi—$800 a month and expenses. Why don't you take that over? You can do the things for the needle company and at the same time call on other customers that we're interested in.'

"I had decided to leave Cordis, so I went with Bill. Cordis was paying me $800 a month and expenses, plus commission on every unit I sold, whereas Bill said $800 a month and expenses . . . and that's it. I said, 'Well, I'm in on the ground floor.'

"At that time, I'm 30-something, my wife, Marjorie, and I have our two children, and some way I am sure he's going to make this thing grow." That's what he told Marjorie—not of the time the topic of the company's future came up and Cook blithely said, 'Miles, no sweat. If it fails, we can always pump gas.'"

Kanne used the Hypo connection only to get started. He was still living in Chicago and, when necessary, sleeping overnight in the Cook apartment. In mid-1964 he went on the payroll as Cook Inc.'s sales representative at large—"New York, Boston, Pittsburgh, Richmond, Miami, Atlanta, Houston, Fort Worth, Oklahoma City, Minneapolis, Detroit. I knew pretty well which hospitals in those places I should call on, locate a physician, get information to him—then I wouldn't have to go back for maybe six months. That allowed me to go all over the country."

Cook was the company's only other salesman, making many of his calls by airplane, flying solo. He did his early company flying in one of the most popular aircraft of the day, a Mooney Mark 20—first in a Mooney he shared with two Bloomington friends: Gene Bayless, a professor at the Indiana University School of Music, and Bob Irie, manager of the Bloomington Sears store then, later a Cook Inc. executive. "I was flying all over the country, putting hour after hour after hour into Bayless and Irie's airplane, and I said, 'I've got to get one of my own.' I didn't want to make them mad."

In the company's second year, he paid the $12,000 price tag for a "pretty green Mooney I thoroughly enjoyed." The Mooney Mark 20, he said, "is a single-engine airplane, low wing, built in Texas, a very, very pretty, fast airplane [180 miles an hour cruising speed]. This company has operated in aircraft ever since those first two Mooneys."

Start of a Dust Trail

In mid-1964, Tom Osborne joined the workforce. Tom's father, Dick, owned a jewelry store in downtown Bloomington. Bill sought him out one day to seek some guidance on soldering the tiny stainless steel wire guides he was working with. Dick Osborne answered Cook's questions and asked a favor in return: consideration of his son for a summer job doing the kind of work Cook was inquiring about.

"I was 18, just about to graduate from Bloomington High School," Tom said. He had no college plans, little thought of getting started on anything until the army inevitably called, in those early years of Vietnam. His father's recommendation to Cook wasn't based on anything he had seen from Tom in the store. "I never did any jewelry work or watch repair. It looked like really hard and tedious work. I was interested in electronics, building things, technical things, mechanisms, things like that. I learned a lot from my dad about tools. He had a contract with the city to overhaul parking meters. He worked on some at home. It was interesting to look inside and see how they worked. One time. But parking meter after parking meter—I thought, 'Man, that's got to be boring.'"

At home the evening after his conversation with Cook at the store, Dick Osborne relayed to Tom what had happened. "He told me this guy Bill Cook made medical instruments and was looking for somebody to help him during the summer, and he was interested in meeting me. I rode my motorcycle over to Bart Villa Apartments, found apartment No. 10, and stood there looking at the door for a minute, a little bit apprehensive. I didn't understand what kind of work it was or what this guy was going to be like. I rang the doorbell. Gayle came to the door. Carl was inside on the floor."

Gayle walked him to Bill's workroom. Tom Osborne has a technician's eye for details. He remembers walking into "a spare bedroom, pretty small, rectangular. On the north wall, Bill had a big metal desk with a linoleum top and a wooden chair. There was a work bench directly opposite on the south wall.

"When we talked about the job, he wasn't very detailed. He showed me what wire guides looked like, explained what they were, and showed me how he made them. He dipped coils into the solder pot; he had a blowtorch, wires, cutters, grinders and things, and he showed me how he did it. I made some, based on what he showed me, and apparently he was satisfied with them. I kept on making wire guides." Tom was an immediate hire, the company's first outside-the-family production employee. "He showed me how to form catheter tips, how to form curves—it wasn't very long before I started doing all those things. In those days, a dozen wire guides was a good day."

After their first year together, Tom Osborne said, "My duties were essentially set—being involved with manufacturing processes for all the new products" and "working on manufacturing processes to keep up as the building expanded, training people—all the way up to what I do today.

"We got a lot of requests for modifying products or whole new product ideas. Bill would give me some directions, some suggestions, and I'd go try that. If it worked, great. But before I went back and told him it didn't work, I'd have an alternative for him. We found a way.

"In those days we were totally immersed in the daily jobs. We never saw the dust trail we were leaving behind us. We never looked there." That "dust trail" leads from the apartment bedroom to today's sales topping a billion dollars a year. Cognizance of that developing phenomenon by the people in the middle of it didn't sink in at any particular time, Tom Osborne says.

"I don't know if it ever really has. This company has been changing every day, since I first started. We're adding something every day. It's not like we stepped out of the apartment and came to where we are today."

Time to Move On

Speaking of stepping out of the apartment . . .

In its second year, Cook Inc. was still operating out of Bart Villa, but expansion had begun. Bill wasn't confining all of his manufacturing work to the bedroom.

"In the kitchen, he and Tom began to use the oven to heat the catheters so they could assume the curve they needed," Gayle said. "They had to be careful. The stove was very hot.

"We had a kiddy extension gate so Carl couldn't get to the bathroom; he wasn't using the bathroom yet anyway." So the bathroom became a work area, too. "We used the bathtub to clean our wire guides," Bill says. "There was a wash pan in there, and right in front of it was a five-gallon bucket, which had nitric acid in it. We would run water over the wire guides to get rid of the acid—we did take some of the chrome off the fixtures with the stuff."

So it was when Bill's mother came over from Illinois for one of her regular visits. "Mom was taking a shower," Bill said. "Bless her heart, Mom was legally blind. She had cataracts, and her retinas were giving up. So she didn't see too well. She knew where the soap was, she started soaping up, and she dropped the soap in the bucket of acid. It started foaming and just bubbled up. The whole bathtub filled up with suds. She was screaming. She jumped out of the shower yelling, 'Bill! Bill!' By the time I got in there, the suds were coming over the side. And it's a reaction, so it gets hot."

It wasn't the first incident. "Bill began to have more and more chemicals and pressurized gas in that work room," Gayle said. "He knocked over a canister once." It was an oxygen tank that he accidentally dropped, Bill said. "If that thing had blown, it would have blown a hole right through the wall.

"I think that's when Gayle said, 'It might be time that you move out.'"

Ain't but One Bill Cook

I asked them to build a work table for me. They did, and when
they handed it to me and I asked them what I owed them,
Charlie just said, "Cook, you can't afford us."
And walked away.

—*Bill Cook*

In Cook Inc. legendry, right up there with the bedroom beginning is the
introduction of Bill Cook to Richard and Charlie Pritchett, whose construction company at that time was at about the same point of its entrepreneurial
infancy as was Bill Cook's.

It's a bonding of business styles that belongs in textbooks.

In 1963, the Pritchetts were working on their first big job—as construction subcontractors under general contractor Dick Bartlett—on the Bart
Villa Apartments when the Cooks moved into one of the apartments, and
the work table conversation came. Charlie Pritchett's version: "Bill likes
construction. We got acquainted with him—talking with us, like everyone
else does. One day he told us he said he needed this little table."

Richard Pritchett gave a no-big-deal shrug. "At that time a two-by-four
was thirty cents, and a piece of plywood was maybe $2. We didn't have
$4 in the material. And it didn't take us long to put four legs on a piece of
plywood."

It was a cornerstone of sorts, the first acquired construction piece in
what is a worldwide empire of buildings and specialty devices today.

Pritchett Bros. Co. also is a big deal now—a business born more out of
desperation than inspiration.

"I was working at a stone mill—about 1960," Charlie said. "I got laid off
on a Friday evening. Richard lived next door. I went over to tell him my
story, and when I got done, he said, 'Well, I got laid off today, too.' He was
working at General Motors.

Richard (*left*) and Charlie Pritchett, builders

"So we sat out there on his porch, a-swinging and a-talking, and we decided right then to go into business for ourselves."

Richard was the second-born and Charlie the third in a family of six children who grew up in a rural area near Needmore, a crossroad community between Bloomington and the next city to the south, Bedford. They went into business knowing they had woodworking talent. "The only thing I ever made an A in was Shop," Richard said. "When I was a freshman, we built a set of cabinets for the trustee's house and went over there and installed them. I was pretty handy on those things. Even when I worked at General Motors, Charlie and I did that kind of work on the side." On weekends or after work, Charlie said, "we'd put in windows or build cabinets for somebody." But in business for themselves—"We were greenhorns," Charlie said.

"We kept talking that night and finally set our salaries at $50 a week. Started the company right then. Neither one of us can remember where we got the money to put in the bank to get started.

"Our first job was building a set of cabinets for Doc Watson [Needmore's only physician]. After that, we just kept going. Never missed a payday." The business grew. "Just word of mouth, I guess. Never advertised any. We tried to do good work."

And the $50-a-week paycheck—"we enlarged it. We got to working with Cook, and we enlarged it quite a bit."

Richard thought back on the twin layoffs that caused their business. "General Motors is a good place to work. There was just a slow-up at the time. You have them every three or four years. Turned out to be good for us, I guess." And his eyes twinkled.

We Need another Building, Boys

The Pritchetts' breakthrough was landing the $35,000 installation project for an organ at the Indiana University Auditorium—"big for us at the time," Charlie said. Their next major project was Bart Villa: four linked apartment buildings that went up one at a time for immediate occupancy. The Cooks' No. 10 apartment was in the third one that was built.

"When Bill came to town, he had a little old Chevy Corvair with a little motor in the back," Charlie said. "He didn't have a heck of a lot of money then."

About a year after The Table, Bill came over one morning and said, "I've got a little room over on Jordan. I want you to panel it and put a telephone and some things in it."

"We put some old cheap paneling in it and rewired it for him," Charlie said. "I forget what it cost. It wasn't too much. He needed the money in those days. That was the first paid job we did for him."

The converted dentist's office (its formal address 300 South Swain Street) was the first Cook Inc. manufacturing operation outside the family apartment. "He wasn't there very long," Charlie said. "From there, on we went to the house he bought out on Curry Pike—just a little three-bedroom house with a double garage. We made a production area out of it.

"He kept growing. When he got to where he was going to town real good, he'd say, 'Well, I gotta go. Gotta go collect money.' He'd fly off to a hospital somewhere, collect money, and come back happy as a lark.

"We built four buildings out there for him over the years. We built the first one onto that house, about 5,000 square feet. We got that done, and it wasn't long before he said, 'I need more room.' So we built another one,

5,000 square feet. We're connecting them all together. We had a design. Then they hired Joe Witkiewicz [and started Sabin Manufacturing Co. in 1969], and Bill said, 'Well, we need another building, boys.' So we built another building there.

"We got that built, and I said, 'Bill, we've got all four buildings done. We ought to tie them together. It wouldn't cost very much to build the other part and you'll have it for storage.'

"He said, 'Charlie, that's a good idea. Won't cost much, huh?'

"So we got it done, got a roof on it, got the concrete all poured—no furnace, no nothing. He came out one day and said, 'Charlie, do you know how much money you've spent here?' I said, 'No, not very much.' He said, 'You've spent $30,000!'

"It wasn't long before he ran out of room again. We had a corridor out in the middle of all that. Wasn't long before we had that enclosed, with a roof on it—everything under one roof. Eventually.

"We never did stop. And it still ain't stopped today, forty years later."

"After we got with Cook, it seemed like there wasn't any stopping us," Richard said.

The same thing was happening for Bill Cook.

"Who'd have ever thought he'd do what he's done," Charlie said. "When we first got started together, you'd never know he'd be worth a quarter. He was trying, I'll put it that way. And it worked out great for him. Worked out good for us, too."

"We were in business probably eight years before we knew we really had something," Richard said. That would have been 1968, the year when Cook Inc.'s sales volume doubled to nearly $500,000. Well before that, the Pritchetts knew Bill Cook was on his way.

"After he quit going and collecting off hospitals, we knew he was doing pretty good," Charlie said. "He'd made it."

An Amazing Story

The handshake man, Bill Cook, had found the ideal operating partner in the Pritchetts. From the beginning, all the way up through multimillion dollar projects, they operated with plans and cost estimates but not tight budgets, and—with no stockholders for Cook to answer to—almost entirely without bids. If there was a building to build, the Pritchetts got the job.

"They have built almost all of our plants and done practically all of the restoration," Cook says. "No project was too big for them. The two brothers just worked so well together. Then later the sons came in. What makes them unique is they don't need plans. They can work off of a sheet of paper and hand drawings on it. Many times in restoration you work with a little drawing, sometimes just a verbal description."

"We knew what Cook wanted," Charlie said. "He always wanted the best. He never questioned the money. He wanted it done right."

That kept up when a new generation of Pritchett brothers took over the company. "We have bid some jobs, but a lot of it is trust," said Joe Pritchett, Richard's son.

Joe's younger brother, Jon, heads the business end of the company now. "I'm honored to have that kind of trust," Jon said. "But in my mind, it's an open book. It's always been an open book. In most jobs, they say, 'Give me some idea what it's going to run.' I usually know what the scope's going to be because I've worked around the Cook family so much. When I get told to do something, I know what to do—I don't ask when, it's how fast? I would hear about not doing it right and not doing it fast more than anything.

"It's pretty nice that with Bill and Gayle Cook, and Carl, you never have fear of talking to them. You always look forward to seeing them. 'Hey, how's it going today?' And they care. That means a lot to me. It's an incredible feeling to know that. The status they have in life is very hard to tell. I don't know how other people feel about that, because I've known them all my life. But it appears they just open up to everybody.

"When we were working down at West Baden in 1996, we'd sometimes have meetings with Bill before we'd start—if a meeting started at 7, he'd be in there at 6:30. Every morning we'd have coffee and doughnuts with some of the construction guys, and I'd tell them, 'Whenever we get our meeting with Mr. Cook started, you may have to leave.' The time came and I said to this guy, 'You need to go so we can get the meeting going.' He said, 'Where's Mr. Cook? He never has shown up.' I said, 'You've been eating doughnuts with him for half an hour.'"

"They like to keep things simple," Joe said. "They're *very* nice people. They've been good to the Pritchetts."

That feeling is mutual. "The Pritchett Brothers over the years have been part of the fabric of our company," Bill Cook said.

"I think it's an amazing story—since 1963, to keep working for one company," Jon said.

Estimates on what percentage of their company's year-to-year business is with Cook vary from Pritchett to Pritchett, but not by much. "Probably 80 percent," Charlie said. "Bill would say, 'I'm coming up on this,' or 'I'm gonna do this.' And he would." Joe says, "I'd say on the average we do 75 percent with them. Sometimes we put all our eggs in one basket, and we gamble a little bit." Jon puts the usual percentage lower, "around 60," although the concentration on getting the French Lick and West Baden hotels going moved that figure upward considerably during 2005, 2006, and 2007. "We always have to be careful," Jon said, "but we're not stupid. We know who to take care of."

Original partners Charlie and Richard have a third brother, Earl, who also worked with them. All of the brothers in the next generation—Richard's sons Joe, Jon, Ron, Ed, and Scott—"have worked for our dad since we were old enough to swing a hammer," Joe said. "I was about 14 when I first met Bill Cook. I mowed the yards on the property they bought on Curry Pike. Even then he'd tell me what limbs to cut off the trees to make sure I cut the right ones."

Jon is six-feet-four, a basketball player who started on some outstanding teams under Indiana Hall of Fame coach Danny Bush at Bedford North Lawrence High and later, while working full-time with the family company, was a part-time assistant coach for Bush. Basketball had altered his route to joining the family company. He got a scholarship at Oakland City College—"I had no idea I was going to play basketball in college; it just kinda happened"—and used it to get his degree in business administration. As the business is structured now, he is the president, and he does most of the cost estimating, but it's a tight partnership with no hierarchy. For example, Jon said, "I can't say enough about what Joe does. All day long he's writing stuff down. I do a lot of cheerleading."

There was one Bill Cook project when—to their mild surprise—the Pritchetts were told they would have to draw up specs and present a bid, just like normal real-world jobs. That was when the Cooks decided in 2007 to build a garage.

Richard loves to tell that story. "Jon and Joe had a meeting with him, and they asked him, 'Now do you *really* want a bid?'

"'Yeah!' he said, 'this is *my* money.'

"There ain't but one Bill Cook."

Moving Up

I wore so many coats and ties and got so damn hot. . . .
I swore to God if I ever got out of that apartment,
I'd just quit wearing those things.
It also saved some money.

—*Bill Cook*

Cook Inc.'s second "factory" was more a matter of relocation than expansion. The family residency stayed in the apartment, but in late 1964 Bill Cook and Tom Osborne's work area moved a few blocks west—to half of what had been a dentist's office. Cook split the space with a fellow tenant at Bart Villa, Jack Walters, who needed an office for a real estate investment business he had started.

Back at Bart Villa, Gayle still was playing all her wife, mother, and company roles. "Every day Bill would bring home everything I needed to do in a big box, like a banker's box. Every piece of paper that had ever been generated to that point was in that box—so he brought the 'office' home every night. I did my work that evening. Plus whatever he wanted me to inspect. We reached a level where we could afford an office person. Then Bill didn't have to carry everything home. I phased out the daily paperwork and inspection and did the advertising and copy work and our primitive catalog."

She also was the bookkeeper. Forty years later she had no problem find-ing the ledger she kept in those opening days. She translated its entries:

"Here's the amount paid to the Indiana Secretary of State for incorpora-tion [$23] . . . and here's $33 to Dick Bartlett as the company's share of the Bart Villa apartment rental . . . and here, in December, our product sales start coming in—$34, $71, $45."

That meant three McDonald's trips?

"Yes," she said, though the money spent for burgers was recorded in another household ledger that she maintained. "When we first got married we kept a tally of our money, down to the penny. At the end of the week, I could account for everything we spent. I might say, 'I'm fifteen cents short.' We'd think, and one of us would say, 'Oh, I put that into a parking meter.' We wanted to know exactly how much money we needed, because there was a period when we were not making any money."

She went back to the company ledger, her sliding finger pointing out: "The first mention of Miles Kanne is here in March, paid $42.12—he had taken over the Hypo agreement. He was still with Cordis, so I don't know technically whether he's an employee at that point, but there's an associa-tion that early. Tom started in June."

Company records show that in the calendar year 1964, the first full year of business, sales totaled $18,000. The next year, with Tom Osborne and Miles Kanne full-time, the sales number jumped to $113,000, then to $132,000 in 1966.[1] "From there," Kanne said, "it really took off."

That take-off required some runway time. Tom Osborne recalls of those first mid-sixties days on Swain: "It was still just Bill and me then. As I started doing more production things, Bill did more office things—invoic-ing and all that. It wasn't a very high-volume business at that point. He spent a lot of time on the phone selling. We hired someone to help with those duties. Went through two or three people there. We hired somebody to help me in production. The first guy who came in lasted about a month." Why? "Pretty much a personality thing. In those days, especially, Bill was somewhat demanding. He had a knack for either driving you out or getting the best out of you. I never took it personally, I guess. I went to St. Charles School, completely staffed by nuns, Sisters of Providence. That was a pretty regimented existence. This wasn't much of a stretch for me.

"If you didn't follow directions, if you did something stupid, Bill could be pretty pyrotechnic. Sometimes I would think, 'He's going to get out a ruler and start whacking my knuckles. He's going to plant his shoe to my rear end, literally.'"

Miles Kanne described Cook's temper as "mercurial." Osborne heard that and smiled. "That fits," he said. "But he has mellowed. Anybody who's worked here a while would tell you that. He can still let you know if you screw up."

End of the Neckties

At Swain, the orders at first came in at a trickle. "We'd get orders for three wire guides or three catheters, or six of each. A dozen wire guides was a big order," Osborne said. "One day we got an order for four dozen wire guides. That one order put a lot of stress on my capabilities. That's when I really began to think, 'There's got to be a better way to do this.' I played around with other techniques. Instead of grinding the tips on wire guides one at a time, I learned how to stack them up just right and do ten at a time. That was how I became product development and manufacturing engineer, all of a sudden."

Swain sufficed for only about six months. In that short period, one lasting thing happened. "The neckties disappeared," Cook says. "And they've never been on since.

"That's just the company style. There's no dress requirement. Some of the women still dress up, but for the most part the men just come casual. We don't have many customers coming into the plant, but the ones who do, we ask them not to dress up—to wear a sport coat if they want. Most of them show up that way. Now, that doesn't mean we aren't dressed in coats and ties when we go to a meeting outside the building. We do *own* coats and ties. We just don't wear them here."

Before the move to Swain, Cook had asked a realtor friend, Steve Riggins, to find him a place to escape the cramped quarters of Dart Villa. Less than a year later, he got back in contact with Riggins with the same need for more work space. Riggins says their conversation ran:

"Why don't you buy your own place?"

"I don't have any money."

"I know you were in the army. Have you used any of your veterans' benefits?"

That was a previously unexplored area, and it helped honorably discharged Private W. A. Cook finance purchase price $15,000, bargained down from $15,950—a five-room, one-story house, with a garage, on Bloomington's west side. It was just outside the city limits, at 925 Curry Pike. The road was already a growing industrial row. Bloomington's biggest factories—major manufacturing locations for Westinghouse, GE, and Otis Elevator—also were on Curry Pike. That made the site perfect for the growth Bill Cook dreamed of for his company. The two-and-a-half-acre lot already was properly zoned for industry. Expanding was not going to be a zoning problem.

This property, on Bloomington's west side in an area zoned for industrial use, became an improvised office and production facility and eventually the first major Cook Inc. factory.

Evolution of a Genius

The manufacturing workforce that had been "just Bill and me" on the move to Swain expanded exponentially to "three or four of us," Osborne said, with the move to Curry Pike. That wasn't enough, when the company's sales began to build. And the manufacturing methods weren't sufficient, either.

"Bill had been having his wire guide coils made at the Myers Spring Company in Logansport," Osborne said. "They were using standard industrial spring-winding machines that were suited for bigger springs—an eighth of an inch in diameter at the smallest. We were asking them to make springs a sixteenth of an inch, a thirty-second, or less. They gave it a good try. They modified one of their machines. Sometimes they could make good coils, sometimes they couldn't. It got to be a big problem for them, because they were making more rejects than good wires and they wanted out of it."

The owner of the spring company told Cook his lawyer had warned him to cancel their relationship for liability reasons. "He sold me the machine for $10,000," Cook said. "I brought it to Van Westrum Manufacturing Corporation, an engineering development shop in Indianapolis we already had been working with, and started coiling wire guides myself. Five days a week I made the trip to Indianapolis [two hours, up and back] to coil springs in a dingy room that had one light bulb.

"I invested $50,000 with Van Westrum to build a second-generation coiler. They had a nice tool shop and some good tool makers. They were going to make essentially the same machine only with greater precision. We'd be able to make micro-adjustments, and the tools would be much more refined."

Ultimately, while awaiting the new Van Westrum machine, Cook moved the Myers coiler to Bloomington and put it to use in the garage at the Curry Pike site. "None of us knew anything about spring-coiling," Osborne said, "so we really struggled. It got to a point where I was spending all of my time trying to keep that machine running. I kept thinking, 'We're just trying to make straight wire into a coil. There has to be a simple way to do it.'

"The natural thing to think of is winding it around a mandrel. I worked on that every minute I had. I rigged up a mandrel, some tools, an electric motor, and tested it to see if it would even work. It did. So I expanded on it a little bit and showed it to Bill. He told me to go ahead and try to develop it, and gave me $50 for materials. I got some two-by-fours, made it even bigger, and got it to work. The big challenge was making it a continuous operation. I spent a month or two trying to figure that out. When I stumbled on the idea that made it work, we started making coils in a way that we could keep up."

That quickly, Bill Cook's biggest investment up to then was obsolete and his respect for Osborne skyrocketed. That inventiveness—and what he kept finding out over the years when puzzling problems were repeatedly turned into salable products—convinced Cook: "Tom Osborne is a genius."

Forty-plus years later, as a company vice president whom Cook says he won't allow to retire, Osborne hesitates to call the coiling machine the breakthrough—for him or the company.

"*The* breakthrough?" he repeated. "We were scrambling every day. When we talk about the business and how it grew, people get the idea that everything was very organized. Well, it wasn't. We were panicked all the time. There was always a crisis to take care of. And most of the time it related to making enough product.

"The 'breakthrough' with Bill is if you're with him through all those crises, if you're with him scrambling. If you go home and say, 'Let me know when you get that figured out and I'll help you,' you won't know Bill for long. But if you're right there trying to be a solution and be constructive, that's a 'breakthrough' with Bill. We've been down that road a lot of times."

Employment Could Reach at Least One Hundred

A small manufacturing operation in an unfamiliar product field doesn't wind up in the newspapers very often. Two years into business, Cook Inc. finally made some headlines. The Bloomington *Courier-Tribune* played high on its front page on September 7, 1967:

COMPANY PLANS PLANT

$250,000 PLANT TO EMPLOY 80 HERE

This was an industrial development that hadn't been wooed from outside but had sprung up from within a community that was just beginning to learn of its existence, let alone its polysyllabic product. The reporter let Cook himself describe the newness of it all: "The manufacture of cardio-vascular equipment did not come onto the medical scene until about four years ago. I guess you could say we were pioneers in the field. It's strictly a noncompetitive field, due to the complexity of the equipment."

The other community newspaper, the Bloomington *Herald-Telephone*, also announced the expansion on its September 7 front page: "The company presently employs fifteen to twenty; but with construction of the first stage of the complex employment of thirty-five to forty will be possible." Project architect Richard Hartung was quoted: "When the entire complex is completed, possibly within the next ten years, employment could reach at least one hundred."

Four months later, a January 3, 1968, *Herald-Telephone* story quoted Cook: "I had very little idea whether this business would go. This particular product line was new and was being manufactured by doctors in their own laboratories—mainly in training centers."

Doctors, he said, seemed happy to get out of building their own percu-taneous-entry equipment. "We can give them a standardized high-quality product cheaper than the labs can." He said his company had found an important middle ground in a communications gap between the medical and engineering professions. "They don't understand each other's language. They need someone to interpret for them."

Adding a Salesman Who Wasn't

A key to enough sales growth to justify the building additions was expanding the sales force. Ross Jennings, one of the company's first customers, came on board as a salesman in 1968, albeit a bit reluctantly.

For all the work Jennings was doing in cardiology (much of it with Cook products) at Indiana University Hospital in Indianapolis, he was not a doctor. "I was born and grew up in Texas, and I have a degree in microbiology from the University of Texas. I had a biological medical background, and I came to IU with Dr. Walter Judson in 1956."

He and Judson, eminent in medical research, worked together success-fully for more than a decade. "In 1968, our laboratory was largely supported by research grants from the American Heart Association and the National Institute of Health. That was the golden age of grants. But as those began to dry up, I saw the handwriting on the wall, and I thought, 'I've got to get out of here.'

"We had been working with Bill all along, and he suggested now and then that I come with the company." So when Cook came up one day and said to Jennings, "What's new?" the conversation went:

"I'm going to leave."

"Where are you going?"

"To Cook Inc., if you'll still have me."

"Let me check on it."

Cook went back to Bloomington, talked with Miles Kanne, and both went to dinner with Jennings the next evening. "I told him, 'I'm not a salesman, Bill. I've never sold anybody anything in my life.'" That was no deterrent.

"Bill and I agreed early that we didn't want to pursue sales for sales' sake," Kanne said. "We wanted to present enough information to the physi-cian that he could see it was to his advantage to buy our product. Answer his questions, give him samples to try out—that's all we tried to do.

"So when Ross said, 'Bill, I can't ask a person to buy anything,' Bill said, 'We don't *want* you to.' We felt if you gave physicians, highly educated peo-ple, enough information that was verifiable, they were going to buy."

Jennings accepted an assignment as the company's West Coast repre-sentative, based in San Francisco. "I loved it. I adjusted to it very quickly. I followed Bill's advice—to this day, I've never asked anybody to buy a Cook product. But if they hadn't bought a Cook product as the result of my being there, I don't think I'd be sitting here talking."

There was another part to the Cook Inc. sales plan that all three—Cook, Kanne, and Jennings—bought into immediately: aim young.

"Doctors just out of medical school, that was our market," Cook said. "We thought percutaneous entry, because of its newness, would be taught in the medical schools. We concentrated on the young doctors coming out in radiology and in cardiology, the residents. Made sure to take them out for a good dinner, invite them to our parties, invite them to come visit our company. We'd even bring them to the plant and pay for their expenses—unheard of in those days. It cost us some money, but it paid off in the years to come."

"If you got a link with those guys, they eventually were going to leave and go someplace," Kanne said.

Talking and Listening

Spreading the word to established doctors about their small, little-known Indiana operation was another challenge. "Of every four calls I'd make," Kanne said, "I'd find one physician who would say, 'This is a passing fad. It's not going to stay around.' Most of those were older. Then I'd get a couple of young guys who were really interested but couldn't convince their hospitals to get involved. And I'd find one young guy who had just received his training, had been hired by a hospital, and wanted to get supplies so he could start doing his stuff.

"I would go to a university medical facility and try to meet the fellows who were doing the work, but also the physicians who were in training. After a couple of calls I could ask, 'Where are your students going?' And sometimes I would get a list of where they *had* gone. That was my sales list."

Jennings was a master two-way conversationalist, taking more away from his sales contacts than just orders. "Explaining about your product also included asking, 'What are problems you have that we might be able to solve with our technology?' You'd get some pretty good ideas for new products. Every now and then we might get an idea that was good but beyond our capability. We kept in pretty good touch with what was going on in the medical instrument business throughout the country. I'd get them the name of a company—it might be one of our competitors—that could do that job and say, 'You ought to talk to these people.'"

Jennings had a short career on the road as a salesman, about five years. But on the road or back in the office, he had gifts that paid off in introducing Cook Inc.

"Ross has a great mind, a memory, never forgets names," Cook says. "And he was a chemist. He led me by the hand through all of this at the beginning. Ross's main function after he came out of sales was to take care of up-and-coming young physicians that he knew were going to have a position of influence. Ross pinpointed these bright guys who were going into academic medicine. He'd say, 'Let's spend some time with this guy.' Sure enough, in about three, four, or five years, we'd see these guys climbing up. That's one of the ways we got our procedures into hospitals all over the country. His later role mainly was to take care of our researchers and people outside of the organization who he thought could contribute to the company in the future.

"A second job for him was to find any technology that was moving along that we should know about. He went to all the scientific meetings and thoroughly enjoyed them. He wrote summaries of what he heard at these meetings. As more and more of our business was coming out of academic institutions, Ross was perfect as our representative to those institutions. An indication of how much he was respected was that he was asked to be on several committees—responsible committees—at Brigham and Women's Hospital in Boston.

"Ross is not a PhD, but he has his master's degree. He served in France in World War II and speaks fluent French—I mean fluent, without an accent. He was a very good person to take care of people on an intellectual plane. If someone with him in Vienna wanted to go to an opera, or a symphony orchestra, or to a particular restaurant, Ross would arrange that and go with them.

"We were a good team. Miles just knew innately what to do. He had experience as an engineer. And he loved to be around people. He liked being out on the road. But as years went by and he became sales manager, he didn't have to be on the road as much. Between 1964 and 1976 there was a lot of road work for Miles and Ross. After that, management was more important, so they stayed in Bloomington."

Some Limitations

Osborne, Kanne, and Jennings were the first products of the uncanny Bill Cook selection method that found and brought aboard management talent which professional "head-hunting" firms and sophisticated systems would never have noticed.

"He has managed to build a group of people around him who are working for a common goal and have the right agenda in mind. That's what has made him successful," Osborne said.

Cook's "gift" is not infallible, Osborne says. "What you don't see are the ones who don't make it. There are a lot of them, too. Some just didn't adapt to that personality. It hasn't all been successes. It hasn't all been fun. There have been sleepless nights. There has been panic.

"We had an old guy who worked for us on Curry Pike, Larry Gray. He had been an engineer on the Monon Railroad, and he retired. He lived right across the street from us in Highland Village. He got curious one day and came over, looking in windows to see what was going on in that old house. Bill met Larry, got to like him, and offered him a job making wire guides. He took the job and worked with us for a while. He was way up in his years then.

"He used to watch all of these crises we were handling, all this worrying and fretting and scrambling. We had a paging system. Any kind of crisis, Bill would page me. I could tell from the tone in his voice what was coming.

"Larry was running a coiling machine, I was working on a machine right next to him, and Bill paged me: 'Tom Osborne, telephone, Line 1.' Larry knew it was just another crisis; I guess he saw that in my face, too. He said,

'Tom, you know, they may be able to kill you, but they can't eat you.' That sounds ridiculous, but at the time it made perfect sense. I didn't answer the phone, and I didn't care what was coming. 'He can't eat me.'"

Finding a Family Home, for Good

One other major, lasting move came in 1967. With Carl approaching school age, Bill and Gayle looked around for something more than an apartment as home. They stayed in the same general area as Bart Villa, buying a two-story home a few blocks south and west. It was on Wylie Street, named for Indiana University's first president, in an area populated in great part by university people.

The house that cost $36,750 is still their home. Not until their fortieth year there did they grace it with almost the minimal modern homeowner's convenience: a garage. Until 2007, winter nights included, Bill and Gayle parked their two cars on the street in front of their home. "Those two scraped ice for years," company architect George Ridgway said. The last few winters weren't as bad for them as before. "I have an automatic starter on my car and I can melt the ice," Gayle said. Ridgway said, "Bill just started his car with the defroster on and let it warm up."

They thought about moving once. "We actually bought a lot on Moores Pike [on the city's southeastern edge]," Gayle said, "but we stayed here because we realized as an only child it was good for Carl to be independent and able to walk to places . . . go places on his own, have kids to play with, go to Bryan Park [a nearby city park] on his own and not always with his mother taking him over.

"This house just fits us. It's close to everything. My 12-year-old car just passed 30,000 miles, and I drive it every day. Which tells you it doesn't have to go very far.

"So we have stayed here. We've talked about going in one direction or the other. Maybe someday we will. It might be fun to design a house—make it contemporary, change styles.

"But we don't need any more living space. I am not crazy about having help in the house all the time and losing privacy. Until recent years when we began traveling, I did all our yard work because we have such a tiny yard. And I can take care of the house, except for six hours once a week."

An Ow, a Bow-Wow, a Hoosegow

Some of our best discoveries were the
result of unplanned meandering.

—*Gayle Cook,*
A Guide to Southern Indiana

The weeklong tensions of getting Cook Inc. launched in the 1960s led Bill
and Gayle Cook to a Sunday habit.

Once they were in Bloomington, almost every Sunday they and Carl got
into the family car and headed out for a long drive. "That was our amuse-
ment," Gayle said.

Carl is one year older than the company, so its infancy was his, and its
years of early growth were his as well. "Carl has always been kind of an
easy, happy kid, even as a baby," Gayle said. "Carl was a turning point in
our lives. I'd had two miscarriages before that, so he was much hoped for.
And he's always been fun to have around. He was born in just the seventh
month, weighing three pounds, two ounces, and needing the special care
given to premature babies. The day we carried him home from the hospital,
the nurse said, 'That's going to be a good-natured child.' And I thought, 'Oh,
sure, how could she know?' But she was right. He was. So on those Sundays,
we were always able to travel with him."

Almost from the start, the relaxation took on a side-purpose. They didn't
just head out into the countryside. Bill did the driving, and Gayle was the
navigator and note-taker. Gayle saved clippings and literature on points of
interest and did library research to learn the history behind various sites.

The more they traveled, the more people heard what they were doing and looked them up to suggest places they wouldn't want to miss. Sometimes they just happened onto things. Ross Jennings was an occasional passenger. "They would spot something of interest, they would drive up to a house, and Gayle would knock on the door and get the information," Jennings said. "In those days they had plenty of time to do that on a Sunday. So they turned that time into something they enjoyed, and that turned into something useful."

What it "turned into" after all those years of Sunday drives was *A Guide to Southern Indiana*, a $1.50 soft-backed book principally written by Gayle but co-authored by Bill. Its tone is Hoosier. Evansville native Gayle knew—and shared—the laid-back pride that the state's less-populated geographic half feels for its links with a slower, less sophisticated day. She captured it with brief eloquence in the introduction to the book: "There are many surprises awaiting the traveler who takes the side roads and lingers in the villages along the way. He should not be afraid to get lost. Some of our best discoveries were the result of unplanned meandering."

The guide came out in 1972 to superb reviews. The travels continued, and it was updated. "It was a big job to put out new editions because we had to check everything—hours of restaurants, everything," Gayle said. Bill's interest in flying is reflected in the guide's listing of airfields and whether those airfields had (1) a restaurant and (2) a courtesy car for getting out on the roads to utilize the rest of the guide.

The original book listed 94 covered bridges and another 155 attractions. A sample, in a section on the Ohio River town of Tell City:

> The Tell City Chair Company, 417 Seventh Street, has been in business since 1865. It manufactured the dainty "Jackie Kennedy" ballroom chairs ordered in 1962 for the White House by the former First Lady. 425 of the wooden chairs were supplied.

In Gayle's hometown newspaper, the *Evansville Press,* columnist Bish Thompson said (under the headline GUIDE TO AREA AUTHORED BY BOSSE GRAD) he had learned some things about the southern Indiana he thought he knew well:

> I didn't know there were several Italian restaurants in the little town of Clinton. They are operated for the most part by descendants of Italian coal miners who settled there long ago. Nor was I aware that the village of Fontanet, a few miles northeast of Terre Haute, once prospered because of a gunpowder plant there. It prospered, that is, until the whole works blew up. That sort of discouraged the population. . . .
> A leisurely browse through the Cooks' booklet is quite enough to convince a person that, with the price of gasoline and the 55 mph speed limit, there is no need to drive to New England or the Grand Canyon merely to see the sights.

Nothing to Worry About, Unless . . .

One of the Cooks' totally unplanned discoveries never made the book.

A tip took them one Sunday to a rural home near Brazil, north and west of Bloomington. "Supposedly, there was a historic building there, a little building no longer used where it was rumored Abraham Lincoln had once stopped." That was enough to excite Gayle, a Lincoln-in-Indiana enthusiast. She had enough advance information that she spotted the prized building as they arrived at the driveway—in a backcountry setting.

"We drove in—trailer, dogs running around, cars parked on blocks," she said. Next to the family home was the target building: "a shack, no longer used," she said. "There was a woman in the yard, and I got out of the car to ask her if I could photograph the building. She came up to speak to me, and her dogs were running around with her. I said, 'Do these dogs bite?' She said, 'No.' Whereupon they converged on me and one of them bit me on the back of a leg. My leg was bleeding. The woman said, 'The dog didn't *bite* you. He just scratched you.' You could see *teeth* marks—you could see the *rows* of teeth. "I thought, 'Oh, boy, rabies. I'm sure these dogs haven't had shots.' And she's still denying the dog bit me—'Oh no, no, it didn't bite you.' I thought, 'This is a bad scene. I'm getting out of here.'

"All this time Bill's sitting safe in the car. I got in the car, and we drove into Brazil to the Clay County Sheriff's Office." The office was in the county jail. This was a Sunday afternoon; most public offices were closed, but not the jail. Gayle charged in and still remembers what she saw.

"It was just like Mayberry. The sheriff was sitting there with his feet up on the desk, a couple of his friends were there talking to him, and you could see down the corridor to the jail cells.

"Bill again is sitting in the car.

"I said, 'I have just been bitten by a dog.' I showed him that my hose were torn and I was bleeding. I wanted him to order the dog quarantined. A dog that hasn't had shots has to be watched for a couple of weeks. And I said, 'I need someone to watch these dogs.'

"'Oh,' he said, 'I don't think you have anything to worry about . . . until you start chasing cars.'" And he and his friends howled.

Steaming, Gayle walked out. "I went to get Bill and told him, 'You've got to come in and see this.' We walked into the sheriff's office, and he saw them all still laughing.

"The sheriff finally said, 'Okay, I'll send a deputy out there.' He got on the radio and told a guy to drive out to the place and find out what he could about the dogs. The deputy called back a few minutes later and said, 'I'm out here, but I can't get out of my car. I'm surrounded by dogs.'

"The sheriff said, 'That's why you're there.'

"There was a pause on the radio. Then the guy came back and said, 'Well, I took care of the dogs.'

"The sheriff had a panicked look. He was afraid the guy had shot the dogs. He said, 'What . . . did you do?'

"The deputy said, 'I turned on my siren and the dogs ran away.'

"Then he told the woman she had to keep all the dogs penned up because they didn't know which one did the biting. Penning them all up did worry me a little bit, but it seemed obvious by then that they were nipping at a stranger, not because they had rabies and were mad.

"So I lived."

And never, ever chased a car.

Team Taking Shape

Phyllis McCullough came here as a receptionist-secretary. Kem
Hawkins was a band director. The vice president for regulatory
affairs, April Lavender, came here as a receptionist. The current
director of human resources, Connie Jackson, came as a
receptionist. There are just many stories like that.

—*Ross Jennings*

For Cook Inc., the 1960s closed on an unimaginable surge. Year-to-year
sales increases of 75.8 percent in 1967, 103.9 percent in 1968, and 94.9 percent
in 1969 shot the annual sales figure from $132,000 to $922,000—a three-
year jump of almost exactly 600 percent.

Take-off had been achieved.

Not just sales climbed. So had employment, most of it added conven-
tionally, but not all. Legends float around among Cook Inc. people about
the most bizarre ways Bill Cook found employees who wound up rising to
high positions.

Michael Boo, who met Bill through Drum Corps International but also
developed a familiarity with Cook operations by helping produce a book for
Bill, has a personal favorite: Bob Lendman, who for several years headed one
of Cook Inc.'s main plants, Sabin Corporation, which manufactures plastic
parts and tubing for Cook's medical companies. "Bob was a really good

The early leaders of Cook Inc. *From left:* Brian Bates, Miles Kanne, Phyllis McCullough, Bill Cook, Tom Osborne, and Ross Jennings.

executive who loved to organize things," Cook says. "He was the head of a small drum corps. I met him at one of our early shows in Bloomington."

Lendman brought his drum corps to Bloomington for a local competition sponsored by Cook Inc., before Bill and Gayle Cook jumped whole-heartedly into the sport with Star of Indiana. Lendman's corps was rehearsing in a field on the Indiana University campus, and the campus police wanted him to move his buses from where they were parked.

"Bob was convinced they were supposed to be there," Boo says. "They were rehearsing, and he wasn't going to move all their equipment and screw up their rehearsal. The police called Bill and asked, 'Could you come down and talk to this guy? We can't get him to cooperate. Maybe he just needs somebody from drum corps to relate to at his level.'

"Bill came down, and Bob was pretty much unapologetic. Bill saw this was a man who had conviction to accomplish things, and . . .

"Out of the blue Bob Lendman ended up running Sabin.

"Bill can spot people."

Company pilot Bob Harbstreit calls that Cook knack "an uncanny ability to look at somebody, talk to them a few minutes, and know what they can do and what he wants them to do. I've seen Bill put people in positions they may not have been trained for, they may not have the sheepskin that everybody else wants. Most of those people have worked out very well. He told me one time, 'It's much harder to untrain somebody to do things the way you want them done than it is to hire a fresh person and teach them.'"

It wasn't always just the hirings but sometimes also the unexpected heights reached that set some people apart during the 1960s and 1970s.

Phil Hathaway

> Phil Hathaway was quiet but very bright. CPA. He had
> his own business, and he worked here—helped us open
> Monroe Guaranty Insurance Company. Miles Kanne, Tom
> Osborne, Ross Jennings, Phil Hathaway—they were there at
> the dawning, the individuals making this thing happen.
>
> —*Bill Cook*

By 1967, Cook Inc. needed a company accountant. Phil Hathaway came from South Whitley in northern Indiana. He got a degree in agriculture from Purdue, spent some time on the road as a milk plant inspector, then operated a drive-in restaurant with his wife. Along the way, he expanded the six hours of bookkeeping he had taken at Purdue with part-time post-graduate studies that ultimately made him a CPA. He was on his own, just starting to build a private accounting practice in Bloomington, when another new businessman in town, Bill Cook, called—"to see if he would handle our books," Cook recalls.

What was to become a major position with a fast-rising international company began quietly for Hathaway. "When I got it, the job was simple. Bill's bookkeeper-receptionist would give me a tape of the checks they wrote—'we spent this for inventory, this for utilities, this for salaries . . .' I converted it into a journal and made a general ledger. They had an acquaintance in Chicago who was doing their annual tax return. I think they were just sending things up to him."

The Bill Cook he met then and took on as a client left a quick impression on Hathaway: "I thought he was kind of laid-back . . . just a good guy. He hadn't been a client very long before several times a week Miles, Bill, and I would go out to Holiday Inn for lunch. One of those lunches at the Holiday Inn, one of the Pritchetts—I think it was Charlie—showed up with some moonshine they bought someplace down in Lawrence County. They loaded up the orange juice, and we all had to have a real stiff screwdriver. Man, that sucker was mean."

"That," Bill Cook says, "was a very bad day."

After a few years, Cook business grew so diverse and complex that Hathaway sold his own practice and became the Cook Inc. treasurer. Then, and as the company's surging growth continued, Hathaway felt the same way—"just amazed," he said. "In 1967, they were operating out of a house. Within a year or two after I was with them, they put an addition on the south end of that house. Just on and on it goes.

"To think we started out using manual general ledgers. Thank God for computers."

Steve Ferguson

Steve's contribution to the company has been immense—CFC, his prime interest, and Cook Group, where his aim was to get the group to harmonize and become more cohesive worldwide. With Steve we got a lot of financial things in order. His influence has just been fantastic—legislative and legal. He's been active on the Washington scene, trying to keep legislations from eating us alive. When he gets out of the casino and golfing business, maybe he'll go back and concentrate on Medicare and Medicaid, trying to straighten it out.

—*Bill Cook*

The Steve Ferguson–Bill Cook friendship preceded any Steve Ferguson–Cook Inc. ties by several years. "Steve's first wife, Jean, was a sorority sister of Gayle's in Alpha Omicron Pi," Cook said. "We got to know each other at an alumni party in 1963. He was still in college."

After Ferguson and Cook met at the party, their wives' involvement with their sorority had further impact on the relationship, Ferguson says. "We started a Gourmet Club of A O Pi alums. We got together pretty regularly. Nobody had any money, so everybody would bring a dish. Then with Bill's interest in sports, and mine, we started doing things together. We went to Illinois to see the high school basketball championship there. Then I'd get tickets to the Indiana high school finals. And we started going to IU football games and to bowl games. We'd pick a different bowl every year."

Ferguson still hadn't completed law school when he first ran for political office. "I ran for the legislature my senior year of law school. Five of us ran in the Republican primary for two seats. That fall [1966], I graduated and took the bar." And passed. And won election to the Indiana House of Representatives, too.

Ferguson served four two-year House terms, during which he also got his own private law practice going. Cook Inc. was an occasional client. "Bill was giving me constant reminders: 'You ought to get out of the legislature because I need you more. You can always go back and do that.' He's pretty diligent. Whenever he needed something, he'd call. And Bill doesn't want you to say, 'I'll get to it tomorrow.'"

Cook said, "For many years Steve served as our attorney and would not accept any remuneration in the form of stock in the company."

While Ferguson was still in private practice, he got a phone call from Cook. "There was something going on in Europe," Ferguson remembers. "He said, 'I want you to go to Europe with me.' I go, just because he asked me. I wasn't charging him. On the plane going over, Bill gives me an envelope, and he says, 'I just want you to feel comfortable doing things like this.' I said, 'Bill, I'm happy to do it.' He said, 'I want you to have this.' I opened it up, and it was a check for $15,000.

"Now, to put that in perspective, I had built my own house, a big house in Marlin Hills [an upscale subdivision on Bloomington's north side]. The cost of that house was $30,000. That check was for more than my year's salary."

When Ferguson did join Cook Inc. full-time, he took on a new area of operation that on paper would have a Rube Goldberg look—built originally for one purpose and expanded and reconfigured to do much more. It's the wing of the business that still has the title CFC.

"CFC started as Cook Financial Corporation for employees—because employees couldn't get bank loans," Cook said. Cook Inc.'s first treasurer, Phil Hathaway, said, "We formed Cook Financial Co. with the idea that we would loan employees up to $1,000. We changed it to CFC because Bill didn't want his name in it. Employees could withhold up to $25 a week. I was bookkeeper, and each one would give me a list and a check. No questions asked. Cook or Miles Kanne would call me and say, 'So-and-so needs a thousand bucks.' We'd just loan it to them, interest-free."

Cook says the beginning intent of CFC was to tie two things together: the company was looking for a way to put to work some accumulating capital from growing profits, and "our employees were having difficulty getting loans even for cars." Employment at this new place called Cook didn't impress Bloomington banks. Bill Cook found ways to fight back. "We raised enough hell with the banks that we actually embarrassed them—'If you can't take a small risk on a Cook employee, on a home or a car, I don't want to do business with you.' We took all of our money out of here and started doing our business in Indianapolis. Later on, we put money back. But in that period we pulled our payroll and everything out. It's a very powerful tool. They got the picture. In the 1970s we got up to an employment level where it was no longer necessary.

"We did these things knowing that people have to have loans, have to have medical care, have to have a feeling that they're wanted, have to be able to go home and forget their worries—these are all very important things. What the banks were doing to me back in the 1960s and 1970s was almost criminal, because they would not loan money to these people who would come in. When they'd come in, they'd want their house for equity. Half these people were renting houses; they didn't have any equity. They'd go in with furniture, and they'd laugh at them. You know how that would make somebody feel."

A defaulted loan moved CFC from the no-longer-needed employee help plan to its present role: property acquisition and management. Cook loaned a builder $50,000 for purchase of some apartments. The builder defaulted, so Cook had some apartments on his hands. "He had Steve Ferguson, Dan Sterner, and me put in $500 each to form CFC," Hathaway said. "He put in the rest. We capitalized it at $10,000. That's how we got into the apartment business. And not long after that, Steve said, 'It's not too bad a business.' Cook Inc. was generating a lot of money, so Bill just kept putting money into CFC, and we'd buy some more apartments."

Cook said, "CFC became the corporate shell that we made for the real estate arm. We began to buy apartments and buildings around the city—that was all Steve's work." Then when the Cooks began to get into renovation and restoration, Ferguson was the primary negotiator. Ferguson also was spending time in Washington, where "the years and years that he put in paid off in legislation and regulations that we as manufacturers can live with," Cook said. "Through Steve, we were a driving force for a change in FDA and the regulations within the FDA. He was the one who helped guide all of that. He testified before Congress. Later Steve came in as president of Cook Group. In the mid-1980s and 1990s, he operated the company and made a great contribution in the solidification and the role of all the European distributors and the defining of their goals."

Phyllis McCullough

Phyllis grew up poor, and she had a terrific mind. She also had a realization of people's needs. She had empathy with employees, and she could identify with their situations. Phyllis made a stamp on the company by hiring the right kind of people in management. Practically all of the managers today and employees in positions of authority were hired by Phyllis. She also developed a large volume of work in product development. Those products are the ones we're reaping benefits from today.

—*Bill Cook*

The day Phyllis McCullough's eyes scanned the newspaper classified ads, she was neither hopeful nor hopeless—somewhere in between, an undesperate housewife thinking there might be something interesting. Her chances of finding the key to the future in the classifieds were tiny. She was, after all, (1) a woman (2) with not the first hour toward a college degree.

Then fast-forward to where the job she found in a want ad ultimately took her: president of a major global corporation and chairman of the board.

A trip like that wasn't even in Phyllis McCullough's dreams—not that day, nor in her much earlier ones as a little girl whose uppermost hope was someday not to be poor.

The Arthur family on Indianapolis's north side had seven children and lost all their possessions in a house fire. Twice. Phyllis was born in 1944, the sixth of those kids, who up to that point had been coming fast: within seven years. She was 6 years old, a first-grader, when their first house burned. All of a sudden she found herself wearing "what people gave you that they didn't want" and living in a garage. "I was thinking, 'I want to do better than this.'" Half a lifetime later, at a Cook Inc. function, her brother supplied a picture of her and her family in those days. It shocked her. "I knew we were poor. I just never knew that we looked so poor."

Her electrician father ultimately built a house around the garage, and Phyllis advanced through elementary grades and junior high to Lawrence Central High School, when that northeastern Marion County area was just starting to be affluent. She was a junior, working nonschool hours at a Kresge 5&10, when one afternoon a winter storm hit. She couldn't get home, so she stayed the night at her sister's house. During that night, a space heater—called into use because the storm had knocked the power out—touched off a fire that consumed the family's house again.

She coped. She finished her junior year two classes short of a diploma, got permission to complete those with night classes at Indianapolis Tech High School, and entered the job market half a year ahead of her class—a self-declared "B–C student in most subjects." She was fondest of typing, shorthand, general business, accounting—the curriculum known as "girls' classes," as opposed to boy things like chemistry, physics, and advanced mathematics that could lead to medical or law school, the academic gender railroading that was the real reason—not athletics—why within a decade the nation had a Title IX federal education law.

After graduation she first worked at American United Life Insurance Co., then at Rough Notes Publishing Co., where Phyllis Arthur met salesman Jerry McCullough. Marriage followed within a few months. Next came a job as secretary to the executive director of the Indiana Bankers Association. "I stayed there until 1968, and I learned . . . just a hell of a lot."

Jerry had moved into the computer world's infancy with Agency Records Control. The McCulloughs moved from an apartment into an eastside home, and Phyllis left the bankers for more pay in a job with Alcoa. She became pregnant and learned that Alcoa's policies said five months into a pregnancy a woman's job was over. Daughter Julie was born in 1972. When Julie was 3, Jerry got a job transfer to Bloomington, and there they were that day, Mom at home with child, in a brand-new town, knowing nobody, when the thought of a job—for reasons that only started with extra income—led her to the classified ads. "I found one seeking a secretary-receptionist at

Cook Inc." She interviewed on a Monday and started work that Wednesday—June 29, 1972.

"Work" was at the converted but still-recognizable house on Curry Pike. "The master bedroom, I guess, was Bill's office. What had been the dining room was the office where Miles Kanne and Ross Jennings worked. A wall had been taken down, and two girls worked in what would have been two more bedrooms.

"I mailed invoices to customers, answered the phone taking orders, and typed basically for Miles and Ross. There were two of us typists. The other one typed Bill's letters. He wrote out most of them in longhand. Another fellow in the office did accounting and the payroll."

That was the nerve center of Cook Inc. in mid-summer 1972. "Shortly after I started I was pregnant again. I had to go in and tell Bill. I was all upset. I thought, 'This is the end.' He told me, 'If you want to keep working, keep working. We don't care.'"

Six months later, Kanne asked her to become office manager. "I took that over in January, I was gone in February for Elizabeth's birth, and I was back after a month as office manager."

In the next couple of years, she said, "Bill and I became good friends, and we talked a lot. I asked a lot of questions. He thought the company was going to do maybe $7 million in 1974 [not quite—$6.176 million that year, up more than 50 percent from the year before], and he felt it had pretty well peaked. It didn't seem that way from where I was sitting. It seemed like it was growing."

It was one of the rare times the vaunted Cook vision was fuzzy. Sales jumped from $6 million to $60 million in the next six years.

All those years later, when the want-ad applicant became president, she looked around and found little company among female presidents of corporations. Men in such positions form fraternal groups. She never found one for women. "There were four of us in the medical device business," she said. "But there was no one who could give me any support or talk about what it was like for us in the business. I became president in 1988, the twenty-fifth year for the company. Bill had been grooming me for this. I didn't know when he was going to do it, but he had been talking about it. He announced it at the company's twenty-fifth anniversary meeting at Palm Springs, and at the same time he made some other organizational changes.

"Bill was always a mentor. I got a lot of strength and satisfaction from internally developing people to do jobs. I knew I was being successful at what I needed to do when I could grow the company and grow management. I think I always had a knack for not only being able to pick the personalities but also understand what their strengths and weaknesses were and try to utilize the strengths and diminish the weaknesses."

Brian Bates

Brian is very methodical—but very inventive and creative.
He can recognize a new product in a minute . . . identify
a new product as having potential or not having potential.

—Bill Cook

Newly married, newly graduated from Eastern Michigan University, transplanted and jobless in the San Francisco Bay area, Brian Bates one bright 1968 morning "walked into the Stanford Med Center in a suit—the only suit I'd ever owned, bought by my parents when I was in the ninth grade. A lady said to me, 'What do you know about electrical engineering?' I said, 'Nothing.' She said, 'I think you should talk to the business manager in the Department of Cardiology.' I did, and they hired me, at $400 a month, for pharmacological research on animals."

Three years later, as a representative of Stanford at a dinner party at the American Heart Association meeting at Anaheim, he met Ross Jennings. "There was no great future for me at Stanford, and I knew about Cook, so I told Ross I'd be interested in joining Cook." Jennings set up a breakfast meeting that also involved Miles Kanne, and within a few days Bates and his wife, Gail, were in Bloomington to see the company and meet Bill Cook.

When they arrived, "I looked into his office," Bates said. "Two men were sitting there. One had a coat and tie on, and the other looked sorta like a

UPS guy, brown shirt and brown pants. I figured the guy with the tie was Bill Cook. Their meeting ended, that guy walked out, and the guy in the brown shirt said, 'Hi, I'm Bill Cook.'"

Cook offered Bates the regional sales manager position either in the Midwest or on the West Coast. "Gail had a good job at Stanford, so I took the West Coast position, which at the time was everything west of the Mississippi River. There were three other reps then: Tom Bowen [Middle Atlantic states], Wayne Vaughan [South], and Henry Kahn [Northeast]. Ross had already left San Francisco to go back to Bloomington, so no one was representing Cook on the West Coast, other than a distributor in Los Angeles. That's where I stayed for another three years."

Born, raised, and educated in Michigan (college major in the sciences and minor in business), Brian Bates joined Cook Inc. much as had Jennings and others who didn't consider themselves salesmen but wound up as key parts of one of America's great sales success stories.

"Both Miles and Ross assured me it wasn't a typical sales position; it wasn't commissioned, it was salaried. If I represented the company well from a technical standpoint, if I knew the devices and how they worked, I would be doing my job properly. That made me feel more comfortable, and that's just the way it was.

"One of the keys to success and growth was to learn from the physicians what kind of problems they were having and what we could do to help them." That way customers became key parts of what amounted to a volunteer research and development department for Cook Inc. in the new fields that percutaneous entry opened up.

"Bill had set up basically a custom shop. No ideas were turned down. If we could do it technically, we did it. Cook became recognized as a company that listened and was responsive and sensitive to the needs of the physician and the patient as well.

"Those were glorious days. We had no constraints on what we did, no regulatory obstacles. We never had committees. We never went through a marketing analysis. We never had budgets. We don't to this day. If we wanted to develop a product, we simply developed the product."

In 1974, Cook asked Bates to move to Bloomington. Bates remembers asking what his job would be and being told, "Look, you won't have any trouble finding work."

"He was right," Bates said. "There was an awful lot to do. Bill and I shared the same office. My desk was next to his. My involvement was and still is marketing and sales. In the 1980s, I became V.P. of product development. Since the early 1980s, I've been involved in large part in assessing new ideas.

"I've never looked back. I always had a comfort level that Cook would have a strong position. I had a great deal of confidence in Bill as a leader, as an entrepreneur, when I first met him. I saw a fearlessness.

An early Cook company sales team. *From left:* Tom Bowen, Stefan Grigholm, Gene DeVane, Jerry Williams, Wayne Vaughan, Frank Longson, and Rick Grenfell.

"Bill's decisions baffled me. His foresight in moving the company ahead was astounding. Every day we had a 2 o'clock meeting—six or eight people. Bill ran the meetings.

"One day Russ East from the machine shop suggested the need for a piece of heavy equipment that would speed up our operations. It cost $250,000. Our annual sales were, maybe, $3 million. After about a two-minute discussion, Bill said, 'Buy it.' I thought, 'Buy it? Spend $250,000 for a piece of equipment in the machine shop?' In his mind there was no question.

"I saw that a lot. All of a sudden, workers would show up, adding a couple of thousand square feet to the garage. I would think, 'It seems like we're going along just fine.' Then six months later, I would think, 'I'm sure glad we've got that space, the way our sales are going.'"

(It's a trait that didn't dim as new Cook Inc. generations came on. Chuck Franz, hired almost twenty years after Bates, said, "With Bill in business, so many times he's just out there in front of you. When I was young, I'd think, 'Why are we doing this?' Now, after twenty years with him, it's 'Okay, I may not understand it, but I know I'm going to. At some point, I'm going to figure this out.'")

Brian Bates has figured one thing out: "Bill never seems to be influenced by the monetary side of things. He's fearless."

Gene DeVane

If we wanted to increase our sales, we just split
Gene DeVane's territory. Because he would increase
the volume accordingly. He probably was our No. 1
salesman—very sales-conscious, sales-efficient.
He covered all the Midwest for us and eventually
became a vice president. He finished his career in
Japan, and that was because the Japanese asked
for him.

—Bill Cook

A North Carolina native, Gene DeVane went to Creighton University (a Jesuit school in Nebraska, which in the DeVane household made it Mama-approved) on his way to California, planning to be part of a medical clinic with some college friends whose specialties meshed perfectly with his.

Salesman extraordinaire DeVane qualifies as one of Bill Cook's accidental aces. "We were in Bloomington because my wife, Gladys, came to IU to get her master's in speech pathology. Going to be a short stop. Things just sorta went haywire."

Ah, those California plans, put together by three Creighton student-friends. One with a medical degree would head the clinic. DeVane's undergraduate degree was in biology, which advanced him to Creighton's school of medical technology and professional standing as a laboratory technician—his role in the planned clinic. The third friend was a pharmacist. "We would have a complete clinic." However, the physician was injured in Vietnam. He survived to enjoy his own success story as a doctor and teacher, but the clinic plan was dropped. "Then Bill Cook came along," DeVane says. "My life started one way and changed rather rapidly."

During Gladys DeVane's IU years, husband Gene first worked at the university in microbiology research, with some part-time hours at Bloomington Hospital. More fate. The government grant that enabled his hiring at the university ran out. He passed a federal test and became an air traffic controller, working at the Bloomington airport tower. That put him in frequent contact with pilot Cook in the early 1960s, when Cook Inc. was just beginning. "We would talk at the airport, and that was about it," DeVane recalls. "He never indicated he was interested in bringing me on board."

After a few years, he did. DeVane accepted and started in an all-new field for him on October 1, 1971. "I knew the physiology involved but not so much the anatomy. Most of the things I had done in the lab were blood chemistries, analyses of the various disease processes. I had never approached the body from the standpoint of intervention, going through the vascular system.

"I had no sales training at all. I looked at that as a help. My thought was parallel to Bill's: if you provide a service, the business end will take care of itself. I was providing an informational service, and, yes, that was sales. But I wasn't pushing you to sign on the dotted line. We're communicating—I provide the information, you tell me what you need. Many times with a physician, I would throw out an idea and just sit back. Physicians love to talk, as much as I do. They'd tell *me* exactly what they needed."

"Ross Jennings and Miles Kanne always put in our minds: 'Get to know the people you're going to do business with.' And, of course, Bill put an emphasis on that, too. For me, to sit down and talk with a physician was just easy. I often thought, 'I'm making a *living* doing this. All I'm doing is talking with people.'"

The Cook payroll plan also made his salesmen different. "Straight salary, no commission," DeVane said. "I enjoyed that. Really and truly. I'm not a holier-than-thou SOB, but I think commissions make people do things they wouldn't normally do in order to make money. With a commission, the temptation is there, I'm sure."

DeVane is in his seventies now. "I look back and I realize that the whole key for me was learning to fly [leading to the job at the airport and meeting Cook]. As a child, in my little town in North Carolina, St. Pauls, south of Raleigh on I-95, I used to dream that I was flying. I'd read in the comic books about flying, then later it was reinforced by the airmen from Tuskegee [a renowned all–African American air wing during World War II]. They were prevalent in my mind." The never-trumpeted part of the Cook Inc.–Gene DeVane relationship is that he was the company's first key black employee.

"My mom never wanted me to stay in St. Pauls. She didn't want me to go away, but she didn't really want me to stay. Creighton was the only integrated school open to me. I couldn't go to North Carolina or Duke at that time. I'm Catholic now. I wasn't then. I got to Creighton through a nun. She thought I was going to become a priest. There is a divinity school there, but I was in liberal arts. But that's how I got out of St. Pauls. Mom did not really want me to leave, but it was out of necessity."

He had been raised in a "pretty progressive" family. "My grandfather had a cleaners and a farm. I can't say exactly what I had in mind to do with my life when I left there, but I knew I had to get the heck out. Nebraska looked different—cornfields, rolling hills. But Omaha was quite segregated. Everything north of Farham Street was all-black. Creighton sat right on the dividing line. The campus was integrated. My dorm was integrated." Future Hall of Fame pitcher Bob Gibson was a baseball and basketball player at Creighton just ahead of DeVane. Future pro-basketball great Paul Silas dominated the backboards for Creighton just after DeVane. But his time there did introduce him to another all-time great athlete. Football Hall of Famer Gale Sayers played at Kansas but lived in Omaha. "I met Gale—in fact, I used to date the woman he married."

Taking Flight

Flying was an integral part of this company. All during the 1960s
I was flying by myself. One day I'd be one place and the next
one someplace else. I'd go from Fargo to Minneapolis, maybe,
then out to Oregon. To this day, there are customers that never
knew we didn't have eight or ten people running around.
I was at a meeting down in Florida, and someone said,
"How many salesmen do you have?" I didn't want to tell them,
so I just said, "Well, we're doing pretty well." But it was me.

—*Bill Cook*

Professional pilot Bob Harbstreit is retired now, after twenty-one years
with Bill Cook, a lot of that time just the two of them side-by-side in an
airplane.

A professional pilot couldn't find a boss with more simpatico. From those
beginning days, when solo flights were his way of spreading the Cook Inc.
sales market, Bill Cook put his love for flying to work for him—a love that
predated even his relationship with Gayle. It was a fondness that grew as
his company's assets grew, to the point where a virtual Cook Inc. air force
made no city on the globe out of reach. "Bill called his airplanes a weapon,"
Harbstreit—"commander" of the "fleet" at the apex for both—said.

From 65 Miles Per Hour to Jets

Bill Cook was still a student at Northwestern University when he and the
skies met.

"I learned to fly in 1952," he says. "I was out at the airport at Canton. I
had some money in my pocket, I had already paid my tuition, and a fellow
came up to me and said, 'You wouldn't want to buy an airplane, would
you? I've had a heart attack, and I can't fly anymore. I've got to get rid of
my Taylorcraft.' I thought, boy, that sounds like a good deal. So he sold it
to me for $450.

"Then I asked the fellow who ran the airport to teach me how to fly. I said, 'I've got two weeks to learn. Can you teach me?' He said, 'Sure.' So we flew every day for two weeks, and I got my license. I took my dad up for a ride; he was nuts. Then I went over and took my granddad for a ride. We had a great time.

After his first airplane purchase, Cook took his grandfather Charles DeLong for a ride.

"I had that plane for a couple of years in college, then sold it for $475 to an airport broker at Palwaukee Airport in Chicago. I had my money back.

"The next plane I bought was an Air Coupe shortly after that, from the same broker. I was still in college, my senior year. I sold it when I went into the army. I bought an interest in a Cessna 170, my first four-place airplane. Probably twenty people had an interest in that airplane. I usually tried to take it on a Wednesday afternoon, when everybody else was working.

Bill Cook and his first Mooney plane

"When I came out of the army, I had no money at all. I owned a BT 13 [Boeing trainer] for a week. I bought it for $350, and I had to sell it just to pay the gas bill. It burned something like twenty-eight gallons an hour. Such a beautiful airplane. I just had more fun with it."

Once he was settled in Bloomington, he bought a Mooney in partnership with two other pilots, but as company business grew, Cook was monopolizing the plane. So, he bought his own plane, another Mooney—"a little green one, new. After that I bought a Cessna Skymaster. I owned two of those."

He was stepping up in speed, hence sales range. The beginning Taylorcraft was slower than highway speeds—"about 65 mph," he said. "The BT 13, about the best you could get out of it was 130—and it landed about the same speed. The idea was to learn how to fly a heavy airplane. You learned the hard way. The stick was hard to pull. It was hard to fly. It's a wonder I didn't kill myself in it.

"The Mooneys were 165 to 170. The second Skymaster was turbocharged so I could get it up high and I could get 200 miles an hour out of it. Then I transitioned into a Conquest jet, then an Astrojet. We bought a series of Astrojets." There the cruising speed was 600 miles per hour.

By then, a lot had happened to his company (its sales had become global) and to him (a 1974 heart bypass had meant no solo flights for five years). But he almost always sat up front with the pilot on his own company flights and took his turn in control, even with the jets.

"It's easier to fly a jet than it is a smaller aircraft, because you have more power and more automatic systems. Because of its power and its characteristics—as long as you understand its characteristics—it's very difficult to stall. Small aircraft have a tendency to stall because you don't have enough power to get yourself out of that. A jet's power can usually get you out of any situation. There are a lot of accidents in single-engine and small twins, but very few in jets."

The Cook "fleet" had as many as five planes at one time. The biggest were a BAC 111 (British Air Corporation) that seated thirty-two and three Boeing 727s that seated thirty-six. The 2007 fleet, available to Cook and company personnel, included three jets (one Israeli Astrojet and two Challenger 604s) configured inside to seat six to nine comfortably.

It's *the* way to travel, luxury living compared to commercial regulations and lines, and waits.

Company in the Air

Before the fleet expanded, the company's roster of pilot/salesmen did. Cook Inc. was early in its ninth year when Gene DeVane joined it.

"I had Indiana, Illinois, Ohio, Michigan, and part of Missouri," DeVane says. "I had an airplane, a Cessna 210 [bought for him by Cook]—my 'company car,' and I used it. One week out of every month, I was in Chicago. I would fly to Meigs or Midway [airports], check into a hotel, and work that whole week in Chicago. Or I would fly to Galesburg or Peoria.

"I set up my system, but if someone would call and say, 'I need to see you,' if I didn't have a hard appointment with someone, I would just deviate and go take care of that. I'd get in my airplane and, whammo, I was there."

He used his airplane judiciously, eyes always on the weather. "I didn't have any scares from weather problems because I never forced anything. Because I love me. I didn't have '*have*-to-get-there-itis.' Bill trusted me to make the decision when to go. If I couldn't fly my plane, I might go to Indianapolis and fly commercially. Bill didn't ever say, 'You have an airplane. Why did you fly commercial?'"

Airplanes were "a very important tool for the company" in a variety of ways, Harbstreit said. "We could bring groups of customer technicians in to see how the products they were buying from us were being made. Once that happened, they felt very comfortable with the quality control of the stuff that Cook was putting out. We did that all over the United States. Field reps from hospitals that were using our product would set up a trip, we'd fly out, pick them up, they'd spend a day at the plant, and we'd take them back at night. If there was a problem with, maybe, a catheter, in the field—unlike a lot of companies, where the company would request that they send the catheter back and it would be two weeks before anything was done—we'd send an airplane out, pick it up, and a lot of times start working on it the same day.

"By 1982 we had a Conquest Turbojet that could reach California or Oregon much quicker. Then another year passed, things were going well, and we got a full jet, a Westwind. We could leave Bloomington for San Diego and in three and a half hours we'd be sitting on the ground out there. We could fly our people in, spend most of the day in the plant, then fly them back. Or, if someone had a new idea for a product, we'd fly someone out to discuss it. If Bill thought it was viable, we'd bring them back and let the person work with our R&D department."

Knew Exactly Where You Stood

If it was just the two of them in the airplane, for business or pleasure, "Bill always sat in the pilot's seat," Harbstreit said. "He enjoyed taking off and landing. A lot of the Mickey Mouse stuff in between, like radio conversations, I always took care of that for him. Bill was a good pilot. I don't ever recall what I would call a bad landing."

Cook does recall a few uneasy moments, some when he was doing a lot of solo flying. In the early 1970s, he said, "I got Gayle, Carl, and myself into a pickle down in Arkansas. The three of us were going out West, not on business, and got into unexpected thunderstorms. It was very turbulent, and I couldn't keep radio contact with air traffic control, so I decided to go low rather than stay up in very rough air. We finally got into Fort Smith and had to wait a day.

"In the Mooney, I was flying by myself to Biloxi, and I got into a very turbulent cloud—it just spit me out. Fortunately, it was not a big cloud, but it did scare me. I had a little bit of disorientation, but it was at 3,000 feet, so there was not any real danger. That's when I decided I'd better have an instrument license.

"Another kind of scary one [in the late 1980s] was when I tried to go overseas the first time. We were in the Conquest—Bob Harbstreit was with me, and [pilot] Gil Holt, and Carl. We were about 200 miles out over water, headed for Reykjavik, Iceland, and the battery overheated. We turned around and did what the book told us to do: turn off the electronic controllers that controlled the pitch, and it went immediately into deep, takeoff pitch."

Harbstreit said, "In those early Conquests, the batteries had a tendency once in a while to start charging and you couldn't stop it. They would explode or burn you clear out of the airplane. That time we got to Bangor, Maine, and landed. The computers were off, of course, so Bill had to manually ride the brakes. The left brake locked up and we made a 90-degree turn and ran into a sign." Literally. "It took out the prop and put a dent in the wing," Cook said.

The sign that caused the damage said: "Welcome to Bangor, Maine."

Today, health problems have taken Bill Cook out of the pilot seat altogether, and he misses those times when he went up just for the fun of flying. Like most pilots, he had a fascination for the feeling of freedom at altitude and, when the need was there, used the friendly skies as a retreat.

"If a problem came up that unnerved him a little bit, he'd go out, get in an airplane, fly around about fifteen minutes, and he'd be at peace with the world," Harbstreit said.

"I understand how it made him feel. I did the same thing. If I got wound up, or something happened that bothered me, I'd hop in an airplane and just fly around for twenty minutes or so. It's so peaceful and beautiful up there. That's a good way to wind down.

"One time about 1981 we flew down to the Ohio River, and we circled an old mansion. Bill looked at that place and said, 'Bob, one of these days I'm going to own that.'" Not long after that, Cedar Farm was no longer looking old, and it was what it is today: the beautifully restored weekend retreat home for Bill and Gayle Cook.

"Another day Bill said, 'Whenever I can slow down, I want to get a boat. I want to cruise the inland waterways. I don't want to go out on the ocean. You can't see anything but water out there. I want to see what the waterways look like.'

"I consider myself to have been working with Bill during the early growing years, when things really started falling into place, and they started expanding.

"He has a vision, he goes after it, and he gets it done.

"I was with him when we were looking down at bare ground, empty fields where company plants are now—Winston-Salem, Spencer. To see all this stuff come about has been a treat for me. It was just marvelous to watch him, to hear some of the ideas he would come up with and start talking about, and then to see them materialize.

Bill Cook and Bob Harbstreit, company pilot

"Most corporate pilots, when they fly an executive someplace, have to wait at the airport until he comes back. I didn't have to do that. Bill always took me with him, which was much appreciated. I got to hear and see a lot of things."

Taking Harbstreit along to important meetings was tactical for Bill Cook. "Bob has a very good memory. I'd take him to meetings—'By the way, this is Bob Harbstreit. He and I flew out here together.' Then at a break I'd ask Bob, 'Did you get that?' 'What do you think he meant by that?' 'Did you really hear him say that?' We hung a lot of people that way."

"I would say my whole working career with Bill was fun—enjoyable and educational," Harbstreit says. "We had some bad times. One time we left San Diego and forty-five minutes into the flight, Bill said, 'Where's my briefcase?' I said, 'I don't know. I'm not your keeper.' I meant it kidding, but, boy, he got mad. We looked out each other's windshield the rest of the way. Didn't say a word.

"When we got out of the airplane, nothing was said. Two or three days later, his secretary called me and said, 'Bill wants to see you.' I walked into his office. He was on his computer. He looked up and said, 'I'm over my mad now. How about you?'

"If you had a problem, or you did something maybe you shouldn't have, you didn't have to wait for a chewing-out. When Bill found out about it, it was instant, right then. You just knew you were going to die in a minute. As soon as it was over, he'd look at you, put his arm on your shoulder, and he'd say, 'Let's do it right the next time.' You knew exactly where you stood with Bill. Constantly."

He talked of another Cook trait, in the area of inspiration. "Bill made you feel like you could do the impossible," Harbstreit said, aware that in his particular relationship with Cook—boss to pilot—that wouldn't necessarily be a good thing. But he wasn't talking about life-risking impossibilities. "He had a knack. He gave you the assignment, something you might not think you could do, but for Bill you worked on it extra hard, you'd get it done, and you'd feel good about it."

Foothold in Europe

There was a lot of tension, almost like a mystery . . .

—*Bill Cook*

An unspectacular announcement appeared in the English-language Denmark trade publication *Udenrigs Handel and Industri Information* in 1969, under the headline HEART-LUNG EQUIPMENT AND EXPLANATION:

> Polystan has entered into a companionship with the firm of Cook, Incorporated, USA, and has established the firm Cook Europe with headquarters at the Polystan works, Generatorvej 41, Copenhagen. This new firm is a joint partnership between Polystan and Cook Incorporated and will produce and market the Cook line of cardiovascular products for the radiologist, cardiologist, and surgeon. This partnership in effect means that a full line of tubing, catheters, wire guides, lymphangiographic sets, needles, tip deflecting devices, duodenal intubation sets, transluminal dilation equipment, fittings, injectors, gas syringes, and various accessories is available for the European market.
>
> Polystan—Copenhagen and London—produces a specialized series of heart-lung machines, arterial pumps, cardiotomy suction devices, blood flow meters, mixing valves, oxygenators, accessories, and equipment in many materials—in use in thoracic surgery departments at five Danish clinics as well as many hospitals and institutions throughout the world.

It didn't make a ripple in the *Wall Street Journal*. But almost forty years later, Bill Cook said, "It was pretty big for me because that gave us presence in Europe."

Behind it was a border-straddling business friendship Cook had formed with Don Wilson of Toronto. "Bill had known Don since 1963," Phyllis McCullough said. "Don introduced Bill to Erik Kyvsgaard, the owner of Polystan."

Wilson was president of Cardiovascular Specialties, his own Canadian company formed for sales and distribution of Cook products in Canada. Wilson's business had a similar arrangement with Kyvsgaard. "Don Wilson's sales company was purchasing from Denmark the oxygenator they made," Cook said. "It was being shipped into Canada, and he was selling it in Canada and in the United States as the North American distributor for their product. That's how he knew about Polystan, and he knew I was looking for a place to manufacture in Europe."

Foothold Established

Cook's first choice had been Ireland. "I went to Ireland to look at what they could offer a small company. As good as they are now in attracting manufacturing, Ireland then was not quite ready—not very adept at bringing people in with an assurance that they could produce there and produce well. They're the premier country for that very thing now, bringing in industries. At the time, they seemed disorganized, so I didn't go any farther.

"Then Denmark came along. They were a member of the Outer Seven, as opposed to the European Common Market countries. They had free trade without restriction in both organizations. We wanted to go there to manufacture because we paid a 30 percent duty to sell over there our product manufactured here—that was European protectionism. That 30 percent was almost the margin of profit. It forced you to manufacture over there." Cook says Don Wilson told him, "Why don't you go meet Erik Kyvsgaard and his family and see if you can work out a deal with them?"

Cook went. "They were very much interested in manufacturing product for us eventually, but in the meantime we could ship and they would distribute for us. I came home December 21, 1969. The company [Cook Europe, announced in the Danish trade publication] was formed in 1970. It just didn't work out."

Operating styles collided. After a few months, Cook realized that Kyvsgaard "was selling our product at a very, very low margin, like 5 percent, to a subsidiary that he owned in England, and the subsidiary marked it up there probably 80 to 200 percent. I kept replenishing the inventory from here, and he was draining out the inventory and never putting any working capital in the business we had.

"He was an opportunist. He thought he would just keep a lot of the money over there and not put more money into the Cook business in Denmark. We sold product, but none of that money came back. It stayed in the bank over there. So we had no reinvested earnings in Denmark. For us, in our business ethics in the United States, we wouldn't have done it that way. We would have brought the money back to be reinvested. It was a matter of opinion."

Cook's college friend and fraternity roommate lawyer Dan Sterner, feels age and ambition had something to do with the split, too. "Erik was old, and Bill was young and bushy-tailed," said Sterner, who spent a lot of time in Denmark as the Cook Inc. lawyer cleaning up after the split. "All Erik wanted to do was wait it out, and Bill wanted to dig in there and go, go, go. They came to a parting of the ways. That was kind of painful."

Clandestine Success

The whistleblower who tipped Cook off to what was happening was a Polystan engineer, Chris Simonsgaard. "Chris was a fine engineer—very gruff and abrupt, and that in the end was his downfall. He was so abrupt with his people that it was difficult for him to manage, and we eventually had to terminate him. But he was the one who honestly told me what the problem was."

When time came to end the relationship, Cook says, "There was a lot of tension, almost like a mystery, because Kyvsgaard knew that I knew what he had been doing." He didn't know Cook would fly to Denmark to seize sole control of Cook Europe overnight. He and Sterner showed up unexpectedly in Copenhagen after operations had been suddenly moved to a new site that had been lined up by Simonsgaard and the company's Danish lawyer, Erik Munter.

Then the mystery almost became comedy. While the Cooks—Bill, Gayle, and son Carl—were in the new building the night before the switch took place, a group of employees showed up, with beer, partying. "We actually hid in the bathroom for thirty minutes, because no one was supposed to know I was in Denmark." The bathroom wouldn't appear to be the best place to hide during a beer party. Obviously, the building had more than one.

The next morning, Munter announced the change of Cook Europe management to Simonsgaard and employees, and ultimately Sterner negotiated settlement of Kyvsgaard's part of the company. The quick change was possible because Cook was the majority owner, with 52 percent to Kyvsgaard's 48. In its own facility, the new business grew, expanding Cook's presence in European markets.

Erik Munter was more than an attorney. "He was a bona fide World War II hero," Cook said. Rather than go to war against the invading Nazi troops in April 1940, Denmark's royal government worked out a "peaceful occupation" agreement with Germany that lasted through the end of the European phase of World War II in 1945. Not every Dane bought into the peaceful part. "Erik was part of the Danish underground," Cook said. "They operated as six- or eight-person cells, and they didn't always know who they were working with.

"About the only thing they could do was disrupt the Germans, and they did a heck of a job of that. They completely crippled Danish transportation. They'd blow up the railroads and bridges; the next day they'd be repaired, and they'd be blown up again. The Germans couldn't stop them. Erik blew up a big Ford factory in Denmark.

"After the war, he became the most prominent lawyer in Denmark. His law firm was very small then, maybe fifteen lawyers. When he retired, it had grown to more than four hundred. Erik died in 2006. He's missed by all of us."

Best Prospect of All

Munter played a major role in Cook Europe's stickiest Danish moment. He put a man who was the designated head of Cook operations over there in jail: Robert George Squires—or Wesley Darrell Squires, or Darrell Wesley Squires, or Darrell W., or D.W., or Wayne Kent Darrel Squires, or William Squires.

After Chris Simonsgaard had been removed, Copenhagen operations flourished under American Jeff McGough, then—in his introduction to Cook Inc. high-management challenges and responsibilities—Kem Hawkins.

Hawkins had joined Cook Inc. as a management trainee in 1981. In 1983 he accepted the job as operations manager for William Cook Europe in Denmark—"two years over there, that was the deal," he says. In those two years, he left Bill Cook with no doubt that his hunch hiring was a good one. Quickly, Hawkins strengthened the operations in the Denmark plant and the ties with European sales.

And he had fun. He, wife Mary, and their three children all made the move and did their best to learn some Danish before going and absorbing the culture while there. "It was the greatest family experience, a tremendous growing opportunity for our kids. Christy was in the fourth and fifth grade, Ryan was in the second and third, and Mary Michelle was 4 and 5."

"Robert G. Squires" was hired in 1985 to direct Cook operations in Denmark.

But two years was the deal, and as May 1985 approached, Hawkins looked forward to turning things over to the man hired back in Bloomington as his replacement. The advance buildup couldn't have been more glowing. The Cook Inc. in-house publication is the *Angio-Gram*, and its announcement of the impending change in its November/December 1984 issue read:

> Robert G. (Bob) Squires has joined the Cook Group companies as Managing Director of William Cook Europe and will report to his new assignment in Copenhagen on approximately April 1, after completing two to three months of training here in Bloomington and other U.S. and Canadian offices. A native of Pennsylvania, Bob has an extensive background in senior manufacturing management abroad, including Japan, Singapore, Latin America, and Europe. He holds Master's degrees in mechanical and chemical engineering and a doctorate in mathematics. A former Air Force pilot and nuclear safety officer, Bob is also multilingual. His personal interests are varied and range from gourmet cookery to writing, home-built aircraft, power boats, and amateur theater productions.

That was just a start. The résumé "addenda" supplied by Squires also claimed he was a "licensed commercial pilot with 7,800 hours of command pilot time, ATR rating, and certification in six types of aircraft through B-707" and "the named-inventor of twenty-three U.S. and foreign patents, the published author of two books and numerous technical papers; fluent in four foreign languages. . . . Having lived abroad for some fifteen years, I have a keen interest and work well with other races and cultures."[1]

"I thought he was the Second Coming," Hawkins said. "I was impressed." Everybody who had been in on the hiring was.

The Cook advertisement in the *Wall Street Journal* that Squires responded to read:

An American-owned medium-sized medical instrument manufacturer located in Denmark is seeking an experienced manager, preferably with engineering background, to assume the position of Managing Director. Individual must speak Danish and be willing to live and work in Denmark. Manufacturing plant is located twenty miles from Copenhagen and employs 170 in Denmark with sales offices in other European countries. Long-term employment with excellent salary and benefits.

His letter responding to the ad read in part:

My present position is that of Executive Operations Manager with a New York diversified manufacturer, with three plants in the U.S. plus one each in Japan and Puerto Rico. During my nine years with the company, I have held Managing Directors positions with both the Japanese and a since-closed location in England, and was promoted to my present assignment two years ago. The company produces electro-mechanical assemblies for the telecommunications and automotive applications, as well as health care industry lines. Among the latter are optical diagnostic instruments, neo-natal life-support units, stainless steel hospital utensils, dental units & chairs, a series of hospital disposables, and an extensive array of surgical instruments.

While born in the United States, I have dual national status with the U.K. since my father was British. My mother was Danish and taught me the language since birth. I also speak four other languages. Coincidentally, I still own ancestral property in Viborg, in the western part of Denmark, and some commercial interests in Copenhagen.

My work experience since early teens has been in the metal trades; I was a journeyman tool-maker at twenty, having been brought up in our family-owned business. I have two Master's degrees in Mechanical and Chemical Engineering from Cambridge University and Rensselaer Polytechnic, and a Doctorate from the University of Michigan. As for my personal statistics, I am forty-eight years of age, a widower for the past seven years, and I have no situation precluding a permanent move to Europe. Nearly all of my family still living are either in England or Denmark.

His letters of application and résumé submissions were read by other Cook Inc. executives whose separate handwritten personal observations were on the top or bottom of the page when they arrived at Bill Cook's desk:

"Best prospect of all."

"Lots of depth to this man."

"Looks good."

Of course there had been routine checks of his application-form claims. And they had checked out. Robert Squires did have the degrees claimed, the impressive job background. And from former employers came telephone recommendations written down as "sound engineer," "broad background," and "dynamic."

It turned out that the new employee who seemed too good to be true was.

The Name *Was* Squires

Even in Squires's few months of early Cook Inc. employment while in the United States, "He came so close—over and over—to being caught," Gayle Cook says. "I was taking Danish at the time, because we spent so much time over there. The ad for the job that he had answered said 'Danish-speaking.' He claimed to have a Danish mother. I said to him in Danish, 'How are you?' Anyone who knows any Danish at all can answer, 'Fine, thanks.' But he didn't answer in Danish. He said, 'No, no, don't make me speak Danish yet. I want to freshen up.' There was a clue. But am I going to say, 'Okay, *you* say it in Danish now'?"

Bill Cook, flying once with Squires in the co-pilot seat, offered him a chance to take control. Squires declined, which Cook considered strange because Squires's résumé claimed time as a B-25 bomber pilot. Cook had offered many other flying veterans a chance to take control of the jet. Each had jumped at the chance.

Squires also claimed experience as a deputy sheriff, but when Cook Inc. security chief Dennis Troy—a sheriff's deputy himself early in his career— tried to talk to him about that, the subject changed. Again, an alarm went off. "Cops love to talk shop with other cops," Troy's years had taught him, but Squires pointedly did not want to. Later in his own Cook Inc. employment, Troy said, he would have stepped up at that point and voiced suspicions. But he was brand-new. Troy's own picture and company introduction ran in the same *Angio-Gram* with Squires's. He kept quiet.

One red flag after another had gone up, separately, to different people, the dots unconnected. "It shows how much you take for granted," Gayle Cook said.

In a few overlapping weeks with Hawkins in Denmark, Squires worked fast. He made promises to key employees—new offices, first-class flying, big raises, more than $500,000 in new equipment—that made him an instant favorite over the guy who was leaving. That guy, Hawkins, didn't learn about those things until later because the recipients had been sworn to secrecy by their generous new buddy, Bob Squires.

What Hawkins did know was that Squires, though present, had stayed mysteriously absent from expected participation in a major sales show in Vienna. The more he learned of things Squires was doing and not doing, the more Hawkins suspected, then felt sickeningly sure, that a hoax had been pulled. The weekend he was supposed to leave for America, Hawkins called Bill Cook about his uneasiness, and Cook reacted quickly. "Bill listened to me for two or three minutes, never said a word. Then he said, 'He's a crook. We're going to be over there to fire him. Hang in there.'"

Afraid he might have overreacted, Hawkins spent the next day on an unannounced audit and found far more than he expected. Squires had submitted a fraudulent invoice, then pocketed a $24,000 payment check. "He had bought a 740 GLE Volvo, through the company, and he bought a house, through the company. And he was trying to sell the company in England.

"The going-away party for me [the night of the phone call] was at one of the finest restaurants. We had our own beautiful room, all the management and wives and husbands were there, and he had a stripper come in." Mary Hawkins was there, and steamed. She knew what Squires didn't yet know and told her husband, "I'm glad he's going to get his."

Lawyer Erik Munter was Bill Cook's hero of the piece. "He was the one who put the impostor in jail," Cook said. Munter had Squires come to his office on a ruse, then confronted him with the evidence. "The guy denied everything, and Erik just picked up the telephone and told the police to arrest him on a warrant. You're guilty until proven innocent in Denmark. They threw him in the slammer. That's the power the man had. If Erik Munter wanted him thrown in jail, he went to jail."

One Smart Cookie

From his jail cell, Squires barraged Cook with letters that changed in tone from early belligerence, angrily attacking Kem Hawkins, to confession and contrition, and then to defiant boasting.

June 5 [1985]:
I am not going to see my professional career destroyed by a totally unqualified judge who measures my performance against Danish standarts [sic] and music teacher mentality. Kem Hawkins has undermined my role here since day one and boasted of it to staff. He may be your protégé, but he has impeded this company beyond measure.

June 23:
I have been locked up in solitary confinement for sixteen days, and under Danish law am denied bail or any contact with the outside world

except by letter. . . . This cell is full of lice and fleas and the food cannot be eaten. . . .

My correct name is Wesley Darrell Kent Squires.

December 8:

I have served my time in Denmark, and although you will never believe me, I did not steal from you or the company. . . . I lied to you only to get a job, to be able to work, not to cheat you.

January 30, 1986:

In a truly desperate frame of mind, I told SMP [his employer for nine years, Standard Motor Products of Long Island City, New York] that I was Robert George Squires, five years younger than my true age, and that I had an engineering degree.

I was extensively tested by SMP on a full spectrum of technical abilities, and because of a lifetime of good solid practical experience, I passed those tests easily. In all humility, I can tell you that my actual skills are substantial.

Cook says in retrospect, "Now there was one smart cookie. He knew what he was doing and what he wanted, and he was able to do it. He had that car, a house in his own name—we had a hell of a time getting that house back. He had already sold $75,000 worth of what we called trade secrets. He was going to sell a whole bunch of machines to a company. Oh, man, he was smart. He got away with $300,000 very quickly.

"We were lucky to get hold of him, to keep him from running away. He took risks. He took gambles. He knew how to do just about everything."

Through all the months of letter-writing, Hawkins recalls, "Dennis Troy was going crazy back home trying to figure out who he really was." The name he had used, Robert G. Squires, and the credentials in his résumé—the ones that weren't totally fictitious—were in *Who's Who*, describing a professor of electrical engineering at Purdue University who at the time of the ruse was in Europe on sabbatical leave. At his court arraignment, Wesley Squires had demanded the return of personal effects taken on his arrest. He got them. Police noticed him fish through some things to locate a piece of paper. They confiscated it. It was a clipping from a yearbook: biographical data alongside a picture of Robert Squires.

Troy found that Wesley Darrell Squires had served in Air Force Intelligence. A passport check showed he had traveled to places uncommon in those Cold War days—East Germany, the Soviet Union, China. Other checks brought the other aliases to the surface.

"We suspect that he was once CIA, a contract guy, because his record just disappears," Cook said. "Back in the late 1940s, when he would have been a very young man and when it was time for him to go into the military, his whole military record just disappears. There's no record of this guy. He didn't exist. We know that he grew up in South Dakota. Beyond that, we don't know a whole lot about him."

Troy worked at building a case for making him face charges back in the United States, as soon as he was released from the year of imprisonment in Denmark. Four federal counts—two of mail fraud and one each of tax fraud and credit card fraud—were brought against him, so FBI agents were alerted to be at John F. Kennedy Airport in New York when Squires came home.

That was its own little adventure.

One Last Try

"I went to New York because I knew he would try something," Troy said. "I met with the FBI guys in New York the day he was to arrive and said, 'We've got to get out to the airport because he's going to try something.' The young agents looked at me. An older agent listened. He called flight operations at Kennedy, and sure enough, the airplane had a passenger on board who had a heart attack and had asked for a landing in Canada.

"But instead of diverting the flight, they had cleared the air space so the plane could go straight in to Kennedy, which meant the arrival was going to be early. We hopped in cars and ran red-light-and-siren out to Kennedy. We ran through customs and immigration, and all the FBI guys had credentials. I didn't have anything. One of the customs guys tried to grab me, and one of the FBI guys said, 'Leave him alone. He's CIA.'

"We got there just in the nick of time. The airline already had an ambulance outside the airplane and a ladder up to the plane. We got to the top of the stairs just as the door opened, and there was Robert Squires. I was the first guy he saw. He looked and me and said, 'Oh, shit.'

"The FBI agents placed him under arrest, but because he was claiming to have a heart attack, they had to take him to a hospital. This was two days before Thanksgiving, and these guys had planned to have Thanksgiving off with their families. Instead, they had to sit with him until he got the all-clear, which was the day after Thanksgiving. I don't think those agents were too nice to him when they took him downtown in New York and locked him up. U.S. marshals eventually brought him out to Indianapolis, he copped a plea, and got three years to serve in Lexington, Kentucky."

More than twenty years later—in May 2007, when he was nearly 80 years old—Wesley Darrell Kent Squires was living in an apartment on East Eighteenth in New York City. Troy knew. He keeps an active file. Once crossed, real cops tend to be bulldogs.

Ireland, at Last

By 1990, through its own sales representatives or foreign dealers, Cook products were being sold in Japan, Australia, South America, the Far East, the Soviet Union, and most of Europe, expanded from the early bases in Canada and Denmark.

Miles Kanne, executive vice president of Cook Group, said at a 1989 conference:

> We did not have any intent of doing exports until we became a viable business in Bloomington and the United States.
>
> But after some time, the grapevine of physicians who had heard of our products really helped. Within nine months of showing products around, Japan, Australia, and Europe all became interested in our products. . . . For us it was relatively easy because we didn't have to go looking for the customer, they came looking for us.[2]

Internationally, Bill Cook did some looking of his own. More than twenty years after his first attempt to put a plant in Ireland—the attempt that wound up locating in Denmark—he was back in Ireland taking a second look. This time he took company architect George Ridgway and others, a total party of twenty-two who flew to Ireland on a Cook airplane.

"The trip was to look at buildings to buy—to renovate into a factory," Ridgway said. "The Irish government was taking us around—the Irish Development Authority. We stayed at Castle Troy.

"A really nice lady, Mary Burton, was showing us the buildings. We went into one that was really cut up, wasn't going to work too well. Went into another one: dark, dingy, big.

"We stopped for lunch at the Lame Duck Tavern. We're sitting there and Mary said, 'Now, Mr. Cook, what would be your thoughts on the last two buildings?'

"He said, 'Mary, they suck.'

"Just took her aback. She was aghast.

"We go on to County Cork on the bus to look at a building there. She turned to Bill and said, 'Now, Mr. Cook, the owner of this building is driving up here—probably a two-hour drive—and I would appreciate it if you would not be so . . . forthright.'

"He allowed that he'd behave himself.

"We got there and walked down to this tilt-up, pre-cast building—really bad. He leaned over to me and said, 'This building sucks, too.'"

"So at the end of the trip he decided to buy some land and build his own. We built a factory, and it has done well. We've added on to it twice."

Twenty-fifth anniversary drawing, 1988, which includes a tribute to doctors (*clockwise, from top left*) Sven-Ivar Seldinger, Charles Dotter, and Cesare Gianturco, and company founders Bill and Gayle Cook. Also featured are other enterprises into which Cook Inc. had expanded by that year.

Doctors

One hundred percent of doctors, when Gruentzig started doing
coronary angioplasty in Zurich in 1977, said it won't work. The
FDA [had it had its present teeth in the early days of intervention]
would have said, "Our panel says it won't work. Our panel says
it's dangerous. Our panel says the heart will go into fibrillation
and the patient will die." All of those things contribute to people
not making major medical breakthroughs today. There may
be an idea or a concept that is out there today and
will never see the light of day.

—*Bill Cook*

Not all the key finds by Bill Cook were employees.

The same mysterious combination of hunch, insight, and luck that so
improbably landed many who became major Cook Inc. leaders linked him,
too, with some doctors who—in separate experiments and discoveries that
frequently meshed through him—unlocked some medical mysteries within
the field that Cook chose, intervention.

Cook's doctors group—Dr. Charles Dotter, Dr. Cesare Gianturco, Dr.
Andreas Gruentzig, and some more—started to form for him when he
was 32. Ten years earlier, Swedish radiologist Dr. Sven-Ivar Seldinger—at
32—had invented their playing field. The Seldinger technique "gave ready

access to all the vessels throughout the body, easily—without cutting down on the vessel, or cutting down in different places in the body, just to put a catheter in," college biology major Bill Cook grasped quickly.

Dotter was 43 when he and Cook met at Cook's low-budget product display booth at a November 1963 radiologists' convention in Chicago. Vision, on the part of both, locked them together for mutual success.

Vision that amounted to alert recognition also introduced the generally unknown young Indiana businessman to:

- Gianturco, an Italian whose breakthroughs in the Seldinger-keyed field began early and were still coming in his eighties;

- Gruentzig, a German already widely recognized in Europe by the time he met Cook;

- Dr. Josef Rösch, who in Cook's early years was a young military doctor in his native Czechoslovakia.

All were to be linked with percutaneous entry and Bill Cook. All were to be helped in their research and discoveries by Bill Cook. All were to help make Bill Cook rich. And all, with their findings and—much of it through Cook devices—implementation, were to save an incalculable number of lives.

"That whole breed of men went through a brief era, starting about the time that I went into business," Cook says. "Actually it started with Seldinger in 1953 but really got going in 1960—running through 1985 to 1990."

Charles Dotter "Had Darting Eyes"

In November 1963, four months into the field, independent medical devices manufacturer Bill Cook finessed his way to booth space at the Radiological Society of North America (RSNA) convention at the Palmer House in Chicago. "We spent $300 for a booth when they didn't have booth space for us. I had been trying to get a spot there since the summer. On the Wednesday before the convention was to start that Sunday, the doctor who ran exhibit rentals for the society called me and said, 'Bill, we have a place for you at the RSNA. We've got one little problem. You're behind a pillar. That's the bad news. The good news is you're right across the way from a Coke booth.'"

Few had heard of Cook Inc. before that convention. There, word got around fast, helped by the location. "The free Coke booth brought people in," Cook said. And they stayed, wowed by the manufacturing process that took place before their eyes. "People piled in there watching me make cath-

Radiological Society of North America convention, Palmer House Hotel, Chicago, November 1963. Bill Cook staffed the demonstration booth.

eters—I had a blowtorch, I had wire guides, I had needles. They were fascinated. It was a free-for-all around that booth. They took our small catalogs and our literature. I got my first career spike in sales after that meeting."

One man who stayed toward the rear of the audience particularly caught his attention, even scared him a little. "He stood back there looking at me. He had darting eyes."

At Cook's first demonstration, the man stayed around till the end, then approached him. After an exchange of introductions, Dr. Charles Dotter asked if he could borrow Cook's blowtorch for the night. Cook said, "Sure," and thought he might have just kissed a blowtorch goodbye, but the next morning Dotter gave him his blowtorch back, with a bonus: ten perfectly made catheters. "I sold them that day for $10 each—almost enough to pay for the booth."

Bill Cook made more than that little bit of money that day. He also made a lasting, invaluable friendship with Dotter, who already was an established pioneer in radiology. "From the very beginning we hit it off, but how we started being together so much kind of sinks into the sunset. We were just good friends. He was my kind of person, easy for me to be with and always a challenge, because we respected each other."

In the 1993 book *The Catheter Introducers,* Cook tells of how Dotter "took me mountain-climbing in Oregon—once. There we were on Three-Fingered Jack in a blizzard. Never again! He also tried to talk me into flying under a bridge so he could take pictures for one of his films. I wouldn't do it. Next, he asked if I would fly him near several mountain peaks in southern Oregon. I did, but he couldn't take pictures because of the turbulence and snow. He was a bird-watcher, artist, music lover, photographer, car buff, and mountain climber. He constantly challenged his body and mind."[1]

Cook said Dotter "was difficult for a lot of people to be with, but easy for me simply because I took him for what he was. I didn't ask anything from him, nor did he ask anything really from me. We were just together and enjoyed it."

That kinship began almost immediately. Once they had met, the two exchanged ideas long into the night throughout the weekend convention in Chicago. In *The Catheter Introducers,* Cook said: "We discussed wire guide and catheter manufacture and what he thought the future would be for angiography. He became excited when he talked of his work, and yes, we discussed angioplasty. Once started, his mind went nonstop."

Dotter invited Cook to come to Oregon to further the discussions. Cook had to admit he couldn't afford the flight. "He paid my expenses out there," Cook said.

In *The Catheter Introducers,* Cook said he found on arrival that Dotter's laboratory "was the state of the art, the finest in the United States. His technicians made their own wire guides. They were producing their own

Teflon® catheters using a recently purchased blowtorch and our Teflon® tubing. Charles was making the catheters."

Cook looks back on the friendship now and says, "I don't know exactly how it kept going, but the next thing I knew we were taking vacations together. Charles was competitive, always a friend. He became one of my very closest friends. He would tell me about his insecurities, his problems, and I would tell him about my problems. We just were very, very close."

After those days in Chicago, Cook, who calls Dotter the father of interventional medicine, knew for sure he had found the perfect niche for an infant company with ambitious growth plans. And he had started at the best possible time

"The field was so new, it was not difficult to catch up. There really was no past.

"Seldinger made his discovery in 1953, and I entered the field in 1963. Even Dotter did not really get started in working with the percutaneous technique until 1958.

"A catheter was rarely used in the blood system until 1941. Then it became a diagnostic tool. Dotter hypothesized that it could be used not only for diagnosis but also for therapeutic use [treating and curing, directly attacking a problem rather than just revealing it]. That's where Dotter started in and made things successful." That Dotter revolution happened at almost the precise time Bill Cook was getting his company started.

According to Dr. Josef Rösch, a Czechoslovakian who came to the United States as a Dotter disciple and early Seldinger practitioner, Dotter's advancement of percutaneous entry into therapeutic use had a birthday: June 19, 1963, twelve days before Cook Inc. was officially chartered as a corporation.

In a paper titled "The Birth, Early Years, and Future of Interventional Radiology," Rösch said Dotter "first officially spoke about" therapeutic applications of the new technique at the Czechoslovak Radiological Congress in Karlovy Vary. Rösch, who was listening raptly, said Dotter closed his one-hour talk by saying, "The angiographic catheter can be more than a tool for passive means for diagnostic observation; used with imagination, it can become an important surgical instrument." Rösch said, "For those of us in the audience, it was like a bomb had been dropped. At that time, all angiographers had only one thing in mind, to deliver an exact diagnosis to our referring clinical colleagues, internists and surgeons, thereby allowing them to select proper treatment. Until then, none of us had even thought that we might be able to treat patients ourselves percutaneously. . . . Charles received a standing ovation."[2]

Dotter then and Cook Inc. later ran into some medical community/ fraternity opposition—"particularly when we were doing therapeutic, and particularly when we were getting in between the surgeons and their pocketbooks," Cook said. "Surgeons made good money cutting off legs. Here was Dotter taking ten minutes of his time and opening up a vessel, eliminating huge amounts of surgery, and saving thousands of legs. It was quite original."

In their Chicago and subsequent conversations, Cook learned Charles Dotter's background. Born in Boston, he studied medicine and radiology at Cornell, where he had a staff position from 1950 to 1952. From there he went west to be a professor and chairman of radiology at the University of Oregon Medical School in Portland for thirty-three years until his death. During his tenure, the Portland institution's name was formally changed to Oregon Health Sciences University, Oregon's only state-backed medical school.

Cook remembers Dotter as "a fascinating character. He climbed every 14,000-foot mountain in the United States, was a military officer in the medical corps, and was an inventor. He was featured in a major story in *Life* magazine (for his discoveries in intervention—his darting eyes a mischievous highlight of the photos that ran with the story).

"Charles always felt a pipe wrench and a pipe represented simplicity. He showed them with every speech he ever did in making the point that it's better to be simple and effective than be complex and kill someone. In all the procedures that he ever devised—there were many of them, and we made millions and millions of dollars from his inventions—he would never take a dollar from us or anyone. He was a wealthy man, but he made his money not in radiology or being the head of the Department of Radiology at the University of Oregon Medical School—he made it in gold and silver speculation. He became a millionaire as a very young man."

The friendship lasted twenty-two years. "Charles Dotter died a Samurai death in 1985. He should have lived to be a lot older. Unfortunately, when he had bypass surgery, he forgot to tell people he was on amphetamines, and they didn't know what was wrong with him when he came out of surgery. He survived but lost most of his lung capacity. He went back to Oregon, and six months later he went to the hospital. He pulled his lung-assist tube off one night and just ended it all.

"Charles Dotter was an individual I admired greatly. I'm sorry he died the way he did. It was an unnecessary death. Had he waited another five years, he would have found something to get him along with a nice life, the cardiac stent that Gianturco had been working on since 1972."

Josef Rösch: Willing to Lie in Front of a Train

Czechoslovakian transplant Josef Rösch is a living continuance of the Dotter mission, with a life story about as engaging as Dotter's—and about as intertwined with Bill Cook. "A fascinating guy," Cook calls Rösch. "He and I got the Dotter Institute started." That is the Dotter Institute of Interventional Therapy in Portland, Oregon, which opened its doors in April 1990—not without a fight.

Rösch was a military officer and a young doctor in Czechoslovakia when he attended that "birth of interventionalism" radiological congress in 1963. He and Dotter became such friends that Dotter made frequent return trips to Czechoslovakia—not just to see Rösch but also to deliver him some help. Illegally. "They were so short over there on products for percutaneous entry—needles, wire guides, catheters—that Dotter would smuggle them in to Josef, hidden in the hubcaps of his car," Cook said.

"People did that kind of thing. Erik Kyvsgaard, when he was our partner in Cook Denmark, once used a false gas tank in his car to smuggle things into East Berlin." False was a good word for Kyvsgaard's commerce: his contraband, which sold quickly, was two hundred breast prostheses—falsies, snapped up quickly by East German frauleins.

Dotter timed one of his visits to Rösch for December so that he could hide plastic tubing under a bulky winter coat as well as the wire guides under his hubcaps. "Charles just gave all those things to Josef," Cook said. "They were so valuable and so rare over there that they were reused time and time again."

It was daring and risky for Dotter, unbridled independence for Rösch. "Josef," Cook said, "wanted no part of communism."

As soon as he and Dotter could work it out, Rösch immigrated to the United States, first to study radiology under Dotter, then to move south to a job at UCLA. "Josef is a superb clinician and a very good researcher," Cook said.

Although Dotter had envisioned greater uses for it in 1963, even years later when Rösch arrived in the United States, "percutaneous entry itself was pretty much research," Cook said. Diagnosis was accomplished by use of a dye carried to the trouble area by the catheter and wire guide, where it was released to form a contrasting background of black and white for X-ray study. "But a lot of times when they diagnosed with contrast media, they really didn't know how to treat the abnormalities. It was a diagnostic tool; you could see plaque, you could see the abnormalities, but as far as heart disease was concerned, there was nothing you could treat it with to help the patient yet. It wasn't until 1969 that they did the first coronary artery surgical bypass at Cleveland Clinic."

Not long after Dotter's death in 1985, Rösch and Cook met to discuss establishment of a research institute in his name, at his Portland workplace. "We conceptualized the whole thing one day out in Tucson," Cook said. Characteristic of both Cook and Rösch, things moved fast after that meeting. Opposition came, but it was left strewn behind like road kill.

In *The History of the Dotter Interventional Institute, 1990–2005,* authors Jan Greene and Otha Linton capture the personalities as well as the indomitable wills of Rösch and Cook, once they had determined how best to memorialize Dotter. Cook was on the speakers' list at a 1989 Charles Dotter Memorial Days event in Portland. He became *the* speaker, the one who dropped a bombshell: he announced a $2 million gift to Oregon Health Sciences University toward establishment of the Dotter Institute—a surprise even to the school's new president, Dr. Peter Kohler, "with whom he had sat down for lunch just minutes before," the book says.

The two hundred at the luncheon responded to the Cook pledge with a standing ovation. They didn't know then what Rösch learned when he accompanied Cook to the airport: the proposed institute would get another $2 million from Cook if it was a fait accompli within a year—a $4 million gift in all.

Rösch went to work fast. Just as fast, opposition within the university's radiological hierarchy developed over the Cook insistence that the Dotter Institute be administered by Rösch—part of the medical school but separate from the radiology department. The school's new radiology chairman, Richard Katzberg, "along with most of the other diagnostic radiologists, believed that splitting the department would divert important income, prestige, and research" and ultimately "ruin the department," Greene and Linton said.

Rösch, aware of his deadline for the extra $2 million, plunged ahead with his plans, which he took to President Kohler, a career endocrinologist who had gone away from the Dotter Days luncheon pleased by both the surprise proposal and the time he had spent with Cook and Rösch. "I liked the idea," Greene and Linton quoted Kohler. "It would give us an edge, a specialty center." However, out of a meeting involving Katzberg in July came a revised plan that essentially eliminated Rösch from clinical control and proposed recruiting a faculty member to run a division of interventional radiology.

That's not the way Cook makes focused donations. In a two-page letter to Kohler, he said: "The proposal does not show a sincere effort of OHSU to support development of the institute and its work, both in research and clinical activities. The proposal looks as though the reverse is true." His letter and its implied threat of revocation included his own cheeky revision of the Katzberg proposal, reestablishing Rösch as the director and head of interventional radiology at the institute, along with some other changes. Kohler sought advice from outside experts in the field, including Dr. Ernest Ring, an interventionalist from the University of California, San Francisco. "Dr. Ring supported the separate institute and urged Dr. Kohler to do the same," Greene and Linton said.

Kohler did, putting his administrative powers on the side of Cook and Rösch. On April 1, 1990, just inside the one-year deadline Cook had mentioned to Rösch as a requisite for the second $2 million gift, the Oregon Board of Higher Education approved the institute's formation. "The bitter controversy left a bad taste behind," Greene and Linton wrote, "and several opponents of the plan—including Dr. Katzberg—left soon after."

The institute that stands today as a leader in the field is a monument not just to Dotter but also to the willingness of both Cook and Rösch to fight for their dream. Leslie Pollick was new on the job as OHSU provost when the controversy boiled up. Pollick, a bench scientist, helped effect the solution and "added language in the ever-changing drafts," Greene and Linton said, quoting her on the issue:

> Dr. Rösch would come charging into the office. You thought you'd all agreed, but it would all fly apart.
>
> He was very willing to rock the boat a little bit.
>
> Josef had a passion for the vision of noninvasive surgery. He was willing to lie down in front of a train to keep it from moving.[3]

Bill Cook's kind of man.

Cesare Gianturco: So Underappreciated by the World

For more than sixty years, Cesare Gianturco's creative imagination has given rise to a wide variety of original interventional techniques and devices, including the cotton-tail embolus, wool coils, the Bird's Nest filter, expandable stents, and the first balloon catheter.

—Leslie A. Geddes and LeNelle E. Geddes,
The Catheter Introducers (1993)

Cesare Gianturco was a little man with a giant intellect, a gentleman always. Cook remembers the time he pulled up in his car for a visit at Dr. Gianturco's Champaign, Illinois, home and found him working in his yard, in full suit, white shirt, and tie.

He was born and educated in Italy, getting his doctorate in medicine from the University of Naples in 1927 at 22. He came to the United States and was practicing at the Mayo Clinic in the early 1930s when Cook was born. He entered the field of radiology while at Mayo, then in 1934 went to the Carle Clinic in Urbana, Illinois, as a founding member and chief of radiology. He retired at Carle in 1965 and moved to the University of Texas system's Cancer Center, the M. D. Anderson Hospital at Houston. He still was making invaluable medical discoveries and breakthroughs there in his eighties.

"I and a lot of others owe our lives to Cesare Gianturco," Cook says. "I'd probably have been dead in my forties without the discoveries he made." At 77, Cook was saying that, and that was thirteen years after Gianturco's death, at 90.

Leslie and LeNelle Geddes' quick and understated summary of Gianturco's achievements tends to sail over a layman's understanding. His ingenuity affected many medical areas, but in Cook's medical device world, Gianturco's major contributions were finding ways to shut off (embolize) arteries and veins when it was needed and to open them when needed.

"He invented the first embolization coils, which is a huge business for us today," Cook said. "You put these coils in a blood vessel, and it stops the flow. If you have an aneurysm, it will shrink the aneurysm; if you have a tumor, it will shrink the tumor. And if you want to decrease the flow of blood to the spleen, you put in a few of these coils and it will slow the blood. He invented coronary artery and vascular stenting, including what is called the Z stent, which is incorporated into every Cook abdominal aortic aneurysm [Triple-A] stent.

"With people who have had injuries to their blood vessels, we've actually walled off the injury and closed off circulation to cancers with these coils. That's the Gianturco coil. It's probably a thirty-year-old product, but interventionalists are learning how to use them more and more. The Japanese are using them a lot to wall off things, particularly in the brain. It's a multimillion-dollar market for us. Huge."

Some of the new uses are cosmetic. "People who have redness in an area of their skin, like [former Soviet Union president Mikhail] Gorbachev—we could take that redness out of Gorbachev's scalp in just a matter of an hour or two. It's blood vessels that have run rampant. There are more blood vessels than there should be. The blood backs up in there and makes you flush. With a Gorbachev, it's there permanently until the veins can get rid of it.

"Kem Hawkins delights in talking about products that have been around for a long time that we've found different uses for and now are on the move. It's one of the reasons our company continues to grow. Brian Bates, Kem Hawkins, and I were talking just recently about making a video of Cesare Gianturco's life, because he's so underappreciated by the world—how great he was, what an impact he made."

The Arrival of Stents

From the blood-stopping coils, former Cook Inc. president Phyllis McCullough said, the Gianturco mind reasoned, "if we can close blood vessels, we ought to be able to open them up. That's when he started working on stents."

Stent was a word almost unheard of in public health until miracle-working products began to emerge in the late 1970s and early 1980s because of the work of Gianturco and other pioneers. Two were Charles Dotter and a young German genius in the field, Andreas Gruentzig, who were nominated in 1978 for the Nobel Prize in medicine. Those three—Gianturco, Dotter, and Gruentzig—were linked through Bill Cook.

The start of everything was experimentation with balloon catheters to force open clogged blood vessels. That dates to 1971 and Gianturco in his last Carle Clinic years. There was no humor in the classic situation that resulted from his first try at opening an artery with a catheter: the operation was successful, but the patient died. He used a balloon catheter to dilate a thigh artery of a woman who was facing amputation of the leg. The improved blood flow that was sought was achieved, but, Cook said, "unfortunately she died that night. The wound came open because the sutures broke. But it was a successful dilatation with the balloon catheter."

Gianturco (and Cook Inc.) had used polyolefin for his balloon catheter, fabricated from a piece of electrical shrink tubing. Others worked on the same principle with different material. Dotter and Dr. Melvyn Judkins teamed up in using "telescopic and caged balloon catheters to dilate peripheral vessels," according to *The Catheter Introducers*. "This procedure came to be known as dottering." And when Gruentzig came out with his versions (the original using balloons from William Cook Europe in Denmark), he gave credit to Dotter and Cook Denmark.

"I heard of Gruentzig through Chris Simonsgaard—letters between the two of them and contracts with us for catheters," Cook said. "Chris asked, 'Could you come over and meet this guy in Switzerland?' I went over, then they got some agreements together." Included was a letter of agreement signed by Gruentzig giving William Cook Europe sales and manufacturing rights on his balloon catheter products.

"He and Chris did not get along," Cook said. "There were a lot of people Andreas didn't get along with, and Chris was one of them. I said, 'Okay, that's fine, Dr. Gruentzig, you go your way and we'll go ours.'"

Cook regularly attached to a product the name of the physician who developed or suggested it, so a Gruentzig balloon catheter was in the Cook catalog when the breakup occurred. In 1981 Gruentzig told Cook to pull his name off the catheter because he had contracted with another company, U.S. Catheter and Instrument Company. Cook felt the 1975 agreement gave him grounds to fight Gruentzig's new contract, but in a memo to Ross Jennings on October 13, 1980, he suggested that Jennings and Simonsgaard "could meet with Gruentzig to determine his wishes. He appears to be in a box, and we should let him decide if we should take over the litigation to protect our rights to produce. . . . We've been had by USCI, but I want to do what is best for Gruentzig. Knowing USCI's track record, I would say he will get the shaft from them." On November 6, 1981, Cook received a Telex from

Gruentzig demanding an end to the use of his name. "It looks like good old USCI got us on this one," Cook said in a Telex he sent that day.

Cook complied and moved on. "I took the very same balloon catheters that we were making at the time in the United States, and I just put Dotter's name on them. We never missed a beat."

Gianturco at the time was at work on another breakthrough. The challenge was stopping blood clots from getting to the heart through the vena cava, the large veins that take blood on the circulatory trip back to the heart. By 1980, he had drawn up the requirements for what he thought would work. In 1984, he and Cook Inc. came out with the "bird's nest filter," so named because three wires the width of a human hair were situated in a tangle within the catheter to filter out clots.

"The vena cava filter was the first device we took to PMA," McCullough said. (That's a Pre-Market Approval application, a step in U.S. Food and Drug Administration procedures after trials have been successfully completed.) "That filter was a breakthrough product for us, because it was the first device of its kind that could be placed percutaneously. All the others required surgery. In 1989, we got it approved."

TV comic Johnny Carson's surgeon installed one in him, and it made the national news wires. President Richard Nixon, after his White House years, got one, with similar national news notice. "It's still a big sales item for us," McCullough said. "And it got us into the next big product that Dr. Gianturco started working on, the coronary stent." That was Cook Inc.'s national headline-maker, and it also was a scientific pursuit that brought Cook and Gruentzig back together again.

The idea of a coronary stent was to reduce the number of heart bypass operations needed by declogging heart arteries with percutaneous entry and catheter-delivered stents that widened the vessels, without the major intrusion into the heart cavity—and the high cost, and considerable internal structural damage, and long recovery time—of a bypass operation. Balloon angioplasty was one way, but that didn't work well in some patients. The stent sought would save the lives of patients for whom angioplasty failed.

Gianturco began working in the early 1970s on an idea he had for such a device. Animal trials testing it began in 1984, involving Gruentzig, who was by then a research doctor at Emory Institute in Atlanta. In 1985, the year of Dotter's death, Gruentzig also died—killed with his wife in the crash of an airplane he was piloting.

The testing of the coronary stent went on, with Gruentzig's assistant, Gary Roubin, joining Gianturco and making key contributions. Laboratory studies began; clinical tests on patients began in 1987. In June 1991, the tests had been successful enough for Cook Inc. to file its PMA with the federal agency.

No word came back for months that became years. "On average, a hundred people die of failed angioplasties every month," McCullough said at the time in harsh public criticism of the FDA's delay in giving a go-ahead.

In May 1993, Sen. Howell Heflin of Alabama was admitted to Bethesda Naval Hospital for balloon angioplasty to unclog heart arteries. It didn't work on him; his vessels would open with the balloon, then collapse again. Five times it happened. In a speech on the Senate floor that is part of the *Congressional Record* for June 7, 1993, Heflin said his doctors told him "what might work for me was a new—and as yet unapproved by the Federal Drug Administration—procedure known as stenting. . . . A stent is a metallic, springlike device as fine as a cotton thread inserted into the artery to prevent it from collapsing. It acts as a scaffold to ensure that the vessel remains open, and eventually it is absorbed into the walls of the artery." Heflin had his stent surgery, was back to work in two weeks, and said in his Senate speech, "Not only am I feeling well and happy to be back on the job, I am pleased to report that on June 2, the Food and Drug Administration announced its approval of the flex-stent for use in patients."

Miracle of miracles. Coincidence of coincidences. Almost ten years after FDA approval of the stent had been requested and just before Heflin was to take the case for release of stents to the Senate floor, out came a release from FDA Commissioner David Kessler.

Howell made a point of placing in the *Congressional Record* adjacent to his remarks the full text of the FDA news release, which began:

> The Food and Drug Administration today announced the approval of a new medical device to help keep open blocked heart arteries.
>
> The Gianturco-Roubin Flex Stent Coronary Stent, made by Cook Inc. of Bloomington, Ind., was approved for use with balloon angioplasty in patients whose heart vessels close back up or threaten to close back up during the procedure. This occurs in two to eleven percent of the patients.

"That was the most astonishing day of my life," Phyllis McCullough says. The company had heard the FDA was about to approve the stent, but nothing came from Kessler or the FDA to confirm that, so no word went out from Cook Inc.

"Senator Heflin had his problem on a Friday. He went into the hospital, and they put the stent in. His son was there, and he made the announcement that his father was feeling good, was going home, and after the Memorial Day break he was going to go on the floor of the Senate and ask why the FDA could not approve this stent faster. The next thing I knew [business reporter] Brian Werth called from the local newspaper and said they'd received word from the FDA that we were cleared to go and asked for a comment. It was a funny way to find out. Dr. Kessler obviously wanted

Dr. Barry Katzen, head of the Miami Baptist Hospital's interventional section/
cardiovascular group (*center*), with Ross Jennings and Bill Cook

public relations more than anything, and he did not want Senator Heflin on
the floor of the Senate talking about it."

Although the coronary stent's approval was for limited use, it was a major victory. Cook Inc. had been in a race with Johnson & Johnson to market
one. "We were the first manufacturer in the world to produce balloon-in-
flated coronary stents," Cook said. "We did our clinical trials here. It took
us about a year longer to get our approval, but we got our approval first in
the United States—before J&J or anybody else. J&J got their approval about
the same time in Europe—maybe six months' difference."

Shortly after Johnson & Johnson put its stent on the market, the company filed a suit to stop Cook Inc.'s sales, alleging patent infringement.
Cook countersued, but Johnson & Johnson won court backing for an injunction that shut off Cook's cardiac stent sales while the suit was fought
out in court.

Meanwhile, a race was on to get FDA approval for a second-generation
stent, which Cook hoped would enter it into a more general market than it
had before—a race to get approval *and* a patent. "That to me is just fascinating: you can be first, you can be a creator, but if you don't have your patents
in line, if you don't make your patent applications—and evidently we didn't
do the job we should have on patents—you can lose the ballgame. We don't
do that now. We are making patents as fast as we can and as many as we can.
We have two hundred to three hundred patent applications a year."

Thus lawyers became almost as important to Cook Inc. as its vista-changing array of brilliant doctors, a list that extended far beyond Dotter, Gianturco, Gruentzig, Rösch, and Roubin. One was Dr. Sidney Wallace. After Gianturco's retirement from the Carle Clinic in Champaign and his relocation in Houston, he teamed with Wallace in research that produced, among other things, the "bird's nest" filter and several stents. Like Gianturco—and Bill Cook, the only nonphysician so honored—Wallace received the most prestigious award in their jointly targeted field, the gold medal from the Society for Interventional Radiology.

A key doctor in Cook Inc. history was the man who suggested entering intervention: Bill's cousin, Van Fucilla. He also was an early investor and a supporter.

And there were many others. Fred Keller became chief of radiology at the Dotter Institute at Oregon Health Science University. Barry Katzen heads the interventional section of the cardiovascular surgery group at Miami Baptist Hospital, another place where major Cook gifts have gone. Keller and Katzen represent a harvest of sorts from the early Cook Inc. days and one last confirmation of great business-launching strategy. "Fred and Barry were two of those young doctors that Ross Jennings, Miles Kanne, and I courted," Cook said.

GRII®

CORONARY STENT

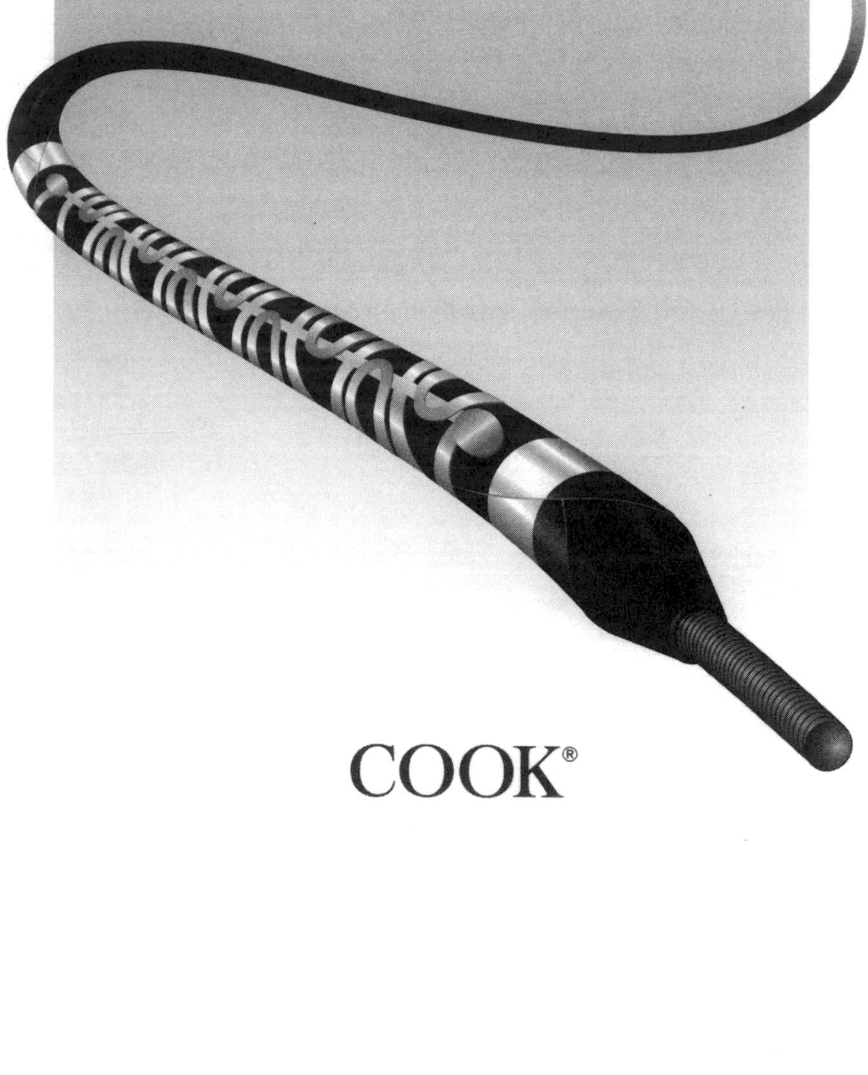

COOK®

Stents and Suits

*From 1988 to 1997 was just hell with lawsuits—and the
damage done to us internally and monetarily
by all the legal fees we were paying.*

—*Phyllis McCullough*

Lawsuits were part of the forced introduction of Bill Cook, a believer in handshake agreements, to a more crass and complicated world.

Cook and Brian Baldwin, his Northwestern fraternity brother, had founded MPL, Inc., a sterile hypodermic needle manufacturing company, before Cook went out on his own. In 1974, the two teamed again to launch a business in Denmark, where Cook Inc. was already established.

Baldwin had sold MPL and started a new company, Baxa Corporation, packaging sterile water in prefilled syringes. The 1974 idea he presented to Cook was for joint operation of a European company to manufacture and sell to doctors disposable needles and syringes prefilled with both sterile water and medicine. Cook liked the plan. "They had this needle-grinding machine built and were getting ready to ship it to Europe," Steve Ferguson says. "At that point, they got sued."

Bernard Fine, the new owner of MPL, filed a claim that Baldwin's new business included trade secrets stolen from him. "The 'trade secrets' covered the whole process of manufacturing hypodermic needles, which was idiotic," Cook said. The machine at the heart of it all, however, was a different matter. The suit played out in Chicago's Cook County Court. It set a record there: it went unresolved for ten years. "They had an attorney, Ron Wilder, who was really a bear," Cook said. "Terrible. A good lawyer. Very frankly, he made my two or three lawyers look like pretzels. He'd just twist them around and throw them out, or take a bite out of them and spit them out. I mean, the guy was good."

Ferguson was still in private practice then, with Cook Inc. as one of his clients. "I'd been on the fringes of the Chicago case," Ferguson said, "and Bill asked me to go see what was going on. Wilder had us stopped with an injunction, and he wasn't anxious to get on from there because he had us locked up. Just as a tactical matter, he was pretty effective, and he was particularly effective in the Chicago courts, so we had our tit in the wringer."

Ferguson started his own investigation of how things had reached that point. "Information tends to have a little bit of a flavor by the time it gets to Bill's desk. So I went to Chicago to do an analysis. Bill and Brian felt they were right and the other guys were wrong. But there were some drawings that came from the other people in our files, which indicated maybe we *had* copied their machine.

"Our attorney was pretty straight: 'Yeah, we've got some problems in this case.' At the same time, these guys from the company that sued us had been bitter. There had been a bad separation. So there was an emotional side that we had to get over."

It might still be injunction-locked—*Affiliated Hospital Products vs. Brian Baldwin and William Cook*—if Fine hadn't sold his company to Smith & Nephew, a conglomerate from England. When the sale happened, Cook suspected the new owners wouldn't care as much about the emotional side of the issue as Fine had. "I ran over to England with Steve almost immediately upon hearing Bernie had sold," Cook said. "Steve wrote up a short contract, and we settled the suit for $1 million. The new people were happy; they didn't want to go ahead with the litigation.

"But the judge still had to rule what the trade secret was. The only 'trade secret' ever found was a drawing of the fixture that held the needles and the rotating mechanism, which was not novel or unique. So I had two of those fixtures all wrapped up and packaged—they weighed about forty pounds. I sent them to Ron Wilder and enclosed a letter: 'Dear Mr. Wilder, here is your booty.' It was fun writing. And when we had other litigation in the future, I hired Wilder to help us. That guy was something else. He and Aaron Kramer, a fellow legal associate, tried cases for us for many years. Ron was a labor law expert, and Aaron was a litigator. The two of them made a superb team. They could blow away almost anybody."

McCullough remembers the first Wilder–Cook Inc. link-up: "A guy in

Illinois called and said he was going to sue us for stealing his product. I had never heard of him. I talked about it with Bill, and he joked, 'We need somebody like Ron Wilder.' I called Ron, and he took on that first case for us." And won it swiftly.

The ten-year suit did bring a new understanding within Cook Inc. of the need to protect proprietary information—inventions that were patentable and trade secrets. For the first time, signing noncompete and nondisclosure agreements became part of the requisite hiring process. Employees already on board were given financial incentives to sign similar agreements.

The long Affiliated suit ultimately cost Cook Inc. $8.5 million—$7.5 million in court-related costs plus the willingly anted-up $1 million in settlement. Cook did end up absorbing K-Tube Corporation in California in settlement with Baldwin for legal fees paid out. The San Diego area company, technologically advanced in laser welding for production of thin-walled steel medical tubing, has since been its own success story under the Cook Inc. umbrella. It's not a large plant, but its employment has tripled—to more than eighty—since the ownership change.

K-Tube was embroiled in yet another suit, which Cook Inc. filed and won against Wall Street giant ITT and one of its subsidiaries, Sterling Tube. The Cook suit charged theft and use of trade secrets involving a former K-Tube employee and a patented process of precise welding for small-diameter stainless steel tubing. After a five-week trial, a federal court jury in San Diego ordered Sterling and ITT to pay Cook Inc. more than $13 million.[1]

A Good Liaison Person

Patent filing was all but overlooked by Cook Inc. in the early years, when the young company's strength was custom-making doctors' requests into unpatented devices and moving on to new requests and needs. "We did a lot of work and a lot of inventing in those days and never thought about patents," Tom Osborne says. "That's one place where we really got bit."

"People came along and saw what we were doing. They jumped in and started copying us. In the 1970s and 1980s, whenever we would go to trade shows or medical meetings with all these medical device exhibitors, I'd wander around and look at everybody else's products and I'd see our product everywhere. People had picked up on all kinds of things. You could just see what they had taken from our product and carried into theirs, then sent their reps out saying, 'Look what we've invented.'" Any device on the market and in the public domain for a year, even if unpatented, by law couldn't be exactly copied and patented, but all that was needed was a small change. "Then *they* would patent it," Osborne said. "It was frustrating. We spend a lot more time with patents now."

Where there are patents, there are lawyers: filing for them, protecting them with suits, defending against infringement charges. Phyllis McCullough had a full taste of involvement in every one of those areas, and she was not a lawyer. The woman whom Cook named Cook Inc. president in 1988 was also his choice to coordinate most legal actions involving the company, despite an educational background that didn't include one day in a law class. "I was the one Bill called on for coordinating litigation. I don't know *how* that happened."

Cook does: "Lawsuits require a great deal of organization. She had a capability of keeping the files, reading the files, and putting them in her memory. Then when the attorneys needed the material, she would always have it available. So she was always our lead person in litigation, the one who would say, 'Okay, lawyers, you take this part, I'll do this part.'

"She even did one case without much legal assistance. She and April Lavender (the company's chief representative in dealings with the FDA) went to New Jersey and won a case all on their own. It involved a company that said we had shipped them more than a million dollars worth of stuff that they said did not meet specifications, even though the specs were spelled out and there was never one that was out of specs. I'm sure they thought, 'This small company in Bloomington—we'll just say we're not going to pay the bill.' So Phyllis and April went, won the case, and we made some money out of it."

McCullough thinks there might be another reason she became Cook's quarterback of litigation. "I was always the one who was cautious—much more intuitive and much more suspicious than Bill ever was. He always trusted everyone. It seemed like I was always spotting something that could turn into a lawsuit, so Bill trusted me to take that over.

"I was a good liaison person with Bill and the legal people. I always felt good that the lawyers trusted me. They could have said, 'Who are you?' I understood the business and what they were telling me. I took copious notes, so I could always explain everything to Bill."

And, in the most critical years of legal battling, she was the Cook Inc. president.

A Very Stressful Time

What McCullough calls the "Jon Wilson lawsuit" involved protection of company secrets. It cost the company $5 million, she estimates.

Jon Wilson's father, Don, was associated with Bill Cook in Cook Canada and was a key man in the 1970s negotiations that put the Cook name in Europe. In Toronto in 1981, Don and Jon Wilson talked with Cook, then formed Wilson-Cook, specializing in products treating diseases of the gastrointestinal tract. Jon was named Wilson-Cook's first president, and in 1984 its operations moved to the Research Triangle in North Carolina, building a new facility in Winston-Salem and incorporating in the United States. In 1989, Cook Group fired Jon Wilson. Then, McCullough said, "Jon started his own company in North Carolina, basically copying what we were doing. We tried to get an injunction and couldn't. Then it was into an actual lawsuit.

"The day before we were to go to trial, Jon filed for personal bankruptcy. So from then on the trial had to go through bankruptcy court, where we were able to prove to the bankruptcy judge the theft of some trade secrets by Jon Wilson but couldn't get an injunction stopping his other business activities. He ended up selling his business to another competitor of Cook Group, C. R. Bard. Bard never did anything with it. He got a little bit of money, and that was it.

"That trial was long and drawn out [from 1989 through 1992]. It required a lot of our time—Scott Eells, Tom Osborne, and I—in North Carolina. Basically, we found out, by putting Jon Wilson through what we had to, he never really learned as much as he thought he did. But the suit was critical to the company as a test of whether we could protect our sales and trade secrets. And it was very nasty, because it involved a father and son. It was difficult and sad for Bill and others at Cook Group, because we were all caught up in a family in distress."

The suits kept coming. Milos Sovak, a Czechoslovakia-born doctor, met Bill Cook through Charles Dotter and worked out the sale of a formula for production of a contrast dye that fit into Cook Inc.'s interventional plans. It was called Oxilan. A company was formed, Cook Imaging, and within a few years, Sovak and Cook Inc. were at odds over everything, starting with management of the company. "Milos was a shareholder with Bill in Cook Imaging," said Dan Sterner, the Indianapolis lawyer who was Cook's Northwestern roommate and a Cook Inc. lawyer from the company's start. "Milos started kicking up his heels. We didn't feel we were being treated right and wanted to part ways, and he made it difficult to do that—plus we had many other protracted arguments and disagreements concerning rights."

Sovak went to court. "He appealed all the way to the Supreme Court and lost in every court," Cook said.

The distractions of the lawsuits came at a time when Cook Inc. was involved in what McCullough called "the most important developments in interventional medicine." This was make-or-break time for the company Bill Cook had dreamed up and carefully puffed from a spark into a flame.

Cook already had two heart bypass operations behind him when the suits and the intervention growth potential converged. "I think your cholesterol level goes up as a result of stress, no question," he said. "And this was a very stressful time in my life."

The Great Stent Rollercoaster

The lifesaving device called the coronary stent will always represent wildly conflicting dimensions of victory and defeat for Bill Cook and others of Cook Inc. who won and lost and puzzled right along with him.

Consider the case—more specifically, the chest—of Steve Ferguson, whose heart problems were corrected long, long ago by a stent Cook Inc. had to take off the market because the market considered it obsolete. "Yeah, my stent's still in there," Ferguson said in 2007, fourteen years after its insertion. "They don't go away. The only time they take them out is during an autopsy."

Then there's Bill Cook, whose heart was and is helped by a stent from Johnson & Johnson Company, with which Cook Inc. fought and lost an expensive suit—over rights to manufacture and sell stents. Cook will never believe impropriety didn't play a part in that suit, which centered on a patent infringement claim involving the Palmaz-Schatz coronary stent that Johnson & Johnson was marketing. "The claim in their suit, which the patent court held that we violated, was use of balloons to expand the stent," he says.

That idea was Cesare Gianturco's, not Julio Palmaz's, Cook maintains. "Cesare Gianturco was around 80 years old in the mid-1970s when he developed the concept of coronary catheterization and placement of these coronary stents into the heart, using a balloon to expand the stent." He cited Gianturco's surgical procedure on a woman's leg in 1971. When the testing and experimentation moved into the area of the heart, Cook says, "the natural transition thought was to put a stent on a balloon, which Cesare Gianturco did." Other researchers were working on similar procedures, including Ulrich Sigwart in Geneva, French cardiologist Jacques Puel, and Richard Schatz and Julio Palmaz in Texas.

Palmaz had a Cook Inc. connection. Commonly, the company worked in confidentiality with doctors pursuing similar ideas and offered separate patenting assistance. Gianturco in 1978 began development of a coronary stent; Palmaz, a radiologist from San Antonio, came to Cook with a different design, also using a balloon catheter. Both received patent attorneys' assistance from Cook. Both reported on their progress at the 1989 Radiological Society of North America meeting. Palmaz ultimately notified Cook he was discontinuing testing and patent services with Cook Inc. and assigning the patent to Johnson & Johnson.

"It was a patent that was very difficult to break," Cook said. "Palmaz's main patent was the ability to deliver, even though we had been doing it for a long time as the work of Cesare Gianturco. Palmaz got a patent, and he was able to protect it, putting a stent on a balloon, delivering it to the site, and deploying it."

The Johnson & Johnson suit and Cook countersuit stretched over months, then years. "We had a lot of prior history that was all dragged up," Phyllis McCullough said. "There was a lot of discovery and a lot of depositions, a lot of time. As small a company as we were, we didn't have enough people with enough knowledge for us to be sitting out all that time testifying. It took a lot of my time. Tom Osborne's, Brian Bates's, and Bill's, too. We all had to be deposed. Finally, in early January 1997, we were able to settle it with J&J. Bill to this day hates the fact that we settled that suit. He thought we should have gone on, and probably we should have."

Bill Cook has his own summation of the situation that he lays out with precision, his irritations plain: "Cook Inc. was the first company in the world to develop a coronary artery stent and also the first to sell one in the United States. Even though Cook Inc. paid for patenting Julio Palmaz's stent, he sold the rights to Johnson & Johnson. It didn't take long for J&J to sue Cook Inc. for patent infringement on a patent Cook Inc. paid for. Because we were eager to begin selling our product in the United States, we settled with J&J, thereby giving up rights to a patent that Cook Inc. may have owned."

McCullough agrees. "We were in such a hurry to stay in the stent market with our second-generation stent, which we had on the market in Europe at that time, and it was being well received. Customers were looking for the next generation, and J&J had nothing new. But we were frozen on doing anything with that in the United States [by the patent-infringement suit]. We wanted to get it on the market, and we wanted to get it through the FDA. It was easier to settle with J&J than draw it out in trial. We settled and went on the market with our GR II stent in July."

Ferguson a Believer

Steve Ferguson was one in Cook Inc. who was uneasy about the new Cook product. And Ferguson, literally from the heart, was as devout a stent man as there was on earth. "Coronary artery disease is a family problem—my brother, my sister, my dad," he said. Always trim and fit, he felt some discomfort in the 1970s. "Bill sent me up to the Med Center [hospitals of the Indiana University Medical School in Indianapolis]. They ran me through a series of tests and couldn't find anything. In the early 1980s I had an angiogram, and it turned out fine.

"I continued to have problems. I saw [cardiologist] Larry Rink at a football game. I was getting ready to leave for Europe, and I said, 'Larry, something's not feeling right.' We ran a treadmill test, and that was fine. I went to Europe, came back, and a couple of months later I was having tightness. Things just weren't right. I was working out on a Stairmaster—it gets to Level 6, and I feel tight. I backed off and called Larry. He told me to change the time I took medicine before I worked out in the morning.

"Then I went to Florida, but I still thought something wasn't right. So I decided to be pretty careful—walk the beach and play golf, but nothing else. I came back home, and now at Level 5 on the treadmill I had a problem. I called Larry, he put me on a treadmill, and he took me right off. He said, 'I've got to get you to the hospital.'"

During examination, Ferguson knew enough from company experiences to read trouble into what he saw of his heart in action on a screen. He told his wife, "Connie, that's just a mess. That's not the way it's supposed to be, let me tell you."

"Carter Henrich, an associate cardiologist with Rink, sat me down and said, 'You need bypass surgery.' I said, 'Carter, I respect you and all of that. But I'm going up to St. Vincent's Hospital in Indianapolis and see if Cass can put in a coronary stent instead.'"

Dr. Cass Pinkerton was the cardiologist who had headed up Cook Inc.'s clinical trials on its coronary stent. "With me," Ferguson said, "the artery on the back of the heart was completely closed and apparently had been for quite a while. I have an unusually large right coronary artery. The average width may be three millimeters, and mine is five. There was a bend in it that was 95 percent blocked. If a clot had flowed through there, I'd have been dead, and people would have been standing at the funeral home saying, 'Damn, he looks good for somebody who did all those exercises, controls his life. . . . Just shows you never know.'

"I told Cass, 'I don't want a bypass. I believe in the stent.'" The unusually large vein posed a problem. The Cook stent was designed for "about 3.5 millimeters," Ferguson said. "The question was whether it was going to work in such a large vessel. So Cass actually called Palmaz at J&J—the lawsuit hasn't been filed yet, but he knows he's in competition. Cass says, 'What do you think about overextending the stent?' With me lying on the table." Dr. Pinkerton heard back: go ahead.

That green light wasn't the end of Ferguson's problems. Dr. Pinkerton's years of doing procedures in a heavy lead apron had caused "a bad problem up in his neck," Ferguson said. The resultant problem was in using his fingers. "Cass said, 'You know I have this problem,' and he wiggled his fingers [indicating a developing stiffness]. But he did it. And I was the last one he ever did."

Implanted in Ferguson was the first-generation Cook stent, the GRBS. "I've been back in twice for follow-ups. The first time, my arteries were better than before they put the stents in. I think the combination of the stent and Zocor is very good."

A Profit Spike, and a Dip

The second-generation Cook stent was intended to improve the GRBS stent's marketability, because in competition with Johnson & Johnson's, the GRBS looked distorted. "Today, the GRBS stent, the very first stent that we made [the one in Ferguson], was probably the finest stent that was ever built," Bill Cook said. "Its disadvantage was it looked very funny after it was placed in the vessel. It had an unusual contour.

"The GR II, the next generation stent that we had, was like a clam shell; we were trying to make a stent look uniform when they placed it, unlike our GRBS stent."

When the go-ahead came from the FDA for Cook Inc.'s second-generation stent, its GR II went on the market in July and dominated it—for a while. Cook's market share jumped quickly from 10 percent to 70. "Our sales volume became $36 million a month, up from $20 million," Bill Cook said. "That's a *huge* step-up."

But competition was hot in pursuit of a similar but better stent to patent. "By October or November," McCullough said, "Boston Scientific and Guidant had both come out with better versions. And our new one wasn't performing well in patients. We were getting reports of very early restenosis."

Cook said, "We pulled both of our stents from the market because we felt they were not as good as the competition. We accepted back as returns all the stents we had sold and gave credit to the hospitals that wanted to go ahead and use the others. So we were out of the business of coronary stents."

It was a shocking financial experience for a company that had been used to sales and profits going upward, always upward. Here not only were sales suddenly sharply down on a leading product but returns were eroding what had once appeared to be gains. In one year, sales jumped almost $100 million—20.8 percent. But the very next year, for only the second time in company history, the sales volume dropped—by almost the identical dollar figure of the increase the year before, down a record 16.6 percent. "We had to take a lot of product back in return," McCullough said. "We had made a lot of money for a few months, and we paid a lot of incentive, and then we credited a lot the next year."

A Coronary Market Return?

It took another decade for Cook Inc. to even think about returning to the coronary stent market with a drug-coated version, but by then the company had become dominant in other areas. Sales increases were back to double-figure annual percentage jumps by 2002. From just 2002 to 2006, sales almost doubled, reaching the billion dollar mark.

The company's bounce-back was led by new stents, in areas away from the heart. "We're in all kinds of other stents," Cook said. "We have huge numbers of stents that are going down into the legs, and the Triple-A [abdominal aortic aneurysm] stent, which is No. 1 in the world right now. We'll be No. 1 for the leg-vessel stents, too. All in all, we are a huge factor in the stent market today."

Still, despite its stents' legal presence elsewhere in the body, Cook Inc. has stayed out of the coronary stent market, Cook said, "because Boston Scientific, Guidant, Medtronics, and J&J hold most of the patents on the coronary stent and delivery by a balloon. Separate stents [patents] apply to different parts of the body because of configuration and design. But there really is no difference [in the working function of stents, wherever they are placed in the body]. You put the balloon in and expand it."

There remains a question to this day whether the national medical community was right in deciding that Cook Inc.'s rivals truly had a better coronary stent—not better than the GR II, which Cook took back to protect its high-integrity reputation in the marketplace, but the one it had come out with originally, the GRBS.

"They did some reports for the FDA after ten years," Ferguson said, "and the GRBS came out better than all the new technology. It's a very flexible round wire. Gianturco really knew what he was doing. I think the round smooth wire moved with the heart. It's a much better stent."

Cook, who needed surgery during the time his own product was frozen and wound up with a coated Johnson & Johnson stent, said, "For Steve and hundreds of others, their vessels are still open today with that stent, whereas many other stents closed down after seven to nine years."

Health

I don't fear death. I have no control over it other than what I'm
doing now, to try to keep myself happy, content, working, not
overdoing, not be too worried, do my exercises religiously,
eat a reasonable diet—all these things I've tried to do
because I don't particularly want to give it all up.
Now, if I get killed, I'll sure as hell be mad.

—Bill Cook

On January 27, 2008, Bill Cook turned 77. That's not a milestone in most
lives, but it had significance for him. It meant he had spent more than half
his years knowing he had a bad heart. "I've reconciled life and death pretty
well," he said. "The thought of dying has been with me since I first began
having heart problems at 38. My heart is pretty well loused up. I don't know
exactly what can be done about that—I don't think anything less than a
transplant."

That's a possibility he obviously has considered, and decided no. "I could
tolerate the surgery. And I probably could get a heart if I said I wanted one.
If you have money, it's amazing how fast a heart shows up. But I've made up
my mind that I'd just as soon other people have it.

"At 77, the best that heart could give me is twenty years, realistically. That would make me 97 years old. Too many other things are going to go haywire by then. I made up my mind a long time ago that whatever day I die, that's fine."

Happy New Year

Bill Cook has had some extreme life experiences. He is sure that, for a brief time when his heart was stopped during bypass surgery, he hovered in a state of near-death. And another time, under other circumstances, he heard the most chilling of words from the most chilling of sources, his cardiologist: "Get your affairs in order."

Cook heard those words from Dr. Larry Rink the first week in January 1998, about three weeks before his sixty-seventh birthday. They weren't long-ranged or cushioned. "He told Gayle and me, together," Cook recalls. "He said, 'This is it. You'd just as well get things ready.' Gayle had a little cry, and I had a little cry. Then we said, 'Well, we'll get our affairs in order.'"

The word came in Bloomington. Only a few days before, the Cooks had been in London. "We spent a very sedate New Year's Eve at the Dorchester Hotel, where we were staying," Gayle said. "We were with Van and Judy Fucilla. We went back to our room, it happened—not a lot of pain, but shortness of breath—and Bill said, 'I have to go to a hospital.'"

For being so far from home, he and Gayle had reason to feel unusually well covered in the emergency situation. "We had a doctor right there with us, Van Fucilla," Gayle said. "And we had Art Hicks, who was the head of Cook-U.K. with all kinds of connections with doctors there. And we were within easy distance of the hospital where the queen goes.

"But it was New Year's Eve. Nobody could find a doctor they knew. Art Hicks couldn't get hold of anybody he had worked with. We just had to take whatever they had at the hospital.

"Then we found out they didn't use the clot-dissolving therapy they do in the United States. Bill always feels he might have . . . been treated better." Heart muscle had been severely and permanently damaged.

It was a slow-developing crisis. New Year's Day passed and the next day. January 3 was a Sunday. "I called Bill in the hospital in London, and he said, 'I guess I am going to be released and come home,'" Phyllis McCullough recalls, picking up the conversation with her response:

"You're not coming home commercial."

"Yes, I am. It's just too expensive to fly one of our planes over here."

"You've got to be kidding me. I'm sending the plane over, and I'm going to have a doctor and a nurse on board."

Everything but a Donor

By telephone, McCullough ran down Dr. Rink, in Bob Knight's hotel suite in Champaign a few hours before Knight's Indiana University basketball team was to play a Sunday afternoon game against Illinois. Rink's avocation was serving as IU's team doctor at all basketball games, home and road. Rink took the call in a corner of the suite and gave quiet instructions on what he wanted on the plane, including a nurse. It wasn't a crisis atmosphere, more of "Let's get him home and do the testing here." It took time to get all necessary arrangements made before the flight could leave Bloomington. Rink went ahead with his basketball duties and was picked up after the game in Champaign for a direct flight to London.

There, Cook said, "I was ambulatory. I just lay down in the hospital until they arrived, then got in a taxi and headed out to the airport."

The trip back was more grueling than tense, but the mood was light. Gayle remembers Rink said, "In this airplane, I'm equipped to do everything for you except a transplant. We don't have anyone willing to be a donor."

By the time the return flight took off, it was well past midnight in London, into Monday morning.

The plane was equipped with sleeping facilities. Rink says, "At one point I dozed off, and when I looked up, I saw in the dark that Bill was up and walking in the back of the plane, smoking a cigarette. I blew up. I told him if he didn't care enough to give up smoking at a time like this, I was wasting my time and he could get somebody else."

The air cleared, in all ways, and once on the ground in Bloomington, Rink directed a series of hospital tests that led to his grave conclusion. Part of the heart muscle no longer functioned properly. That's when Bill heard that he was not expected to live much longer. "That awakens you. I said to myself, 'Well, I'll do what I can.'"

One of the pragmatic steps he took soon afterward was to hand someone else the reins to his company for the first time. "I turned most of the business over to my associates, and the primary associate was Phyllis McCullough. She could run the business, and I had already named her president.

"I took a more passive approach by becoming the computer programmer, where the pressure was not always on. And, yes, I was still sort of a figurehead at the top, but for the most part, other people operated the businesses—Phyllis, Steve Ferguson, Miles Kanne, Ross Jennings, Phil Hathaway, all of them very close, good people. And, of course, I could still develop product, and Tom Osborne could still manufacture prototypes, so we continued to grow."

Gayle found both realism and some reason for optimism in what else she had heard Rink say that day. "What I remember Larry told us was, 'This number of people in this condition live only a year, this number three years, this number five years. . . .'" Any percentage figure above zero was something to build on, and both she and Bill went to work building.

Rink prescribed for Bill Cook a new list of drugs tailored to his changed conditions. Ten years later, well past Rink's dire probability warnings after the London incident, Bill Cook's "affairs" were still very much in his hands. "The medications, the surgeries, the stents that I have in me have kept me alive."

Like an Idiot

His is some health history—basically uneventful in his first thirty-eight years. But there were moments in even those years when the cowboy in him reared up.

In the Days before the Dream, when he was still working to get MPL going in Chicago, Gayle remembers the time he grabbed his side with the classic sudden pain of appendicitis. "He went to the hospital, and they took his appendix out," she said, "but the trouble was, the next day he had a very important appointment for MPL, and he was still in bed. He got up and dressed, and sat in the chair for a while like they always allow you to do. Then he strolled down the hall, went down the elevator, called a cab, and kept his appointment."

Years later, he and standard hospital decorum had another brush. His mother, in her eighties, was hospitalized in Effingham, Illinois. "For years she had had gall bladder trouble—pain at times, not able to eat what she wanted to," Gayle said. "Bill talked to the doctor, and he said, 'I think all you can do for your mother is make her comfortable now.' Bill said, 'Is there no surgery if it's a gall bladder?' The doctor said, 'No, we wouldn't operate on her at her age.' So Bill called a doctor he knew at St. Vincent's Hospital in Indianapolis and said, 'If I bring my mother there and she does have a gall bladder problem, would you operate on someone that age?' He said, 'Yes, I will.'

"Bill drove to Effingham. We had a car where the seat would go back, and we brought blankets and pillows. Without official release, he wheeled her out of the hospital, put her in the car, and drove straight to Indianapolis [about 150 Interstate highway miles]. She did have gall bladder problems, they did operate, and it was the best thing that ever happened to her. Suddenly she could eat anything she wanted, go out to eat with her friends, and enjoy the last years of her life. It was wonderful."

He grew up with one common health problem, after early introduction to the habit of smoking. "I was 21, taking a test in college. Like an idiot, I picked up a cigarette to try to stay awake, and that was the beginning. I promised my parents I would never smoke until I was 21. But I didn't get much beyond 21. My mother was a nonsmoker. My dad was a very heavy smoker."

And so was Bill—three or four packs of Kents every day. "There was always that itch—I smoked cigarette after cigarette—always edgy, always agitated."

He doesn't blame his own heart problems on smoking, though he understands Rink's frustrations after years of trying to get him, a heart patient, to quit. "Smoking does exacerbate the problem," he said, tapping information he has acquired with his own characteristic research into the subject. "Nicotine is an irritant that over time promotes cracks in the blood vessels. The red and white blood cells fill up the crack, and that in time creates plaque, which is a combination of calcium and a whole bunch of junk that goes in that crack to heal it. So you have scar tissue and calcium that eventually fills up the vessel or creates a clot. There are a lot of ways of causing a heart attack.

"I think most of my heart problems were created by my genetic makeup. Even though my mother lived a long life, she had heart attacks at almost the identical age that I did, and she had other heart attacks like I did. My dad had high blood pressure and died of a cerebral vascular accident. He blew out a vessel in his head.

"That's one of the things that saved my life. Knowing what my dad died of, I was able to keep an eye on my carotid artery. That's where most of the problems creep in, where you end up with a very serious problem—it's blocked, or you throw a clot. Normally it's a clot, and a clot will end up in your head somewhere, you'll have a cerebral vascular accident, which means literally blowing out the artery. The result is you become paralyzed, or you die, like my dad. He lived for a week as a vegetable, and then he died."

After genetics, he considers stress the major contributor to his heart problems. "Your cholesterol level goes up as a result of stress, no question. And a very stressful time in my life was getting this business started. I'm definitely Type A, meaning I agitate myself. It doesn't take anyone else. All my life, I've wanted to get up early because I was afraid I'd miss something. I'll wake up at 3 or 4 AM and think, 'I'm going to get up and see what will happen today.'

"I think those were contributing factors, because I always had an edge about me. And I had an explosive temper. I still do, but I hope I can keep it under control. I snap. All of a sudden, boom, I'm saying things a lot of times I regret, and I turn red in the face. I've spent a lot of time mending fences after I've blown my top."

There is another stress that maybe only the man at the top of a major company—more precisely, a health devices company—can feel. "In this business, where your product is in the body inches away from where it can kill a person if something goes wrong—that for many years bothered me. I thought, 'Whoa! I can wipe somebody out.' I was fearful for several years of my own product. Maybe that wire guide will break, maybe that plastic catheter will shatter. And they do. The point is, it doesn't happen very often. I learned to handle it. But during the years . . ."

A Gathering Storm

Whatever caused them, heart concerns started for Bill Cook shortly after Thanksgiving in 1969. "I was cutting down a Christmas tree with Carl [7 at the time] out on a piece of rural property we owned—nice tree, about six to eight feet tall. It was very cold. I was cutting by hand. I had a light jacket on. I noticed a tightness in the chest and some pain—transient, it lasted just a short time and then was gone. I never mentioned it to anyone. Nothing was done. There was nothing I could do. There wasn't even a treadmill in town yet."

Some heart damage resulted, undetected until later tests. By then, Cook had experienced other problems. In 1971, he took Steve Ferguson along in his Mooney on a flight to Madison, Wisconsin, for an Indiana-Wisconsin football game. "As we were walking to the game, he started feeling pressure," Ferguson said. "I'm not sure that either one of us actually said it was heart, but obviously that was in our minds."

"It did not manifest itself in pain," Cook said, "but when I got to the game, I had an upset stomach and my heart was palpitating. Having been in the business a while, I understood there was something haywire."

They watched the game, and then new anxiety began. "I was looking for somebody to fly us home," Cook said. "I was afraid that I might not get us home because I knew I had a problem."

"We couldn't find anybody," said Ferguson, who is not a pilot. "So we took off and flew back. That's the only time I ever paid a lot of attention to how to get the thing down."

On another New Year's Eve—the night of December 31, 1973—the Cooks and Fergusons were in New Orleans for one of the greatest college football bowl games ever played: Sugar Bowl, 10–0 Notre Dame vs. 11–0 Alabama, Ara Parseghian vs. Bear Bryant. The lead changed hands six times, Notre Dame ahead 24–23 late in the game but pinned at its one-yard line by a punt, only to get out with a gutty pass from the end zone, Tom Clements to tight end Robin Weber, straight up the middle for thirty-five yards and an escape that won the national championship. Breathless stuff, but not the biggest thing on the mind of the Cooks and the Fergusons.

"There was an abrupt change of temperature just before the game started," Bill recalls. "I was walking to my seat, and a cold blast of air hit me. I said, 'Something's wrong.'" But not so wrong that he called for help. "I got up to the top of the stadium and watched the game."

This time, though, the problem couldn't be avoided. Afterward, he cut off the couples' planned holiday trip, lined up a ride to the airport, and flew home. At IU Medical Center in Indianapolis, Dr. Walter Judson and associate Ross Jennings "put me on a treadmill and I didn't do very well. I only lasted two or three minutes. Then they gave me an angiogram, and I had a little problem with allergenic reaction, which again meant shortness of breath and coughing. They finished that and [using some of Cook's own manufactured products in stock at the Medical Center, he was pleased to note] found out I had some pretty serious problems."

The world's first heart bypass operation wasn't performed until 1969, at the Cleveland Clinic. This was early 1974, and Bill Cook needed one. "I had to go to California, because they didn't even do them yet in Indianapolis," he said.

Actually, Cook's friend in intervention, Charles Dotter, got him booked into an Oregon hospital for surgery by a pioneer bypass surgeon, Albert Starr. Time came for the surgery, and Dr. Starr was unavailable; he was having his own bypass operation.

Cook's cousin, Dr. Van Fucilla, stepped in. He was second in charge of radiology at El Camino Hospital in California's Silicon Valley, and that's where Cook had his bypass. "Van introduced me to Dr. Lee Enwright, a surgeon who had worked under the very prominent open-heart surgeon Norman Shumway at Stanford University. Dr. Enwright had done a hundred bypass operations himself when he did me. I recuperated at Van's house in California. I came back, and I was fine until 1983." By then he was in his fifties, with an all-new outlook on taking care of himself physically.

Speed Walking, Alone

He zeroed in on his weight. "My weight has fluctuated," he says. "When I was married, I weighed 235 pounds. Then I went down to 180. I had my first bypass and I went down to 150, because Ken Cooper said, 'You have to go to 150.'"

Kenneth H. Cooper is a retired Air Force colonel—almost exactly Cook's age, Cook the older by thirty-six days. In 1968, the year of Cook's first heart flare-up, Cooper introduced to the world the word *aerobics* and his own program for revitalizing the cardiovascular system. Cooper's "Bedrock Principle No. 1" was that everyone needs regular, moderate exercise. Weight control fit in there somewhere, prominently, Cook concluded after having a physical exam at Cooper's Aerobics Center in Dallas and meeting the man.

On Cooper's program, Cook says, "Actually I went to 143 pounds. Oh, man, I looked like death warmed over. Awful. But this was Cooper talking about how to increase your longevity. If you take that weight off the heart, you probably can get along better. I seemed to get along just fine at 143, but I was hungry all the time." So he eased off a little. "I got up to 160, and I felt pretty darned good. Then it became 170, and then I went back to my stabilized weight, which is anywhere between 180 and 190."

He became a walker—heavy-duty. Walking is another Cooper staple, and Cook met Cooper's recommendations and took them to his own levels. "Bill walked four and a half miles seven days a week, no matter where we were," Gayle said. "If we were in Chicago and it was midnight when we were finished, he'd go out and do his walking. And this was for years and years and years." Gayle almost never made that walk with him, "because he would do fast-walking. I practically had to run if I was 'walking' with him."

The walks had to be suspended temporarily when he ran into another problem: severe back pains. "Charles Dotter called me at home one night and said he hadn't heard from me for a while. I told him I hadn't been to work because I had back problems and couldn't get up. He said, 'Come out here. We've got a good back surgeon. Let him operate on you.' I went out, they X-rayed me, and they did a laminectomy—for a disc in the spinal cord, between two vertebrae. That was done at the University of Oregon in March 1976." Three decades later, Cook is still irritated by the timing. "That's where I was, in bed listening to the game in Oregon, the night we won the national championship in Philadelphia." It wasn't just *a* national college basketball championship, rare as those are. Cook, a rabid fan who loves to be where the action is, was a whole continent away from the most historic athletic moment of his Bloomington years: when Indiana concluded what—thirty-two years later—still is major college basketball's last undefeated season by beating Michigan in the NCAA finals, 86–68.

After the surgery, his back felt fine, and he went back on the brisk-walking regimen, until one day in 1983. "I was walking by myself in Bryan Park [near his home], and I had to sit down; I had to wait for Gayle to drive over and pick me up. I was put on the table at St. Vincent's Hospital in Indianapolis for another bypass surgery."

The second bypass went fine except for one side-effect: "Everything they had done in the laminectomy at Oregon came undone. I don't know why, maybe the way I was flopped on the table, but I came out with a back ache, and I had a weak back from there on. It hurt until I was in my late sixties, and then it stopped. Now I can walk well again."

And then came the New Year's Eve in London, and a radically changed life.

It Worked for a Biker

Bill Cook's "change" could be scored like a major league double play: Mc-Cullough to Mellencamp to Gebhardt.

Rock star John Mellencamp, who was bouncing back from a heart attack, decided he needed to be in better shape while on tour. So, after reading a fitness book by Kris Gebhardt, Mellencamp got the onetime Ball State University football lineman to tour with him and provide personal fitness training, which Gebhardt did for three years. Phyllis McCullough had an off-work role as head of an Indiana University athletics fund-raising group, the Varsity Club, and at the time she was trying to get Mellencamp's name on a donation big enough to get an indoor workout facility built for the IU football team. Mellencamp-Gebhardt meshed; so did Mellencamp-McCullough on their project. Those two relationships were the starting point.

In conversation with McCullough, Mellencamp once mentioned his workout regimen and bet her she couldn't handle a Gebhardt schedule for a year. She won the bet, Mellencamp paid her off with a portrait that had been done of him, and John and his wife, Elaine, became friends of Phyllis and Jerry McCullough—social friends, traveling friends, good friends.

And so it was that when Bill Cook was at his lowest physical point, coming out of his 1997 heart attack with a permanently impaired heart, both John Mellencamp and Phyllis McCullough thought of Kris Gebhardt. McCullough recalls, "John called me and said, 'Why don't we get Bill working out with Kris? It's done so much for Tracy. It has to be a good thing for Bill.'" Tracy Cowles was Mellencamp's cousin and closest friend, and his heart problems were much worse than Cook's when Gebhardt began to work with him. "Tracy was very sick. After three heart attacks, he only had 10 percent pumping capacity left in his heart," Gebhardt said. "This was a guy who couldn't walk across the room. He couldn't lie down and sleep because he would choke on his own blood. He had to sleep propped up in a chair. John told me, 'I'm going to take him on the tour. Otherwise, he's just going to get sick and die. Is there anything you can do with him?'

"I started experimenting, trying things with weights, not treadmill like everybody prescribes. He was my lab. He and John. There was no protocol for this. The normal prescription for somebody with heart disease was to send them to a rehab clinic and put them on a treadmill—back to the days of Kenneth Cooper, all aerobic. I didn't have success with that with John. I had it with weight training and the techniques I was using.

"In about two weeks Tracy was able to lie down, and he was feeling better. He was doing a whole routine of stretching and weight training combined. I was using the basic heavier movements, like chest press and leg press, things you wouldn't think you would put somebody on who has severe cardiovascular disease. I was using amounts of weights where I assist

Physical trainer Kris Gebhardt, a former Ball State football player, and Bill Cook

them. Handing them little three-pound dumbbells just doesn't tax the heart enough. If we use the equipment, and the machine's right and the weight's right, we can create blood flow.

"Tracy was a biker and a tough security guy. He said, 'Kris, my wrist and my upper arm are the same size. That's how sick I am.' He had very little blood flow in his hands. The exercises I would do would force blood flow into them. But this is dangerous stuff. This is a guy doctors didn't even want to do treadmill tests with." In a year, Gebhardt said, Tracy Cowles "was back to 190 pounds, in good shape, and back to work."

That's why Mellencamp and McCullough double-teamed Gebhardt to take on another client.

Ten-Year Plan

"One day Phyllis said, 'You really ought to help Bill Cook,'" Gebhardt said. "I said, 'Who's Bill Cook?' John said, 'He's that rich guy whose planes we use on tours.' 'What's wrong with him?' 'He's like Tracy.' 'How much money does this guy have?' 'He's a billionaire.'

"Oh, no," Gebhardt said, "I'm not taking on that guy's lawyers. If I go over there and kill him . . . forget it."

That's where it stayed for a while. "Then Phyllis asked me one day, 'Do you think you could help Bill? He won't leave his house. He's really sick. Larry Rink has told him to get his affairs in order.'

"So this was my deal. I said, 'We'll get a gym set up over at your office on Curry Pike. I'll come in Monday, Wednesday, and Friday. I'm going to do this for a month.'

"I go in there. Bill's in very bad shape, as bad as Tracy, but a lot older. And a lot richer. It's not very good for business if you kill a billionaire. It's going to be in all the papers.

"The first session with Bill was fine. He was listening. I was controlling the situation; he wasn't. He was great. He didn't try to dictate a thing.

"I remember going home and my wife said, 'What's this Bill Cook like?' I said, 'You know, he's full of piss and vinegar.' No, I think I said, 'He's an ornery bastard.' But he *is* full of piss and vinegar. I just love the guy."

Gebhardt at the time thought of himself as an author first. "I invested everything I owned into that career path. Thought it was my calling to go out and sell books," Gebhardt said. "But that first year I thought, 'Bill Cook touches so many more lives than I could ever touch, with the products that they develop, and the money that his company puts into the economy. And the company has to have him. I'm going to do this for ten years.'

"I told Bill, 'I'm going to get you ten years.' He said, 'Oh, the doctors are giving me a couple.' I told him, 'I'll get you ten years. And that tenth year, you're going to take me to Necker Island.' It's an island that Richard Branson of Virgin Records owns, in the British Virgin Islands—the most beautiful spot in the world, a private island. You rent the island, $27,000 a day. 'We're going to take twenty-five of our friends there and celebrate after ten years.'"

McCullough said, "The first five years passed. Tracy Cowles lived five years after working out with Kris. He stopped working out, and he died. We passed the five-year mark with Bill, and it was, 'Okay, we've got to keep him going.'"

On January 2, 2007, Gebhardt said, "I walked in and said, 'Okay, Bill, this is starting our ninth year.' Next January starts our tenth year. That's my deal. Into the tenth year. We've been through some ordeals—with the kidney, and . . .'

"The ten-year thing was a joke the first couple of years. About the fourth year, Bill came in and said, 'I had my check-up with Larry Rink, and he's starting to believe your ten years.'"

"About Christmas 2007, Bill called me and said, 'I guess we've got to book that island.'

"January 2008 came, the start of our tenth year, and I told him, 'I'm sorry I undershot.' We never even stopped to celebrate. Just went on with what we've been doing. I did put together a plaque and presented it to him, showing what he's done in these years of workouts." That all starts with the top line on the plaque: his weight work from first day on adds up to 48 million pounds.

Rink is not ready to make the Gebhardt system of physical work for cardiac recovery patients his recommended procedure. "But it has seemed to work on Bill. He definitely got much stronger."

End of a Habit

"The kidney" was another major problem for Bill Cook in his seventies. "That was 2002," he remembers. "I was outside the Crazy Horse [a downtown Bloomington restaurant], talking with Connie Ferguson. Steve was paying the bill. I felt a very sharp pain on the left side of my back. Then it dulled down, and I thought maybe it was muscular. That was on a Thursday.

"On Saturday, I was having a meeting at the office with a couple of people, and the pain was so intense I had to go to the hospital. By that time it was too late. The kidney was gone."

With his heart down to 13 percent working capacity and one kidney gone, he finally did stop smoking.

"It was a by-product of being in the hospital for those days and not being *able* to smoke," Gayle Cook said. "He said, 'Well, okay, I've done it for four days. The cold turkey part is over.' So he quit. And he has never complained."

"It wasn't hard," Bill said, "because I knew I had to quit when that kidney failed. When I walked out of the hospital, I didn't have the craving. I had the desire, but I didn't have the craving. I said, 'I'm not going to smoke again.' And I didn't.

"There is still always an appeal, but never a craving. When I get into a place where there is a lot of cigarette smoking, it bothers me. It bothers my eyes, and it stinks. I'm very sensitive to the smoke now."

The failure of his left kidney led to insertion of two renal stents. "He lost a lot of weight, and he was real weak when he came back to work out," Gebhardt said. "He bounced back in a week and a half. That's how good a foundation he has."

"I do feel good," Cook said. "I cannot exercise heavily, because I don't have any appreciable heart capacity left. When they say 'You have between 55 and 60 percent of your capacity,' that means the left ventricle will be pumping 60 percent of your blood. That is the big pump that does the majority of the lifting of the blood, the 'good work.' It shoves the blood up into your head and then through gravity and other ways it comes down, and the right ventricle pushes it on into your vessels. Mine runs between 13 and 18 percent.

"What physical fitness has done is let me have a normal life. Larry Rink has had me on medications, cholesterol-lowering and blood pressure-lowering, for about twelve years. I attribute keeping me alive to both, not just one or the other."

Always One Step Ahead

His surgeries continued. In May 2003, he had his Johnson & Johnson coronary Cypher stent inserted at St. Vincent's Hospital in Indianapolis. In July 2004, he said, "I had two renal stents put in me on the right side at Cleveland Clinic. I'm one of the 25 percent who have two arteries to a kidney."

An irony is that none of the stents in him was Cook-made. "During both of the bypass surgeries, some of our products were used—catheter products: the wire guides, the needles, and the catheters," he said. "But nothing that I have in me as hardware is ours." It was a matter of timing. Cook Inc. wasn't making coronary stents when he needed them or urinary stents when that emergency came.

The key thing keeping him alive and strong, Gayle Cook feels, is the insight that Bill's years in the health business have given him. "He knows when he needs something done, and he's aware of all the procedures that can be done. He has just done everything at every step. Someone else would have been gone long ago. Bill has always stayed just one step ahead. I don't think someone not in the industry would have done that. He knows when to have a check-up and see if anything can be done—opening a vessel, whatever.

"We knew a man who had one of those early bypass surgeries the same time Bill did. Bill had a redo nine years later. They offered this to the other man, and he said, 'No, I don't want to go through that again.' And he died."

The Guidant Fiasco

> *Billionaire* is a made-up term because the asset is in the
> corporation. The only way I would ever gain that number,
> that resource, is to sell the company. And after the
> Guidant fiasco, I have no reason to sell out.
>
> —Bill Cook

There was a *poof!* effect in the headline that Bloomington woke up to on the morning of July 31, 2002:

COOK SOLD FOR $3 BILLION

The magic balloon ride of nearly forty years was over. Bill Cook was climbing out, and who could blame him—especially anyone who knew that the man who had turned billfold money into billions was in his seventies now with major health problems. If there was a public consensus, it probably was "What a ride, Bill Cook! Congratulations. Enjoy yourself."

The sale wasn't just big news in Bloomington. The *Wall Street Journal, New York Times, Financial Times,* and the less-elite dailies led by *USA Today* all gave prominence to a $3 billion business deal. Wall Street noticed, too. Stock prices for the purchaser in the deal, Guidant Corporation, jumped—10 percent in the market's opening hours, still an impressive 5 percent at the close. Three times Cook's size in annual sales, hitherto competitor Guidant's top officials were publicly salivating over what the deal promised to do for them: take the snarl out of a patent knot that had tied up three rivals in their pursuit of primary position in medicine's lucrative Great Cardiac Stent Race.

Then, on the morning of January 3, 2003, the same-sized headline screamed a different message:

COOK-GUIDANT DEAL OFF

In the twenty-two weeks between, a whole lot of roiling was going on.

Key Word: Paclitaxel

From the time when Cook Inc. had, then lost, the cardiac stent market, its research and testing were all-out in pursuit of a stent that would put it back in competition, because the big companies that had shouldered Cook out didn't have anything close to an ideal product, either.

The 1990s patent problem with Dr. Julio Palmaz and Johnson & Johnson was only the beginning. The next key issue was thought to be finding the right drug to coat the stent and reduce a major post-angioplasty risk that had surfaced over the years. Restenosis was the problem: the artery opened by the balloon process collapses, at great risk to the patient. "All the companies were experiencing a high rate of restenosis," Phyllis McCullough recalls. "Coating the stent with a drug was thought to be the key to stopping that." Johnson & Johnson and Guidant were trying different but similar anti-immune coatings. The drug Paclitaxel, produced by a Canadian company, Angiotech, "seemed more promising" to Cook Inc. researchers, McCullough says. "But nobody really knew for sure." Angiotech put rights for use of the drug up for sale for $70 million, plus royalties. Cook and another rival, Boston Scientific, went together, paying $35 million each plus royalties to share the rights.

"When we started doing trials with our stent—bare metal with a Paclitaxel coating on the stent—J&J was in trials with the Palmaz stent with a polymer coating on it," McCullough said. "They were having some issues. Customers were saying they were getting some restenosis problems. We had figured out a way to put Paclitaxel directly on a metal stent without having to use polymer, and that seemed to be doing very well. But we really didn't have a good stent, because we were having to work around everybody else's patents. Guidant had probably the best stent on the market, but they had a drug of their own in trial and it failed. So they were left without a coating."

Guidant came to Cook with a proposal: let's sell our stent with your coating. Under their proposal, McCullough said, Cook would "buy catheters and stents from Guidant, coat the stents, put them on the catheters, and then sell the whole thing back to Guidant, and Guidant would distribute the product."

It sounded sensible and workable, but there were contract entanglements. One of the stipulations in the co-licensing agreement with Boston Scientific was that Cook Inc. could sublicense Paclitaxel usage to its own subsidiaries but couldn't license to anyone else unless the whole Cook organization was sold. Additionally, McCullough said, "We had certain restrictions in our settlement agreement with Johnson & Johnson as to what we could do with other companies. Basically we couldn't sell or distribute to them. In this case we thought we were in pretty good shape because it was Guidant's stent and Guidant's catheter and our coating with our drug that we had a license to. We thought we could do *that* distribution.

"But I was nervous about it because I thought we were going to run into trouble with Boston Scientific." Or Angiotech. "As we got going with the agreement and it was announced, we asked for Angiotech's permission, and they said basically they weren't going to get in the middle of it.

"There were months of just horrible negotiations. We were in European clinical trial with the Guidant stent, not in the United States, when it was fairly certain that Boston Scientific was going to sue—us probably first and Guidant second. They sued us, and we started pursuing the lawsuit.

"Guidant, being the bigger company and feeling they had the most to lose, wanted to take over the lawsuit, which we did not want them to do. It became a difficult situation." In May 2002, Guidant president Ron Dollens went to Bloomington to talk with Cook and McCullough and said he wanted to buy the whole company and eliminate the rights problem.

In Big Trouble

Due diligence is the legal term for the revelation of full details of operations required from a company being purchased. McCullough had the due diligence responsibilities for Cook Inc.

The due diligence process required from Cook Inc.—a company built on handshake agreements and comfortable with operating without a budget— completion of accounting audits from 2001 on back. "Guidant wanted to see if the records were correct, what our write-offs were, what contingency funds we had, just how we generally conducted business," said Dan Sterner, the company attorney from its beginning.

That was the start of the process, the "easy" part, McCullough said. Full revelation of regulatory practices "was critical to Guidant because they were already under the gun with the FDA and I think eventually the Department of Justice. We didn't know that going in. We learned as we were going through due diligence that Guidant had its own reasons for wanting Cook. Guidant was in trouble over *its* Triple-A device."

The sale announcement came while "we were still fighting the lawsuit with Boston Scientific and we were going through the process of due diligence, or trying to," McCullough said.

The sale was complicated. "The sale price was $3.2 billion," Bill Cook said. "The story can be told now that we had an agreement that if we sold to them, after a three-year period we could buy back all of the assets—with the exception of the Triple-A stent, Paclitaxel technology, and one other product—for $375 million, and go on just as we were. Otherwise, I would have never sold."

Essentially, the agreed deal split the Cook companies between those that were producing medical devices and those that weren't—biomedical being the broad term to cover Cook MyoSite, Cook Biotech, Cook Pharmica, Global Therapeutics, and areas reaching far ahead in gene therapy and other exploratory fields aimed at answering a range of questions that have baffled medical science for years. Those areas particularly excited Bill Cook and would have come back to him after a three-year wait.

McCullough said, "Bill asked me to go with Guidant in the deal, and he, Carl Cook, Steve Ferguson, and Kem Hawkins would be a management group that would run those other companies for Guidant and eventually buy them back. It got to be a very difficult diligence process. Ron Dollens sent Ginger Graham, one of his top executives, in here. Ginger is a Harvard MBA grad—very aggressive and very much a go-getter. She was trying to push the due diligence, and there was resistance within our people. There was just one agony after another trying to go through this process. It was a difficult time for me internally. I was looked at by some here as being on Guidant's side of the process—leaning too far that way."

That, she says, was never the case. "I didn't want the company to be sold. I loved Cook. I grew up with it. But I was really trying to do the job. If we were going to do due diligence, I had to provide the information. I truly believed the combination of Cook and Guidant would be a good thing. They needed us, not only for the stent coating but we obviously had the best Triple-A device, and they had the market strength and power—in cardiology particularly and with vascular surgeons. From a marketing standpoint, it was a good match."

Still, Bill Cook was pessimistic about the Guidant sale going through. "We had already lost the first round of the Boston Scientific lawsuit [a few weeks after announcement of the sale]," McCullough said. "They got basically a temporary injunction, and we were preparing an appeal. Bill, I think, was frustrated with the whole thing, frustrated with the perceived problems of me and Kem Hawkins and Steve Ferguson in the middle doing all the negotiations and [company treasurers] John Kamstra and Rob Santa doing all the accounting and everyone being gripy. Our inside counsel at the time, Pete Yonkman, got into a big fight with the lawyer for Guidant. And our trials [the stent-testing going on in Europe] were showing that our coating process had some flaws in it. The product never failed. We just had what I considered ramp-up problems in going from doing small quantities of stent coating to very large quantities. It was just an awful mess. The farther you went along, the more you knew, 'This thing is in big trouble.'"

Just Nightmares

It wasn't the only mess for McCullough. "In September," she recalls, "we were notified about Kevin Scott and his problem with PERF," the multimillion dollar Public Employees Retirement Fund.

Scott was an impressive young lawyer who in 1998 had been hired to a top position at Cook Inc. Turned out he was (1) not a practicing lawyer—he had never passed the bar, and (2) a felon who had served a prison term in Cincinnati during the years 1993–97 when his application said he had been working for Procter & Gamble there. Dennis Troy and Fred Hayes from Cook's security staff, acting on a tip, went to Cincinnati and brought back the court records on Scott's conviction.

"Bill said, 'Call him in, confront him with all of this, and see what he says—see if he admits it,'" McCullough said. "In Bill's office, he basically 'fessed up to everything. He said he hadn't told us because he had to have a good reputation for five years before he could apply for the bar again, and he wanted to earn an opportunity to do that with our job.

"So we gave him a second chance. And we agreed we wouldn't discuss his history with anyone else, but he could not represent himself as a lawyer for Cook Inc. He turned out to be an embezzler. I didn't know that."

After the confrontation, McCullough said Dan Peterson, a Cook Inc. manager, "told me and some other executives in our company that Kevin had an opportunity to take a state government job with PERF in Indianapolis. He said Kevin had told the PERF people everything about his background, but they still wanted to talk to people at Cook. I agreed to talk to them." So did some others, in separate telephone conversations.

In the conversations with PERF representatives, she said, "None of us mentioned the previous felony because we had been assured he had already told them. So I got duped a couple of times." Scott's hiring came to light in an unrelated newspaper investigation: in a budget crunch, Democratic governor Frank O'Bannon announced a hiring freeze. When the *India-*

napolis Star learned some public officials had been hired after the freeze, the newspaper ran a screening test on them. W. Kevin Scott was one, and the *Star*'s computer check came up with Scott's penal background—a major story because he was handling millions of public dollars in his PERF role.[1] McCullough was pinpointed in the story as "the Cook executive who gave him a great recommendation after I knew he was a convicted felon."

A state investigation followed. McCullough was identified as at least a material witness, with suggestions she might face prosecution. "Just nightmares," she said. "And right in the middle of the Guidant deal."

At the time, McCullough was no longer Cook Inc. president. That was another element of the tensions. She had moved over to chairman of the board, and John DeFord had been promoted from within the Cook ranks to take her place. But after only three months, DeFord was fired, and Kem Hawkins moved up from Cook Group president to take over the full company.

"John had worked here about nine years," Hawkins said. "He had a PhD, incredible intelligence. Phyllis and Bill made the selection of DeFord together, and they decided after three months it wasn't going to work."

It was a rare personnel misstep on the remarkable Bill Cook record. It was more painful for Phyllis McCullough. DeFord was her nephew.

And the Guidant deal was still going on.

In her personal gathering storm, everything converged one morning when a delegation of fifteen from Guidant came to the Cook office, and from Indianapolis a State Police investigator, a representative of the U.S. Attorney's Office, and two lawyers arrived to interview McCullough on the Scott matter—all this at a time when migraine headaches were already sporadically incapacitating her.

At one point in the middle of that tumultuous day, McCullough in frustration resigned and Cook, at least as frustrated, accepted. But when the strain had eased a few days later, McCullough still was chairman of the Cook board.

And the Scott storm passed with the hint of charges against her dispelled.

And the Guidant deal was dead.

All of that in five months.

A $50 Million Aspirin

The negotiations with Guidant ended when Boston Scientific was declared the winner in its suit against Cook. Judge Charles Kocoras of the U.S. District Court in Northern Illinois ruled that Cook Inc. could not be sold to

Guidant—"that the distribution agreement violated our Angiotech agreement, and that buying Cook was simply a way to get around that," McCullough told the *Herald-Times*. Hence the "deal's off" headline.

Cook wasn't shocked by the deal-killing ruling by the Chicago judge. "Basically, we were caught between two agreements," he says. "The Johnson & Johnson settlement said we couldn't sell stents to anybody unless the entire Cook Group was sold. The Boston Scientific–Angiotech agreement said we couldn't sublicense to anybody but a subsidiary of Cook unless all of Cook Inc. was sold. Then Ron Dollens came in and said, 'We'll just buy it all.' The judge ruled that we couldn't play games, and what we were really doing was selling Paclitaxel. He equated the deal to a painter purchasing a house, painting it, then selling the house back to the original owner. He said 'It doesn't make sense.'"

Neither side worked at pursuing new negotiations. Publicly, Dollens said that Cook's European stent testing problems chilled his company's interest. "We let Guidant say the stent wasn't working, they paid a $50-million break-up fee, and that was it," McCullough said.[2]

The break-up fee was a powerful aspirin for Cook's five-month headache. And the future brought other reasons the deal not made looked like one of the best ever for Cook Inc.

"Guidant's history from there was just downhill," McCullough said. "They were without a coating for their stent product. Boston Scientific got its Paclitaxel-coated stent on the market and took a lot of Guidant's market. Boston Scientific was gloating and happy to bury Guidant. Johnson & Johnson made an offer to buy Guidant, and at the last minute Boston Scientific offered more money and ended up buying it. Then, because of the acquisition, Boston Scientific's stock went down.

"There's no question we are far better off now [than if the sale to Guidant had gone through]," McCullough says. "The structure of the company today is much stronger. The problems that Guidant was in that we didn't know about would have been there. We would have been dragged through an awful lot trying to fix things, and we would not have had control. Johnson & Johnson still could have made a bid for Guidant, with us as a part of it. Boston Scientific would have done the same thing. So, in the long run, the way it all worked out, it's a blessing in disguise. However stressful things were, it came out right."

The whole key to Cook Inc.'s subsequent success, Bill Cook says, "was what we had in our pipeline at the time. We had a whole bunch of products that were just ready to come out then. After the sale did not go through, we brought them out quite successfully. One was the Triple-A stent. Once we were free to turn all those things loose," including the biomedical areas, "we just took off."

Not a Fan

The man who will own the company next was not unhappy to see the deal crash. "I hated it," Carl Cook said. "Let me back up a second: I didn't think the Paclitaxel deal was a good idea. And I thought the Guidant thing was the worst idea ever. I am not a fan of the coronary stent market. You either own it or you have none of it. If you show yourself to be a thousandth-of-a-percent better than everybody else, you get 90 percent of the market. As soon as somebody else comes up with something a tiny bit better than you have, they get it all and you lose it all. None of our other products behaves that way. If you're good, you're competitive in the market and you'll get a percentage of the business.

"The only means of judging a coronary stent is its long-term closure complication rate. Nobody wants to have a stent in them that is not as good as another one, because that means you have a higher chance of having an issue that may be fatal. So I didn't like the coronary stent market. It took our eyes off the ball on our other products because it generated so much more money than anything else we were doing at the time."

Pretty Good Return

The conclusion in looking back at the Guidant deal and litigation years is that the luckiest thing—the near-miracle—for the Cook company of today is a stark one: that Bill Cook survived it.

Pete Yonkman is less than half Cook's age, but even to him, the five years of legal wrangling were "just awful." In the real crisis months, he said, "I would wake up in the middle of the night with just panic attacks. There was too much drama on a daily basis."

And Bill Cook—in his seventies, with a badly damaged heart and his life's work in the chips on the high-stakes poker table where he had sat—made it through.

The Guidant-sale experience did show him one other thing that he hadn't fully gauged before—about the widespread feeling about him, personally, and the company he personified, among employees who had grown in number as Cook Inc.'s sales grew—many of them still around from the company's early days and others second-, even third-generation members of the Cook Inc. employee family.

"I learned there was a lot of heartache on many people's part when we began to sell," he said. "And I couldn't tell them about the other deal—that part of the company would later return to the Cook corporation."

The image was that the man they had worked for all those years was getting out—taking his money and running. "That was the image, and I never realized just how much that hurt a lot of people. I've gotten sort of used to the idea now that there are a lot of people dependent upon the company—what we do and how we do it."

The experience also gave him a gauge of his company's worth—and therefore, realistically, his family's, since the company is fully owned by them. It's a gauge much more valid than the *Forbes* magazine guessing. "Unless you go to the market place, you have no idea. It was worth every cent to Guidant at the time they made that offer—$3.2 billion. Now, would it be worth more to another company today? The answer probably is yes, but I can't—nor can anyone, really—evaluate what the company is worth today. We've more than doubled in our sales, and we have a much stronger product line."

In the year of the proposed deal, 2002, sales wound up at $574 million. The company's first billion-dollar sales year was 2006, at $1.053 billion. Then sales in 2007 rose another 18 percent, to $1.247 billion. "So maybe now it's worth $5 billion. I don't know." He does know one thing: "It is a pretty good return on a $1,500 investment." That's 3.3 million to one. And rising.

The Band Director

We have a lot of schoolteachers in this management. And we
have a lot of music majors. Music majors conceptualize differently
than a lot of us. Why, I don't know. The artistic side of the brain,
I think, makes people creative. People who draw visualize in
three dimensions. They make very good businesspeople,
and they could make good engineers as well.

—*Bill Cook*

In its post-Guidant years—"after the Guidant debacle," as Bill Cook phrases it—he loosely puts a half-again-higher estimate on the company's value than the $3.2 billion figure that seemed mutually agreeable to seller and buyer in 2002. One of the reasons for the increase is a subsequent decision that restructured the company's European operations, to great success.

"We knew we were going to have to change the way that we sold. We were going to have to close offices in Europe and go direct," Cook said. "There were no longer any barriers, such as duty or inspections. If you entered one European Common country, it was good for all the Common. And the currency then was Common.

"Up to then, we had our own distributors, marketing, and our own buildings and office staff in virtually every major country in Europe. We never made a profit. The overhead was too high. It was a different way of marketing: they didn't sell the way we did, and they didn't close sales. They didn't come up with new products."

It meant streamlining, eliminating a layer between Cook and customer—a high-level layer, involving longtime friends. "We had to get rid of the sales agents. We had to have strategic business units as opposed to sales offices," Cook said.

Kem Hawkins,
president of Cook Inc.

"After the European Common came into existence, we could go right across country limits without any problem whatsoever. But it took us fifteen years to even begin dismantling this ponderous organization we had. We had to terminate a lot of people. Peer Daamen, who had been one of our key men in Europe—Steve Ferguson didn't want to get rid of him, but he was one of the main stumbling blocks to reorganization. I had to ask Geoff Reeves to retire in Australia, because we were going to change the way they marketed over there and close some of their offices. Those were tough and sad decisions that had to be made.

"Kem was probably the only person who could make those hard decisions then, and he did. That was five years ago. Now Europe is more lucrative for us than the United States. There we make about 20 percent after tax, better than we do here. But, of course, we support all the research and development here."

The Guy Hanging on the Fence

Kem is Kem Hawkins, the band director-turned-president among Bill Cook's unorthodox-hiring successes. And, of course, it's a neat story.

For Bill Cook, it dates to his own fight back from heart problems, when he put himself on a rigid regimen of brisk walking, more than four miles each night—*every* night, wherever he was. At the time, Carl was a member of the Bloomington High School South marching band, and Kem Hawkins was its director.

"When I took my long walks on late summer evenings, I'd always stop and watch the band practice. There were Kem and Carl out there in the middle of the field. I didn't think Kem ever noticed me, but he did." But barely, according to Hawkins. "I found out later Bill was the guy who, when we were rehearsing at night, was hanging on the fence watching. I was always the last one out there after practice, turning out the lights, and he would be there saying, 'That was a great rehearsal. Boy, they're getting better.' And we'd talk for a few minutes."

The talks registered in the someday segment of Cook's mind, ever alert to possible future employees. A mutual friend was lawyer Harold "Skip" Harrell. "After Carl graduated from high school, I asked Skip about Kem—whether or not I should talk to him about coming with us. Skip said 'Definitely.' Kem was of the same mind. He had to get out of teaching, because he couldn't make enough money. He was making $18,000 a year. He had three kids. He just had so many bills to pay he couldn't make it as a schoolteacher. It didn't take long to convince Kem it wouldn't be a bad idea to give this a try."

His rocket rise from trainee to president followed—No. 3 in a line of presidents that started when health problems prompted Cook to create the spot so he could shed some administrative responsibilities while refocusing (on personally designing a new companywide computer system), not in any way retiring. There were Phyllis McCullough, for a few bumpy weeks John DeFord, and then "the band director."

As a schoolteacher and band director, Hawkins may have fit the Bill Cook mold better than most MBAs or engineers. "I find schoolteachers and musicians make excellent businessmen for whatever reason," Cook said, "if they're not contaminated by being too long in the system. I like that combination—people who like to teach, like a schoolteacher; and who like to perform, like a musician. Musicians are usually big hams, love to perform—get 'em on stage, turn the lights on, light 'em up, and let 'em perform. Musicians are just superb.

"As a band director, Kem was always aggressive, always wanted to win and compete, competed in the best way, and was always friendly. As president, Kem keeps the organization relaxed and going, but he has a slightly different way of doing things—more excitement involved. And he is a disciplinarian—kindly and nice, not overbearing. It's a 'Why don't you . . .' type of discipline, or 'I'd like for you to do this. . . .' Phyllis relied on employees and put a great deal of responsibility on individual managers, which is how they were able to develop. Like Scott Eells.

"So, sometimes you hear, 'A band director runs Cook, Inc.' I challenge anyone to find anybody who has more interest and more understanding than Kem Hawkins. Guys with all kinds of PhD or MBA or MD degrees can't even begin to have the understanding that he has.

"Yeah, the way I do things drives people at IU nuts. I tell them, 'You don't have to have a degree to work here and become a manager or become a president.' You don't pick degrees. You pick people—people who have a desire to *do* and to enjoy what they're doing. It's really not difficult to tell that, if you don't let degrees and that type of thing get in the way of looking at the person."

In some hirings that paid off with longtime key employees, Cook says, "I liked the people. It was not their educational level. April Lavender, our senior vice president, regulatory affairs, has only a high school education. Aimee Hawkins, our executive assistant, made her freshman year in college, and that's about it. Jim Heckman, our senior vice president for marketing and communication, had four years of college and became a teacher. I could go on and on with people who are not supposed to be business people."

When Aimee Hawkins grew up in Bloomington, her mother worked for Indiana University president Herman B Wells. Aimee started as a secretary and now is Cook's equivalent of a congressman's administrative assistant. She is responsible for making the inner core of the Cook hierarchy work. "Aimee handles all of the office personnel," he says, "anyone considered to be an office person [for company executives]. She has about a dozen people directly under her and a lot more than that she's responsible for, probably fifty. That's her job. And one day she will be a vice president."

Heckman, first baseman on the Spencer team that reached the Final Four in the 1968 state high school baseball tournament, came out of Ball State as an art teacher. He needed more money than his teaching career could produce, so he joined Cook Inc. at a starting level. Every Cook employee knows that tardiness is unacceptable; Jim Heckman was stuck with a 1972 Pinto that didn't always start on winter mornings—and he lived a good twenty miles from his job. He took to parking it atop a hill so he could give it a shove and use the downhill momentum to get his engine turning over. On cold nights he disconnected the battery and kept it warm inside the house. He didn't fully trust either method, so he usually left home very early for some leeway time. On a day when everything worked and he arrived much earlier than his shift schedule, he was having coffee in the company cafeteria when he was joined by another early riser, Bill Cook. Their conversation led to one of those Bill Cook decisions. Heckman went into the art department, and after a little time there Cook took him to lunch, and after eating he turned his placemat over and wrote out in longhand Heckman's new job responsibilities in a promotion to management. He has been a company executive for years now—one more on that unorthodox list of Cook ten-strikes.

Eyeing the Next Forty-four Years

And then there is the band director–president. Kem Hawkins was born December 8, 1947, son of a neighborhood grocery owner in Richmond on central Indiana's eastern border. His brother and sister were born on the other side of World War II—ages 11 and 13 when he arrived. His was a "great home life, a good experience in school. I was a musical genius in that area of the world—pipe organ and trumpet. I was featured with the symphony orchestras.

"Then I came to IU. They had the best young organist out of Russia, and I'm coming from Richmond, Indiana. Big difference." He learned quickly that those people from all over the globe who chose IU's School of Music brought with them more than just overwhelming talent. "When I saw the same kids in the practice rooms on Sundays at 10 AM as I did at 6 PM, I realized that even though I might have the talent, I didn't have the heart." He decided to become a teacher, not a performer.

And he had some learning to do about that, too. The first day of his junior year in a music education class taught by Dr. Leon Fosha, he remembers that Fosha "looked down through the list of people in the class and he said: 'Kem Hawkins, you're going to be dealing with kids. What's your philosophy of life as it pertains to education?' I had to say, 'I don't know that I can give you an intelligible answer.' There are moments that are life-changing. That was one. I realized I had to have a philosophy underpinning everything that allows me to deal with all the different kinds of things that are going to happen."

He had a successful teaching career in middle school and then high school. Then, through Skip Harrell's intervention, he sat down to talk with Bill Cook. A job offer came in the mail a few days later, and that spring when school ended on a Friday, the band director started a new profession on the next Monday—as a management trainee.

Learning while Lunching

"I started in the stock department. In a couple of months I was manager of the department, with more responsibility. Within the first year, I was named plant operations manager. After two years, I was asked to go over to Europe and served as managing director over there." Two years later, "I came back and got Cook Critical Care started. Got Cook Surgical started. Became vice president of Cook Inc. Was asked to be president of Wilson-Cook in Winston-Salem, still serving in the other roles. Did that for five years. Toward the end of the fifth year I was asked to be president of Cook Group."

And then he became president of the entire operation—all of that in less than twenty years.

"During my early tenure, Phyllis, Bill, Miles Kanne, Brian Bates, sometimes Tom Osborne, Don Hollinger, myself—we would all go to lunch. Everybody would have a glass of white wine, and then Bill would hold court. He would say, 'Brian, what's going on?' Brian would say he talked to so and so, and Bill would say, 'You know, I remember about five years ago . . .' He was leading and providing insight. I don't think any of us really understood how valuable that was.

"Institutional memory is what we value here—how we keep who we are. I am absolutely possessed to make sure that during my tenure we set this 44-year-old company up to survive for the *next* forty-four years. The way to do that is to preserve who you are, to do the right thing all the time, for the right reasons.

"I'm the only president in the world—that I know of—who has had the owner of the company say to him: 'I've got enough money. Don't ever make a decision based on money. Make the decision only on the basis of the patient.' Do you know how rare that is? 'I don't care what the ramifications are to the company financially. Do the right thing.' I'm a steward of the office, passing through. My name is not on the front of this building. Cook is. You can't forget that. You have to make sure that everybody understands from whence we came. The story of Miles Kanne, working for free. The story of Charles Dotter, who refused to take a royalty because he wanted to do the right thing for the patients, and the money wasn't important. And when Bill Cook told Dr. Dotter, 'I can't afford to go out to your lab in Oregon,' Charles Dotter paying his way. It wasn't a matter of 'How would that look?' It was about two people trying to do the right thing for patients and sharing a dream. That dream is what this whole thing is about."

Philosophy

If I could only get IU to believe: you learn business;
it's not taught in a classroom environment.

—*Bill Cook*

Carl Cook, who one day will run the family business, sees the most unusual of his father's strengths with the clarity of an intended emulator. One of those strengths, hence one of Cook Inc.'s, is "thinking a little bit outside the box," Carl says. "We like to hit 'em where they ain't. The crazier an idea is, if it works it's going to be that much more successful. Nobody else will have it, because everybody else will say, 'That's a crazy idea. Get out of here.' So No. 1 is ability to spot when a crazy idea might actually work. A corollary to that is being able to see talent in people that other people aren't seeing.

"That's a huge criticism I have of résumé-based hiring. In a lot of companies you cannot be in an executive managerial position without an MBA. Have to have an MBA. Won't even talk to you unless you have one. And yet an MBA doesn't mean you can lead. I've seen a lot of guys with MBAs who are absolutely worthless in management jobs because they have no leadership, no insight. They are 'by the book.' They don't know what to do. You can get a guy with only a high school education, who has worked several jobs, maybe was in the army—put him in that same role, and he'll do a much better job."

Carl's views on degree overvaluing are in no way defensive. He has an electrical engineering degree and an MBA.

In Cook MyoSite, the futuristic small company he has been given to build within the Cook Inc. empire, he has attempted to employ his dad's imaginative insight. "He has made some very unusual hires that a lot of people don't understand—nothing on the résumé to indicate that they would be any good at the job they're in. I'm not going to say I have inherited that, but I know you need to keep an open mind.

"That's been one of the fun things at MyoSite, because I hired all of the people. The first two people came right out of the lab where the technology was developed. I had to have them because I had to have somebody who knew how to do it. Everybody else from that point I hired.

"A couple of times a bunch of people came in for a situation. We all interviewed them, to make sure they had the right background. Then we sat down and went over them all. From an education background, everybody was about the same—they had graduated within the last eight years, and they had roughly the same degrees. There was a consensus: 'This is the person.'

"And I said, 'No, we want *this* guy.' They looked at me, and I said, 'We want this guy.'

"I thought he had more maturity than the others. In the job he had lost when the plant closed, he had been exposed to a lot more things than the others had. He just seemed to me to have a much broader view of life and the world than the others. They all probably would have done fine, but the other interviewers came to me later and said, 'Thank God you got him. He's saving our ass right now.'

"I've picked some stinkers, too. Nobody bats 1.000."

I Have to Like the Person

His father wouldn't dispute that, nor would he back off from basic hiring philosophies that start with Bill Cook's credo: "You bet on the jockey, not the horse."

"To hire someone just because he or she came out of Yale, Harvard, Northwestern, graduate school at IU, the School of Law—you can't do that," Bill Cook says. "You have to bet on the person, the individual. I've come across people who have come here—both employees and doctors wanting products—and I've thought to myself, 'That idea is not particularly red-hot, but, boy, are they smart.' So you take a gamble and say, 'Hey, how about coming to work here or doing some research for us?' Then I'll get them a project to work on. The idea may not be the best in the world, but if you have a bright person you can depend upon . . . that's what I'm speaking of.

"Of all the people we have in the company, I'd say the ones in the top echelon are mostly people who have come from disciplines other than business, but they're bright and they have a drive and motivation to learn. I think that's more important than a college degree or what the degree is."

He's not talking solely of hiring administrators. He also thinks he can spot a good person for production, or business, or sales. "First of all, I have to like the person—somebody who is friendly, more or less outgoing in the sense of venturing forth with their ideas, people who are not suspicious of trying something new and different.

"I look for people who have common sense and common interests with mine. If I find a person interesting and find what they have to say interesting, I bond up with them. It's a two-way conversation. It goes to almost everything I do.

"I should caution, however, that being friendly is very important, but becoming a friend can be dangerous when running a business. A friendship can sour if some unpleasant event takes place between the one who employs and the one who is employed.

"You have to find what it is that you like about that person. There have been people I've hired that I didn't especially like personally, but some attribute they had I knew would make them good on the job."

Carl understands what his father is saying with "First of all, I have to like the person."

"That's true," he said, "and he has the advantage that he likes almost anybody. You have to be careful how you say that. Some people take that in the wrong direction. But that's a good way of summarizing."

The future is always on Carl Cook's mind. "One of the things we have tried to do is make a conscious effort to grow internally, but you also want some people from outside so you don't have in-breeding. In a company the size of ours, it takes longer to move up the ladder of responsibility. When we were small, they could see their chance to move up. When you get bigger, there's more uncertainty. The people who are the real go-getters, who have the leadership and think outside the box, who have all the things that you need for somebody in top management—those people might not stay with us.

"In this day and age, you can get a much bigger raise moving from company to company than moving from one job to the next within a company. Some people I thought were good prospects left because they could get that opportunity sooner at another company. We're going to lose some talented people because we can't promote them fast enough. And we've brought some people back. But I have to hope we can always keep strong leadership in the company, people with quick judgment."

His father is confident about the Cook Inc. of tomorrow. "The beauty of this company is it will go on well past me, because there's a whole group, a whole legion of young people coming into management, and I think most of them will stay with us. Things may not remain the same. They never do. But I think this company has a great future."

A Student Advocate

Indiana University is the state's educational giant, dominant in Bloomington for almost 150 years before Bill Cook found it as a great place to live. His hiring practices may stray from the school's recommended norms, but in general he has the school's ear. Over the years, he and Gayle, mostly through Cook Inc., have donated more than $25 million to IU. He also served five years as a member of the school's nine-member board of trustees. He went into the trustee job ambitious to make a difference. "[Democrat governor] Evan Bayh appointed me. I thought there was a lot of money we would be able to control and make a real good impact. But at the time I was a trustee, there was only a few million dollars available in the budget that we controlled. The rest was preordained, already spent."

During his trustee years, he was involved with one university program that he enthusiastically supported, Faculty and Staff for Student Excellence Mentoring (FASE), and it still thrives as part of the school's retention program. Its intent is to keep freshmen in school; its method is to pair freshmen with professors, students, and community leaders as their mentors.

His first year as a trustee (1995), he underwrote a party for the FASE program participants: dinner at the Bloomington Convention Center, dancing with the John Mellencamp band, and an offer from the trustee-host. After telling the students his uncle gave him a clock when he enrolled in school, Cook gave one to each student at the dinner and said: "You have four years to enjoy yourself. When you get out, bring me your diploma and this clock, and I'll give you a watch." He threw the party annually even into his post-trustee years, and the watch agreement hasn't ended yet. Through spring 2008 he had given out 840 Seiko watches to FASE Mentoring enrollees who advanced to diplomas—840 successes, 840 graduates from a high-risk academic group unlikely to have produced anything close to that number without the FASE program's individual attention.

"That FASE program—that's the thing I was most proud of," he said. "With it we were able to take the freshman retention rate from 65 percent to 94 percent, within the program's constituency. Those kids were all at risk. They weren't staying in school. With FASE Mentoring, we were able to keep them there. Dr. June Cargile made it work. She was a mother hen. She made the phone calls that were necessary to get those kids up and get them to school. That was just a wonderful experience, the best time I had at IU."

Exposure to students wasn't any part of his trustee turnoff. "I just detested the meetings—they were boring, committeelike. I got out." His spot was filled by Ferguson, who has been reappointed three times. The most recent reappointment was in 2007, and the board elected him president. "Steve has done a great job," Cook said.

Professor Bill Cook

Just as he has his own divergent ideas about how to run a business, Bill Cook has his own ideas about a class he would like to teach at IU—about how, indeed, he would restructure the degree programs at IU's Kelley School of Business, always ranked among the nation's twenty or so best.

He would realign the whole process, starting by eliminating the four undergraduate years of the business school.

"You don't get a good undergraduate education in any business school. At Cook there are very few opportunities for four-year graduates of business. I have always said your undergraduate years should be completely spent in liberal arts, the sciences, or education.

"I think the business education should all be concentrated in two years of graduate instruction—a graduate school of business, 1,500 to 2,000 graduate students, who learn business in a work or cooperative educational environment. They could either come back to college after working for a few years or they could alternate semesters where they spend part of their graduate years in school and the other part at work.

"If I could only get IU to believe—you *learn* business; it's not taught in a classroom environment. 'How to get along with people'—what a waste of time, for four years trying to learn how to get along with people. If you can't get along with them, don't go into business.

"I used to teach a two-hour seminar at Rose-Hulman [a small, renowned engineering school at Terre Haute]. We'd meet from two to four times a year. Occasionally I would talk about aspects of business—what it takes to raise capital, if you need to. But for the most part we would concentrate on product evolution and engineering. The class consisted of about forty students, and I'd usually have about a hundred people in the room. We were talking to engineering students, but also to many faculty members who would show up. Everyone found an interest because it was sort of a dog-and-pony show. We'd bring things to them that they'd never seen before. They'd be captivated by the novelty of our products."

It was a "we" production, not just I, Bill Cook. "I brought April Lavender to talk about clinical regulations and dealing with the FDA, or Phyllis McCullough to talk about being a woman president of a corporation. Or I would take an engineer who had a product under development.

"Just recently we invited an IU business class to our plant because I wanted the students to see what a privately held company is like. I wanted them to feel and touch what it is like to be entrepreneurial. What is not being taught about an entrepreneur business is how the company is operated, how psychology is important in dealing with employees, why significant donations are made to universities and institutions with the stipulation that applied research will be used for a specific product, process, or objective. Most universities today, particularly the medical schools, will accept that type of funding."

In a pamphlet entitled *The Leader Determines Company Behavior,* he laid out some basic tenets—some "Values for Living"—that would be taught in a Bill Cook classroom:

- *"Don't be in a hurry to begin your life's work*—take time to look around as an adult. Experiment, be a job hopper, or a professional student for a while. Taking the time now to find out what you want from life will be a fantastic learning experience. I was 32 years old before I quit going to school and job-hopping, and I have never regretted it. But, remember, it may befuddle your parents for a time."

- *"Never plan too far ahead, or too precisely, because you can lose sight of your goals and dreams.* Dreams can die because 'plans' make them seem insurmountable." He sees another hazard: "A business or a personal plan is a perfect excuse for not seeking a better, alternative direction." And another: "When I see people making long-range plans, I see so many pitfalls that can make those plans go awry. I see it in government, I see it in everyday business life: people making long-range plans and making investments in something that, halfway down the road, they find doesn't work. A lot of that has to do with not concentrating on the element of today—always thinking about tomorrow. I think you always have to have a little of tomorrow in mind, but you shouldn't plan too heavily and make decisions that way. You can get $15 million or $20 million into a product and all of a sudden wake up one morning and the product isn't right. Concentrate only on today, solve today's problems, and don't worry about what's going to happen tomorrow until tomorrow. I call it segmental thinking."

- *"Plans made by a committee remove part of the responsibility that should be yours alone."* That's a particular stickler for him. "If I make a plan, if I have an insight for a goal, it's mine. If you have committee goals, you have everybody's ideas of what they think the goal ought to be. That's one of the reasons I think the federal government doesn't work too well—too much committee and not enough people assuming responsibility, and *taking* responsibility, for a job."

• "*A business or a personal plan is a perfect excuse for not seeking a better, alternative direction.*" No "five-year plans" for him. "I get no pleasure from making out a business plan. I've made one or two in my life, and I thought to myself, 'How ridiculous! If I get halfway down this thing and what I'm saying doesn't work . . . ?' So why make long-range business plans—one, two, three, four years? I try not to go too far ahead in my thoughts, even when I invest up to $100 million, $200 million. My only thinking is how to get the plant built, what kind of money will be needed for that plant, and how to get from one day to the next, financially, until you're getting product. I don't think of tomorrow. I think eventually there will be a return."

• "*Know history, because the past helps you foresee your future.*" That belief is why he fights to keep the pioneers of his company on site, or at least on call—"history" in this sense a synonym for experience with connotations of "Those who forget the lessons of history are condemned to repeat it." Cook says, "As you get older and you rely upon your past, it certainly helps. How did you get where you are? Hardly a day goes by that I don't call Phyllis McCullough [who lives in retirement in Florida] for a piece of history. And I won't *let* Tom Osborne retire; he keeps wanting to get out on his motorcycle and ride, and I say, 'Tom! Who's going to be the historian?' Brian Bates has already made a commitment that he will stay forever, as long as I will. Those people are historians; you don't make mistakes when you rely on history. There are too many places where you repeat mistakes again and again and again and again."

• "*Try to keep your family above the business.* There was a time in my life when I kept my business in front of my family, a little bit. There were times during the early years when I could not be around, when I was gone for long periods of time. But you do have to work hard to make your dreams come alive and be real. If you are going into a creative occupation, you have to expect to be a workaholic where time means little to you."

• "*Always be competitive—you always want to compete, not necessarily with others, sometimes with yourself.* But most *certainly* you want to compete against your competitors. You don't want to like your competitors too much. You want to be friendly to them, but you don't want them being your friend. And if you can bury them, do so."

And, maybe his favorite:

- *"Ready, fire, aim."* The key word is the first one. "That's right. Ready means preparation. Get yourself ready to do something, then do it. If you screw up, you go back and see what happened. What I call 'aim' is hindsight—you find out where you screwed up, and you can correct it much easier. A lot of people would rather sit and prepare. They can prepare all their life. You've got to feel a little uncertainty, a little risk, and then say, 'Okay, I'm ready to risk this. And when I'm done, I'll figure out: Did I do it right, or did I do it wrong?' One of the key elements is: Did you make your risk with good common sense, based on history?"

That willingness to accept the financial losses of a failing project and change directions—"If you screw up, go back and see what happened"—is a Bill Cook strength that Steve Ferguson cites. "Somebody told me early on that most people can't cut their losses soon enough, and that's why they can't ever reach success. Bill can cut his losses at any point. There were a lot of times when we started down a path and by the next morning, he said, 'Oh, no, wait a minute.'"

Virtues of Privacy

From Cook Inc.'s start, Bill and Gayle Cook have operated with a steadfast determination to stay unencumbered—by debt or by stockholders, which meant staying a private company, not public. "One of the reasons I've always stayed private and never gone with investors is I don't want to serve two masters," Bill says. "Brian Baldwin [his partner in MPL, Inc., his last employment before setting out on his own] and I had shareholders. They were constantly asking questions, constantly wanting us to grow more. I learned early on in my business life, 'Gee, they can sure be troublesome.' That has proven true today. When publicly held companies don't make their forecasted sales or forecasted profits, they get hammered—even if they had a good year. Their stock goes down, and the shareholders are jumping up and down yelling for the president's head. It's terrible. That's one of the reasons I believe that companies have people who make mistakes—very, very serious production mistakes, quality-control mistakes, clinical mistakes, business mistakes. They're under the pressure to produce, can't produce, and do funny things.

"I can think of any number of public-company managers who have done some very strange things with their product problems—such as a serious product quality deficiency or an adverse clinical report pointing toward product failure. Sometimes they don't investigate or report the problem properly or, worse, they might even try to cover it up.

"As a private company, the only master you have to serve is the customer. You don't have to worry about the shareholder or the banks holding notes coming due."

It's the difference between short-term thinking and long-term planning, Bill Cook feels. He looks around in his own medical devices field and looks outside it—and names names.

"Some companies' short-term thinking works to their detriment—thinking based on pleasing the shareholder. To the shareholder, increasing the price of the share is quite important. Because of that, time and time again you see companies make short-term decisions when they should be developing long-term goals.

"Short-term to me means a period of a year or two, in which company executives try to inflate their stock prices by announcing a corporate acquisition, or progress on development of a new product, or imminent approval by the FDA for a clinical trial. The executives' income may be based largely on stock market price increases. So, in anticipation, some stock prices just skyrocket thirty, forty, fifty times company earnings.

"When Guidant was going to acquire us, their stock shot up immediately, simply because they were acquiring technology that they didn't have. Then, when it was found out they would not be successful in the acquisition, their stock plunged.

"To meet shareholder expectations, Boston Scientific has historically gone with short-term objectives. Over short-term they have been successful, but long-term they probably have hurt their future. They bought Guidant and acquired a huge debt load. They purchased technology rather than developing their own, and it appears that they paid too much money for it [$25 billion].

"A company that is traded on the market has to be extremely careful of not overextending its debt. When a company is overleveraged, the stock goes down in value. On the other hand, when public companies don't have enough debt, corporate raiders can buy them—in some cases for below their asset value—then split up the assets and sell them to other companies for a quick profit. That's easy to do when there isn't sufficient corporate debt to prevent a bargain-basement corporate raid.

"Johnson & Johnson continues to be a success story because they continue to improve all of their product lines as well as acquire companies that have technology they need. They acquire and develop technologies to stimulate corporate growth and shareholder interest. I believe Johnson &

Johnson is a well-run stock company, which makes it different from many of the investor-held medical corporations. Over the last forty years, their investment decisions for the most part have been sound. Summarizing, I'd say that the biggest hurdle for public company management is a common inability to separate what is best for their customers and what is best for their shareholders."

Waxing on Johnson

He has an admiration list of big private companies that were not so much models for him to follow in building his company but—as he has read up on them—convince him that high standards of responsibility and profits can be maintained in virtual perpetuity.

"I like to think of S. C. Johnson and some of the other privates that for many, many years have survived. Mars Candy is a private company like that. 3-M is not a private company, but I've always admired them. They have scientists they just turn loose and say, 'All right, go out and invent something.' Post-It, Scotch Tape, and their wound bandages are just the best in the world because they've gone the extra mile to know adhesives and understand their place in the market.

"S. C. Johnson of Racine, Wisconsin, is best known for its leading product, Johnson's Wax, but its different product lines, such as Raid, go on and on. That's a family-owned company that everyone in business should study. They put out great products and know how to sell them. Their research-and-development is exceptional. They try things that no one else tries.

"I don't know the family. I know about them just from reading about them, and I've thought, 'Gee, that's a nice group of people. They've done a wonderful job.' I've seen pictures of where they live in Racine—unpretentious homes. And their company buildings are unpretentious, except that one is now a museum designed by Frank Lloyd Wright.

"From what I've read, their philosophies pretty much coincide with mine. I think that's true of most family businesses. However, a lot of family businesses have gotten in trouble as a result of not having good employee relations or trying to milk out every last dollar. And family businesses tend to disappear or be sold when family members cannot agree on vital business decisions.

"You can put the customer before the shareholder when the shareholder is family. It's under your family's control, and the decisions are yours to make. And you must remain open to investment at all times."

Shut Out of the Financial Press

The chief disadvantage to staying private, in Bill Cook's view, is not having access to equity capital. He avoided that with the simplicity of his start—"all I needed was a blowtorch, a soldering iron, and a few little tools and fixtures I could make myself"—but he recognizes it as a potential problem for most business start-ups.

"Another disadvantage for the private company starting up is that there's no financial press [headed by the *Wall Street Journal* but also including business pages or sections of major newspapers or journals] that can help you by promoting your stock and your products. The financial press generates a lot of interest in public companies, particularly IPOs [initial public offerings of stock], where the company has just reached the market. During the initial offering, a new stock company and the financial writers drive up the stock by discussing perceived and real advantages of the company's product or service. The financial press is very influential in helping do that.

"A company can rise and fall on what the *Wall Street Journal* and some of the analysts and brokerage houses say about it. If they don't like your company or your industry, they can really do some damage. A private company doesn't get that advantage or disadvantage. We're never on their radar. We have to work very hard to get there.

"We're starting investment broker seminars so we can meet their analysts and writers and try to give them a better understanding of how a private organization like ours operates. Then they can compare our products better with some of the products that public companies are touting. We can say we have this product and we think it has the following features, by comparing our products to, for example, those of Medtronics, a public company."

Carnegie, Gates, and Bill Cook

Extreme wealth took on a Scrooge image in early twentieth-century America because of a superrich group called "robber barons"—multimillionaires Andrew Carnegie (whose fortune came primarily in steel), John D. Rockefeller (oil), J. P. Morgan (banking), Jay Gould (finance), and Cornelius Vanderbilt (shipping). Railroads built the fortunes of Edward H. Harriman and Leland Stanford (whose wealth created the California university as a memorial tribute after the death of his young son Leland Jr.) and added greatly to the wealth of Carnegie, Gould, and Vanderbilt.

Carnegie has had the most recent notoriety of that group; a couple of new biographies were bestsellers. Historically, he's also one of the most noted national benefactors, because of his endowment that was responsible for the construction of public libraries in communities across America. "He was a hero to a lot of small towns that never heard of his reputation," Cook said. "Just about every town in the country, from two thousand on, has a Carnegie library. I think that was a late-life image, a late-life decision.

"With the libraries, he more or less originated the idea of matching funds: you put up some money, and I'll put up some money. [Carnegie had the same deal for all communities: he would build and equip the libraries if the town would provide site and maintenance.] Bill Gates, I think, leans more toward putting up his own money without requiring matching resources from the recipients."

Gates is America's contemporary symbol of great wealth, without the "robber baron" baggage that Carnegie carried at a similar age. "The big difference between Carnegie and Bill Gates is that Bill Gates realized while he was young that he wanted to give away most of his fortune. When Bill Gates worked in the business every day, he made some very aggressive moves against his competition. His competitive nature gave him a bad public relations rap that was not to his liking or choosing. He always had the belief that somebody was moving in on one of his patents. Or, if it was one of his operating systems, he believed he was free to dictate what went on that system. That proved not to be the case. The operating system governs how the computer runs, but it does not necessarily give an individual the right to say, 'Only my programs should work on this system.'

"Bill Gates found out the hard way. He was busting antitrust laws right and left, and he did a very effective job of putting fear into his competitors. However, unlike Carnegie, he got out early, and he started to give away his billions. He's highly respected now for that. He has very little to do with the day-to-day business, but I believe he still is very influential in his company's governance.

"Carnegie was an older man when he began to give away his millions. I think when he was king of the pile in steel, he felt people owed him a living. Somewhere along the line he decided it was time to live down his reputation. He'd had some terrible strikes and a lot of things against him. He did not treat his employees well. He tried to extract too much work out of them for the amount of money he paid. I don't believe his benefits were attractive, unlike Henry Ford, who I thought was a real good employer. Henry Ford did a great job in bringing his employees many company benefits, and they in turn helped him build his corporation."

Bill Cook, accumulator of his own fortune, has been watching. "You learn from these people, in knowing about them—not that I ever read much in-depth about them. But I did have an understanding of mistakes that were made. I tried not to make those mistakes."

Religion

I've had a great time and enjoyed every minute
of my life. If that's heaven, I've had enough of it.
And if there is an afterlife, that's great.

—*Bill Cook*

For most people, one of the most private of personal matters is religion. Sometimes it's not left that way, even among the best of friends.

Bill Carper and Bill Cook grew up together in Canton, Illinois. The closeness they have maintained has put Carper in an awkward spot a few times in recent years. "At our church, or even in other things around town," Carper said, "when we're raising money to pay for special projects, people know we're good friends, so they look at me and say, 'Bill Cook has all kinds of money. Why don't you see if you can get something from him?' I always say, 'No way. He's a friend. I'm not going to do that.'

"But a few years ago, our church had a major building campaign. This *is* the church he went to when he was a kid, and he was very active in it. You never know. I thought there was at least a chance he would *want* to do something. So I let myself be talked into saying I would see. And the next time I talked to him I said, 'Here's the deal . . .' and told him the details of what we were doing. Bill listened, laughed a little bit, and said very nicely, 'Well, I'll tell you what: you do churches, and I'll do schools.' And that was fine. I hated like the dickens to impose."

I Believe in God

Bill Cook doesn't go to church anywhere very often anymore. It has nothing to do with disbelief. Cook considers himself a man of faith, although his is nondenominational. He and wife Gayle spend most of their Sundays in their own cathedral, Cedar Farm, their restored antebellum home that overlooks the Ohio River at a serene point about 100 miles south and a little bit east of Bloomington—which is maybe 150 meandering river miles upstream from Gayle's native Evansville.

It has been a while since they regularly attended a church. Both did as kids. In Canton, Bill walked with his mother to First Methodist Church. Methodism's roots reach—like the Cook ancestry—to England. In Evansville, Gayle and her brother, Glenn, went with their parents to St. John's Evangelical and Reformed Church, a denomination that, like the Karch family, had roots in Germany.

There's no statement, no declaration intended in their church attendance pattern today. "I don't think there is any reason," Bill said. "I believe in God. I have, I think, a very comfortable relationship with God. My mother was religious, always church-going. My dad was not particularly religious, but he believed in God.

"I went to Sunday school. I sang in the choir. I played the piano at church. I was the pianist for the Sunday school, back in the days when I was a pretty good pianist. I could read music, but I wasn't particularly good at interpretation of music. And I had an organ. I still have an organ, although I haven't played it for years.

"I always enjoyed the musical part of the program in church, and I would find certain sermons that were appealing to me. But, for me, the Bible we have isn't really the Gospel. So many things in the Bible are interpretations. You don't know for certain what even the original King James Version said. I think scholars are getting back to the original.

"You have to remember that the Bible was one of the first attempts to bring together science and a belief in a higher being. Some of those things I could say okay to, some I didn't know, and a lot of other things I didn't care about.

"I like the Twenty-third Psalm, because it's beautiful ['The Lord is my shepherd, I shall not want; He maketh me to lie down in green pastures; He leadeth me beside still waters . . .']. But there are so many parts of the Bible that you read, and when you get done you really don't know what it said. You listen to five different ministers on one paragraph, and they'll give you five different interpretations. As a believer, I don't subscribe to any particular religion, but I think people who do not accept science—who say science is a sacrilege—have rocks in their head. And a lot of evangelicals do that."

I Believe in God

Bill Cook doesn't go to church anywhere very often anymore. It has nothing to do with disbelief. Cook considers himself a man of faith, although his is nondenominational. He and wife Gayle spend most of their Sundays in their own cathedral, Cedar Farm, their restored antebellum home that overlooks the Ohio River at a serene point about 100 miles south and a little bit east of Bloomington—which is maybe 150 meandering river miles upstream from Gayle's native Evansville.

It works the other way for him, too: knowledge and understanding of science in Bill Cook's world work for, not against, a belief in God. He has lasting impressions of when science and religion were blended in a lecture hall during his student days at Northwestern. "You have to gather an understanding of life and the world around," he said. "I'm no great thinker. I just happened to be around people, like professors. I've mentioned science professors Albert Watterson and Ray Wolfson, and Bergen Evans.

"Bergen Evans was an English teacher who professed to be an agnostic or an atheist. The two scientists both believed in God. They would take you into the beyond. And you wouldn't even know that you went there.

"Watterson, on one of his last lectures during my sophomore year, talked about the stars and the way things could have existed. It was so beautiful. On the screen, we also had beautiful pictures of stars. Then, as his parting shot, he offered a prayer for all of us. He prayed for us. He prayed for himself. He prayed for a better world. And he said, 'Many of you here will make a better world.' It really got to you. Man! I'll never forget that last lecture my sophomore year. I'll *never* forget it. Fantastic!"

He's not at all sure that a 1950s-stature Watterson couldn't deliver the same lecture even in today's politically correct climate. "If you're that big a man, you can do anything you want. You're the reigning elephant."

What Bill Cook heard that day and what he has learned in life experiences since leave him with a question. "It makes you wonder why people *don't* believe in God. When you think about all the different combinations—that even in all this chaos there had to be an order, way back when. How people can become agnostics I don't understand. It's all there. It all fits. You look at it and say to yourself, 'What are these people talking about?'

"They just don't get it. The guys who get it are the true theoretical physicists and the true biologists. There is an order; there is a higher being. Nobody tries to describe it, because you don't really care. But you can't have all of this chaos and then all of a sudden an orderly progression of things begins to happen, from inorganic things—like iron and like potassium. They come together and start creating proteins? It boggles the mind.

"If the ministers themselves would take a few courses and come to understand that chaos and order go hand to hand—somehow it all comes together, and you have this body of energy. One moment it's inorganic, and the next moment it's alive. You see it in fungus, in mold. People are so surprised when they find bugs that once lived on the moon. What do you expect? Of course they did. The universe all came from one place. When the big bang came . . ."

Today, if he were to become active in a church, he says, "I probably would be a better Catholic than I am a Methodist. I believe in structure of the church—the formality, the mystery. I think that's something that we all miss greatly."

His friend and longtime associate with the Star of Indiana drum corps, Jim Mason, was married in a ceremony at St. Patrick's Cathedral in New York City recently. The Cooks attended, and that day reinforced Bill's fond feelings toward the Catholic Church. "The comfort that I felt . . . a beautiful, beautiful church . . . we sat there, and what a wonderful feeling it was, in that ceremony . . . the church, the pomp, circumstance . . . a Catholic girl marrying a Protestant boy. . . . There was a very high element of comfort that I had not seen in years. It was a beautiful service. Then they opened up these magnificent doors, and you could see all of New York on a perfect, sunshiny day. It was incredible."

A Holy Place of Beauty

He experiences another moment like that each time he steps into one of Indiana's most beautiful holy secrets: the church inside the dark brick, almost foreboding (from the outside) monastery of the Sisters of St. Benedict, which sits high on a hill just inside the eastern edge of the tiny southwestern Indiana town of Ferdinand (population 2,277). Those visits by Bill and Gayle Cook happen irregularly but not infrequently.

The monastery dates to 1886. The present church within the monastery was built between 1915 and 1924, but its awe is as new as each dawn's. Its pews will hold about three hundred worshipers. On Christmas Eve, from as far away as Louisville, five hundred pack in, and Easter Sunday isn't much behind. The Wikipedia website under "attractions in the town of Ferdinand" lists just one: the monastery, with its glorious church. Towns much bigger have much less to offer.

The church's age was showing when the millennia changed. "Parts of the ceiling were falling down," Sister Rose Mary Rexing said. "In the winter the radiators clanked in the middle of services, and in the summer it was hotter than blazes. It just didn't *feel* as holy."

For eighteen months, the Sisters had their services as well as their three-times-daily prayers elsewhere in the monastery while construction did far more than repair the old church. When the time came in August 2005 to dedicate the renewed church, the approximately 120 in residence at the monastery were the first to worship there, "at a little prayer service—I still remember the night," Sister Rose Mary says. "It was so lovely. I literally sobbed and sobbed.

"So warm . . . so peaceful."

So breathtakingly beautiful and holy.

Towering overhead in the sanctuary, the equivalent of almost eight stories up, is a dome 87 feet high and 32.5 feet in its base diameter. The circular dome has sixteen stained glass windows with angels. That spectacularly impressive dome is a link between Bill Cook and the Sisters of St. Benedict. He knew of their refurbishing plans and their dome, and he suggested to them the Conrad Schmitt company of Milwaukee. That was the firm that handled the restoration of both the dome in his West Baden hotel and the one in the courthouse in Bloomington (as well as major restoration work at Radio City Music Hall in New York and the Basilica of the Sacred Heart on the University of Notre Dame campus). Its workmen-artists achieved the same restoration wonders in painting and lighting at Ferdinand as they did in their other jobs.

The full restoration cost $7 million. It was a major leap of faith by the Sisters from a tiny town in the middle of one of Indiana's primary centers of unemployment and low income. Making the challenge infinitely greater was timing: the exterior work on the project began September 9, 2001, two days before the Al Qaeda strike on New York City that traumatized America and—for a brief time, at least—derailed the American economy.

The project went on and was completed (and underwritten) in just over four years. A booklet describing the project, *Restoring a Sacred Place,* lists about 10,000 donors, counting couples and families. Among the 10,000 were William and Gayle Cook.

Generosity and a Little Bit of Teasing

Before all that, before their recommendation of Conrad Schmitt, the Cooks had been there. "Our first contact with Bill and Gayle was when two sisters from here were at the West Baden atrium and introduced themselves," Sister Rose Mary said. "Bill told them they had prayed in our chapel, stopping off on the way to their home on the river." (Cook says he and Gayle discovered the church in their mid-1960s travels researching for their 1972 *Guide to Southern Indiana,* which includes the monastery as a recommended site.)

"My own first impression of him," Sister Rose Mary said, "came when I stopped by his office in Bloomington to say thank you for something they had done for us. Aimee Hawkins, Bill's executive assistant, took me for a quick tour of the building, and when we came back, Bill was there. He showed me his office, and he walked with me on my way out. We passed by some woman employees with their hair in nets, and he greeted each of them with so much obvious respect. I could not forget that.

"For me, he's just down to earth. He and we Sisters of St. Benedict have a common value of caring about the people of southern Indiana. We take a vow of stability, promising that we will not move around and we will serve the people around us. That's the same thing I see in Bill and Gayle."

She, as the director of mission advancement, and Sister Kristine Anne Harpenau, prioress of the monastery, attended a 2006 Chamber of Commerce luncheon at nearby Jasper when Cook was the speaker. They were seated in the first table in front of the speaker's rostrum, in full view of the audience.

"I see Sister Rose Mary here," Cook told the gathering of Jasper businesspeople, bringing her into his talk before he had even introduced Gayle. "We all know Sister is in the good works of raising money. I'm sure many of you here have had Sister Rose Mary in to talk about your pocketbook. We're all very happy to see you, Sister Rose Mary."

Illustrative slides played on a giant screen as he talked. "My first company was Balco. I do hope the good Sisters will put their hands over their eyes. I was in the shot glass business. We manufactured *nude* shot glasses. Gayle and I—forgive me, Sister—had a good time with friends. We had eight hundred of these art pictures that we had to evaluate. It took us quite a long time in the evening to go through these—we repeated several times to view them for their art."[1]

The kidding continued an hour after his talk when he and Gayle met with the two Sisters at the monastery, about thirteen miles from Jasper. Since the 1970s, Catholic nuns have been freed from having to wear the traditional habit whenever they appear in public. The two were at the luncheon in simple black and white apparel, but not habits, and at the monastery Bill expressed his disapproval—lightly, teasingly, but clearly recommending a return to tradition. The "mystery" of the church, he said, is served best by wearing the habit.

No objections came back—just smiles, and no subsequent plans to do as he suggested. "No," Sister Rose Mary said months later, "although I do understand what he is saying."

Maybe not every non-Catholic would have the cheek to so advise Sisters or to chide them.

"Oh," Sister Rose Mary said, "my dad [in her growing-up days in Evansville] always told me, 'You tease the ones you love.' Now, I don't know about publicly." She laughed. "I do think now he ought to show me those shot glasses."

A Long White Tunnel

Legend says the threat of death gives the issue of personal faith a priority that sometimes even lasts. Hence the saying: "There are no atheists in a foxhole."

Bill Cook's health scares had nothing to do with foxholes, but one made him a believer in tales told by some who hovered on the brink of death but came back—and talked of seeing a white tunnel when life had all but slipped away and they were unconscious. "I had the white tunnel in 1974," he said, referring to when he was one of the first Americans to undergo heart bypass surgery. "I suppose that was at the moment that the pump turned on and they stopped my heart. I don't know what happened, but they said they lost me for a small period of time. I just saw this white tunnel, probably forty feet in diameter, stretched out endlessly. There was blue at the end, and white on both sides. I don't recall what I looked like. All I can remember is looking at that tunnel, and there was blue in the background and white all around.

"A lot of people have had it. If you have a heart attack and your heart stops, some people get that tunnel effect. Somebody said I had a few bad moments. But it was transient. I don't know how long it was."

It's not a subject he has brought up often, but he did once: to another who had known the effect, Ellen Ehrlich, wife of Indiana University's fifteenth president, Thomas Ehrlich. "Gayle and I went for a walk one night, and when we went by their house, we saw them both reading in their library. We knocked on the door and spent maybe three or four hours with them. Ellen and I got to talking, and Ellen mentioned her bypass. We realized we had had the same experience. We went through the tunnel.

"We talked about the brain cells we probably lost, the vital things. She feels she may have lost some of her ability to reason. I never thought that way. I felt if anything my ability to reason was improved. That sounds weird. But I think what I lost—I used to have an excellent memory for names, but after that surgery . . . I surmised that some of those bubbles that were in my head from the oxygenator got somewhere and knocked out those little neurons that tell me something. Gayle laughs at me. She says, 'You know everybody.' But not like I used to."

He senses one other effect from his "white tunnel" experience. "I think it's the reason I've never feared death after that. I feel when it happens, it happens. That's it. I used to say that when I die, I'm going to be mad as hell. But I don't think I'm going to be quite as irritated. I'm reconciled."

As for Heaven . . .

Christianity—Methodist or Catholic—talks of an after-life, a heaven.

When death comes, Bill Cook says, "I'll take it either way. If heaven's there, I'll take it. If it's not there, I think that's all right, too. When you're dead, you won't care anyway."

Politics

He does not fit in government.

—Charlotte Zietlow, 1982

His extreme success as a businessman leaves no room for second-guessing about career paths. But there was a time when Bill Cook was looking around for a career direction, so the question came: Did you ever think about entering politics? "Only to the extent that I never wanted to be a politician," he said.

Not that he hasn't kept track of politics, and politicians, and formed strong views—conservative views, definitely right-of-center views, not necessarily Republican, but Republican far more often than not.

"I've never really had time for politics. I do donate. I'm a switch-hitter. I voted for Kennedy the first time, and I voted for Nixon the second time. That's kind of my politics. I donate to people not by party but by the type of person I think they are. I've been an admirer of Evan Bayh [Indiana's junior senator, a Democrat in his second term, and a two-term governor before that] ever since he has been a politician. I've talked with Evan a lot. Evan is conservative, part-Republican at heart. That's why he wins so big in this state.

"I was a great admirer of Doc Bowen [Dr. Otis Bowen, a small-town medical doctor, two-term Indiana governor, and a member of the Reagan cabinet]. I'm pretty apolitical. I vote for the person. I don't vote for the principle of the party, because the party is led by the guy who runs the country. However that man leads the country, the party follows. If he doesn't like the policies of the party, he changes them—maybe not when he's running, but later."

He has views on each of the ten presidents of his adulthood, from Dwight D. Eisenhower through George W. Bush. He questioned the 2002 entry into Iraq ("I'd have stuck in Afghanistan") but opposed a 2008 pullout ("He made an error, and now we have to stay there, because if we pull out, whatever president comes in, we have to prepare for a bunch of these people coming in and doing some rather nasty things"). These are views of one citizen, not one wealthy citizen with clout and a pipeline to the White House. This is a surprise, given the introductory powers that great wealth is presumed to carry in American politics: billionaire Bill Cook has never met a president.

"The only president I've even seen personally was Reagan," he says. When Indiana won the 1987 NCAA basketball championship, the team was flown to Washington in a Cook Inc. plane, with Bill Cook as pilot, four days after its victory for a meeting with President Ronald Reagan and Vice President George Bush in the White House Rose Garden. The players and Coach Bob Knight shook hands with Reagan and exchanged gifts and friendly remarks. Cook was in a group of IU fans watching from a distance—"150 to 200 feet away," he says. "There were a lot of Hoosiers there. Everybody came in red." One other time, from his own plane he looked across and saw Reagan leaving Air Force One at a New York airport. That's it for his live views of a president.

The Man and the Sewer

The man who "never wanted to be a politician" has served in a public position or two and had his local political battles. He won some, lost more, lost his temper once or twice, but at least as often—especially after he had achieved business eminence, financial security, and seniorhood—his quirky humor showed through, not his anger, as he tweaked his adversaries, particularly on civic issues. Pulling their chain, it's called.

"A lot of times I didn't do myself any good, but Steve Ferguson and I had a lot of fun. In many respects I was frustrated. I just didn't have the patience, so I figured I'd give everybody a rough time who was giving me a rough time. It became a combination: 'Okay, you frustrate me, and I'll pull your chain.'"

The give-and-take began when he accepted an appointment as a Republican member of the first Bloomington Utilities Board in 1973. It was politically balanced with three Democrats and two Republicans, three (two

Democrats and a Republican) picked by Democratic mayor Frank McClo-skey, the other two (Cook and Democrat Patricia Gross) chosen by the Democrat-controlled city council.

That was in April 1973. The board's first meeting occurred the same week that Cook's appointment was announced, and the headline over the news-paper story the following day was PICTURE ISN'T ROSY. Before the year was out, the board's stamp was on a move doubling the sewer rate in Bloom-ington, which meant for Indiana University an overnight increase of about $250,000.

On September 5, 1973, Governor Bowen appointed Cook to the Lake Monroe Regional Waste District Board.

It was a stormy year. On November 16, front-page local newspaper stories announced Cook had abruptly resigned from the City Utilities Board over a funding fuss with the city council. He was quoted: "They refused our budget and are going to let another three weeks go by before deciding on it. That's a bit much." Next day, he was back on the board. Three months later, on February 22, 1974, he was elected its president.

Cook was soon on the front page again for his candid phrasing at a committee meeting. The chapter of the National Audubon Society filed a report on a fringe-of-Bloomington lake (Lemon), and Cook called the report "garbage" that "turned my stomach" and "drove me up a wall." A day or two later, city council president Jim Ackerman was so mortified by council-appointed Utilities Board member Cook's comments that he publicly apologized to the city's environmental commission, which had received the report. A March 8 *Herald-Telephone* story led off: "The head of one city board apologized to another city board for comments made by a member of another city board."

His biggest civic battles then involved location of a sewage treatment plant on the city's south side. Bloomington through all its early history—and Indiana University's as well—had been hampered in growth and at times had its very survival threatened by water shortages. In the 1950s, the federal government chose to attack the problem of almost annual flood damage along major Indiana rivers with a flood-control program that in-cluded construction of huge reservoirs—three in north-central Indiana and one, the largest of all, in Monroe County, south of Bloomington. Monroe Reservoir became Lake Monroe. A flood control project became one of Indiana's primary water recreation areas, with boating and beaches and swimming on what became the biggest "lake" inside the state's borders.

It also seemed to represent a permanent end to Bloomington's water worries. Almost instantly, like newly irrigated crops in a desert, both the city and IU grew as never before.

Land development around the lake, above all protection of the waters from pollution, became a concern that put a spotlight on those committees to which Cook had been appointed. Location of a water treatment plan became a headlined issue.

"We [mostly Republicans on the committee] came up with a plan for the plant to be below Lake Monroe," Cook says. "We had some Democratic councilmen who apparently wanted to make an issue of the money." The plan Cook supported would have cost more originally, but he felt it would have proved economical over the years. It was a battle he ultimately lost, and nearly a decade later, he called that "one of my greatest disappointments . . . my first foray in not having the opportunity to have people accept what I said as being realistic and rational."[1]

Now he says, "My exasperation was just that I wanted to save money with a very efficient utility, and I felt we got a hodgepodge with an expensive facility in the wrong location. I've never changed that opinion. I had my first heart attack about the time that was happening. I felt it just wasn't worth the pain and misery to keep that up, so I resigned after four years of it."

He Does Not Fit in Government

Bill Cook's primary adversary in the sewer-plant issue was Charlotte Zietlow, who at the time was serving on the Bloomington City Council, which had legislative and funding controls over the Utilities Board. Cook and Zietlow are perfectly cast to be adversaries. Zietlow is a liberal Democrat with a doctorate in linguistics and a long career in political life. Yes, she said, in recalling her public collision with Cook over the building location issue, protection of Lake Monroe was a concern. "But that was a secondary thing to me. My concern was the process. I wanted to hold public hearings. Bill very clearly wanted to bypass that.

"Bill is a 'ready-fire-aim' guy. He says so himself. And the hell with whoever is in his way. That has worked out great for him in business. He's gotten a lot done that way. But he does not fit in government, he does not fit on committees, and he doesn't deny that."

She had said in a May 25, 1982, *Herald-Telephone* interview:

I have nothing but the highest respect for Bill Cook. He's a phenomenon . . . a true American success story. He is autocratic.

I can't imagine him ever wanting to be in a position where he didn't have controlling authority.

And twenty-five years later: "I still say that."

Zietlow, who operated some successful small businesses of her own, was in another public role (serving on the Monroe County board of commissioners) when she and Cook were matched up again in a front-page exchange in the early 1980s. The present Monroe County Courthouse was built in 1907, in an era when Indiana's ninety-two counties seemed in competition to see which among them could build the most ornate, impressive headquarters for court and government activities. Classically, the building went up in the heart of downtown in the town that was the official "county seat." Bloomington's courthouse was classic in all those ways, but in its eighties it was deteriorating fast. The three-person board of commissioners, publicly elected, had among its responsibilities providing adequate office space for county officeholders, the primary "tenants" of the courthouse. The overly spacious building, with its granite steps and high rotunda ceiling, flunked every heating and cooling efficiency test, and its developing ugliness and deterioration risks made its retention and repair questionable.

"Had we not intervened, the courthouse would have been gone," Cook says. "The architects had already come out and said they couldn't save it because it was just structurally unsound. All of us knew that was untrue. They backed up Charlotte. Charlotte said it should come down."

Zietlow, a member of the commissioners' board, remembers it differently, and her *vox populi* convictions again divided the two. "Yes," she said in 2007, "there definitely was some thought of tearing it down. I thought it was my job to go around and talk to as many 'powers that were' as I could to see how they felt about it. I talked to bankers, lawyers, Scott Schurz [publisher of the Bloomington *Herald-Telephone*], and Bill Cook, and not just Bill but other business leaders, too. There was an overwhelming feeling among those people—Bill was an exception—that 'the building is useless, tear it down.' Personally, I wanted the building to be saved. But that wasn't what I was hearing. They wanted it torn down and a new county office building built on the site. We had to do something. We had county offices in little rabbit warrens all around the downtown."

By then, Cook was embarked on a series of downtown renovation projects that included the once-glorious downtown landmark, the Graham Hotel. Every town, especially every midwestern university town, once had a Graham-type downtown hotel. In the 1930s, Hollywood stars stayed at Bloomington's Graham before performing at nearby theaters. By the 1980s, it was a ramshackle blight among the antiquated buildings on the four blocks facing into Courthouse Square.

All it took was a political handshake—Bill Cook with Democratic mayor Frank McCloskey—and the building was on its way to resuscitation. "Here was a fine example of people who just got together," Cook says. "After we had bought the building, Frank said, 'Bill, what are you going to do with the Graham Hotel?' I said, 'I'm going to fix it up, but only if I can get a commitment from you. Would you build a parking garage next to the hotel?' Frank said, 'Bill, shake hands on it, and we'll do it.'

"Frank and I shook hands, and after fifteen minutes of talking, there was a parking lot on the way right next to us. We built those two things almost simultaneously."

That was Bill Cook's idea of how business and government could work. McCloskey was a liberal, later serving four terms in Congress, but he had lined up with Cook in trying to get the sewer building project through, and Zietlow didn't forget. She ran against McCloskey in the next Democratic mayor primary. McCloskey won.

Ultimate Victory in Tweaking

McCloskey was in Congress when the courthouse issue surfaced just before Christmas 1982. With the restored Graham Plaza about to open, Cook and Steve Ferguson let it be known publicly that Cook Inc. through its wing CFC could alleviate the county's immediate space needs by making the hotel open for use as office space. They also offered to renovate the courthouse for $2 million, guaranteeing that it would be ready in a year.

Daily, comments went back and forth among the officeholders. Commissioner Warren Henegar said Cook's proposal, if accepted, "would solve a lot of problems. I suspect it's a lot cheaper than it could be done otherwise." Henegar wasn't for razing the courthouse. "I have an emotional attachment," he said.[2] County council president Rodney Young said flatly, "We are not going to tear down the Courthouse. We are out to provide more space at a reasonable cost."[3]

By late spring 1983, a "Save Our Courthouse Committee" had been formed—more than 150 names on the committee list, including Bloomington mayor Tomilea Allison, former Indiana University president Herman B Wells, not newspaper publisher Schurz but his editor, Bill Schrader, plus both Cook and Zietlow.

It was saved and handsomely renovated. The offer of availability of office space in the new Graham Plaza was declined, and a modern office building was built in the downtown area near the courthouse.

Cook's memory of the evolution of the courthouse project is: "We had all of these people rumbling around, saying, 'Let's tear it down and get a parking garage.' I told Steve Ferguson, 'Let's come up with a quote that we will rehab the courthouse for a couple of million bucks,' and when we said that, everybody stood up and said they wanted to preserve the courthouse but that 'Cook has no right to take that job—that needs to go out on bid.' It worked perfectly. I told Charlotte, 'You have to do what you think is best.'"

Zietlow was quoted at the time: "We appreciate Mr. Cook's interest, naturally. I don't think we're in a position where we can say, 'You're a really good guy, and we'll give you the job.' We're a government, not a business, and we have rules and regulations we have to follow."[4]

Cook says, "Bloomington Restorations Inc. and the Monroe County Historical Society got busy, they stirred up the crowd, and we had the courthouse saved." A key member of both preservation groups is Gayle Cook. "She was right in the thick of all of this. I was doing some kind-of-tricky things, and honest Gayle was just doing what comes naturally."

It was, for Bill Cook, the ultimate victory in tweaking. "We helped them through all the kind of desperate stages—there was even a lot of conversation about having Ralph Rogers [a Bloomington-based construction company] come in and blow the rock out from under the building, then build a parking garage underneath, or even blow up the whole courthouse, which was ridiculous. We made our $2 million offer to the community to do the courthouse. That got all the contractors up in arms: 'Oh, no, you can't allow Cook to do that. Let us bid, too.' We knew exactly what the reaction would be. We had no reason to do it. We didn't want to do it.

"And on the hotel-as-annex possibility, we made them an offer. But they made what I think was a better decision: to go ahead and put up a new building nearby for additional necessary judicial use. A very good time was had by all."

A Mural Issue

After the restoration work was completed, a discovery was made: a set of four murals painted specifically for the new building and a trademark of it ever since its opening was missing. "That's another story," Cook says. "Those beautiful murals on the interior of the courthouse dome had been removed and not replaced in the restoration."

The four 8 × 16 foot murals were the creation of German artist Gustav Brand in 1907 and 1908—each representing a special facet of Bloomington and Monroe County. They were entitled *Stone Industry* (a seated old man, representing the Stone Age, with other figures and tools in the foreground and a quarry in the background), *Justice* (the Goddess of Justice holding the sword of righteousness, and other figures, male and female, representing everything from truth to treachery), *Education* (Indiana University saluted with figures seated on stones carrying the words *Knowledge, History,* and *Science*), and *Agriculture* (more figures, with harvested grain, a cornucopia, a handplow, and a scythe).

The murals hadn't truly been lost. They were stored while the county pondered ways to pay for restoring them. "Somehow they had been stored at the unused Brown School," Gayle says. "We found them when we bought the school as a headquarters for Star of Indiana. Advisories on the huge canvases to store them at archival humidity and temperature had not exactly been followed."

The oil-on-canvas murals had been taken down and stored in the early 1980s—"in terrible condition," a Monroe County official, Virginia Rose, told a newspaper interviewer. "They were badly water-damaged . . . at least six inches of paint around the edges of every one of them because the walls had been painted around them. In certain areas, the picture was almost entirely gone."

"Gayle sent the murals up to Conrad Schmitt Studios in Milwaukee, a firm specializing in restorations," Bill said. "They repaired them and rehung them in the courthouse." This $70,000 project was underwritten largely by the Cooks.

In 1993, they were put in place just below stained glass windows that arched up to the building's dome. Which was another story. "The dome [on its exterior] was patched, aging copper," Cook said. "Everybody was jumping up and down, saying that we had to do this and do that to restore it—had to pick a bright new color to paint over all the metal, which should have been the soft natural green of copper patina. Gayle went to a meeting of county officials, and she was armed with photos of other domes with natural patina. The result was they painted all the metal copper and non-copper patches in perfectly matching patina green." In 2007, the dome got a totally new copper roof.

A Tower and Babble

Cook and the city squared off in early 1994 with less pleasing results for him. CFC announced plans to build a $10 million thirteen-story residential building about four blocks north of the courthouse—a skyscraper by downtown Bloomington standards. The spectacularly Old World Gothic structure was just one governmental step away from construction: a zoning change for the site, from commercial to residential use because it included twenty-three condominiums.

Two months after plans for the building were announced, the heavily Democratic city council (8 to 1 majority) rejected the rezoning request, 5 to 4. The council's public hearing on the issue drew an overflow crowd and lasted until after 2 AM. Bill Cook was not there—"because I have a tendency to get irritated," he told a newspaper interviewer. Could have happened. The comments included some that were personal and hostile: Bill was "on an ego trip," and Gayle was "a Leona Helmsley." The vote was 4 to 4 when the deciding vote came from Democrat Iris Kiesling, who said she opposed "the immense mass and height" of the 177-foot building.

The two months between announcement and rejection had Bloomington talking. The structure, one line of speculation ran, was going to have a personal penthouse at its pinnacle for the Cooks. "Just myths that somehow got kicked around," Cook told a reporter. "I am very happy where I live, thank you."[5]

The building died that night, but the issue didn't. Cook immediately spiked all talk of a revision of plans and resubmission. A next-day *Herald-Times* story quoted him: "It is just pure and simple—it is not going to happen again. I have never based a decision on emotion, and that is one of the things that hit here. Personal preference seemed to take priority over the logic of the building and the economics of the building."

Bloomington *Herald-Times* editor Bill Schrader called the vote "wrong-headed." He wrote, "It is no secret that this council has a no-growth reputation. . . . [R]ejecting millions of dollars in property taxes the project would generate says volumes about that reputation."[6]

A newspaper advertisement carried the five no-voters' pictures and labeled them the "Fatal Five." A billboard on the side of a downtown building carried a similar message. Letters to the editor for and against the building kept the topic hot for weeks. The ad and the billboard listed as sponsors a group called "Positive Progress Incorporated." Few doubted that there was at least a wink of acquiescence behind the vindictiveness from the man who has said of his tendency to tweak, "*Okay, you frustrate me and I'll pull your chain. . . . I figured I'll give everybody a rough time who's giving me a rough time.*" But it was and is a suspicion that both Cooks, winged as they were in the episode, stoutly deny, including even specific knowledge—then or now—of who made up "Positive Progress Incorporated."

Eighteen months after the vote, one of the council members who opposed the tower was defeated for reelection, and a second chose not to run again. The other three were reelected in what became a 6 to 3 Democratic majority under a newly elected mayor (another Democrat). Steadily over the years several big (but not *as* big) newly built downtown apartment buildings went up in the same general area, meeting the need the Cooks said all along their building was meant to address: getting more people to live and—by their presence and purchasing power—revitalize the downtown.

Father of the Bloomington Y

One of Bill Cook's biggest civic achievements had a minimum of government involvement. The huge Bloomington YMCA, on the city's south side, has Bill Cook all over its DNA. It probably had roots dating to the high school Bill Cook who stood up in the chambers of government in Canton, Illinois, and told the city fathers they needed a youth center—which was ultimately built. And all along, Canton did have a Y.

"I grew up in YMCAs," Cook says. "The fellow who ran the Canton YMCA—his name was Patterson—gave me a free scholarship because my parents couldn't afford the YMCA dues. I always appreciated that. I had a scholarship from the time I was in sixth grade until after my eighth grade when my dad paid. But there really was no Y here. There was an organizational framework for the YMCA that was attached to the university. They invited me to a meeting. I went, and a man on their board asked what I thought we could do.

"A YMCA analyst came in and wrote a report that said we didn't need a Y because townspeople could use the facilities at the university and the high schools—which was a bunch of hogwash. We just went ahead anyway, irrespective of what the report said.

"Cook Inc. put down the seed money—I think we put in $1 million at the start—and the community raised the rest. And off we went. It's now the largest Y in Indiana." It's a 130,000 square foot structure with more than 11,000 members.

"I think there's a total of $3.5 to $4 million in the facility that's there now, and we've put in about $2 million. The community and membership dues have raised the rest.

"Right at the start, we [in the Bloomington YMCA hierarchy] made a pledge that we wouldn't borrow from anyone, and we wouldn't take from United Way, and we never have. So everything that we have done at the Y, including scholarships for people who can't afford the membership fee, has come out of dues. Those run about $300 a year, which is very, very low. We have so many members we never have had a money problem. There has always been a surplus.

"It's a family YMCA, where the family goes together. The dad may go to the weightlifting room, the mom may walk, and the kids may play basketball or run. There are no ping-pong tables or pool tables—no real place for recreation, only places for sport and physical activities. There's a swimming pool, but the pool is used for laps, not for fun and games."

It's not a Y of the Canton type, which was a social hub, a dancing center, for Canton teens. "I don't know if there's any *Dancing with the Stars* down there or not. But dancing is a good physical activity," he said.

"It's surprising how many people say, 'We should have this or that for kids to hang out after school.' If people want to play pool or do that type of thing, they're just going to have to go someplace else, because the Y is not the place for it. It's set up for physical fitness.

"We also have a medical component with it that Dr. Larry Rink has set up. After people graduate from the regimen of exercise the hospital has set up, they go into the YMCA programs, and some of them stay in it twenty-five to thirty years. Some of the very first people who came into that Y program are still there."

Cook, the man who brought it into existence, no longer goes there. "I had a problem when I went down there, after five or six years. Somebody always would stop me and want to talk, or they'd want to walk with me and talk, or run with me and talk. It just didn't work out. When you do exercise, you almost have to be alone. Sometimes you like companionship when you're walking, but many times you just want to get that over and leave, particularly if you're in a regimen. That's why I left. Many people thought it was a social opportunity to talk, I guess."

The workout center he built into Park 48, the Cook Inc. headquarters in Bloomington, is where he does his physical conditioning now—he and a whole lot of Cook employees in a separate big one, well equipped. "One of the most serious problems we face as a society is overweight, and we're addressing that here through physical fitness and having our own training facilities, plus having our own trained nurse to help people with things like self-consciousness. Go over there after work, and you have difficulty getting in. People take a half-hour of their lunch hour working out or maybe fifteen minutes."

In August 2007, plans were announced for a second Bloomington Y, but the deal for the site planned then was cancelled before any construction. A second Y still is likely. "It should have been started fifteen to twenty years ago to take the pressure off," Cook says. "There are just too many people down there now. You size your Y for the peaks, not necessarily for the way it is during the day. There are times when people can hardly get on the track or on the basketball court.

"They will have to do some fund-raising, but they have always had enough money to keep up the other facility. That's why it looks so nice. They have been able to put small additions on it, and they have not had to raise dues too often to make that happen.

"Ever since the Y started, there has been someone from our company on the board. I'm pleased with our contribution. It really was not planned. We found that there was a need for a Y, and we had enough financial resources to make it happen."

Uncle Matt's Relative

The Graham Plaza and the public parking lot across from it, plus the restored courthouse at the city's hub, represent just the liftoff point for a mostly harmonious linkage of Bill Cook and government in changing a fading, deteriorating, suburban mall–victimized downtown from dilapidating like almost all the other Bloomington-size towns across the United States.

The Bloomington of the 1920s, 1930s, 1940s, 1950s, and 1960s had a downtown of character: Faris Market, a classic old family grocery with cut-to-

George Ridgway, chief architect

order fresh meats and a delivery truck and local ownership, squeezed in between other shops right on the main street; theater houses, of course, the handsomest tastefully preserved in décor later and converted into an elite Italian restaurant; clothing stores—men's and women's, some with generations of family histories; and small restaurants, including Bender's Cafeteria and Burgher's Grill, where IU basketball players hung out and proprietress Mildred "Mid" Burgher never missed a game or saw a Hoosier free throw, because she never looked, fearing the worst. Hinkle's Hamburgers was there, too, as purely Bloomington as Cresent Donuts—which its operators always, stubbornly, spelled without the second *c,* a one-word experience in difficulty for Bloomington spelling teachers but a place with its own ultimate stamp of coffee-shop approval: cops hung out there a lot.

One by one, even the character places left. The owners died off, or they moved to the town's mall-ish edges, or the chains won out with their cut rates and national advertising. "The downtown was falling apart," Bill Cook says. "I never rehabbed a downtown before in my life, but at the time it seemed like the right idea—to try to keep the central part of the downtown.

"At that time, the square didn't look like much, and there were few stores left—only about thirteen in four blocks. There were a couple of restaurants, and that was about it. When Hinkle's Hamburgers moved out to the west side, that was just about the *coup de grace.* That was almost the last thing standing downtown."

The block of buildings facing the courthouse from its south side ranged from aging to collapsing. That became a foothold for Cook through CFC and its head, Steve Ferguson.

"We had an opportunity to pick up all the buildings on the south side of the square in the 1980s," Cook said. "We knew we had to start somewhere on rehabilitation of the downtown. We had the Graham Hotel on the north side of the square, we had J. C. Penney on the west side, and then the buildings became available on the south side. Steve did all the negotiation on that."

A savings and loan institution, Fountain Federal, sold the block to CFC. Some store buildings in that single block had to be gutted—and then rebuilt. It became an $11 million project, and from the previous owner came the block's name, Fountain Square.

It was the first project in the relationship between Bill Cook and the new Cook Inc. chief architect, George Ridgway—Ridgway, without an e, like the general Harry Truman elevated to run the Korean fighting when Truman fired Douglas MacArthur in 1951. Exactly like General Matthew Ridgway, which came in handy for George's father, Steve, when he was serving in the artillery under General Mark Clark at the Battle of Monte Cassino in Italy during World War II. "They were sending 6 × 6's pulling 150mm howitzers down through the valley trying to get better positions, and the Germans were sitting up on Monte Cassino mountain just blasting away, like sitting ducks," George says. "His commanding officer told him, 'We want to get these howitzers to the other side. I want you to lead.'

"Dad said, 'I don't think Uncle Matt would like me to be on the point.'

"'Your uncle is Matthew Ridgway?'

"'Yeah.'

"'You're probably right.'"

Subsequent genealogy searches indicate there is a distant relationship, but "uncle" worked just fine at a key time, or maybe there wouldn't have been a George Ridgway who had fifteen years in as an architecture teacher at Vincennes University and his own private practice going when Bill Cook heard of him and asked him to come up for an interview for the company architect job that had opened with Ken Wolverton's retirement.

"I showed up, bright and early, at 7, in a three-piece suit, not knowing about Bill Cook. I've only seen him in a tie three times since then. We sat down in Bill's office—Bill, Steve Ferguson, Charlie and Richard Pritchett—and talked about everything but architecture. Bill had sung in a barbershop quartet; I was still in a barbershop quartet. 'Do you like drum corps music?' So we watched drum corps, at full volume—you don't listen to it, you feel it, usually against the chest. Never asked about credentials, even if I had a license. Just talked.

"He said, 'Well, when can you start?' I said, 'When do you need me?' He said, 'By God, right now!' I said, 'Well then, Mr. Cook, we've just burned two hours of daylight.' He said, 'Charlie, take him to work.'"

The Golden Rule

"Work" then was the Fountain Square project, where the first major job was keeping the east side of the block from caving in. Steel braces from street level up kept the building upright until reinforcement could be established. "We pushed it back and rimmed the entire square with steel, and anchored it to, of all places, the former jail," Cook recalls. "The jail is all concrete. You would have to have a major, major catastrophe for anything to happen to any of those buildings now. That entire block is rimmed in steel."

For $11 million, Cook intended to have his say in how the reconstruction went. Ferguson had his views, too.

Cook doesn't even try to hold back a grin as he recalls some days when neither one was laughing a lot. "Steve and I had a running battle. Whoever got there at 4 PM, quitting time, normally what he said then would be what would be in the next day's work. So if Steve wanted a valve put at a certain place, he would be there right at 4 PM, making sure I wasn't going to be there at 4:15, because I might want it someplace else. A couple of times Steve put the valves in rather strange places. And other times, he made great decisions."

Ridgway recalls, "I couldn't have been working for Bill for six months when one day Steve and I were at Fountain Square. A monumental stair goes up through the middle of the three-story building, with skylights at the top. The stair was painted light blue. Bill came walking through—he had been to the dentist so he was in kind of a bad mood—and he said, 'Ferguson! I thought we said we were going to paint that stairway canary yellow.'

"Steve said, 'Well, Bill, we were talking about how that blue going up there kinda fades into the sky through the skylights, and we thought we'd take a look at it—it's just primer anyway, we'd see what it looked like.'

"Bill said, 'Ferguson, I thought we were going to paint the damned thing canary yellow.'

"Steve tried to smooth it over again. Bill spun on his heels, looked at me, and said, 'You're the damned architect. What do you think?'

"I said, 'Mr. Cook, I believe in the Golden Rule.' He said, 'What's that?' I said, 'He who has the gold makes the rules.'

"He turned right back to Steve and said, 'Canary yellow. Before the day's over.'"

The project introduced Ridgway to the way Bill Cook, through his building partners from Pritchett Bros. Construction Company, does things—eye always on the highest quality, but not necessarily as drawn up. "A lot of times—a *lot* of times—the drawings weren't complete until the job was done, because of changes that came," Ridgway said.

"A wall in Fountain Square runs around the restroom. Bill would say one thing. Steve would say another. The wall got moved two or three times. I came in one morning, and Earl Pritchett had put the wall on wheels—'Until they decide where that wall goes, I'm putting it on wheels.' Good idea."

The Good and the Bad

Bill Cook's jousts with local governmental restraints take on new dimensions these days. "After my heart attack, and after the building of the downtown area and the YMCA, I began to move away from trying to fight these kinds of problems. The people operating Bloomington have done many things I agree with, but there are so many things that have hurt our town—for example, 'historic preservation,' which in my opinion is a lack of judgment by people who don't want to make a judgment call."

That's an eyebrow-raiser from one of the two most recognized preservationists in the state—and husband of the other.

"Gayle and I *are* preservationists, but both of us have an understanding of what should be preserved and what shouldn't. It should have historical significance, or it should have some architectural value. If it can be replicated in reasonable form with existing talent, then that's not historically significant. The requirements are very easy."

Cook shakes his head over city decrees that have blocked property owners from taking down old houses in some residential neighborhoods to build new homes. "We're ruining our neighborhoods by not upgrading. We need to clean up the town. We need to tear some of this junk down, and the city doesn't realize it. If you get older and older houses instead of upgrading with a $400,000 house, you end up paying more taxes on a $150,000 house. It's crazy. It doesn't make sense."

And that comment: "*The people operating Bloomington have done many things I agree with*"? "They have done a good job with parks and recreation. Phenomenal. The community does encourage people to come here because of its beauty. A lot of people come to this community who have picked it out of a magazine. They read, 'This is a good place to live,' they come see it, and they move here. There are just droves of these people.

"Fourth Street [with blocks of ethnic restaurants between downtown and the IU campus] has grown very well. I think that is a very strong asset. I think the continued use of the courthouse square for a restaurant district is an excellent idea. I'd like to see more retail downtown, but that may be impractical. Some places have closed down, but little bagel shops and places where you can pick up food have opened."

Not so Cook-approved is a city project from the 1990s still prominent on the north entrance toward downtown—Bloomington's dominant entry point, from the Indianapolis side. The two parallel north/south streets through the downtown, Walnut and College, become one-way on the city's northern edge, and where they split once was a green area a block wide and about three blocks long. In that green space, a city administration built a water retaining pool, for reasons that included improved drainage and fire protection for the neighborhood. The project uprooted and removed about 100 trees that had lined the area's east and west borders—a job carried out pretty much in an ill-timed one-day swoop: it happened on Arbor Day.

Bill Cook, whose sentimental gift to his hometown of Canton, Illinois, was funding to replace hundreds of trees lost to a 1975 tornado, doesn't even include the lost trees in his broadside at the lagoon that now greets Bloomington's northside arrivals. "That should have remained a very pretty boulevard—not the open concrete sewer they have out there now, with some nice little wildflowers and a lot of dirty water. We have a concrete monster. It gives no one any benefit. It's not pretty. It's so stark. It looks like some of those catch basins that L.A. is trying to take out. They sold the idea to us."

Second-Hand Smoke, Global Warming, Etc.

Politically correct is not a term ever applied to Bill Cook. On the subject of secondhand smoking as a cause of lung cancer, for example, ex-smoker Cook says, "When I get into a place where there is a lot of cigarette smoking, it bothers me. It bothers my eyes, and it stinks. I have no problem at all about craving. I'm very sensitive to the smoke. I *don't* yet believe that secondhand smoke is going to give me cancer. A lot of people can find work checking theories like that out. A research project is a good way to do it. I'm waiting for better information."

Which gets him to this: "It's like global warming. About all that whole issue is going to do is employ a lot of people. They're going to research the heck out of it. It's so foolish. We'll spend billions of dollars. We can clean up the air. That's fine. If they want to clean up the air for better health, that's good. But if they think they're going to do anything about 'global warming' . . ."

Off-the-cuff reactions can and do come from Bill Cook frequently. That isn't one of them. He has done his own reading, his own intellectual investigating, and formed opinions. "You get in trouble looking at global warming through a certain time span of, say, 100 years. If you look over a period of 15,000 years or 20,000 years, you see this fluctuation of temperature.

"You also see another thing: the possibility of 100 million years ago—or even 500 million years ago—a meteorite striking the earth and churning up dirt and dust in such a way that it blanked out the sun. The Gulf of Mexico is believed to be a huge meteorite site that put the sun out for, I think, ten years.

"From 1500 to the 1900s we were in a mini Ice Age. We see the fields in Holland, all the beautiful pictures in the 1400s, 1500s, 1600s, where they were speeding on these frozen fields. Hell, we were in an Ice Age. And that was a normal cyclic thing. Then gradually it warmed up.

"If there's a magnetic change, then it's very easy to think there can be a slight tilt of the earth. Or you could actually knock the earth off its axis. You could have a meteor strike, or you could have what they call a celestial wobble. At certain times there will be pressure waves coming in from outer space that smack the earth and move it. One or two degrees can really get your attention, particularly with weather."

Celestial wobble, which is Google-able, seems an odd term and topic for use by a man who says impaired vision has him reading little these days. It has not dulled his curiosities. "Somebody will say 'global warming.' I will research that. I suspect there are natural reasons for at least some of it."

Google is one primary source for him. Others are less predictable. "If I'm interested in a subject, *Popular Mechanics* is another place I'll look. I'll pick that up at the barber shop. I retain scientific things in my mind.

"But reading *is* very difficult for me today. I can't read a book. After about twenty minutes, my eyes lose focus. But I will read a newspaper and other periodicals every day. On medical subjects, I get information in a number of ways. I watch TV, the Discovery Channel, the History Channel, and read medical periodicals.

"A lot of things I have in my mind are from the days when I did read a lot. Not too long after college, reading became very difficult for me. I have trifocals, and with glasses I have 20/20 eyesight for driving. But it's difficult to get these trifocals in a position where I can read. I had to have trifocals so with the intermediate I could read an instrument panel on an airplane. But I like to read from another range.

"Gayle will read a book a week at least. She points me to things she's interested in, and I find an interest in, too. But I suppose my scientific things come from periodicals and journals and the History and Discovery channels."

And a memory enriched by those unforgotten vista-expanding Wolfson and Watterson days at Northwestern.

Cook Clinic

When I started this clinic in 1993, everybody in town thought
I was nuttier than a fruitcake. We would go broke. It would
cost us too much money. And the doctors and the hospital
got mad at us for doing it. Those doctors love us now
because we pay cash. If we refer one of our patients to them
for specialty treatment, they see the patient, we get the bill,
and we send the doctor a check. And we get a
discount for quick payment. It works.

—*Bill Cook*

It looks like an ordinary doctor's waiting room, except:

- It's a little bigger, with nineteen chairs.
- It has a sign saying, "We Welcome Our Walk-In Patients."
- It's open Monday through Friday from 8 AM until 8 PM—
  not until 3, not until 4 or 5, until 8 PM. And from 8 until noon
  on Saturday.

Cook Clinic is more than one company's attempt to combat and control rising health costs. It's Bill Cook's microcosmic offering as Exhibit A that the
health problem—which neither government nor private medical practice
nor any of the profits-through-the-roof insurance companies has begun to
dent—is not insurmountable at all.

Cook Family Health Clinic

Affordable health care "is not a problem," he says. "Political expediency makes people think it's a problem. Politicians do not understand medicine, nor should they ever have tampered with it. It is a problem very easily solved, and we've proved it with our clinic. We've had just over half the cost that we would pay to an outside organization to have medical care for our employees here because good access leads to quicker diagnosis and treatment."

Cook Clinic—which serves nearly 5,000 employees and their dependents—is a passion for Bill Cook.

Every American bill payer will understand how and why the clinic began: in response to one more rate increase from a health insurance company. Blue Cross–Blue Shield had a blanket policy covering Cook employees in 1981. At renewal time, the insurer laid out a list of Cook-related bills it had paid the previous year and raised its charge for the coming year by 10 or 12 percent, Phyllis McCullough recalls. It was a "hmmm" moment. "Bill and I looked at that and thought, 'If we were self-insured and used the same pricing that Blue Cross uses . . .'"

Cook Group Health Plan Trust was formed, with the same benefits and coverage as before, but it eliminated the middle man. "When they're spending less on you than you're paying them, you're paying their overhead," McCullough said. "We decided to do it ourselves."

Care was taken that all labor and insurance laws and regulations were followed. Community acceptance wasn't automatic. It took time, McCullough said, "to get recognition from the doctors and the Bloomington health community that we were a viable insurance company." Quick payment of bills established that rapidly. Not far down that same road was the idea of making health care more accessible for employees—i.e., ultimately, the Cook Clinic.

A lot of economic realities combined to justify the clinic's ultimate formation in 1993—primarily the need to keep employees on the job. "It was all tied around: we want to be progressive, but we are a hand-craft company, and we need our employees at work," McCullough said. "With every absence, you could never make up the time lost.

"In the first year we were self-insured, I came up with the idea that we would pay a bonus to employees who didn't have to use their health insurance—up to $500 at the end of the year from the premiums that they and we had paid in. That worked so well I almost broke the plan, so we had to do away with that kind of wellness plan. But we've always tried to get our employees to focus on preventive health maintenance. Adding the clinic was a big step toward maintaining at least a handle on health care costs. We need the employees. They need health care. They need access morning and night. The whole thing came together."

There were inevitable collisions in the relationship between the clinic and the Bloomington medical community. Ever-climbing health care costs led to a variety of counter moves by all parties involved. "Preferred providers" became a hot term—designated doctors would agree to accept lower established fees in return for getting the business of cooperating insurance companies or employer groups. The participating doctors were the "preferred providers."

Initially with the clinic, Bill Cook says that doctors told him, "You can't do that. You'll never get a doctor to work for it." That did not prove to be true.

The clinic was in its early years when cardiologist Larry Rink and eye surgeon Dan Grossman, two of his friends, came to Cook with Unity, a preferred-provider plan they were attempting to get off the ground. Cook listened, thought it was headed directly opposite from the clinic concept in solving the medical costs problem, and exploded. Phyllis McCullough breaks into a grin as she recalls an aftermath. "I went to a Super Bowl party at Larry's house, and somebody brought up something about Unity. He couldn't understand why Cook didn't go along. Danny said, 'Hey! If *you* want to talk to Bill Cook, *you* go talk to Bill Cook. I tried, and there's still a chunk missing out of my ass.'"

The Company Clinic Trend

The bulky Sunday *New York Times* on January 14, 2007, headlined one of its lead stories COMPANY CLINICS CUT HEALTH COSTS. Reporter Milt Freudenheim's story began: "Frustrated by runaway health costs, the nation's largest employers are moving rapidly to open more primary care medical centers in their offices and factories as a way to offer convenient service and free or low-cost health care." Of America's 1,000 biggest employers, 100 now have on-site primary care or preventive health services, and the number is likely to grow to 250 by 2008, the story said. Held up as a spotlighted example, "the biggest primary care clinic so far" was a medical center that Toyota built in San Antonio alongside its new truck assembly plant. "Unlike most of the new medical offices—which are staffed by nurse practitioners and in some cases a part-time doctor—Toyota's San Antonio health center has two full-time doctors, a part-time physician, a blood-test lab, and an X-ray center," Freudenheim wrote, quoting an expert in health care benefits who called it "a clinic on steroids."

"The biggest"?

For fourteen years, Cook Clinic has operated with three full-time doctors and a blood-test lab. Now there's a fourth doctor part-time, the full-time nursing staff stands at ten, and there's a pharmacy staffed by one full-time pharmacist and two part-timers. There is also a room for intravenous treatment. "If a patient comes in dehydrated, we can put them in the IV room and give intravenous fluid," Cook Clinic's lead physician, Dr. Tom Hollingsworth, said. "That can be terribly expensive at a hospital emergency room—$500, maybe $1,000. What does it cost us? A couple of bags of fluid . . . a nurse's time, but she's already here . . . a doctor's time, but the doctor's already here."

Everything—eleven examination rooms, the IV room, the blood-test equipment, and the pharmacy—is in one building, easily accessible just northwest of Bloomington's downtown.

The fourth doctor was added in August 2007, "so there's always somebody for walk-ins," Hollingsworth said. "One of our early promises was that you would never have to wait." Prior to the latest hiring, he said, "That wasn't altogether true. Some people have sat out there, embarrassingly, for up to two hours. We just can't have that."

Wait-familiar patients no doubt share that sentiment, but few would expect to hear it from a doctor—which may be why Bill Cook says, "If you listen to our employees, the sun rises and sets with Tom Hollingsworth."

No Stockholders, No Hurdle

Dr. Tom Hollingsworth looks like Central Casting or Norman Rockwell supplied him to Cook. He has a veteran doctor's soothing appearance: graying hair, Santa-friendly eyes that twinkle, a merry voice, and a manner that radiates and generates confidence. For twenty-three years he was a "real" doctor, an orthodox family doctor, private practice and all, in Muncie, In-

Dr. Tom Hollingsworth, lead
physician of Cook Clinic
in Bloomington

diana, the area where he had grown up. One day at lunch with a doctor friend from Bloomington, Mike Aronoff, Hollingsworth mentioned he was looking at Bloomington as a possible place to relocate in about five years as a slowdown job. Aronoff said he didn't know about that far into the future, but a Bloomington doctor named Bill Cutshall was putting together a staff to open a clinic for a local industrialist named Bill Cook. Hollingsworth talked to Cutshall; in July, Cutshall and Dr. Neal Rogers got the clinic going, and by October Hollingsworth had been able to shut his Muncie practice down and join them.

After leading in getting the clinic started and directing its operation in the early years, Cutshall retired and was replaced in 1999 by Dr. Terri Brown, the first female physician on the clinic staff. Rogers had retired in July 1998. His replacement, Dr. Dan Fagan, left after seven years to practice at the Indiana University Medical Group in Indianapolis. Dr. Rick Schilling, a Bloomington native who had practiced in Michigan, joined the staff in 2005. The 2007 addition was Dr. Mary Van Kooten, a onetime registered nurse who returned to medical school and—with two teenage children— completed a family practice residency.

"We're very happy to have female doctors," Hollingsworth said. "When I retire, a female probably will be my replacement. Look at the demographics—50 percent of medical school graduates are female, and 70 percent of Cook employees are female. Naturally a lot of them are more comfortable with a female doctor."

In his Muncie years, Hollingsworth augmented his private practice by working from 7 to 9 AM three days a week as a company doctor at a West-inghouse plant. That primarily involved workmen's compensation cases, "taking care of people who had been injured on the job and were coming back to work. We do that here, too, as well as the other work."

His experience inside private industry gave Hollingsworth an apprecia-tion for what Cook set out to do with his clinic and accomplished. "Bill Cook has the advantage of his company being privately held," Hollings-worth said. "How could you set this thing up if a board of directors was overseeing your bottom line? How do you say to them, 'Over the next fifteen or twenty years, this is going to save money,' when the next quarterly bot-tom line is not good?"

Don't Say Cheaper

Getting the near-unanimous employee participation that was needed to make the clinic cost-effective was a potential early problem. "Early on, peo-ple would say, 'You mean I can't go to my own doctor?'" Hollingsworth said. "But that didn't take very long—I'd say a year, maybe two years max."

"One of the things you hate to give up is the doctor you've been treated by, someone you have confidence in," said Francie Hurst, who heads up the clinic's nursing staff as nurse manager. She was one of the clinic's first employees, there before it opened, involved in putting the first nursing staff together—and in selling the clinic to those initial participating em-ployees, not greatly different from what still happens today with each new employee.

"They come to an employer who says, 'If you take our insurance, the clinic plan, you will need to see the doctors at our health center'—and they say, 'No! I can't do that! I just don't want to leave my doctor!'" Hurst said. "I ex-plain that it is a challenge, but we've all done it, because the clinic offers such a wonderful, vast array of services, in a family-oriented environment."

And it's cheaper, too.

"It's the right thing," Hurst corrects. "I don't like the word *cheaper*. Pa-tients hear *cheap* and think, 'I get what I pay for.' I say it's cost-effective and advantageous for everybody."

And it *is* cheaper.

For family coverage, an employee in 2007 paid a maximum of $279 a month; $12.50 was taken off if the employee would commit to participation in a wellness program that includes all the basic tests (blood pressure, heart rate, even blood sugar and body fat) and offers corrective programs and support groups where needed. There is a $300 annual deductible for special-ist care ($600 family), with the policy covering 80 percent of the specialty costs after the deductible (up to $900 out-of-pocket, anything more fully paid by the policy). It's the same for drugs at the pharmacy.

That one policy allows any covered member of the family to get a doctor's treatment at the clinic for a $15 co-pay. "It doesn't matter what we do for that patient," Hurst said. "The patient sees the doctor, we draw labs that typically would cost around $500 somewhere else, and the patient doesn't pay any more than the $15. If it's a problem needing a specialist, the clinic doctor recommends one—in Bloomington if possible, elsewhere if necessary—and we make the connection with the specialist, leaving the patient only to work out a time of appointment."

Hollingsworth offers an example: "Let's say you have abdominal pain. You think: 'Who do I go see if I don't have a G.P.?' It could be a gastroenterologist, a surgeon, or a gynecologist. If you go to the wrong one to begin with, he or she is going to say they can't help you, and you have to go to another specialist. We can start the workup on the cause of the abdominal pain, narrow it down to what we think it is, and try to make an appointment with the appropriate specialist the first time. Even that is not always easy."

A Specialists' Specialist

Before the clinic, Cook said, "Many of our employees couldn't find a family practitioner or anyone to accept them as their patient. Let's say their child has pneumonia. They take him to the emergency room, they give him a few shots, and send him home. They tell him to come back, but the parents can't afford it because they've already spent $500 to get the child in, take some shots, and get some penicillin. They can't afford another $500. So the child keeps his pneumonia, he gets an enlarged heart, he gets an inflamed liver, or he might even die. All of these things can happen as a result of having an infection. It's a never-ending circle. You have to have family practice.

"In those days, a person who didn't have a referral doctor couldn't get into the hospital. You could get into the emergency room, but after that you were at their mercy. Prior to 1986, they could kick you out if you didn't have enough money, or they could refer you to some doctor who was going to take you for every dime you had. There are doctors in this town today that we will not do business with because they price-gouge. They set you up for a procedure you don't need. We don't need that nonsense.

"You go to our clinic and get treated at a fraction of the cost. You say, 'I don't feel good.' You are treated right there for what's wrong with you. They already have your history because you've been there before. If you have a serious problem, the clinic will send you up to Indianapolis or if necessary down to Florida for treatment. Then you come back and get well."

In Bill Cook's mind, making the crucial contact with a specialist is Francie Hurst's own specialty. "Francie knows where all the hot-dog doctors are and the best prices. If a patient needs special treatment, our people make all the arrangements. They don't get put off. Not Francie."

"Hot-dog doctors," Hurst repeated and laughed. "I like that."

"We do have open doors that others might not have," Hollingsworth said. "Cook insurance pays well and pays quickly. That puts us at the top of the acceptance list. I think we've gained credibility with specialists over time. They know we refer appropriately; they know we're not just kicking somebody over to them because they're a problem to deal with. Then, when they're done with the specialty care, they send them back to us."

A Controlled Forty-Hour Week

And that predicted problem of finding qualified doctors to staff the clinic? "We've proven that there are plenty of doctors out there who would give their right arm to be able to practice with our clinic," Cook said.

Hurst calls it "a wonderful opportunity for physicians to practice medicine the way they feel medicine needs to be practiced. They don't have to worry about insurance companies breathing down their necks. They don't have to worry about asking for a patient to have a particular referral and the insurance company saying they can't do that."

Hollingsworth recalls that when he talked with Dr. Cutshall, heard about the clinic's intentions, and got an invitation to join, "I was really excited—a controlled forty-hour week! For a doctor, the idea of having every holiday off, and every Sunday off, and of working every third Saturday until noon— that was great. And the idea of somebody walking up once a month and putting a check on my desk and dealing with only one insurer . . .

"I don't know that there's any physician in this town who wouldn't at least listen if you said: 'Average your last five years' income; once a month I will come in and lay a check on your desk to cover that monthly average, and you won't have to deal with insurance; you'll only have to practice medicine.' I can't imagine anybody not wanting to do this—just practice medicine, leave the business aside.

"We *are* seeing a diminishing number of young physicians going into primary care. They all want to go into specialties where they obviously make more money. We tell them, 'If you join us, we're going to compensate you well, and we'll give you a life you can predict.' I think that would be very attractive."

Bill Cook says, "When you get people the caliber of Tom Hollingsworth, you're getting the cream of the crop. You're getting sympathetic people, people who are good leaders, people who have an idea about families, because they wanted to spend more time with their own families. Like Tom: he was killing himself in Muncie trying to make a living being a doctor. He comes down here, 9 to 5. You talk about a beautiful way to practice."

Walk-ins Really Are Welcome

Well, not exactly 9 to 5.

Monday through Thursday from 10 AM to noon and 4 PM to 6, two doctors are on duty. All three full-time doctors—Hollingsworth, Brown, and Schilling—are there those days from noon to 4 PM. The busiest period is 3 to 6 PM, Hollingsworth says. "The kids come home from school, you get off work, you get the child from daycare—it's 4 PM, and most doctors' offices are shutting off."

Only early and late Mondays through Thursdays—from 8 to 10 AM and 6 to 8 PM—is there just one doctor at the clinic. The three full-time doctors' on-duty schedules (8 to 4, 10 to 6, noon to 8, the first four days) rotate each week. One shift includes a three-day weekend off, starting Friday. The noon to 8 PM shift also gets Saturday duty. "So there's one 'bad' week every three weeks and one great week," Hollingsworth said. "Mondays are always busy. It's to be expected. We close at noon on Saturday and there is all day Sunday."

Hurst's job includes knowing the numbers. "Mondays and Friday are typically busiest," she said, pulling out up-to-date records. "This Monday we saw eighty-four patients. Between 4 and 8, we had twenty-eight patients. If those patients had not had access to us, they would have gone to Prompt-Care or the hospital emergency room."

The term *family practice* is not misapplied. Sue Ellen Wasick, a receptionist since 2002, says, "You grow to really care about patients. They know me, and I know them. We become very good friends."

Hurst says, "We *are* a family. We're all Cook employees. Our job is to help keep Cook employees healthy and on the job. That's very important. Cook is lean. They don't have a lot of extra people. Their jobs are very specific, very skilled labor. We get them back to work as fast as we can. When they're off, we call to see how they're feeling. We don't just leave them out there. We want to make sure we're doing the right thing.

"From the beginning, everything we did was focused on what was right for the patient, because that's what Mr. Cook wanted—extremely good care and continuity of care. He saw fourteen years ago what was necessary. He wanted employees to be able to come to the doctor's office when they were off, rather than having to take off. So we're here twelve hours a day."

And that "We Welcome Walk-Ins" sign in the office? It's not misleading, Hurst says. "We prefer an appointment for patients who have chronic illness—high blood pressure, high cholesterol, heart disease, diabetes. We like patients to have appointments for those things because they typically take so long. But some things like sore throat, earache, stomachache, you woke up not feeling well—we like to see those as walk-ins."

The Bill Cook Plan for America

Now: The pertinence of Cook Clinic. For America.

The man who dreamed it up has four major targets in mind:

1. The high number of Americans without health insurance.
2. The rising cost of medical care for both individuals and employers.
3. Runaway drug costs.
4. The shaky status of the Social Security program.

By using Cook Clinic as a national model and putting it to work throughout the country, Bill Cook says, all four could be addressed and either eliminated (1 and 4) or greatly alleviated (2 and 3).

With a bonus: Personal 401k plans that would mean a savings plan for all participants.

The cost to individuals is "22 to 25 percent of their income," he says, "no more than 25."

The cost to employers is a matching figure for the employee's cost, but a firm handle on what is uncontrolled and ever-rising now: medical and insurance costs.

Required would be supportive national legislation making participation as near-unanimous and mandatory as Social Security enrollment is now—right from age 18, or the first paycheck if it comes sooner.

"There's no better place to see the medical problem being solved than right here, with the Cook Clinic," he says. "The solution is here."

A Problem: Invincibility of Youth

He speaks to the America whose politicians have been throwing up their hands in frustrated failure every time the subject of a national health program comes up. And that means constantly for the last sixty years.

Such talk first was heard from Harry Truman. The last presidential attempt at a true national health program was in 1993, with First Lady Hillary Clinton steering. That ship was scuttled before it ever got out of port. Coincidentally, 1993 was the same year the Cook Clinic began. It's still afloat, full-steam ahead.

Cook's plan would require every corporation, and every group of small related companies, to take the health-cost problem into its own hands, as he did, and open a clinic for its employees. It's a step he feels would have immediate coverage benefits but also long-term health payoffs. "That would be a way of getting all those young families that have no insurance now the entry-level medical treatment that is so important for their kids and for them. That would take care of probably 70 to 90 percent of all illnesses, particularly with young people. And you won't have the cost of the emergency room and the cost of kids getting sick and remaining sick or permanently hurting them in the future."

His plan would require every worker 18 and up to get in. Starting with the 18-year-olds, overcoming the disinclinations of youthful invincibility, is a key—maybe the most important one, Cook feels. "You hear, 'All over the country people are uninsured.' They never tell you that 80 percent of the young people are uninsured because of choice."

The 80 percent figure is debatable. His point is less so. Not until reaching a predictable point in life do many Americans start thinking in terms of spending their own money to insure themselves. "They're invincible," Cook says. "So many people 18, up through the age of 38—don't ask me why 38, but up to 38—don't feel that they need insurance, so they don't take it out.

"The federal government has to mandate that once you have a job and once you hit 18, you're paying into an insurance program. That's exactly what happens here [at Cook's plants in and around Bloomington]. If you come to work here at 18, you're paying into health insurance and Social Security.

"If the federal government wants to solve the problem, I'm saying, 'I'll solve your problem. But you've got to do what I tell you to do: set up these clinics all over the country.'

"They say, 'We can't do that.'

"You're not doing what I've told you when you say that to me."

In addition to the clinics by employers for employees, Cook's plan would include federally built clinics in every community for people outside the parameters who are too young for Social Security and Medicare—free clinics, with volunteer doctors. Those free clinics "would also take Medicare and Medicaid patients. The doctors would get paid for that by existing government programs. They'd have volunteers to fill out the papers."

He has seen it at work. A free clinic just like that opened in Bloomington in 2007, staffed by volunteer doctors. The clinic is part of a national Volunteers in Medicine project. Bloomington was the fifty-first community to open one since the first started at Hilton Head, South Carolina, in 1993. Bloomington joined Columbus and Indianapolis as Indiana cities with a volunteer clinic. The Bloomington clinic figured on a $9 million annual operating budget, all but $1.5 million of it covered by "in-kind" volunteering from doctors and medical professionals. The rest was to be funded mostly by corporate sources, among them Cook Inc. (which was in quickly with a check for $600,000). But also coming in were some $100 and $200 checks from individuals. Dr. Rajih Haddawi was the Bloomington doctor who got that clinic going, and its patient participation rate right from the start ran about double the national average. "Haddawi is just a great guy. He'll make that a success," Cook said.

"That's the solution for people who don't have jobs or are underinsured—people who were indigent or who did not have money to be cared for, because they were not working for an employer who had a clinic of its own."

Mandate, then Get the Hell Out

Attached to an effective national program of clinics in the Cook plan "would be continuation of Social Security, Medicare, and Medicaid but also mandated 401k plans for everyone. I believe a mandatory 401k is necessary to make Social Security work properly. It's my belief that if you have all of those working people involved, from age 18 up, and they have to allocate about 25 percent of their paycheck—Medicare, Medicaid, health care, and 401k—you can accomplish all of these tasks and people will be much happier. The employer and employee match contributions. It's also a savings plan. There are really two parts to the plan: 401k and Social Security. Everyone says we can't afford that. I say we can't afford not to have it."

In November 2006, Democrats took control of both houses of Congress from Republicans by arguing for sweeping change, starting in Iraq but specifically targeting the national health problem. Cook saw little in the first year that encouraged him to think an effective health care program was coming. "The Democrats were all talking about a raise in minimum pay, and they got it," he said. "The dumb butts—what they ought to do is say, 'Everybody has to have health insurance.' That would be the biggest single thing that could happen to health care in this country. In my dream, it will be a combination plan of Social Security, Medicare, Medicaid, and health insurance all during your life, and to start paying for that from the time you are 18, or 16—whenever you go to work.

"When we were growing up, our parents didn't mention not being able to pay for medical care. We have to take a giant step backward and ask why? Nobody seems to want to attack the problem. It's not a problem. It's political expediency perpetuated by unknowing people. Maybe uncaring. This is less costly, and you will have a happier and better population, a well population. It just requires time." Time and a program-launching federal mandate, a hard word for a sincere conservative to use.

"I guess that has to be," he said. "But the federal government, once it mandates it, has to get the hell out. The federal government *is* the cost now. You spend huge amounts of money taking care of nothing but paper. And we don't need all the overlapping things the federal government mandates, all the regulations, all the numbers that tell you what a disease is."

He cites a personal check-up on a kidney problem in 2006. "I went to the Cleveland Clinic. That three-day treatment cost $40,000! Doing the same thing [without redundant federal requirements] in a smaller hospital would have been much less.

"When you see the different numbers that they put together on mandated procedures and combinations, it drives you crazy. Our people don't have to worry about that. Our rates aren't anywhere near everybody else's. The employees are satisfied with the service. The doctors are satisfied with it. And I've been able to use it as the basis of my thoughts on how to improve medicine. I've learned a lot from that."

That Bugaboo Term

One of the things that doomed Harry Truman's first attempts and rose up again when Bill-through-Hillary Clinton tried in 1993 was the anathema America has built up for the term *socialized medicine,* although democratic nations with federal health programs all over the globe haven't seemed nearly so cost-clobbered for both medical care and medications as staunchly private America.

Bill Cook definitely does not consider his plan or his clinic "socialized medicine" or a step toward it. "It's not. Is it any different for me to pay a wage to a person here and then that person pays part of that wage to be insured? It's pure insurance. It has nothing to do with socialization."

Dr. Tom Hollingsworth smiles at the injection of an inflammatory term in connection with a program he strongly advocates. "People getting together in some way and taking care of a problem—you can call that whatever," he said.

The national disinclination toward anything smacking of socialized medicine has traditionally been led by the American Medical Association—doctors, Hollingsworth's colleagues in the practice of medicine. In Bloomington he doesn't feel any such pressures now, although he suspects Cutshall did in getting the clinic going. "I think Bill Cutshall took some heat—'What are you doing?' Almost like he had become a Commie."

But not anymore and not for very long then. "Within a year, I was president of the Monroe County Medical Society," Hollingsworth said. "But, to be honest, I think that was really a case of 'Oh, you raised your hand at the wrong time.'

"This *is* sort of like socialized medicine, because I practice medicine and never talk to a person about insurance. Everybody who walks through that door has the same insurance, which happens to be through Cook. So it's Cook's form of—whatever you want to call it—Universal Health Care."

McCullough calls it "bizarre that the idea of universal health care is so wrong. This is not the federal government. Bill has exactly the right idea: you start locally."

She said other companies have inquired about the program, but few go beyond an inquiry. "We always heard, 'You can do that if you're a private company, but not if you're a public company.' The public companies could do it. They don't want to tell their shareholders exactly what they're spending on health insurance. I can't believe there's a stockholder out there in any big company who would not want their company to participate in bringing down health care costs. They wouldn't be spending as much money as they're spending now, and they would cover people who aren't covered.

"You have to spend some money to make some money. We had to spend the money in the beginning to get this working. It's a benefit—not a right, a benefit—that the employee pays for, along with us. But it is not a profit center for the company. We never expected the Cook Clinic to be a profit center. Unfortunately, our medical societies and hospitals are looking for profit, because Medicaid and Medicare are so screwed up.

"Doctors don't like the present system. They don't like getting paid nineteen cents on the dollar from Medicare. They are so afraid of 'socialized medicine' that they don't look at other ways to do it that could cost so much less."

The word may be getting around, but at the moment the Cook Inc. version of a universal health plan is a long way from universal—even with the trend among big corporations that the *New York Times* story (by Freudenheim in January 2007) cited.

"There's nothing like this that I know of," Bill Cook said. "Kaiser started something like this in World War II. It later became Kaiser-Permanente Medical Group. It entailed clinics and hospitals, and it is still around." Kaiser-Permanente is one of the Michael Moore targets in his 2007 movie *Sicko*, a movie that—considering the wide ideological separation between Moore and Bill Cook—makes a remarkable number of points similar to Cook regarding public and private failures that have made the national health care problem seem insoluble when it isn't. Cook clearly has more admiration for Kaiser-Permanente than Moore does, but mostly for its employee clinics, not the hospital that Moore denounced.

"Ours is not necessarily a hospital plan," Cook said. "It's a plan that would get people to a doctor so they could (1) practice wellness and (2) have a better referral service to a specialist if they needed it. Plus, we have a pharmacy, which is extremely beneficial in holding prices down.

"I don't know of many companies that have tried it in a small way, as we have. I just don't think people understand it is relatively easy to do. But you have to have enough participants to do it. I think 5,000 would be plenty—that's employees and their families, their dependents. Beyond that, it's just gravy. Three doctors can take care of 5,000 very adequately, provided that the referral system works. We've proven that."

He waits for Washington to notice. "The only chance we have is with our own Indiana senators championing such a cause in Congress," he said. He's a major supporter of both Republican Richard Lugar and Democrat Evan Bayh, and he's confident they will remain in office as long as they want, which means they would have seniority and credibility within their separate parties—both of which could translate to across-the-aisle clout in backing groundbreaking legislation. That's part of the Bill Cook dream.

Not Always Right, But . . .

Lugar and Bayh don't represent his only hope. Cook also has his legislative ambassador to Washington, Steve Ferguson, warming up in the bullpen.

Ferguson's focus was on getting the French Lick–West Baden hotel and casino projects on the way and through the courts, until the last round of lawsuit hassles there ended in June 2007. "Steve was active on the Washington scene for about ten years, trying to keep legislation from eating us alive," Cook said. "Now, when he's out of the casino business, maybe he'll go back and concentrate on Medicare and Medicaid."

And on the national clinic plan: "I think he's right about reforming health care, but he's out in front of the posse," Ferguson said. "Our clinic is a way for us to stabilize costs and to deliver better health care to our employees. The *New York Times* article said that other employers are starting to see the same thing. I think ten years from now everybody's going to be doing it. And that, I think, is the solution. Bill is just fifteen years ahead of everybody on what it is and the politics of it. But everybody's going to get there. It's the way to go.

"The problem is getting people-access. When we started our clinic, we had coordination with General Electric, Westinghouse, Otis, Indiana University—the major employers in Bloomington. I got a lot of good information then from those other employers."

Among things the data he received showed, he says, was that "if the Bloomington GE plant had had the same health costs per employee that Cook did, they would have had $5 million more annually on their bottom line. IU's health care costs then were about $2,700 per employee, and we were about $3,500. Now IU is up to about $7,000, and we're at a little less than $5,000." So, yes, even with the clinic, Cook's health cost over fourteen years went up—about 42 percent. But the university's increase—much more reflective of the national average—was up almost 160 percent. That's a difference of just under 4 to 1.

"A lot of times he's just too far in front of everybody," Ferguson said. "I say to people: 'He's not always right, but he's right often enough you'd better listen.'"

The day revisited

KIDNAPPING REDUX

The kidnapping part of Arthur Curry's intrusion into the lives of Gayle and Bill Cook had lasted just twenty-six hours. Unimaginable hours, to be sure—unforgettable hours, taut and tense every tick of the clock during those two mid-March days in 1989. Unending hours, too. For long days, then weeks and then months after the first twenty-six hours ended, the tension didn't stop, stretching through each new day's headlines, and each day of mixing with longtime friends and some people who had walked and shopped and dined and watched sports events with them all along and now were newly aware of these two middle-aged people, so insistently unaffected by their own millionaire status but affected by it, nonetheless, because of Arthur Curry's criminal greed. The nightmare didn't end for Gayle with Curry's capture and her freedom. That, in Churchillian terms, was just the end of the beginning.

The Trial

First, for Gayle Cook, there was euphoria.

Behind that blindfold, of course she thought many times that her ordeal might end in death. "You know that you—the victim—are the most significant witness in a kidnapping," she said. "That's why they're often killed."

But she hadn't been killed, and when her shackles were off and she was out of Curry's van, life got fast-paced for her. She was interrogated briefly by FBI agents at the scene of her release, then taken home in an FBI car where—after a shower and change of clothes—she answered more questions, laying out as best she could recall details of hours that tended to compress together, although some memories were clear.

And finally, they were alone—Bill, Gayle, and Carl Cook, Steve and Connie Ferguson. They drove to a nearby health facility, Promptcare, to get treatment for Gayle's forehead wound and hand paralysis from all those hours with tight binding on her wrists. It was early evening, and they were hungry. They went to an Italian restaurant, Grisanti's, down the street from the Jewel store where she had bought groceries a long, long day before. Dinner was relaxed. So was conversation. "The event was over. We talked about it," Bill said. "Gayle has never had any hesitancy talking about it."

Bill was the driver and Gayle was in the front seat when they went east down Wylie Street on their five-minute ride to Promptcare. No one noticed—especially Gayle, the one who might have, maybe traumatically—that they passed a car parked on Wylie, a blue 1978 Toyota Corolla, the one she had been crammed into at the start of everything. It had been left there after her transfer into the van, and it wasn't found by police until the next morning.

Almost a year later, when the case against Arthur Curry came to trial, the Cooks' failure to notice the Corolla was among things raised as a conspiracy insinuation in the defense's grasp for a shadow-of-a-doubt in the mind of just one juror, to avoid a guilty verdict.

The abduction was on Wednesday, March 15, 1989; the arrest on Thursday, March 16. The U.S. attorney's office in Indianapolis had immediately waived jurisdiction to the state. "For a federal crime, there has to be some kind of interstate connection—even by telephone," Dennis Troy said. "That does not preclude the FBI from coming in and conducting the investigation. You just can't prosecute in federal court." Curry crossed no state line, but he came close. Terre Haute bumps up against the state's western border with Illinois.

On Friday, March 17, after being held in jail overnight, Arthur Jackson Curry wore black sweatpants and a purple sweatshirt with "Monroe County Jail" stenciled across the back as he was formally charged in Monroe Circuit Court in Bloomington with five felonies: kidnapping, criminal confinement, battery, criminal recklessness, and auto theft. Kidnapping was the only one of the five counts that was a Class A felony. In Indiana it carried a maximum sentence of thirty years, with a possibility of another twenty for aggravating circumstances (e.g., injury to the victim). Criminal confinement (later dropped because it had the effect of duplicating the kidnapping charge), battery, and criminal recklessness all were Class B felonies, and auto theft was a Class C. Judge James Dixon set bond at $1 million. Curry said he was "broke and in bankruptcy," and Dixon agreed to name a public defender to represent him. That didn't prove necessary. Curry engaged Robert Saint, from a small Indianapolis law firm, to take the job, with help from associate David Smith.[1]

Curry spent the next 362 days in the downtown Bloomington jail.

The Cooks' gratitude showed in personal letters Bill wrote a week after the experience to each of the four police agency heads who were with him when plans were first made—Police Chief Steve Sharp, Sheriff Jimmy Young, State Police Lieutenant Ken Fowler, FBI Special Agent in Charge Bill Ervin—and to Ervin's ultimate boss, FBI Director William Sessions in Washington.

THE DAY REVISITED

Gayle says immediately after the arrest, the FBI's standard operating protocol was made clear to them—"Not only shouldn't we tell anyone what the FBI did but we also shouldn't name names because they should be anonymous.

"We said, 'What *can* we do? These people did everything right.' They said, 'Write a letter to the Director of the FBI, praising the team that was sent to Indiana. That letter will be read into the Congressional Record. And then come to the FBI office in Indianapolis, let the people meet you, and you can tell them that whole story.' We did. And we sent boxes of candy."

The letter to Sessions was written and sent on March 24 and read into the Congressional Record by Indiana representative John Myers on April 4, 1989. In it, Bill Cook told Sessions of the call he had received, informing him of the kidnapping, and his letter said in part:

> Even though kidnapping is uncommon, your Special Agents' knowledge, skill, and professionalism were incredible. Their kindness and intelligence were disarming. Each had a personality and a face that was different, but their love of their organization and its mission were demonstrated in everything they did.
>
> Mr. Bill Ervin, Special Agent in Charge . . . is special. He is a man whose intelligence and kindness are obvious, but I will remember him as a friend who gave leadership to a group of trained professional Federal Officers. When I looked at Bill and his associates surrounding the Ford van where Gayle was held, I saw happiness in each face. They had succeeded. A few moments before, they stood ready to kill or be killed. . . .
>
> If at all possible, I would most appreciate having all agents involved with this project recognized in a manner which is appropriate to the Bureau.

"It was a huge group," Gayle Cook said of just the FBI agents involved in the case. She was told, "If you thank the person who made the arrest, you don't realize there was someone up in an airplane, there was the whole radio crew, the people who took care of communications, the people who did the phone-tapping. . . ."

She understood. "There was a kidnapping threat to David Letterman's son. He said very little on TV, but he did say, 'I just want to thank the FBI. They were great.' I know why now. I'm sure he was impressed, but he was told the same thing."

Sessions had known firsthand of the situation. From Washington he made phone calls that kept him apprised hour by hour of the case in progress.

On January 30, 1990, Judge Dixon denied lawyer Saint's request for a change of venue, which Saint had based on a claim that media coverage of the case in the Bloomington area made selection of an unbiased jury impossible. Dixon kept the trial in Bloomington but ordered that jurors be chosen from Bartholomew County, two counties east of Monroe, its biggest city Columbus.

Within a week, ten women and two men had been picked. Gayle Cook was two weeks past her fifty-fifth birthday when the kidnapping occurred. The ten women averaged just under 45 when they were picked. Three of the selected woman jurors were older than Gayle, the oldest 68. One of the others was a 23-year-old waitress with two years of college education at IUPUI—a joint branch extension of Indiana and Purdue universities in Indianapolis. Three were in their thirties. Eight of the ten women were mothers. The two college graduates among the jury selectees were schoolteachers. The two men were fathers, 52 and 53.

Arthur Curry was 42 when he met them in court.

Gayle Cook first took the stand on Tuesday, February 6, 1990, when the trial began. With prosecuting attorney Robert Miller guiding the way with occasional questions, she went through the kidnapping experience as she remembered it, in great detail. News reports noted that the day in court was the first time she had seen Arthur Curry's face. On February 7, the Lafayette *Journal and Courier* announced, KIDNAP VICTIM CAN'T IDENTIFY CURRY. It wasn't a trial-jeopardizing revelation. She readily admitted she couldn't identify his face because it was behind a ski mask when she was abducted and when, a few minutes later, she began more than twenty-four hours in a blindfold and other restraints.

In her testimony, she said she was not given food or water nor was she allowed bathroom breaks. Rather, Curry stopped once to buy adult diapers, put one on her, and changed it once. While he was changing it, she testified that "he said something to the effect that 'I'll change it because I don't want you to spend the rest of your life in a diaper.' I thought that meant I didn't have long to live."

Beginning with the instructions she gave Curry on how to get through to her husband on the telephone, she said she tried to think of ways to cooperate. One was telling Curry what to tell Cook to expect at the kidnap scene—for example, purse on the kitchen table, groceries in the foyer, trunk lid up on the car parked outside—every detail she could think of to try to expedite the ransoming process. "I was terrified. He had weapons, and I didn't know what to do. We just kept talking [when the gag was occasionally loosened] and I tried to think of ways to save myself."

Saint's only contribution to the trial's first day was an opening statement to jurors that was a cold personal assault on Gayle Cook: "Our case is the state doesn't have a case. The state's case is based on the victim, and the victim will not speak with the truth." He waived cross-examination during her testimony, retaining the right to call her back to the stand in defense testimony.

That came two days later, after the trial's focus in the intervening time had been on other witnesses, most of them FBI agents or state or local police, who told what they had observed, primarily during the capture.

Reliving the experience with her testimony her first day on the stand wasn't easy. But doing it again was much worse. She had been warned. The Cooks' attorney, Bill Lloyd, "advised me in preparing for the trial, 'They will say you're lying. That's the only defense.'"

She wasn't prepared for the extent of the attack on her truthfulness and her character. In less than a full day on the witness stand, Saint came at her with 565 questions, rat-a-tat-tat.

She had been on the stand less than a minute on February 8 before a thirty-seven-question barrage began concerning how well Gayle knew Kay Sylvester's cleaning "ritual" and TV-watching habits—to gauge why she decided to put off bringing the groceries in until later. The court transcript records this exchange:

How long does it take to clean the kitchen? I can't tell you exactly. *More than an hour?* I can't tell you. *More than an hour and a half?* I don't know. *What does she do when she cleans the kitchen?* She cleans the counter top and the sink and the floor and the mirrors in the bathroom and the plumbing in the bathroom. *You have cleaned the counter tops, haven't you?* Yes. *And you have cleaned the floor, haven't you?* Yes. *And you have cleaned the hardware in the bathroom, haven't you?* Yes. *And the mirrors. How long does that take?* I don't know. *I thought you were familiar with the ritual?* I don't know it minute by minute.

All of that was almost convivial compared to what came about an hour later.

Mrs. Cook, how did you use the restroom from the time that you were in Mr. Curry's van until approximately 3 o'clock on March 16th? I wasn't allowed to use a restroom. *Did you ever urinate or defecate?* Yes. *And on how many occasions did you urinate?* I don't know. *On how many occasions did you defecate?* I don't know. *And did he get an adult diaper for you?* Yes. He got more than one diaper. *How many?* I don't know how many he had. Two were on me. *He put one on, removed it, and put another one on?* Yes. *At the time that you were originally placed in the van, were your feet bound together?* After he placed me in the van, he bound my feet. *And did he bind your feet so that your two ankles touched together?* They were tightly bound. *Did they touch together?* I think so. *And did they remain together?* That binding remained the same. *And that was made up of cord and tape. Is that correct?* I have not seen that binding. *But you couldn't separate your ankles?* I could not separate my feet. Perhaps my ankles were a half-inch apart, I don't know. I can't tell you that. But I could not separate my feet. *And it is your testimony that you were bound in this captain's chair, too, weren't you?* The upper body. *And you had this coat on. Isn't that correct?* Yes. *And you had a long skirt on, too, didn't you?* Yes. *And he never removed you from that captain's chair until you used the pay telephone at the Travelodge. Isn't that correct?* Until shortly before.

Saint went for the kill:

> *Would you tell the ladies and gentlemen of the jury how it was with your ankles bound together, wearing all this clothing, Mr. Curry was able to put one diaper on you, remove that diaper, and place another diaper upon you, Mrs. Cook?*

The cool answer he got back:

> Do you want it step by step? I was seated in the captain's chair, my feet bound together resting on the floor of the vehicle. My upper body was bound to the chair back which was tilted somewhat backwards. And Mr. Curry took my skirt and my slip and pulled them up. He had a diaper, which as you probably know, opens up flat. You don't step into it like a pair of pants. It opens up flat. I lifted my hips up out of the chair. He put one end underneath me. He brought the other end of the diaper up the front as I spread my legs apart, put the two ends together at the hip and fastened the tabs.

Another eighteen questions got into details of the state of the van's interior at the time of capture:

> *Did it smell in the van?* The odor was very unpleasant. *What did it smell like?* Like a dirty diaper.

A day or two after her release, she laundered the skirt and other clothing she had worn, except for her coat and other items that showed blood and duct tape residue. Those things and the diaper she had saved in a plastic sack she turned over to police a week later when she had a follow-up questioning appointment.

> *Why did you launder it?* I laundered the skirt and the slip and the underpants because they smelled so bad. *Didn't the diaper smell, Mrs. Cook?* I had it in a plastic bag sealed up.

State Police Sergeant Maurice "Bud" Allcron had testified he disposed of the diaper after receiving it because he considered the diaper of "non-evidentiary value." Its absence and Saint's continued questions about its

THE DAY REVISITED

means of application became what Curry later ridiculed as Saint's "diaper defense" that Curry claimed worked against him.

There were innuendoes in Saint's questioning of Gayle Cook that, even with negative answers, seemed designed to hint that maybe she was involved in a two-person plot:

> *Mrs. Cook, how is it that this alleged abductor just happened to be coming by east on Wylie after all the grocery bags made it to the foyer?* (Objection by Prosecutor Miller, sustained by Judge Dixon.) *Now, Mrs. Cook, was Arthur Curry ever in your house?* No. *Was he ever in your kitchen?* No. *Do you recall seeing Mr. Curry's van parked on East Wylie ten to fourteen days before March 15th?* I didn't notice it. *Do you recall a man who came to your home on several different occasions prior to March 15th?* No.

And:

> *Mrs. Cook, you have been described as a very detail-oriented person. Do you agree with those observations of friends?* Yes. *Would you also agree that you are the sort of person that plans and organizes things very well?* Sometimes I do, and sometimes I don't. *Would you also agree that you are the sort of person that carries out the details of those detailed plans?* Sometimes, but I don't do it 100 percent of the time.

That was Saint's 565th question.

> *Your honor, we have no further questions.*

Curry did not testify. Neither had he allowed an interview by police after his arrest, although some of his words went into the trial records via officers who said he volunteered them, either when apprehended or at various points in transportation ("I can't believe this. I can't believe you caught me. I thought I had a perfect plan. I must have underestimated you." And, "I'll bet a hundred times I thought of just letting her go"). Curry's brother, Daniel, said on the stand, "He once told me, 'She didn't deserve this. She's a nice lady.'"[2]

With the jury temporarily out of the courtroom, Saint presented Judge Dixon with a signed waiver by Curry of his right to testify. The waiver said in part Curry had been advised by his attorneys not to testify "in my best interest" and "I understand that I could ignore the advice given me and testify, but I choose to follow their advice freely and voluntarily." Still, after receiving and reading the signed waiver, Judge Dixon asked Curry if waiving his chance to testify was, indeed, his choice.

CURRY: "At the advice of counsel, I have elected not to testify."
DIXON: "And I assume you concur. . . . Is that true?"
CURRY: "They are wiser men than myself, Judge."

KIDNAPPING REDUX

DIXON: "I need to be certain in my own mind, Arthur, that this is a
decision that you are willing to agree to."

CURRY: "It is a decision I have chosen to live with."

Dixon brought the jury back in, sent the case to them, and four hours
later the verdict came in:

Guilty on all counts.

There was a hollowness to victory for Gayle Cook. She termed the whole
trial experience "very traumatic."

Prosecutor Miller wasn't a happy winner, either. He angrily criticized
Saint's line of questions for implying that she wanted to leave her husband
for "a loser from Lafayette." Saint hadn't the "guts" to ask her about that
during her testimony, Miller said.

"As a matter of fact, that's the point of the defense. They want to bad-
mouth the good name of a decent woman. She's a fine and decent woman.
She should not be disgraced in public with the accusations that she herself
was not given the opportunity to respond to."

Gayle Cook's response came sixteen years later, the memories and their
pain still fresh.

"To be attacked by a defense attorney is awful . . . to have your veracity
challenged, to be told you're lying. . . . That was his only defense, that I was
lying. The guy dragged me through the whole scenario of consequences of
not having a bathroom for twenty-six hours. I think he was trying desperately to show that I really *was* allowed to use a restroom, which I wasn't. But
to be attacked, to imply that I knew the guy and was running off . . . that is
all *very* . . . distasteful. The whole thing was just very hard for me."

The Sentencing

Their garageless home was not the only late 1980s sign of unpretentiousness
for the nouveau riche Cooks. Their home address and telephone number
were right there in the phone directories that everyone in Bloomington had
when a flash of news put the kidnapping and recovery of Gayle Cook all
across newspapers' front pages and dominated local telecasts.

"We had our phone disconnected about two days later," Gayle said. "We
were in the phone book. We went to an unpublished number. Both of us just
said, 'Enough.' You don't realize the outpouring from strangers with advice,
criticism, kind words—everything. Nuts came out of the woodwork. One
woman wrote and said, 'You probably wonder why you had to suffer so. It
was God's way of telling me who to ask for money for my church.' Another
woman said, 'Now that you know what it's like to be abused by a man,

please send me $100,000, $200,000, or $300,000 so I can leave my abusive husband.' One man called and said, 'There was a boy who drowned, and he wouldn't have drowned if the FBI hadn't been busy looking for you. You ought to come to the funeral.' We just had enough of these things and said, 'We're going to lie low for a while.'"

Bill said, "The trial and the whole defense were difficult for Gayle. She is a person whose integrity and honesty always show. Those things came through her to Carl; they're basically two peas out of a pod. It's really tough for both of them to lie. They can't even tell a white lie—they're disgustingly honest.

"She wanted to make sure that I didn't believe [the innuendoes]. Well, hell, we knew that was going to be their defense. They were going to come after her with everything they could. It didn't bother me, because it was a defense that I thought was stupid. He didn't have a really bright lawyer. He didn't have a criminal lawyer; he had a corporate lawyer. They just did dumb things. There's no doubt in my mind that he got off easy. But the trial lawyer certainly didn't help him."

Even before the trial, Gayle had begun her own self-therapy program to expunge the horror of fresh memories. "I deliberately did things to get over it. It happened on a quiet afternoon, 2 PM, on our quiet street. I began going out and walking the neighborhood at that time of day. I got out on the street, so I wouldn't jump whenever a car went by or slowed down. I tried to get over the feeling that something could happen on the street, or on the sidewalk, or in the yard."

She even sought out the blue Corolla. "I knew where the student lived, thought it might be parked there, and it was. I took pictures of it, so I wouldn't be startled if I saw that car again."

And there was that Kenny Rogers lyric: "You picked a fine time to leave me, Lucille."

"I went out and got that tape and listened to it, so that wouldn't be a memory I would always have. It was so vivid in the car, to think there was this person sitting in the front of the car, singing, 'You picked a fine time . . .'

"I think it worked. I didn't have repercussions. But I can see, if someone stayed inside for months afterward, you would be paranoid. You have to desensitize yourself to those things associated with it. To me, it was the logical thing to do. Like they say, when you fall off a horse . . .

"But some things we stopped doing, just so we weren't in public for a while." She had responded to almost every speaking invitation before. "I had one right afterward that I did keep, a short course at IU." That went all right, but she declined anything further, graciously but firmly. They even stopped going to IU basketball and football games, a big part of their lives—a big part of all Bloomington's social life—for about as long as they had been in town. "We stopped going to games because we were recognized," she said. "And we never gave an interview, never told the story."

On the day the verdict came in, February 13, 1990, Judge James Dixon closed the trial, dismissed the jurors, and returned Arthur Curry to Monroe County Jail to await sentencing, which was required within thirty days by Indiana law. Dixon met the requirement with the early March date he set for sentencing, but lawyer Robert Saint was granted a delay he requested. By the time the new date came on April 3, Saint had relayed to Dixon his own written request for leniency in the verdict and nineteen letters of support for Curry from friends and past business associates.

The letters were variations on a common theme: shock—certainty that the crime was an aberration, a mental collapse under great financial strain that would never be repeated, and that the longer Arthur Curry was in jail, the longer society would be denied a talented, contributing citizen:

> My feeling is that this illegal act was done while he was temporarily insane. . . . Art should be treated, not punished or incarcerated.

> I'll pray that your sentence will be tempered by the good he has done and can do.

> I would urge . . . a light sentence and extended community service—let society benefit from his mistake.

> I believe he can be a good citizen again. A contributor, teacher, and addition to our world.

Bizarre was a word that showed up in three letters, one bitterly skeptical:

> I know him very well and know in my heart that he did not do that which the prosecutors say he did. . . . I trust you will take the real Arthur Curry into consideration and not focus on a bizarre incident last year and the politics involved.

And some doubted that Gayle Cook had been in any real danger during her captivity.

> He is not a dangerous person, in my opinion.

> I do not believe that Arthur has demonstrated that he is really a danger to society.

> The crime . . . no one was injured.

> Art is not a "hard-core" criminal.[3]

THE DAY REVISITED

Given his own chance to speak at his sentencing hearing on April 3, 1990, Curry said, "Someone asked if I had remorse. How could I not have remorse ... after destroying my family, friends, and all that I care about? I think five seconds after this thing began I had remorse. I wish I could turn the clock back twenty-six hours and make it all go away."[4]

Judge Dixon had little comment in sentencing Curry to thirty-two years (the possibility was fifty-eight) in the state's maximum-security prison at Westville in northwestern Indiana, almost two hundred miles from Bloomington. Curry was given credit for the year he had already served in Monroe County Jail. With time off (50 percent) for good behavior, that left him with just over fifteen years to serve.

"It is a serious offense, there's no question about it," Dixon said. "It is also obvious after the fact that the defendant is not a very good criminal."[5]

That was Bill Cook's appraisal, too. "Curry is a coward. Not too bright. Not even cunning. A lot of really smart crooks can be cunning; they can charm their way out of anything. This guy couldn't. He's an individual who never learned how to be a criminal. He always got caught. He got caught in a couple of bankruptcies. He got caught up in Chicago at the brokerage house, skimming I understand. He'd come across as reasonably bright, effervescent. He'd get you part of the way, but he couldn't get you all of the way. He started believing his own press clippings. I think it started out as a guy who couldn't organize and couldn't do well financially, and he had a father who overshadowed him and probably didn't guide him in the right direction. I think that's pretty evident."

One letter in the batch of nineteen Dixon received—single-spaced and running over to a second page—took on extra significance after the sentencing. It was from Jerry S. Rosenthal, of Woodland Hills, California. A key paragraph said:

> Arthur has been a friend and trusted financial advisor for ten years. And his performance in both capacities was such that I gave him full responsibility for a large investment portfolio. Arthur's candor, integrity, and performance justified this action.

Rosenthal was one who raised the point of Curry's potential for future good:

> This ... should not be considered an end, because Arthur Curry has much to contribute to society in a very positive way. Excessive incarceration can only be detrimental both to Arthur and the public who would stand to benefit from the reservoir of services he can effectively perform.[6]

Nine days after the sentencing, Jerry Rosenthal made his own news in the case. He and partner Gerry Popper owned Alligator Productions Ltd., of Woodland Hills, and the two of them first implied, then later confirmed, plans to make a TV movie. The movie would focus on Curry, they said, and on the thirteen years of his life leading up to the kidnapping. They estimated the cost at $12 million and said it could be out by the spring of 1991. "We just want a good, exciting story, and a regular kidnapping is a boring story," Rosenthal said in an interview. "If it isn't a screenplay, it'll be a book. It's too good."[7]

Good, exciting, and . . . funny?

Oh, yeah, Rosenthal said. "There's the comedy of the exchange of the ransom in the Kmart parking lot. I can just hear the P.A. system: 'Attention, Kmart shoppers. There's a ransom exchange taking place in the parking lot. Please don't go there.'"[8]

"It definitely has its comedic overtones," Popper said.[9]

Rosenthal told one interviewer of knowing Curry through financial dealings for twelve years, jibing with his leniency-request letter to Judge Dixon. What didn't jibe with his message in the letter was his admission that one of his dealings with Curry cost him $500,000.

> . . . a friend and trusted financial advisor . . . I gave him full responsibility for a large investment portfolio . . . his candor, integrity, and performance justified this action.

"My wife would like to castrate me every time I bring up his name," Rosenthal said in the interview.[10]

In prison, Curry made a four-minute tape of his allegations and distributed it to news media and to Alligator Productions. On June 3, 1990, Popper sent Gayle Cook a letter asking for her cooperation ("We have Arthur Curry's story. Now, so that we may effect an unbiased presentation . . ."). On June 8, Rosenthal followed with a similar letter (". . . we find many unanswered questions. . . . Arthur Curry still alleges that you were a co-conspirator in the kidnapping, not an unwilling victim. Have you any comment . . . ?"). On June 14, family lawyer Bill Lloyd fired back a certified letter to both Popper and Rosenthal denying them her "consent or permission," demanding that "all further contact" go through him, and warning that "any attempt to falsify, sensationalize, or exploit Mrs. Cook's ordeal for your profit will result in an appropriate response."[11]

There has been no movie.

Bill and Gayle Cook weren't around for the sentencing or the Alligator Productions letters.

THE DAY REVISITED

"Our reward to ourselves after the trial was the only trip we've ever taken like it—we went to Egypt, with a group, on a cruise," Gayle said. "We were on the Red Sea, on a small boat, about eighty passengers. You put into shore in Egypt, see the sights, then get back on the boat, so you're actually eating and sleeping on a Greek boat even though you're going into Egypt.

"We asked not to be listed on the passenger list, because the trial got national attention, and amounts of money and names were mentioned. So we asked if we could go anonymously. They said, 'Certainly.' I suppose a lot of people do that for other reasons.

"We didn't take false names. Looking back on it, we should have. It would have been easier. The woman who was in charge of the tour had never been told [of the anonymity granted them], and our names were never on anything, so she apologized numerous times.

"Once we were on the boat, acquaintances were first-name anyway. So at the end of the tour, when we were all saying goodbye, I told her, 'You don't have to apologize anymore. We had requested that anonymity.' But I respected them for what they did.

"That was a great trip. We're so glad we did it. We started in Cairo, then went down the coast to Aswan Dam, the Tombs areas, the Pyramids. Also to Petra, in Jordan. It was politically very quiet then. Steve and Connie Ferguson were with us, and Dan and Susan Sterner. So that was a happy result."

They came back to the aftermath of the splashy trial and sentencing coverage. The chinks in the Constitution-protected Great American Free Press armor that the Forbes experience had introduced them to previewed some of the same disappointment with the local and regional coverage, even though it was generally supportive.

"The newspapers . . . they don't always consider the position of the victim," Bill Cook said. "There is all this 'alleging' going on, this 'balanced' reporting that they try to portray, the 'sense of fairness.' I learned the hard way that reporters aren't too prone to check things."

It was harder, more personal for Gayle. "Every accusation the defense made was also in the paper," she said. "So you hear, 'Did you *really* know him?' I got a letter from one woman, 'Why don't you confess? Arthur Curry is such a nice man. I think this has been covered up because your husband is embarrassed.' Now I see why people get so frustrated when they're in the news."

It wasn't that the Cooks had never been in the newspapers. The growth of their company, generally overlooked at first, had taken on full recognition long before the kidnapping. But that recognition was by a wholly different audience, Gayle sensed.

"A funny thing, in journalism . . . all of the publicity we had about expanding the factory, new products, preserving buildings . . . none of that brings out this element. But a sensational crime, a sensational trial—the response is like some people *want* to get involved. While Bill and I were trying to stay out of the public eye, others clamored to get in. One woman, who had no role whatsoever in the case, wanted to appear in the trial."

Nationally, journalism groups have been growing more and more outspoken in support of legislation to permit cameras—TV and still—in all courtrooms, not just the increasing percentage where the prevailing judge now allows them. Gayle Cook fervently opposes such a law. "I feel cameras in the courtroom would create even more sensation seekers."

The Appeal

Arthur Curry was back in Monroe County Circuit Court on March 1, 1993, with a self-argued appeal. He spent three days there making his case for a new trial, basically on grounds of incompetent defense by attorney Robert Saint.

On the first day, Curry had Saint on the stand under his questioning for three hours. The tactic had its price: it freed Saint of lawyer-client obligations while defending himself. While he was on the stand, prosecutor Robert Miller in cross-examination had Saint read into court record the twenty-six pages of Curry's handwritten statement that Curry gave Saint prior to the trial. (In a written statement to a reporter that was not part of the appeal, Cook attorney Bill Lloyd termed it a confession that "says it all. He admits his guilt and the violence with which he harmed Gayle Cook." Lloyd said Curry's "desperate and bizarre fantasies and fraudulent stories all made up in Curry's criminal mind do not deserve comment.")[12]

During his three-day appeal, Curry accused Saint and associate David Smith of coercing him into waiving his right to testify at his trial. That was in a list of twelve complaints he had against the way he had been represented in court. He accused Saint of 202 lies during his defense and of ineptness that "made a mockery" of the trial.[13]

Judge James Dixon took under advisement the testimony and a mass of documents submitted by Curry, promising a verdict within a month. He came back in less than two weeks with a twenty-three-page rejection, addressing each of Curry's charges, citing legal precedents and case law, and including in his firm denial:

> The evidence presented by the state at the trial . . . demonstrated clearly beyond a reasonable doubt that the petitioner abducted Gayle Cook against her will, causing her injury at the time of the abduction; that the petitioner

sought to obtain a ransom through said abduction; that Gayle Cook was abducted and confined against her will in a most disgusting and embarrassing manner; that she was found bound and gagged in a motor vehicle operated by the petitioner at the time of arrest; and that the petitioner abducted Gayle Cook by use of an automobile that the petitioner had stolen.[14]

And so it was that on March 16, 1993, Arthur Curry was sent back to Westville to serve the rest of his sentence. Only Judge Dixon knew whether there was significance or coincidence in the date on which he finally slammed the prison door shut on Arthur Curry.

It was the fourth anniversary of the day Gayle Cook was freed.

There was an adjustment period for the Cooks after the kidnapping and its extended aftermath. It mainly involved only the primary victim, Gayle. "Bill is very good—when something's over, it's over, move on," she said.

Carl isn't bad at that, either. His sense of humor—the one that his dad says mirrors Gayle's, not his—helped in the adjustment in its own way. "I told her how tough it was [during his evening and morning at home during the hushed-up kidnapping] when her friends would call—how I could have said, 'I'm sorry, she can't come to the phone. She's tied up.'"

Bill says, "For about two years, I noticed she always looked behind her and was very conscious when she got out of the car. Now she's just fine.

"She much prefers to go with me, wherever we go. There have been a few trips, not too many, but I'd say several, where there was no need for her to go, other than she just wanted to be with me. That's sort of a hangover. But basically she's over all that—100 percent. And she can talk about it to other people."

Events broke down the last barriers for Gayle.

"We started the West Baden project in 1996," she said, referring to the biggest restoration of all they have taken on. "We had to go public then because we had to publicize the place. Then Bill became an Indiana University trustee—he of course was in the public eye. From there on we just kinda forgot about it."

Even the annual Forbes 400 list, which came out in September 2007, with Bill Cook listed No. 1 in Indiana and No. 65 in the United States with a net worth "guesstimated" at $4.5 billion, is no longer so nettling, Gayle said. "Not anymore, because we're used to it."

Carl Cook does not share his mother's resigned acceptance or her grace on that subject. "I have nothing good to say about Forbes or its list. It's nothing more than a shopping list for all the assholes in the world. Whenever they've contacted us, we've pretty much told them to go to hell. I will continue to do so."

KIDNAPPING REDUX

The Last Acts of Arthur Curry: The Aftermath

Arthur Curry was the thinking man's convict. Behind bars, he adapted to the environment quickly and figured out ways to exploit the system. During his year in the Monroe County Jail, he wrote an essay that authorities made into a book, *I'll Never Come Back,* adopted by the Indiana State Farm for distribution to prisoners about to be released. His yearlong conduct won him the support of Monroe County Jail chaplain J. Wesley Powell ("I don't think there's a harmful bone in his body. . . . Unlike other inmates I've known, his concerns were not about his case or even himself. Instead, he was worried about the other inmates").[15] That had to be an impressive plus for Judge James Dixon when he was weighing how severely to crack down on this model prisoner who had done a very bad thing.

Dixon's thirty-two-year sentence by Indiana law had theoretically guaranteed at least sixteen years with presumed good behavior, which was down to fifteen after the year he had served in Monroe County Jail.

It turned out to be eleven. While at Westville, Curry completed work on two degrees at Purdue University and that won him more points toward release. He was paroled on October 30, 2001. Six weeks ahead of that, under Indiana's victim notification law, Gayle Cook had been apprised.

For parole, Curry had needed a sponsor, someone guaranteeing he would have a job and an element of oversight. He got that in an Indiana University fraternity brother who was a lawyer at Wabash, a northern Indiana community of about 12,000. When he left Westville Correctional Facility, Wabash—in Wabash County, on the Wabash River and the old Wabash Railroad—welcomed Arthur Curry with warm hospitality.

His friend introduced him around Wabash to the town's leaders. He was "very open" about his past, Galen Bremmer, president of the Wabash Chamber of Commerce, told an interviewer—"very open" almost to the point of boasting, telling details of his calamitous life "from the standpoint of picking yourself up and rebuilding your life."[16] He took a sales job at the Wabash Ford dealership. Then he and his brother Daniel combined their middle names to form a construction company called Jackson Wallace. Arthur bought a sweeper store, a dry cleaner's, a big downtown building in which he opened Art's, a grocery, on the first floor, with Art's Apartments—neatly renovated by Jackson Wallace Construction—on the second and third floors. Arthur had just bought three doughnut shops in nearby Marion with plans to open one in Wabash when he sat down, confident and optimistic, with *Wabash Plain Dealer* news editor Roy Church the afternoon of June 10, 2003, to discuss his doughnut plans. Church got a story ready to run in the next day's paper. The story ran, but with a new lead. Arthur Curry and the police had met again.[17]

Not at Wabash—thirty-three miles up State Road 15 at Warsaw, Indiana.

Cook Inc. security director Dennis Troy had never lost track of Arthur Curry. "I followed him while he was in prison. When he got out, I checked up on him because I wanted to know where he was and what he was looking like, up-to-date pictures. I went to Wabash and got some surreptitious pictures of him (working as a Ford salesman). I brought them back so Bill and Gayle could know what he looked like. I found out where he lived, what kind of automobiles he had, just kept an eye on him."

Dennis Troy wasn't nearly as surprised as Wabash people when he heard Warsaw police had arrested Curry for stealing a car. "I went to Warsaw and met with the arresting officer. He told me Curry was driving a late-model GMC Jimmy. He parked it in a motel parking lot and walked across the street to a convenience store early in the morning, about 6 AM. An old car was sitting in the convenience store lot with the engine running. He just hopped in and drove off. People inside the convenience store saw it happen and called 911."

Warsaw is slightly smaller than Wabash. The police spotted the stolen car within minutes and "got in a high-speed chase," Troy said. When Curry lost control and wrecked the car, police ran him down as he fled on foot. When they closed in to make an easy arrest, they couldn't believe what they heard. Curry, hands up, pleaded, "Shoot me, just shoot me."[18]

Nobody thought about shooting. In Warsaw, it was a simple car theft, foiled by alert citizens. When Troy got there and heard the story, he smelled bigger game. "I told the Warsaw officers, 'Guys, he was up to something. That was the same M.O. he had when he grabbed Gayle Cook—he stole a car and used the car for commission of a crime. He was going to go commit another crime, maybe another kidnapping but probably a bank robbery. You might want to check to see if anything like that has happened around here, because I'll bet that's why he said, 'Shoot me.' Car theft alone isn't that big a deal."

He was jailed for car theft. There were no parole-violation strings; those had run out. Friends from Wabash put up $500 to guarantee his $5,000 bail and get him out to face charges the next week. The friends never saw him or their money again. He skipped town, leaving Daniel behind.

Almost three years later, on May 10, 2006, the U.S. attorney's office in Indianapolis announced that Arthur J. Curry, 58, and Daniel W. Curry, 60, had been formally charged with robbing four Indiana banks over a three-year period (2003–2006)—three in Terre Haute, the other in Kokomo—of just over $1 million in cash.

Daniel had been living in Bloomington. Arthur had been living in Greensboro, North Carolina, as Aldine Grey Hege Jr. The real Aldine Grey Hege Jr. was a disabled man who lived in Winston-Salem in the same boarding house with a friendly attorney with an Ivy League education who voluntarily helped him get some benefits. Nice guy, Arthur Curry. "He basically conned me out of my birth certificate and Social Security card," Hege said in an interview. "He was the same age as me, so I guess he thought he could become me."[19]

Before long, the new Aldine Grey Hege Jr. was living in a rented $250,000 home just off the fairway of a country club thirty miles away in Greensboro, active in a Baptist church, and in the luxury car business. "He had a used car lot where he sold high-end cars—Cadillac, Lexus, Mercedes," Troy said. "He was using bank-robbery money to bankroll it."

Arthur's brother wasn't as bright with his money. Repeated trips to Caesar's casino riverboat at Elizabeth, Indiana—in Harrison County, just a few miles from Cedar Farm, the Cooks' weekend home—put the FBI on Daniel's trail because he was spreading around bills that had been stained by the red dye banks use as a theft detector. Daniel was arrested in mid-February 2006, and police found thousands of dollars of the dyed bills in a storage unit he owned. The next month, Arthur Curry's car was stopped in Greensboro, and a routine check uncovered the 2003 Warsaw warrant for skipping out on the stolen-car charge. More checking found bank accounts in his name totaling $300,000. Police seized eleven cars and $89,000 in red-stained bills. Various items of disguise were found among the possessions of both. The federal indictment charged them with taking $301,000 from the Terre Haute First National Bank April 9, 2003 (two months before the Warsaw arrest); $394,000 from Old National Bank in Terre Haute on February 9, 2005; $80,000 from Regions Bank in Kokomo on December 9, 2005; and $225,000 from Fifth Third Bank in Terre Haute on January 19, 2006.[20] Additional charges might never be filed, but the Curry brothers are suspects in another nine bank robberies in Indiana and just over the state line in Louisville during that time.

The "M.O."—*modus operandi:* procedure—was consistent and similar to the kidnapping: disguises worn by both, stolen cars used. This time the guns were unquestionably real, and each warrant charged the two with brandishing the guns during the robbery—*brandishing:* a legal term, not just slang for carrying, meaning shaking or waving a weapon menacingly. Judge James Dixon had died at 72 on November 17, 2001 (three days before Curry's father, William, died at 82 in Sarasota, Florida). Had Dixon been alive at the time of the new arrests, surely he would have remembered those letters recommending leniency for fallen angel Arthur Curry: *not a dangerous person . . . not . . . really a danger to society . . . not a "hard-core" criminal.*

On June 1, 2007, new sentences came down: twenty-two years for Arthur, who had entered a plea of guilty; eighty years for Daniel, who pleaded not guilty and was convicted in federal court in Indianapolis. Federal laws allow no more than 20 percent off for good behavior, not 50 percent as in state courts. That meant a minimum of seventeen and a half years for Arthur, which would make him at least 76 when first eligible for parole in 2025. Daniel was looking at an earliest release of 2071, when he would be 126.

Police might not be done with them yet.

On September 20, 2006, yellow "Caution Police Line Do Not Cross" tapes went up around a downtown Wabash building once owned by Arthur Curry.[21] The remains of a man's body were found in the basement of the building, and police determined the man—identified by DNA evidence as Michael S. Wagner, last address in Fort Wayne—had been murdered. Wagner had been missing since 2002.[22]

The Currys' construction company had remodeled a top-floor apartment in the building, and one of the brothers was believed to have lived there. There was speculation that Wagner might have been murdered in the apartment and the body dragged downstairs. Wabash police said Wagner had worked for the Currys' construction firm.

Wagner was a victim with his own police history. "He was wanted for questioning in the murder of an elderly man and wife in Speedway, Indiana," Dennis Troy said. "It is my understanding that Wagner had befriended the couple." Joseph Krieger, 76, and his 77-year-old wife, Dorothy, were killed in their home the night of October 5–6, 2002.[23] Their car was recovered at Marion, Indiana. One of several guns stolen in the Speedway robbery-murder was in Arthur Curry's possession when he was arrested in North Carolina. On June 16, 2006, he pleaded guilty in a U.S. district court in North Carolina to being a felon in possession of two .38-caliber handguns and a .22-caliber rifle.

Then Wagner's body was discovered, and Wabash was abuzz with Arthur Curry rumors and murder rumors. Were the Currys involved in the Speedway murders *and* Wagner's murder? And there were rumors of the discovery of a second body.

Police weren't talkative. Investigations were unhurried, because authorities knew where to find the two if further prosecution were to come. Life outside prison walls might finally be over for Arthur Jackson Curry, risk-taker, but maybe not time in a courtroom.

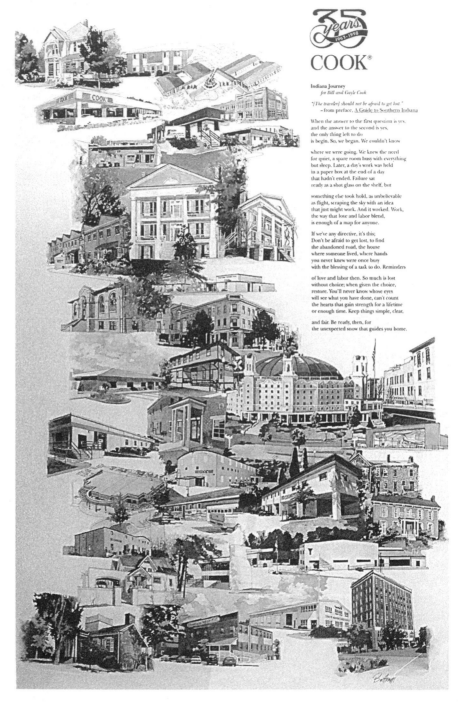

Bill and Gayle Cook's investments in renovation and restoration provided the theme for this painting along with their own poetic message, which was presented to them at the company's thirty-fifth anniversary dinner in 1998.

The Future

We have a good generation of leaders. When those people—Steve
Ferguson, Kem Hawkins, Scott Eells, Brian Bates—when people
like that start to retire, who's going to step in for them?
I'm sure it will work out, but where are they going to come from?
Who are they? Are they already here? That's what you always
worry about. You know that in ten or fifteen years you're
going to have a lot of different people in those very top roles.
Are they going to be as good or better than what we
have now? Because you've got to have that.

—*Carl Cook*

There will be no surprises in passage of the vast Cook Inc. company on Bill
Cook's death. That was one of the things taken care of after cardiologist
Larry Rink's 1998 advisory to him to "get your affairs in order"—after Rink
went to London in response to Cook's New Year's Eve heart attack, brought
him back to Bloomington for tests, and studied the test results.

"We didn't know much of anything then about inheritance laws," Bill
Cook said, "but, being in the financial situation we are, we worked harder
and faster to get our estate in order.

"One of the main things was to get stock transferred to Carl, so family
control would continue should something happen to me. At the time, Gayle
and I had fifty-fifty stock. It took us almost fifteen years to transfer the stock

Carl Cook

to Carl in an equitable way, so the taxes wouldn't kill the company. That can happen. You can kill your company by trying to get the stock transferred or to sell it to your children, because of the estate taxes."

One tax-free "pass-through" is permitted. Ownership could have been passed to Gayle with no complications, "because she is my partner. But there would be only one pass-through, not another one then from her to Carl. We had to bypass Gayle to get the stock to Carl now. That took a long time and a lot of planning and work."

It has been done, though even now it's not a completed process, Carl said. "It never ends. There's always some other maneuver you have to do, or a ruling comes in and you have to adjust something. But the bulk of what needs to be done has been done."

Carl Cook says his father "never said, 'I want you to take over.' He did say it was an option: 'You're going to have to sit down with these attorneys and decide what you want to do, because it's a ten- or fifteen-year process.'" Carl sat down with estate specialists—several times, with one basic choice to make. "The estate planners tell you that you can have either the money or the control," Carl said. "If you want the money, you basically have to sell the company and you get half the money, Uncle Sam gets half. Or you can do a whole bunch of very complicated things and you can keep control of the company, but you're not going to get huge sums of money out of it.

"I was the heir. I had to make the decision. If I hadn't wanted to have anything to do with the company, that would have led to one direction. But

I wanted to see it stay private. The only way to guarantee that was to stay in it. I could take all this money and run, but that would leave everybody else in the company with the very strong possibility that they wouldn't have a job.

"My attitude is that most of the people who work here know that if they don't do their job, they can lose their job and damage the company. But no matter how well they do their job, that's no guarantee they can keep their job if the company gets sold. A decision that we as a family make can completely neutralize all the work that they put into it. They don't control their destiny, beyond just doing their job."

Those Cook employees who have always felt—and been—high on Bill Cook's priority list represent a legacy that Carl prizes. "Yes," he said, "because No. 1, it's just a nicer place to work if everybody is being treated well—attitudes are better, morale is better, everybody helps each other. I don't have a frame of reference. I do visit other companies, and there are some where you think, 'I could fit right in here,' and others where you think, 'God, what an awful place this is. Let's get the hell out of here.'

"Enron had this Darwinistic management theory that they fired 10 percent of the people every year, whether they needed to be fired or not. They would jettison the bottom 10 percent every year. What an asinine idea. You have everybody trying to upstage each other, trying to make the other guy look bad, push themselves up. A lot of other companies have not gone to that extreme, but office politics is a big part of the work day.

"There's politics here, don't get me wrong. But if everybody feels they're going to be treated fairly, to be listened to, there's no such thing as 'That's not my job.' You do the work that needs to be done. It makes everything more pleasant for everybody. I think that's why a lot of people stay here even though they probably could make more money somewhere else. I'm told our health benefits do that as well. If the employees feel part of the company, they're going to make the right decisions. They're going to think of the patient first."

Ah, prevalent pleasance! He heard a comment from an outsider about the unusual ratio of smiles in the Cook Inc. corridors. "That," Carl Cook the engineering graduate said, "is the nitrous oxide in the building." Laughing gas.

For Just $200 Million . . .

He's of the Today Generation, but Carl Cook doesn't seem inclined to depart radically from his father's appreciation for handshake business dealing.

"You do pay a price sometimes for being trusting. And we have. You just have to take that as a cost of doing business. If you like somebody and you trust them, it's a heck of a lot easier to do business with them. And if they like you and trust you, it's a lot easier.

"When you get in a situation where you're either not trusting or you're bound by your own procedures, it gets very hard to do business. 'We're going to have to draw up an agreement for that,' or 'I need that in writing'—you spend more time arguing and doing paperwork than you need. If you can be trusting, it's much more efficient. If you're not trusting, you've always got lawyers in the mix, and that slows everybody down."

His 2008 assessment of the business State of the Company is positive. "I'm very happy with what's going on right now. The key is to always have one or more big products that are in the growth phase. Right now for us it's the Triple-A stent. It's growing, and it's generating a lot of money. It's a new medical procedure that's still got several years of growth and involvement. It will flatten out. We need to have something else then that is big and growing. But for a good long while, it's going to be Triple-A."

He sees some candidates for a product leadership role in the future, "but they're in the research stage. We don't know if they're going to work. We're moving farther up the aorta [with stents]. It's going to be seven to ten years before we've got a full product line that covers all the big aneurysms. I think that's going to dominate for a while. There's always a chance something will turn into a surprise. We've got some products like the vena cava filter that are growing and generate lots of money, but they're not as big as Triple-A."

From its earliest years, Cook Inc. has thrived on ideas coming in from doctors who are familiar with its capabilities as a research company. That's still happening, but not so much—as in the good ol' days—from doctors who in their practice have run into a particular problem and think they have a suggestion that might solve it, with Cook Inc.'s help. Now the aim is bigger, and the "Eureka!" flashes are followed by visions of big, big money. Carl, with his role in running the satellite company MyoSite, already has heard some of those, and he uses his humor to draw up a sardonic scenario: "When a doctor comes in to propose this great idea he has for treating this disease—I'm exaggerating a bit, but the presentation goes something like this:

1. The United States population is 280 million;
2. Out of that number, 300 million are at risk for this disease;
3. Out of that 300 million, 400 million are going to be seeking treatment;
4. And out of that 400 million, 500 million are going to want this device.

"They want $200 million up front, and they'll give you the patent."

MyoSite research in summer 2007 was "in the outer reaches of something I really don't understand—taking your own cells and injecting them into the various sphincters of your body and repairing them," Bill Cook said. Popular usage of *sphincter* (the anus) differs only in breadth from the word's medical definition ("a circular band of muscle that surrounds an opening in the body, especially the anus, and can narrow or close the opening by contracting"). Involuntary urination is among the non-anal problems the research seeks to cure. "It is particularly adaptable to people who have urinary sphincters that have gone haywire for whatever reason. It's had some interesting results in Canada. It has the capability of repairing them, which is a phenomenal advancement if we can pull this off—and if we can get FDA approval to do it."

Therein is an illustration of Carl's scenario in action. "Probably 200,000 people have the problem," Carl said, "but not all of them need to be treated— maybe 50,000. No matter how good our product is, not all of those are going to come to us. I could hope for 30,000. I'd take 10,000."

Carl Cook

We had a little bit of everything in our neighborhood, but it was mostly university. A professor lived across the street from us who was a socialist, but a happy socialist. We got along great with him. In the election of 1972, he put a McGovern sign in our yard, and my dad put a Nixon sign in his. It was a lot of fun.

—*Carl Cook*

No potential owner ever grew up with a company more literally than Carl Alfred Cook, who was born in August 1962, and was still five weeks away from his first birthday when, on July 1, 1963, Cook Inc. came into being.

It's inaccurate to say he grew up as a child of wealth. There was no wealth in his earliest years. When it came, he had parents determined to keep from him its trappings. He grew up in the only house he knew, in a neighborhood close enough to public school he could walk—one of the virtues Gayle Cook prized about Bloomington.

"I don't know if Carl even remembers this, but he walked to Elm Heights [an elementary school], and when he went from there to Binford [for seventh and eighth grades], I told him, 'I'm not going to drive you. We're within a mile, you can walk or ride your bike.'

"So, a year ahead of time, he decided he wanted a bigger bike [replacing one his parents had bought him] for riding to Binford, because not only would he have his backpack of books but he would also be carrying his big saxophone.

"So we said, 'If you want a new bike, you'll have to save your money for it.' There aren't too many ways to save money at that age, but he did some odd jobs—he rewebbed some lawn chairs and did things for the neighbors. Fall came, and the bike was $125. He was $10 short. We didn't hand him the $10. He walked to school until he thought and found something he could do to come up with $10. And, boy, did he take care of that bike. My point is this town allowed us to live very normally. I value that."

He didn't have an RMK label—rich man's kid—with his earliest school peers. His father's financial standing wasn't something that occurred even to him until "Dad spoke at the 1972 company Christmas potluck and said, 'This year we'll be a $4 million company.'" Carl was 10. "A million anything when you're that age is impressive. That's when I realized maybe we were doing a little better than most people.

"By middle school, the company was big enough that there were kids whose parents worked in the company. I started sensing that certain kids were treating me differently than they otherwise would. People started saying my dad was a millionaire—sixth, seventh, eighth grade.

"When I got to high school and had a wider group of friends, there were kids I knew whose parents didn't like me—they were university egalitarian and I was this capitalist. One girl I knew, her mom was far to the left of Karl Marx. Her dad was fine, but her mom—what do you do?"

A Bloomington Man at Purdue

In Carl's junior high and high school years, Indiana University basketball was the biggest thing going in Indiana, let alone Bloomington. He went to every home game, watching the Hoosiers go unbeaten in winning the national championship his seventh-grade year and win the championship again in his senior year at Bloomington High School South (1981).

"I knew fairly early in high school that I probably was going to want to go for engineering as a major. That narrows your schools down right off the bat." For one, it eliminated Indiana University, which has no engineering school. "I didn't want to go to IU. What's the point of that? Our house is closer to the main part of campus than half the dorms. So even though I was going to be an IU fan, I wasn't going to IU.

"I wanted to stay in the Big Ten. Sports was kind of important to me. I figured wherever I went in the Big Ten I would get to see IU play at least once a year.

"Engineering was hard to get into at the time. I only applied to Purdue and Illinois, and at Illinois you apply for an application. I had been accepted at Purdue before the application came from Illinois. I never bothered with it. I figured Purdue was better anyway."

Purdue is a highly respected engineering school. To Carl Cook, everything about that decision was logical, except for the sports part. Indiana and Purdue are two of college athletics' archetype archrivals.

As a Bloomington native and overt IU fan at Purdue, he said, and even when he was away from school back home, "It was a little rough. Up there I was a spy; down here I was a traitor, even though I came back for probably half the home games. Up there or down here I caught all sorts of hell if Purdue beat IU. On the other hand, I remember one time Indiana came up there to play, Purdue was going for the Big Ten championship, and Indiana beat 'em by about twenty-nine points. A guy stuck a note on my door: 'Say one word, Carl, and you're dead meat.'

"I get asked: What's the difference between IU and Purdue? Aside from the majors—one's liberal arts and one's conservative arts—IU at some level subconsciously understands that today's students are tomorrow's alumni, and if you want to raise money from them, you'd better make sure they leave happy. Purdue doesn't understand that. To some professors there, students, particularly undergrads, were these time- and resource-consuming leeches that 'interfere with my research and use up resources, take away my valuable time—I could be writing grants instead of teaching these stupid sophomores.' In the so-called counseling office, if you complained about anything, they would say, 'Look, a hundred guys want your spot. If you don't like it here, leave.' They told me that, to my face. There was absolutely no welcoming attitude for students there once you got out of freshman engineering."

A Secret Kept

By his Purdue years (1981–84), there was wealth in the family, but it wasn't generally known two hours north of Bloomington at Purdue. "I was almost completely anonymous. Aside from the bio-med guys whom Dad had worked with, I had one professor who had met my dad because he was an airplane pilot and had flown to Bloomington."

The virtual anonymity followed him into graduate school at the University of Iowa, where there was less of the "IU fan" stigma, although it is a fellow Big Ten conference member with Indiana and Purdue. At Iowa, he said, "I didn't let on where I was from. A couple of days before I graduated, a woman who was also in the MBA program and her husband threw a party, and she told me her father was head of radiology at one of the big hospitals in Des Moines. So all along she had known me, but she said, 'I could sense you were trying to keep that quiet.' I thanked her for that. It was a nice gesture."

He left Iowa in May 1987, with his master's degree in business administration—and impressed. "The attitude there toward students is very good—much better than Purdue, probably not as good as IU. If I had known then what I know now, I would have gone to Iowa for engineering. You're going to learn the basics at any accredited school, so I don't think it would have made any difference in the long run, and I would have had more fun."

From Iowa, he didn't move straight into a Bloomington office. "I went to Europe to work for a year, then to Pittsburgh for ten years, then to Winston-Salem. I was there about a year and a half. Then I came back here."

It's an early-career hurry-through that his father dissects in a little more detail. "He went out on his own—he spent a year going back and forth from France and Germany, setting up our computers over there. That was his first job, getting a little feel for the company, seeing if he wanted to do it. He was very good with computers. His next job was at Cook Pacemaker Corp. in Leechburg, Pennsylvania. He was instrumental in taking them out of the pacemaker business and into other products. After that, he went to the Cook plant at Winston-Salem; he was there two years. After fourteen years, he came back. He's running the company [MyoSite] now in Pittsburgh."

For the past few years, his duties have included oversight of the extensive renovation projects at the French Lick and West Baden hotels and management of the two operations. Busy schedule.

"I always told Carl it's a lot better to govern than it is to be a part of operations," Bill Cook said. "By govern I mean you set policy and you find good people to do the things that need to be done. For an operations person like I was, you're always looking to the problems of the operation, and you never have time to smell the flowers. I think he has that sense for governing and having the vice presidents do the actual operating. Gayle and I have been very happy. Carl has grown up to be a well-rounded person."

And they were even happier on January 5, 2008, when—in a ceremony at the picturesque West Baden Springs Hotel he had helped to restore—Carl left bachelorhood to marry Marcy Heshelman. They had met when Marcy was working in the auditing department at Cook Inc.

Meeting of the Generations

Carl, the second generation of the Cook family, probably will have a lot of years ahead working with the second generation of the Pritchett Bros. Construction Company.

Carl Cook and Joe, Scott, Eddie, and Jon Pritchett are united by, among other things, pigeon poop.

The four Pritchetts are brothers, sons of Richard Pritchett, who with his own brother, Charlie, has been handling almost all construction for Bill Cook since 1964.

In his early teens Carl worked summers for the older Pritchetts, along-side the younger Pritchetts, starting on the first of the restoration jobs Bill and Gayle Cook took on.

It's called the Cochran House. When it first came to the attention of the Bloomington Restorations organization in the mid-1970s, it was called the Lindley House. It was big and old and threatened, its distinguished history masked by dilapidation. It was in a primary downtown area, where housing starts a few blocks northwest of the courthouse, but it wasn't easy to spot—"this nice house behind nine other buildings, shacks, in the front yard," Gayle Cook said. "We had never noticed it before, but Bloomington Restorations got a little publicity about it in the paper because the owner was threatening to tear it down. Bill and I went past and looked at it. The company was looking for an office at the time for Monroe Guaranty Insurance Co. We thought, why don't we try renovating that?"

Monroe Guaranty was one of the early Cook Inc. satellite companies, formed to handle the young company's own product liability insurance and growing quickly to something much broader. "We got up to about $30 million in premiums—we were writing more outside of Cook than insuring Cook," the company's first treasurer (and Monroe Guaranty operating head) Phil Hathaway said. "It just became a general property and casualty insurance company. We insured the City of Bloomington for a while."

But first there was a lot of work to be done on the Cochran House, starting with clean-up. That's where the second generation of Cooks and Pritchetts came in.

"The Pritchett kids and I worked as laborers [under Pritchett Bros. Construction]," Carl said. "Ed was a year older than me and Jon was a year younger. I was 13, just old enough to legally work. All three of us worked on the Cochran House. We were demolition and sweeping-and-shoveling. When we did the pigeon stuff, we wore masks. We'd knock it out of the ceiling—the easiest way to get it out was to get up above it, stand on the joists, and bang it down with crowbars and hammers. It was waist-high on the floor when it was done. Then we had to shovel it all out the window onto dump trucks."

"Oh," Jon Pritchett says, breaking into a grin, "absolutely I remember that. Carl and I go way back. We worked at the YMCA one whole summer—swept floors, cleaning it every day. That was a fun, long job. It made me figure out I didn't want to be a broom-sweeper the rest of my life."

"The biggest job I worked on was the Graham [restoration of the Graham Hotel]," Carl said. "That was the most fun. We did demolition, and I also ran the manual elevator."

The Start in Restoration

While Carl and the Pritchetts were working on the Cochran House interior, Gayle was tracking down the building's history in old newspaper files and other archives. It was a stately place, three stories and a basement, red brick with white pillars out front. James Cochran, a Connecticut native whose interests included liquor, grist mills, and real estate, was 61 when he built it in 1849 for his wife and their three children. Little more than a year later, Cochran died, and his widow sold the building in 1852 to Andrew Helton, who had moved up from Kentucky. He and wife Hannah had eleven children, but the house survived—sold in 1869 to former Indiana governor Paris Dunning. Two more changes of ownership put it in the hands of Bloomington's first pharmacist, Hiram Lindley, who raised a family that included Ernest Lindley, who taught at IU for twenty-four years before becoming president of the University of Idaho and then chancellor of Kansas University. Buildings at all three places are named for him.

The Lindleys had the house until 1910, hence the Lindley House name it carried when Bloomington Restorations Inc. first set out to save it. By then it desperately needed help. After the Lindleys, it fell on hard times. The Monon Railroad had it for a while, and it went bawdy—a stop-over place for railroad workers, "Monon Flats," a house known for gambling, drinking, and prostitution.[1]

Gayle Cook chose to restore the name of Cochran House. "James Cochran built it. He was quite a well-to-do businessman. He had a lumberyard, and that's why there's nice woodwork in there."

The restoration was going on in 1976 and 1977. Bill Cook by then was taking brisk nightly walks in his recovery from 1974 heart surgery. Gayle tried, then gave up on regularly walking with him because of his swift pace. But, she said, "We often would walk over to the Cochran House at night to see what had been done during the day.

"We kept track of the expenses—the purchase price, everything—to see when we were finished if we had saved money by renovating, rather than putting up a new building. It turned out we had. We made all three floors usable—2,500 square feet on each floor, 7,500 square feet. The cost ["$45 a square foot, finished—not bad," Bill said] was lower than building something like that new. Plus, it got so much free publicity and produced so much goodwill on the west side [the center of Bloomington's early African American community, which included a segregated school and a community center].

"This was really the first improvement in that area. Across the street is the Second Baptist Church. The church was so grateful to get rid of the eyesore.

"Then we bought the property across the street that was the old Seward Machine Shop [built in the early twentieth century]. It was really a hole after years and years of greasy machining. We rebuilt that and bought the property north, which had been Beasley Foods, and made that look better. Then I think next came the old Monon Depot downtown and the Graham Hotel.

"At the same time we were doing the Cochran House, we were doing the Colonel Jones House down in Spencer County. But we weren't rushing that. The Pritchetts did it, too, but only as they had time. We were mainly trying to get the Cochran House done."

And Bill and Gayle Cook were off on the mission that is the distinguishing, satisfying glory of their senior years.

The Guise of Modernization

The 1970s was at the beginning of a national concern for restoration and preservation of sites with at least community history. Gayle said, "I was on the State Historic Preservation Review board for many years, and we've been in touch through the years with the National Trust [for Historic Preservation]."

With his grounding in the pigeon leftovers, Carl Cook acquired his own preservation interests. "I wouldn't say acquired," he said. "I was around it when we did the Cochran House, the Jones House, the Graham Hotel. I thought it was neat to go look at a building and see how it would change. It has always bothered me to look at an old building that had been modernized and think, 'Why did they put that ceiling in like that?' I always think a building looks better the way it was originally built. The upgrade very rarely is an improvement. I've seen a lot of buildings ruined in the guise of modernization."

Pete Yonkman

I've heard people wondering where we're going to get
our next leaders. A lot of them are already here.

—*Bill Cook*

The lawyer who joined the Cook corporation during the Guidant negotiations is one example of the in-place young leaders who could be a part of the Cook Inc. management future.

When the job as president of Cook Urological opened, including management of a 500-employee plant at nearby Spencer, it went to Pete Yonkman, as his introduction outside law practice and into management. Then, in early 2008, Yonkman was named executive vice president of global sales marketing and moved back into Park 48, Cook headquarters in Bloomington; Derek Voskuil replaced him at Spencer.

Yonkman grew up in Indiana (Crown Point, with a county jail that John Dillinger made famous by breaking out of with a phony gun). At IU, he says, "I had a double major in psychology and philosophy. So I was . . . virtually unemployable."

Son of a lawyer, he went to IU Law School. He was practicing on the staff of a Michigan insurance company, about to start a new job in a Detroit law firm, when Phyllis McCullough (who knew him because her daughter Liz married Yonkman's IU roommate) called. "They were going through the original Guidant process, and they decided they needed some additional legal help.

"Amazing timing. The next day I was going to start. And I loved Bloomington. I jumped at the chance to do world-class work in a small midwestern college town, a great place to live."

That was in 2000, when Pete Yonkman was still in his mid-twenties. His next few years were nightmarish. When the Guidant deal finally collapsed, he says, "I don't even remember my original reaction. There was a flurry of activity, then a week when all of a sudden everything was calm. It was just refreshing to be able to go back to regular business, doing the things we like to do.

"One thing it did for me: nothing seems all that daunting anymore. Any project you get into, 'That seems easy . . . relatively speaking.'"

After the Guidant days, his Cook Inc. work focused on "helping to establish Cook Japan and Cook China, working with our distributors over there, which got me into the business side." That came in handy with his job shift in September 2005 to Spencer and a major operation to run. Right away, ready or not. "I plunged right in, in the great Cook tradition of creating jobs and putting people in the deep end to see if they swim."

Yonkman is big, his words come out fast, soft, thought-out, humor-spiced. "Cook Urological to me was a whole new challenge outside legal work. I enjoy legal analysis and problem-solving, but I enjoy working with people more, trying to get what they're capable of doing—build as opposed to tear down, which a lot of times you're doing in legal work.

"This company is getting so big it's hard to know everything that's going on. A legal position is really an interesting seat to have. I'm pretty well integrated into what's happening across the company. We get to know the big issues.

"At Spencer I had this big operational facility. I got to watch over two of the company's business units, women's health and urology, see what happens on that end of the marketplace.

"We're going through a period of really strong growth. We've got a lot of immediate goals for our women's health and urology. We have momentum going. I feel like we're so close to being able to make those two business units something special. We're sort of where Cook Inc. was maybe fifteen years ago. If we can have that one really big product, Spencer can be like Park 48 ten years from now."

It's on its way. In September 2007, the corporation announced expansion that will add 50,000 square feet to the 104,000 square foot Spencer plant. Park 48, after an expansion completed in 2007, is just under 1 million.

Searching for Simple Answers

When Bill Cook was Yonkman's age, Cook Inc. was still just a gleam in his eye. Now he's a working example for the Yonkman generation to observe.

Bill Cook is lawyer Pete Yonkman's business school. As he studies and observes, his own psychology and philosophy learnings come into play.

"I watch the way Bill evaluates people, his understanding of human nature," Yonkman says. "He's able to do a size-up faster than anybody I've ever seen—what they're capable of getting done and whether they're good at doing it. When he finds that combination, he's able to fuel that and make that person successful. He's really good at putting the pieces together and identifying what drives people and how best to use that.

"The most enjoyment I get out of the non-legal part of my job is trying to figure out those triggers that get people to perform at their highest level. I'm obviously not nearly as good as Bill at understanding human nature, and I do know sometimes it doesn't work. But when you have a success, when you really figure it out—they've been in the wrong spot, not achieving what they can, then you see them turn the corner and they're off and running—that is really pretty cool.

"Another thing I've noticed with Bill is that he's extremely curious. That's the core of what drives him, listening to see what's working and what's not working, whatever avenue of life he's talking about.

"And when he has the information and sees an opportunity, he's willing to bet on that. Where some people will just put their toe in the water, he's willing to go all the way."

It's still a spirit he sees in Cook and in Cook Inc. "I've thought a lot about this company's future. We are situated in an interesting spot, with Pharmica, MyoSite, these advanced technologies. You always hear, 'All of these products we have today will be going away. New technologies will come.' But look at these products we've had for forty years, and a lot of them are still around. I'm not sure that isn't going to be the case ten years from now.

"Of course there will be new biologics and drugs that definitely will be a part of where we are headed. But if you look at the cost of health care, I think there will always be room for a company creating simple solutions for problems. Everybody's trying to build the next complex biologic or synthetic, solve all these very complex problems. Obviously we need to be there and understand those technologies.

"But over time the way technology works is the level of complexity rises until somebody comes up with a simple solution, then it drops down, then rises, then drops. We may just be going through a period where everybody is obsessed with advance technologies and really complex solutions. One of our strengths is that we build simple solutions.

"I've always heard Bill talk about that: simple solutions for complex problems. There's a lot to be said for that."

The Basketball Team

Every one of those athletes has just been superb. The four basketball players came in at about the same time—just a perfect time. We were going through a growth phase and had to have more professional-type managers. These are just guys who are bright as they come. They would have excelled anywhere they went. They're all aggressive, and competitors, every one of them. They'll eat you alive.

—*Bill Cook*

The immediate Cook Inc. future will have major involvement that the Bloomington populace—and most of Indiana's—will feel like standing up and cheering for.

Before they became Cook executives-in-training, John Kamstra, Scott Eells, Chuck Franz, and Wayne Radford wore the red and white warm-up pants of Indiana University's basketball team. The four's fifteen cumulative IU varsity years included just one of stardom: Radford's senior season. All four are big stars now at Cook Inc., living rebuttals to "jock" jokes.

Their company success hasn't surprised Bill Cook; their common denominator was selection and retention by one of college athletics' most demanding coaches. "You will notice they are Bob Knight athletes," he semi-jokes. "We felt if they could survive the Bob Knight School of Etiquette, they could survive anything."

Franz said when he was approaching graduation at IU in August 1984, he applied with three companies—RCA and Cook in Bloomington and Cummins Diesel in Columbus. "Coach Knight asked me which one I would prefer, and I said Cook because I knew the other basketball players were out there.

Former Indiana University basketball players who hold key positions at Cook Inc. *From left:* Chuck Franz, Wayne Radford, Scott Eells, and John Kamstra.

"The four of us who work here, and Scott May as well—to be able to grow up with them in this company is just fun. We all went through something basically together. That's the background of 'Let's get tough,' with Coach Knight."

It was part of a universal message in Knight's IU years, but one that came through to Chuck Franz tailored, personal. Franz arrived in the same freshman class with All-American Isiah Thomas and drew the humbling job of guarding instant star Thomas daily in practice. "In the locker room, Coach would get on Isiah—'If you make that mistake in the NBA, Isiah, you think you're going to be on that team, or is that coach just going to trade you?' When he looked at me, he said, 'Chuck, if your boss continually asks you to do something and you don't do it, do you think you're going to have a job?' It was never about the NBA with me. But it's being taught to be a part of a team, and the work ethic—that comes with all of us. We were taught that, we were trained that; it isn't limited to basketball."

Phyllis McCullough, primarily responsible for the hirings, laughs about her basketball "team." "Sometimes I tell them they know too well how to be role players. Their Knight training didn't all wear off. Sometimes they have to break out of the box a little bit.

"One day Bob had a prospect in town on a recruiting visit, and I saw Scott, Wayne, and John standing in the lobby with their coats on. I asked them what they were doing, and they said, 'Coach Knight called and we're going out to Assembly Hall.'

"I said, 'You know, he's not your boss anymore.' Just to jog their memory."

Through Knight's Indiana years, Cook said, "Every year, on the first day of practice in October, those guys would get together, close the door, light up cigars, and the stories would fly."

John Kamstra

Kamstra, the third player recruited by new Indiana coach Knight in the spring of 1971, had his promising basketball career curtailed by a severed Achilles tendon in his sophomore year. Knight—whose long list of outstanding IU guards included four first-round NBA draft picks—always maintained Kamstra would have been one of his best. But for Kamstra, instead of a possible NBA career he was redirected and came out just fine.

"John was the first one of the basketball players we hired," McCullough said. "After he got hurt, he worked part-time for us in the office with his leg in a big cast. In 1975 and 1976, we had an awful lot of money in the bank, and it really wasn't earning anything. John had graduated and gone to work for an Indianapolis accounting firm. I called him about being an inside accounting person for Cook. He interviewed and took the job."

Now he is the company's chief financial officer—"very conservative, so conservative he squeaks," Cook says, "unlike Steve Ferguson and me. We're more aggressive in spending money than I think John would like. He makes a great counterbalance. John is just a superb financial manager who understands how a corporation has to work with money."

Scott Eells and Wayne Radford

After a career mostly as a reserve that did get him a 1976 NCAA championship ring, Scott Eells, six-feet-nine, graduated and took a job in Greensburg, Indiana.

"At almost the same time, Wayne Radford [another '76 Hoosier who had one season in the NBA] was working for Columbus Container, and we were a customer," McCullough said. "I really liked his personality. I thought he was a good sales person. So I had Scott and Wayne both out to dinner, before a basketball game, and we hired them both."

They went on different career paths with Cook Inc. "Scott was much more of a production-oriented, operational-type person," she said. "I offered him a job—to come in and work in management training and operations." Not sales. "Scott just did not have the sales attitude—there was no B.S., no salesmanship to him. He liked mechanical things."

"Because of his general manufacturing ability, Scott could run this company as well as anybody," Cook says. "He doesn't really like sales. He loves manufacturing. And that's exactly what he should be doing. He's a problem-solver. He's executive vice president of operations, second in charge of this company. He could be first except he just gravitates to operations and loves to work with his hands. He's very good with his hands and thinks three-dimensional."

Sales did fit Radford. "Wayne's like the other three, very bright," Cook said. "He runs our Critical Care Division. He takes care of the marketing. He's pretty much the main guy. I was hoping he would have an interest in doing purchasing and all other types of managerial jobs with the exception of production. It didn't take long to figure out that he didn't like that. Wayne wanted to be on the outside. He loved selling, and he was good at it. Still is. But he sat on an airplane too long with his legs crossed (he is six-feet-four), developed phlebitis, and it almost killed him. He *had* to come in off the road."

Chuck Franz

"I found Chuck on a road gang," Bill Cook says.

It's not *that* kind of prototypical Cook-hiring story. Three years into his college career, Franz switched from a business major to computer science. Cook himself was the resident computer specialist at Cook Inc., and he knew of Franz's abilities. Franz indeed was in cutoffs on a hot August afternoon, filling a hole in a gravel road when Cook drove past. "We knew each other. I waved, and he waved," Franz says.

"I went out specifically to see him," Cook said. "I didn't get him then. I think Phyllis ran him down. But I knew he was a computer major, and I knew what people thought of him. Chuck definitely is one of the key players in the company and has been for many years. He has taken over companies we needed somebody to run until we could find a permanent president. He ran Cook Pacemaker in Pennsylvania. He has been overseas in Europe. He operated Cook Urological for years.

"He has a terrific mind, plus he is an absolute computer genius. He can see a problem with a computer and solve that problem, and most of the time he does it himself. He's solving the computer problems down at French Lick—buying and modifying the software. His title is vice president of Cook Group, but it won't surprise me if he goes out to another Cook company and runs it. He can run almost everything. He is sort of like John Kamstra—an egghead, if you will, who has an innate sense of the right things to do."

Dave Volz

Pole-vaulter Dave Volz is the non-basketball player among the IU athletes Bill Cook has assembled—"operations vice president, right under Scott Eells. Same thing—aggressive, competitive, bright, good management skills. Both he and Scott know how to be friendly without being friends, very firm, fair, and they know how to lead."

Volz was the best athlete of the bunch, maybe the best ever to graduate from a Bloomington high school. A state and national pole-vault champion while in high school, he won the NCAA championship as a freshman at IU in 1981. The summer of 1982, he twice broke the American record—20 years old and on track to be the world's first nineteen-foot pole-vaulter when a vaulting pit accident in Europe severely fractured an ankle, effectively ending his championship collegiate career. He was unable to compete for a spot on the 1984 U.S. Olympic team, still wasn't competitive in 1988, but in 1992, ten years after his injury, he won an Olympic berth and at Barcelona used wile and guile under awful vaulting conditions to finish fifth, barely missing a medal.

His comeback got him to Cook Inc., and Cook helped get him to Barcelona.

In the late 1980s, McCullough said, "Sam Bell [Volz's IU coach] called and said Dave needed a job where he could stay in Bloomington and work out at IU for the Olympics. We gave him a job at a warehouse in Ellettsville, where he could make his own hours and leave whenever he had to for training. It was so great when he made the team and got to go to Barcelona. We had a sales office in Barcelona. Our manager over there opened his house to Sam Bell and Marcie [Volz, Dave's wife and Bell's secretary when they met] for them to stay while Dave was there.

"Then he came back with us after the Olympics. We trained him in production management. He became operations manager for our Ellettsville plant, working under Scott Eells. They work well together. That's how Dave moved up."

"Up" is the common direction for Volz. In 2007, Cook said, "He vaulted fifteen feet just to show his kid he could do it. Fifteen feet, and the man is 45 years old!"

Scott May

He's not a direct Cook Inc. employee, but Scott May was the best basketball player of all the Hoosiers with Cook ties—1975–76 College Player of the Year, two-time first-team All-American, an Olympic gold medalist and starter, the second player taken in the NBA college draft. After a twelve-year professional career, an injury-shortened six seasons in the NBA and six as a top American star in Europe, May joined a division of Cook—CFC, whose president, Steve Ferguson, was his attorney and his basketball agent as soon as May's college career ended.

For nearly twenty years, May has been in Bloomington, affiliated with CFC but active on his own as an owner and manager of apartments. "Steve Ferguson, I, CFC, Bob Knight, Mike Woodson, all of us have a financial link with Scott's business, as investors in many of his ventures," Cook says, "and all have paid off. He has picked and bought well and run these things superbly—18 percent return, what more could you ask for? He just has a nose for business. It's pretty unusual, I think, to have a great athlete so interested and so astute as he is. It's just having that innate ability to see things that others don't. And he's tighter than the bark on a tree."

Woodson is another with Cook-IU basketball ties, through investment partnerships with May and Ferguson. After an eleven-year NBA career, he has been head coach of the Atlanta Hawks since 2005. "Mike's an absolutely super person," Cook said. "In my opinion, he could have been the coach at IU [the job was open in the spring of 2006, and again in 2008]. He was ready. His experience in the NBA would help, and he would be a superb recruiter."

The Team That Was

May took on a key role in one of Bill Cook's most bizarre enterprises. "Scott was still playing over in Italy when I decided I wanted to have a pro basketball team, but not in the United States. We found out that Manchester United [in Manchester, England] had a team that was available." Manchester United's big worldwide identification is in soccer, but it did have a British Basketball League franchise. "They offered us the soccer team for $13.5 million and taking over an $11.2 million debt. I turned it down. I hate to think how much it's worth now—many times what it would have cost us.

"They almost gave the basketball team to us; we just took it off their hands because it was losing money. They had never been close to winning anything till we got there.

"Our first game we had three paying spectators."

May became "pretty much the general manager. He played one more year in Italy and then he was commuting to Manchester from Bloomington for about nine years. He wasn't coaching or playing, but he was there all week, and our coaches would listen to him. And he was doing the recruiting.

"We got to where we had some good crowds, 3,500 to 4,000. Several times we made a run for the championship and couldn't quite get there. That's when we decided we'd buy the championship."

The British Basketball League operated with salary limitations (a low-scale version of the NBA's salary cap), but Cook tired of losing to teams he felt were winking at the rule. "We picked up any player who wanted to come, no matter what he charged us."

And on May 7, 2000, a Manchester newspaper story began: "Indiana's winning touch at developing championship-caliber basketball teams even extends overseas, as the Manchester Giants, a professional team owned by Cook Group International, swept to its first ever national championship." Birmingham fell in the final, 76–65, Manchester's 45–7 season setting a league record. The team had no former IU players but did have two from the Big Ten: Roy Hairston of Purdue and Travis Conlan of Michigan.

"Then," Cook said, "the year after we won it, we said, 'This is hopeless.' We couldn't get the people of the league to put in any money. 'Sky,' the big satellite there, like DirecTV here, came in for one year, and it was amazing how things picked up. We had 16,000 at one game. We were wanting to put in money and maybe even get up on a satellite with our own advertising and make something out of the league, but we couldn't do it alone.

"Even the NBA has had problems getting anything going with British basketball. Spain, Germany, Italy, France, Greece—they're all going well with basketball. Basketball never reached those heights there."

Nobody's Going to Argue

> Much of our success against competition derives
> from the ability our computer system gives us
> to process orders and control inventory.
>
> —*Bill Cook*

There are, on the ubiquitous Forbes 400 list, many who got there as computer whizzes. Bill Gates is the king, but there are others not far below him. Two have a link with Bloomington. Mark Cuban and Todd Wagner's passions for Indiana University basketball and their occupational location in Dallas way outside the range of the IU Radio Network led in 1995 to their developing Audionet, which in 1998 became Broadcast.com, and by 1999 was such a mushrooming giant that at the height of the dot-com boom Cuban and Wagner sold out to Yahoo! for more than $6 billion, and each was a Forbesian.

Bill Cook represents the opposite. He built his medical devices company and his fortune, then cultivated a fascination for computers that he personally put to work. In 1976, when Cook Inc. was 13 years old and annual sales for the first time reached $10 million—hallelujah time, but less than 1 percent of today's $1.2 billion—Bill was involved with Phyllis McCullough's

Dairy Lea Trophy won by the Manchester Giants in 2000.
Bill Cook's effort to build interest in professional basketball
in England led to what he calls "the world's ugliest trophy."

husband, Jerry, and his Data Solutions Inc. in bringing computers to the
Cook kingdom.

"I recognized that the computer system was going to be the wave of the
future," Cook says. "I helped develop the system here. I was by myself for
a while." That's why only a few years later the top man himself was driving
on a gravel road on a hot summer day to personally look up a computer
prospect—Chuck Franz, pothole-filler.

In those beginning installation days, Cook says, "We didn't allow any
other type of computer into the company except Microdata until we had
our programs we could use for manufacturing. We wrote our own programs, based upon an operating system that is not generally used—the
Pick system [for originator Dick Pick]. I did have some people from Jerry
McCullough's company who would help me periodically."

Bill Cook at computer (photo by Carl Cook)

One of those was Rick Snapp, who joined Cook Inc. in 1988 and, Cook says, "through the years, built the Cook computer system. He not only specified the equipment and operating systems but also wrote a lot of the key software."

"Pick" is a system that "is more common in the furniture manufacturing industry and government," Snapp says. Cook likes it because "you can modify it without having to change any other parts of the program set."

Simplicity.

That word is Bill Cook's overriding goal, and has been since his ultimate-in-simplicity start. "All of our sales ordering and inventory systems are very simple and basic, but comprehensive and fast," Snapp said.

Snapp came out of Columbus (Indiana) High School in 1973, son of a doctor, grandson of a doctor. He graduated from IU in 1977 as a chemistry major—perfect for pre-med. No, thanks, he said, after growing up watching the long, demanding hours kept by his father, one of two internists in Columbus at the time. Although he took no computer courses in college, afterward he started down a road that led to his career in computers. He joined Cook Inc. at a time when the IT department there—information technology—involved just five people, including Bill Cook.

Maybe not every employee would like to be a leader in an area where the top man of the company is integrally involved. "Having the top guy looking over your shoulder has some disadvantages. You can't bullshit him," says Snapp, the man charged with making the Cook system work. "But the advantage is pretty obvious—ain't nobody gonna argue. I don't have to explain myself. 'This is what we're going to do.' Bill was always involved. He liked it; he knew he could write code, and he could understand how things work. He always said, 'You can control a company if you can control the information in it.'"

"I still want to know about major changes," Cook says. "Just recently I asked Chuck Franz to give me a rundown of what he had done with the FDA on bar-coding. But three people run the computer system now—Chuck Franz analyzes needs, Rick Snapp maintains the operating part of the machines and does programming, and Rob Dorocke does all of our media stuff—our 'king of Mac.'"

The future Bill Cook saw in the 1970s—to link up all of the Cook operations around the globe, coordinated for instant contact—is here. "All the companies share very similar ordering and inventory programs, by Bill's design—by Bill's demand, actually," Snapp says. "He wanted roughly the same thing everywhere. I look for more and more consolidation—more of the one-Cook emphasis and philosophy that has been going on. I've been in all the places in Europe and Australia. I haven't spent any time in Asia. Some things are definitely spinning in that direction."

Antisense—Anticipating Miracles

Antisense is a word so new it's not in some medical dictionaries, even ones that define DNA ("the basic genetic material present in the nucleus of each cell") and tell what those familiar but mysterious initials stand for (deoxyribonucleic acid).

It is, of course, in Google, and Wikipedia: "Antisense molecules interact with complementary strands of nucleic acids, modifying expression of genes. . . . Cells can produce antisense molecules naturally, which interact with complementary molecules and inhibit their expression." It might eventually be a way to arm the body to fight its own problems and cure, not just slow down but cure, a wide variety of deadly health threats—including, Bill Cook says, cancer. And very soon.

It's a thrilling new wave that medical science is riding, and it's a reason why Cook sees great times ahead—not just for Cook Inc., which is antisense-conscious as are all in its field, but also for a world maddeningly frustrated all these years by medical answers not found.

"The antisense drug is a way of preventing duplication of a bad gene, so the body doesn't know the bad gene is there," Cook said. "That's a simplistic way of putting it, but that's essentially what it is. Humans now have the capability of manufacturing a material that can literally stop gene production, saying: 'This is a bad gene. Don't replicate that gene.'

"With these new antisense drugs that are coming on the market, in our lifetime we will see a cure in HIV and Hepatitis C. We'll see a cure for muscular dystrophy, for flu, including Asian flu. Right on the horizon today is a cure for diabetes.

"Ebola—drugs are already going into clinical trials that are a cure, not an arresting measure, a cure. And West Nile virus—there's a cure on the way for that."

And cancer, the eternal frightening anxiety above all human anxieties? "I think there will be a gene tailored to get the cancers. I think that is on the horizon."

The public assumption from medical science's longtime frustrations in seeking a cause—hence a cure—for cancer is that there is no "silver bullet," that the many forms of cancer guarantee there will be no single cure.

"We *think* that, because cancer assumes different characters," Cook said. "But we do know most cancers have the predisposition of growing in an uncontrolled manner. The cancer has a blood supply, in most instances, even though it has a different place in the body—breast cancer, uterine cancer, cancer of the colon, cancer of the lungs. They all have a blood supply, and they are almost uncontrollable. We will be able to shut that down by engineering the genes.

"It may be one elixir, it may be multiple elixirs. But it's going to be some type of gene injection. I think in a matter of ten to fifteen years we will see that.

"We have so much knowledge now about what makes the DNA work. I think we will see more and more cures for disease. So many things that are working now in genetics of plants will be applied to genetics of humans. It is possible now to identify the specific genes, or gene links, that create the disease.

"In forty years, people dying of disease is not going to be a problem. It's going to be a matter of having older people who still are alive but don't have the physical capability to keep on going. I don't know whether we will stop the aging process, although we could. Perhaps there will be a cure for that.

"The first thing we'll probably see is the correction of abnormalities in small babies, where they have a genetic imbalance or genetic problem, and they will be corrected in the womb." He is including chromosome imbalances that lead to Down's Syndrome babies and similar problems that shorten or alter lives. "This DNA and RNA knowledge that we're gaining now is just massive. With computers, we can almost predict which genes and gene links are the problems—the genetics as well as the disease itself."

Already, genetic applications are at work in the newest Cook Inc. facility, Cook Pharmica, in an old factory building about a mile from company headquarters in Bloomington. Jerry Arthur, head of operations there, said the road to cancer cures is being explored there with new findings in production of drugs—pharmaceuticals.

"Pharmaceuticals traditionally are made from plant and animal parts," Arthur said. "Insulin was made from the pancreas of cattle and pigs. Now insulin is made from cell culture. About 35 to 40 percent of the injectables on the market right now are biotech, made from a man-made process rather than part of an animal or a plant.

"All laboratories have cell lockers. You put cells in storage, freeze them, get them out, use them, and multiply them. The cell line we use is called the CHO line. It was derived in the early 1980s from the ovary of a Chinese hamster. That hamster is long out of the picture, but the cells still grow. The scientists will take the nuclei of the cell and genetically engineer one little section of the cell, then hand the cell back to the lab and grow a bunch of them.

"They're already attacking cancers this way. It's all biotech drugs out there, just a wave of new active ingredients. One of the things we're working on is a hemophiliac drug. Another is a bone-fusion drug. Science is learning how to turn off genes, turn on genes. If they can turn off the right genes, a cancer can't spread. Antisense chemistry breaks the reproductive chain. I think that's going to be the key to extending life."

Meanwhile, Cook Pharmica is off to an auspicious start. Monsanto was announced as its first laboratory customer, Inspiration Biologic its first in production, and already an $84-million expansion has been launched. It's expected to be in production by 2010 and to double the plant's income potential, according to Arthur.

Next: The Generation of Regeneration?

The promising future at the Cook Pharmica plant in Bloomington is the delayed payoff of one of those lawsuits in Phyllis McCullough's dizzying decade. It's part of why the decades ahead have their own dizzying promise.

The court fight with Dr. Milos Sovak ran through most of the 1980s. Well into the 1990s, Cook Imaging was still trying to get Oxilan, the object of the battle, going as a profit-maker. It had more than its share of ups and downs for Cook Inc., but today Oxilan is a product with a present (but not with Cook: the French company Guerbet LLC bought patent rights from Cook in 2002 and markets it out of an office in Bloomington), and a humanitarian past (through money-ambivalent Charles Dotter, who died long before it went into production but, with his passion and persuasiveness, had used his own separate relationships to link Sovak's scientific breakthrough and Bill Cook's entrepreneurial skills).

In the early 1980s, private hospitals with expensive dyes could give their affluent, insured patients low-pain radiology treatment that—vital as it was in interventional, surgery-preventing internal "detective" work—wasn't available to indigents and accident victims brought off the streets into public hospitals. They got the treatment, but with cheaper dyes that produced excruciating pain.

Phyllis McCullough attended a Chicago luncheon where she said featured speaker Charles Dotter "was so disgusted with the contrast media manufacturers and their high prices that he didn't say a word as he played a tape of nothing but the sounds of patients being injected with regular contrast media—'Ow!' . . . 'Ohhhh!' . . . 'Ohh-owww!'—screaming, obviously in extreme pain. When he finished the tape, he challenged somebody to *do* something. That somebody, of course, was Bill."

And his answer was Oxilan. But nothing came easily.

AARP, Cook Style

In 1993, Jerry Arthur accepted a buy-out offer from Lilly Pharmaceuticals in Indianapolis and retired after a thirty-one-year career. Along the way, he had spent eleven years in night classes to get a Purdue degree from the university's Indianapolis extension. His job advanced from beginning line work to supervisory roles that included some sales experience. When Lilly made a buy-out offer attractive enough ("They bumped up our retirement and gave us a year's pay—that was too good to pass up"), he took it at age 53 and says, "I was thinking: I won't have to deal with the FDA anymore."

He wasn't an unknown in the Cook hierarchy. Phyllis McCullough is his sister. He went into retirement with plans to go into a house renovation business with another Lilly retiree, but before he ever got into that, "Phyllis called, wanting to talk to me about their management problems at Cook Imaging [where Oxilan was being readied for market]." He promised to get a résumé together, but didn't soon enough for his sister's impatient boss. "I got a call on a Friday from Bill: 'Forget the damn résumé. Get down here on Monday. We need your help.'"

The problem wasn't an FDA-caused delay. There was no Oxilan product to test yet. "They had installed a filling line and a piece of equipment, and they couldn't get it working. I looked at what was wrong. I told Bill I could get four or five guys with different kinds of expertise [who had accepted the same Lilly buy-out] to come with me, and in three months we could get the plant running. One was an excellent mechanic, another an excellent formulation scientist, another was a freeze-dryer authority, one had been assigned to the FDA for a couple of years, and the other one had been my boss—Lilly had sent him all over the world to solve problems. Bill called us AARP—Arthur And Retired People. There were thirty to forty years in every one of those guys. They were fantastic."

The plant was readied for production, but that was just part of meeting the FDA procedural process. "You have to run three lots, called stability lots—prove you can run it consistently, and prove that what you produce is effective and consistently good," Arthur said. "All the documentation and all the tests that your doctors and researchers would have done, if you couldn't run the product, you couldn't submit it to the FDA."

By FDA standards, Oxilan represented Cook Inc.'s first venture into pharmaceuticals. "It wasn't a pharmaceutical," Arthur said, "but it had to meet all the requirements of a pharmaceutical ingredient, because if you inject anything into the bloodstream, you bypass all the immune systems. If you inject bacteria, you've just killed the patient. The body can't react.

"So they were just bleeding red financially. There were sixty employees writing and documenting and testing and setting up the lab, testing all the lab equipment, calibrating the air pressures and all the things that go into sterile rooms, doing smoke tests to see that the room clears. Then you have to get everything involved sterile—the room, the equipment, the people— and prove you can keep it that way. In three months, we were able to submit product to the FDA and wait for their approval. We had proved that the plant was running and was capable." Approval came.

By the mid-1990s Cook was on the market with Oxilan, offering at fifty-three cents a milliliter what similar-effect major companies' products were costing $1.20, cost-prohibitive to "community" hospitals. A boom of sales pushed Cook Inc. to ramp up its production, but sales stopped when suddenly the major companies' prices plummeted, leveling out at nineteen cents a milliliter. "We couldn't compete with that. It was costing us forty-six cents to make it," McCullough says.

So a backlog of Oxilan developed at Cook Inc. Arthur, who was now head of the sixty-employee plant that was turning it out, proposed a new direction: "I'll shut the plant down temporarily. I've got forty people you can use somewhere for about six months, and I'll convert some of the production to do contract manufacturing."

Thus was born Cook Pharmaceutical Solutions. "We started that in the fall of 1996," Arthur said. "It took off like a rocket."

The Undertaker Factor

The new company opened up Cook Inc.'s manufacturing facilities to other companies—to produce "a line of syringes in which we put other people's medicants," Cook said. "Major pharmaceutical companies would ship their product in or we would formulate the medicants for them, package the medicants in a syringe-and-needle combination, and ship. It was an excellent business."

"Lilly was our first customer," Arthur said. "In 1993 Lilly had eight formulation scientists. Seven of them took the buy-out package, and the eighth

Jerry Arthur, head of operations, Cook Pharmica—"This is the biotech industry"

one quit. In 1994, I had one of them come to work for us, and in 1996 I found three more of them. So we had half of their formulation department, and we told Lilly, 'Would you like for us to do some formulation for you?' They said, 'Thank God, yes.'

"From our first customer in 1996, we had grown to 250 customers and 315 employees in 2001 when we sold that operation [Cook Pharmaceutical Solutions] to Baxter. We had about $70 million invested in it, and after four years we sold it to Baxter for $220 million."

Arthur and the employees went to Baxter as part of the sales package, complete with no-raiding and noncompete clauses. However, Arthur said, "I didn't last very long at Baxter. I said I'd work at least a year, but I didn't make it. They bought us under the guise that we would be allowed to run our business our way. Within three or four months, they were changing things. They were emphasizing, 'We want this quarter to be good, so you guys have to do this and this.' Then corporate groups starting coming down and changing the way we did things—on about four fronts. I made some frosty statements, and . . . they didn't like me anymore and I didn't like them. So we went our separate ways. We broke clean, and that was fine. I was 61." That was 2002. "I got a call from Bill in August 2003. We had lunch, and he said, 'This is the first day out of our noncompete agreement. We could go back in business with pharmaceuticals.' I said, 'Okay, let's do it.'

"We started figuring out what and where we could do it. I spent that fall traveling for Bill. Went out to Boulder, Colorado, and looked at a plant; it wasn't a very good one. One in Illinois was in bankruptcy, so that didn't work out. Wyeth had a big plant in New Jersey that was shut down by the FDA—that one could have been fixed. I was sitting in my New Jersey hotel room with my computer, and I wrote to Bill, 'We could buy this plant, and I think we could make it work. I'm going to go down to Puerto Rico and look at a couple of other plants.'"

Cook's return e-mail read: "I vote no. I know location isn't the primary decision-maker on whether we do or don't do a business. But at your age and my age, we need to stay near an undertaker who understands us. So come back to the Midwest."

When one of Bloomington's major employers, RCA, pulled out, the plant it left behind turned out to be perfect—"so much better for what we wanted to do than I anticipated," Arthur said. "The production layout is just outstanding."

Now called Cook Pharmica, the plant is just off the south end of Bloomington's downtown. It is remodeled and redesigned, but it is twenty-first century in look and concept, devoted to producing pharmaceuticals using the cell culture process, and it has put retirement out of Arthur's immediate plans. "This," he said, "is the biotech industry."

Within the biotech world, a national preoccupation is on stem cell research—a political issue, a religious issue, above all an attention-grabbing
issue that suggests all kinds of hope to one side and God-defying invasion
to another, while lots of money is being spent, more is sought, and returns
are scanty.

Dr. David Stocum, director of the Center for Regenerative Biology and
Medicine at IUPUI in Indianapolis, had an especially interested listener
in Bill Cook when Stocum said at a monthly Cook managers' luncheon in
October 2007 that the money and attention focused on stem cell research
would—toward similar goals—more promisingly be spent on researching
and learning about cellular regeneration.

"All of this stem cell stuff is definitely misdirected, greatly overstated,"
Cook said after the luncheon. "We squander money on research on stem
cells when in actuality we should be studying the protein interaction between cells. There are only one or two successful uses of stem cells as yet.
People are being deceived in many respects."

Stocum's talk evolved into an accordant back-and-forth exchange between him and Cook, who was sitting in the audience. On his part Cook,
the man longtime friend John Mutz once called "the best listener I've ever
come across," was tapping more than fifty-year-old memories of prescient
theories he absorbed in the classroom of one of the Northwestern University
professors he reveres, comparative anatomy instructor Albert Wolfson.

"Cellular regeneration is a very interesting area," Cook said later. "We
know the body has the power. We just don't know the combination of proteins needed. And it is the proteins. Some combination of proteins triggers
a reaction in the cells. We just don't know exactly which ones and in what
amounts.

"It's one of the things that Carl and I talked about a year ago, that we've
got to keep doing the types of things that he is doing at MyoSite, and the
people at Cook Biotech in West Lafayette are doing: stay with the cellular
and the organ research, and eventually we will come up with something.
But right at the moment, society is messing around with this stem cell argument—and it *is* an argument, a 'he said/you said' argument—that is gaining nothing for anyone except distracting from science. Embryonic stem
cell research became a political hot issue that nobody should have gotten
involved in. If politicians and people understood what we're talking about,
there wouldn't be this brouhaha."

Cook Biotech was founded in 1995 after Purdue University researchers, partially funded by Cook Inc. grants, discovered remarkable skin regeneration powers—e.g., in cases of severe burns—in the small intestines

of young pigs. The product's name was shortened to SIS—small intestinal submucosa—and it is laid directly onto the burn, never to be removed but, instead, absorbed in the healing process. SIS is not regeneration, Cook says, "although we think there is potential application. At this time SIS stands on its own. It is a matrix that the body's own cells grow into. There is a healing reaction every time SIS is used.

"In the research at MyoSite [founded in 2001], they go into a muscle and select what they believe are cells that have the capability of replicating tissue if you get them in the right proportion with other cells. Wherever the cells are injected, they will replicate the tissue that surrounds it. That has great promise: replicate your own cells in the particular position. If you want to replicate tissue that has been damaged or lost, for example, replace a heart or grow a heart . . . organs, like kidneys, livers, hearts . . . parts of the brain." Or "take a severed neuron—that's where everybody would like to see some major advances, where you can take part of the spinal cord and regenerate. There is great hope there that someday they will find a cell that is capable of regeneration." And victims of severe spinal cord trauma, now facing a lifetime of paralysis, might walk again. That's a foreseeable dream on the regeneration horizon, Stocum said at the luncheon, fortifying Cook's own aims.

"In our case at MyoSite, we're working with autologous grafts from human cells," Cook said. "At Biotech, we're working with a matrix, which is nothing more than a scaffold that cells love to deposit themselves on. The matrix allows ingrowth of blood vessels and the deposit through chemistry of proteins and cells.

"Cook Pharmica works with mammalian cell culture. You take cells from a mammal and multiply them. Then you insert some genetic material into the cells so they produce some desired material, like a specific protein. This used to be done with bacteria or yeast cells. The greatest example is diabetes; they actually make most insulin now from cell cultures, and it's identical to human insulin. Now we're trying to produce other things like that with mammalian cell cultures.

"We're very much involved in any process that does healing or regeneration. We may not be involved in everything going on inside the cell itself. But in Carl's case at MyoSite, where they had certain mixtures of cells, they do know they can regenerate a urethral sphincter.

"We're working with another technology in antisense. Drugs are taken for a lot of reasons. Sometimes they can cure something, like an antibiotic killing infections. Lots of times they don't cure anything; they only treat symptoms. And sometimes drugs like aspirin—the greatest thing ever to come down the pike—aren't that specific. Aspirin can be taken for a lot of reasons—for headache, for fever, to thin the blood. But antisense is different. It works on genetic material inside the cells to keep the body from making bad proteins. We think it can be very specific and cure diseases at their root."

Playing with the Elephants

The morning of October 4, 2006, Bill Cook convened a meeting of some of his top company officials to hear early reports on an antisense project already under way. In opening the meeting, he called antisense "a new technology that could be important not just to Cook but to the world . . . sort of a Buck Rogers outer space thing we've never attacked before. We're playing a new game here. I don't know what the gold standard is."

There to lead in answering questions was Joe Horn, who first came into the Cook Inc. orbit when his company, Global Therapeutics, became the first major outside acquisition in Cook history—and, at $35 million, it is still the biggest. With Global Therapeutics, Cook said, "We bought technology."

Horn came along as vice president of Cook Inc.'s International Clinical Services until the Colorado office was closed in 2004. Now he is president of Global Therapeutics within Cook Medical division. Very early, Bill Cook was and obviously still is impressed by the energetic, bright man, a generation younger than Cook. "Joe is a very talented individual—Type A, very hyper, very driven, has spent a large part of his life working on stents. He's from Wisconsin—just in general a very nice individual. And very hyper."

It was Horn, Cook said at the 2006, meeting, who put him on the antisense project. "Joe called and said 'I've got this great idea.' And he spelled it out."

On the antisense work, Cook said, Horn "operates fairly independent, and we are doing that on purpose because (1) we don't have anybody in the company who is as savvy on this as Joe is, and (2) we are on a fast time schedule, so the fewer people who have to be in the decision process the better. So Joe and I make most of the calls."

Dr. Patrick Iversen was there along with Horn, presenting charts and slides telling of tests under way at three sites in Germany ultimately involving fifty patients who were already showing "symptomatic ischemic heart disease . . . stentatic lesion [stenosis detecting] of native coronary arteries . . . treated by solitary percutaneous bare metal stent."

Months later Cook said the preliminary testing was "getting along very well. It will be a new cobalt chrome stent, rounded unlike any other stent ever built." In a report in December 2007, Horn said, "Our goal is to begin the study in the first quarter of 2008 and complete patient enrollment by the end of 2008."

Cook said, "We think it's going to be a very good product in time. Many people are coming off stents right now. There aren't as many being sold, but who knows? It's a high-risk item, probably something I'd have to make the decision on. I'm going to experiment on myself a little bit, probably inject myself with this material with the idea that it might be able to slow down atherosclerosis [clogged arteries]."

The clinical trials were being done in Germany because "the federal government makes it extremely difficult to do clinicals here. Also, they are so expensive here—$9,000 to $18,000 for one patient. And you might have to do 1,000 patients. The cost can just be horrendous."

Why so high?

It starts, he said, with "the number of nurses required to keep the documentation and keep the project going; the doctor has to be present to supervise installation of the product; the doctor has to follow up, then has to dictate his findings. His follow-ups can be three, six, nine, and twelve months. These patients have to be monitored. There may have to be telephone calls made. And then there's hospital stay involved. If we're putting in a stent, that's a hospital stay, normally an overnight. Very expensive."

There's also a screening process just to find suitable test patients among those with heart disease symptoms. "You have to find people who fit a certain profile. Some would be too sick. Others might be diabetic or have a disease that skews your results. Diabetes and age are both very big factors. Diabetics are much more prone to arteriosclerosis. That doesn't mean they can't get a stent, but in clinical trials it throws off the results because you are looking for normal growth, not abnormal proliferation."

In Cook's own field, he sees one other cost-accelerating factor. "Within the FDA there's a lack of understanding that a device is not a drug. Drugs have an effect that may take ten or twelve years to show up. A device either works or doesn't work. But we are so hidebound by regulations that it's difficult—in some cases impossible—to get a new product through. We have to pick and choose."

The classic case of a drug's delayed signs of danger is thalidomide, a drug developed and first marketed in Germany in the late 1950s, used for expectant mothers as a sleeping pill and a counter to morning sickness. Its success rate was outstanding. Overnight, the wonder drug was rushed into quick usage worldwide, including in the United States, before enough time passed that a horrifying number of birth defects traced to the drug began to show up. The Thalidomide Experience probably was the most influential reason for the strengthening of regulatory agencies such as the U.S. Food and Drug Administration and subsequent tough legislation. With good reason.

Because of the high cost of meeting regulatory demands, bigger-market devices inevitably get top priority, Cook says. "It used to be we could take a device that was life-saving, or life-improving, make it, and market it, and it would be a great device for maybe a few people. But today you can't afford to do that. It's difficult to decide whether to make a product or not to. In our company, we have hundreds of people in regulatory (making sure federal requirements are met). In some products, as much as 25 percent of our product cost is regulatory—actually part of the pricing."

With antisense, Cook said, "We're just moving ahead. It's got me excited. It has exciting potential. I have a lot of confidence in it, but we may not be the one who capitalizes on it. There may be a myriad of reasons why we won't be able to continue this, but I have a lot of confidence that it will work."

His charge to his assemblage that 2006 day of project unveiling came in classic, colorful Bill Cook words: "We're trying to play with marketing and science at the same time. If we're going to be going for the mass market, let's don't play with the pigs. Let's go in and play with the elephants."

Never Mess with Budgets

Bill Cook's direct involvement—one man in a vast enterprise—does show up. Jerry Arthur says when he was at Lilly he once had to make seven presentations at seven levels of authority, over a period of several weeks, before getting permission to buy a $100,000 copying machine. "In the spring of 1998, we were going great with Cook Pharmaceutical Solutions. I told Bill, 'We need to spend $25 million and build a high-speed syringe line. We'd have the only one in the United States. Companies in Europe are selling $100 million a year. I think I could pay for it with my own cash flow when the business gets rolling if you let me plow everything back in.' He said, 'Go ahead and build it. If you run out of money, come see me.'

"That was the approval! That's all it took. That copying machine was $100,000 at Lilly. This was $25 million.

"The first day I met Bill, he said, 'We don't do budgets. If you need something, you buy it. If you don't need it, you don't buy it. Budgets don't help you.' And he said, 'We don't do presentations. If you've got an idea, go do the idea. Don't waste my time telling me about it and waste your time putting a story together.' And he said, 'We don't do business plans. You write things down, they become obsolete, you try to follow them—that's a bad idea.'

"'And take the damned tie off, Jerry. You make me look bad.'

"The cost of our new plant [Cook Pharmica] was estimated at $45 million. The costs reached $45 million, and we weren't even close to done. I was sick. I sent an e-mail apologizing. He sent me back an e-mail: 'Jerry, that's the very reason I never mess with budgets. The costs go somewhere else, and people get all upset. Don't worry about where I stand. I think you and all your guys and gals are doing a terrific job.' I showed that e-mail to our people, and that energized the whole plant. Nobody wants to fail after that.

"He's been an absolute joy to know and work with. When the chips are down, he can really get people's attention. He and I don't always get along.

We've had some awful fights. But I love it. There are certain times you can't argue with the guy. He's not going to *let* you get a word in. Another day, another time . . .

"He has insight that other people aren't blessed with. Very early in my career at Cook, I was having lunch one day. Bill joined me, and we started talking. Another fellow joined us, a supervisor from the lab. He introduced himself to Bill and shook hands. Bill wasn't there five minutes, and he got up and left. I saw him in his office later that afternoon and he said, 'Boy, that guy who sat across from you today is a piece of work. Outwardly he's really friendly and nice. Inside he's got a rage. He won't succeed at anything in life. He won't succeed here, either.' About a month after that, the guy was caught falsifying lab data and was fired. I thought, 'My God, I must be standing naked in front of Bill. I don't know *what* the hell he sees.'

"The guy has an energy, a strength, a vision, and then he has that amazing insight. Somehow, the rest of us are connected at 110, and he's at 440."

Wealth

Power and Opportunity

I never really worked for money.
I worked to exist. I have never particularly
enjoyed things that money brings, but
I do enjoy the power that money can bring.
And if you do have power, you should
exercise it as best you can.

—*Bill Cook*

When power and money are paired in a sentence, the instant mental picture is ugly. Sinister. Power unrestrained by intimidated, winking, bought-off law. But money that is big enough also brings a power to do in an instant what others with similar ideals but ordinary means can only wish. Good things.

In August 2006, Indiana State Trooper Gary Dudley and Deputy Chief Gary Martin of the Lake County Sheriff's Department were giving up their off-duty time to ride with seven other active and retired police officers in a thirteen-day, 1,000-mile cross-state fund-raising bicycle ride for the Indiana chapter of COPS—Concerns of Police Survivors.

At just about noon, on State Road 63 paralleling the Wabash River just inside the state's western border with Illinois, a freight truck rear-ended the riders' support van—despite the van's huge banner and flashing amber lights warning of the cyclists' presence and low traveling speed. The van lurched forward into the pack of cyclists, and Dudley and Martin were struck and killed.

It was a poignantly ironic story—two veteran lawmen killed riding bicycles on behalf of fallen officers—that every Indiana newspaper carried on August 23. The ones with some detail told of how Dudley, 52, had served with the Indiana State Police for twenty-six years. A lieutenant, he had advanced from highway patrol to a training role, and more than half the state troopers in service throughout Indiana in 2006 had trained under him. Dudley had organized that fund-raising ride and rides of the previous two years as well.

And Martin? After he had served in the Gary Police Department for twenty-five years, he had become chief of the Lake County Sheriff's Department. For twenty-seven years, spanning both jobs, he taught criminal justice at Indiana University's northwest Indiana branch. A Gary police detective mourning the accident told of taking Martin's class, of how he was about to drop out because he couldn't afford it, and Martin pulled out his own checkbook and paid the tuition cost. Martin's son was on the Gary police force. The weekend before the accident, Martin had given his daughter away in marriage.

"I saw that story and felt so bad," Bill Cook said. "These guys had taken care of all of us as public servants, given their lives up—killed on their bicycles, trying to get a couple of kids through college. And they were able to raise just a lousy $18,000. That's sad."

Surely nobody reading the story was untouched. Surely most wished they could reach out and do something. Bill Cook did. "We gave a million dollars to COPS, pretty much on the spur of the moment." That's the power of wealth, over wish. "That's exactly right," Cook said. "That's the difference."

The B Word Is Not Dirty

No news release accompanied the check. It wasn't until six weeks later that even members of the Indiana COPS organization were told in a newsletter—astonishment coming through in proper police-report jargon—that the morning after the officers' funerals, secretary Amy Stehr "was contacted by The Cook Group reference making a donation. Amy met with them and after speaking with the board and answering their questions reference COPS and our mission to take care of our survivors, they advised her they wanted to make a sizable donation and named the sum they wished to contribute. Needless to say, Amy was shocked and amazed at their generosity and was able to hold her secret from the rest of the board until yesterday." A letter accompanying the gift said it "is intended to fund an endowment where the interest earned will be utilized for the comfort and welfare of surviving members. It is our sincere hope that individual and other corporate citizens will also contribute to the endowment fund. Our fallen officers must never be forgotten and we must never forget the devastating effect that such a loss has on their families."

It was signed by Bill and Carl Cook and other officers of the organization. It was Bill Cook's gift—in the company's name, as is normal for other philanthropic gifts made by him and Gayle. There are practical reasons beyond modesty. "If we don't give the money, we would have probably taken it in dividends, so in essence, it is our money," Bill said. "But instead, why take it through another taxation? Why not just give it off the bottom line and give it as the company?

"I've always tried to give where there are a large number of people involved—like a university or Star of Indiana—where you can do the most good and have the most impact on the greatest number of people." That's an operating (and gift-giving) principle that keeps him from being an easy mark for every cause. Solicitation "does come at you, and you get used to it. Benevolence to me is certainly not a dirty word. The newspapers like to mention 'Bill Cook's a billionaire.' That does not have a good connotation. Whenever that's mentioned, Gayle and I think, 'Oh my God, here we go again.' On the other hand, if people know that, there are certain things you can do."

Frankel-ly

The Cooks' understandable aversion to the Forbes 400 list got humorous treatment from one of America's most noted newspaper columnists, Max Frankel, in the *New York Times Magazine* on November 19, 1995. Frankel scanned the list freshly released (a list he called "a breezy familiarity with the lives of its subjects, which counts their centimillions with mock precision and delivers its research in a seductive Who's Who patter"), and picked out four as examples. One of them he carried verbatim:

> William A. Cook, Medical supplies . . . ex-cabby . . . hated big-city Chicago . . . spent $1,500 on blowtorch, soldering iron, plastic tubing; made then new cardiovascular catheters . . . new coronary shunt likely home run . . . estimated over $750 million; he denies.

Frankel wrote:

> Cook denies a net worth as great as $750 million? Or as little?
> The fun of The Forbes 400 is that you're never quite sure who has been undervalued and who has lied his way up the ladder. The mystery is why so many of us care: why the wealthy lust after such rank ranking and why the rest of us revel in the revelations of their outlandish affluence. . . .

Why do we pine for Barbara Walters to lead us past the gates of estates? Why do we let the *Wall Street Journal* pretend to be the diary of the American dream? Why do we pay $5 to fondle Forbes's list, upon which none of us will ever appear? . . .

Which fortunes reflect a farsighted vision, and which only the dumbest luck? Which were amassed honestly, and which by tawdry means? Which are spent for noble ends, and which are being squandered?

Why, indeed? Which, indeed? But if those last three questions represent a choice between (a) and (b), William A. Cook would seem to be on that list as (a), (a), (a).

There's a particular satisfaction for both Bill and Gayle Cook in the middle question. Their fortune came from developing and getting into worldwide usage medical devices that served to both prolong life and improve the quality of those prolonged lives. It's a comparatively noble way of getting on a list with some whose stepladder to great wealth was at least as noble—but a whole lot more who got there as heirs to fortunes that they put to effective work, or as overnight riders of real estate or dot-com bubbles who knew when to cash in, even some who got there by the opposite of healthful routes, for example, tobacco.

Of the Forbes 400, the number with similar society-benefiting backgrounds is a subject he doesn't bring up but clearly has thought about. "I've got the Forbes book. There's not too many of them, maybe ten. There's a fellow named Sorenson . . ."

Google says James L. Sorenson grew up poor in Yuba City, California, never went to college, served as a Mormon missionary in New England, sold for Upjohn just after World War II, went into business on his own as Sorenson Research, patented some medical devices (one of them plastic catheters of the sort Cook began with), and sold the business to Abbott Laboratories in 1980. His stake from that sale had an up-to-date value of $2.5 billion, with another $1.8 billion in real estate holdings, the 2006 Forbes report said—when Sorenson was 85.

". . . and the Stryker family . . ."

Surgeon Homer Stryker grew up in a town of under 1,000, Athens, Michigan, about twenty miles north of the Indiana border. An infantryman in World War I, he was in his thirties when he graduated from the University of Michigan Medical Center and 43 when he completed orthopedic studies there. At 46 in 1941, after three years of orthopedic practice, he invented and patented a turning frame that allowed bed-ridden patients to be turned easily, as a preventive to bedsores and stimulation to healing. The same year he formed Orthopedics Frame Company and continued to invent and patent—with the help of his son Lee, expanding his company into a worldwide sales business. In 1964, when Cook Inc. still was a bedroom business with an employment roster of two, Orthopedics Frame became Stryker

Corporation. That was opened to public trading on Nasdaq in 1977, three years before Stryker's death at 85. Lee Stryker was killed in a plane crash in 1975. The family is represented on the Forbes list by three of Lee's children, all billionaires. Homer's granddaughter, Ronda Stryker, is the only one of the three still listed on the Stryker Corporation board.

"... not too many," Cook concluded.

"Most of those Forbes 400 people made their money in real estate or other ventures. Some are from companies sort of like us that you've never heard of—in the medical field, solely owned or they have been acquired by another corporation. Gayle and I have all the money that we can ever use personally. But when they say I am worth $3.2 billion, that's idiotic. *That money is not there.*"

What is there is serving him well—some allowing him to buy and indulge in the use of a toy that fulfilled a lifetime dream, much more to answer dreams of not just him and Gayle but a whole grateful southern Indiana community.

Honors and Gifts

Bill Cook has received honorary degrees from Northwestern University, his alma mater, and from Indiana University, Rose-Hulman Institute, and Vincennes University in Indiana. He doesn't find it coincidental that those four universities are prominent among the educational institutions that have received more than $60 million in gifts from him and Gayle over the years.

"With the exception of the Rose-Hulman degree—which is not honorary, it is an actual degree given in engineering—the honorary degrees were for an amount of money we had given, as opposed to something I had done. Many people receive honorary degrees because they benefited society in some way. In my case, I think the main reason I received them from Indiana, Vincennes, and Northwestern was for financial donations." But the honorary degrees do keep coming—in May 2008 from Marion College in Indianapolis.

Awards and honors also have come, some carrying special meaning. The field he entered as a manufacturing pioneer thanked him in an unprecedented way. The Society for Interventional Radiology made him the first nonphysician to receive its gold medal—"probably the highlight of my business career, because I'm recognized by physicians as being worthy of their society. To be accepted as a fellow and become a gold medalist . . . that didn't come from my peers; it came from people we served. I think that had to do with my ability to translate medicine to product."

He had left high school and even Northwestern with plans to enter medi-

cal school. Those plans changed, but his academic courses aimed at qualifi-cation for medical school benefited him in ways unplanned. "Pre-med gave me the tools with which I could visualize what doctors were telling me, because I understood anatomy and had a fairly good working knowledge of biology and chemistry. When they would talk about the coronary arteries, and the difficulties in manipulation, and why you needed a fulcrum some-place below the left coronary artery, and why you needed a loop in order to twist the catheter into the left coronary—I could visualize that. These are the kinds of things that you learn (1) from knowing a little bit about anatomy and (2) from thinking about it. I had the interest, definitely."

The American Heart Association at a black-tie event in Bloomington gave him and Gayle its Cor Vitae Award for contributions to cardiovascular health care. In July 2006, he and Gayle received Indiana Living Legend rec-ognition by the Indiana Historical Society, putting them in a group of about fifty that includes leaders from government (Senator Richard Lugar, former congressman Lee Hamilton, and former Indiana governor Otis Bowen), education (university presidents Herman B Wells of Indiana and Father Theodore Hesburgh of Notre Dame), entertainment (Jazz Hall of Famer David Baker, composer-artist John Mellencamp, TV's David Letterman, Chris Schenkel, and Jane Pauley, singer Crystal Gayle, and Garfield creator

Jim Davis), plus author Kurt Vonnegut, stars Oscar Robertson, Larry Bird, and George McGinnis, and coaches John Wooden and Bob Knight from basketball, and Carl Erskine from baseball.

In addition, as individuals or as a couple, he and Gayle have been honored as preservationists by the National Trust for Historic Preservation, the National Park Service, Historic Landmarks Foundation of Indiana, and the Indiana Department of Natural Resources. A science hall at Northwestern, a music library at Indiana University, and a stadium at Rose-Hulman carry the Cook name. "All of the awards are very, very significant to me. They reflect a body of work."

One of His Bill Cooks

The Cooks' donations commonly come with strings attached—declared well in advance. There's a history to that.

In the early 1990s, Indiana University's athletic department wanted to equip its football stadium with TV-quality lighting for occasional night games and other uses. Cook agreed to underwrite the $1 million cost and, after personal experiences that included temporarily lighting IU's stadium for Star of Indiana performances, specified that the Musco company from Muscatine, Iowa, get the assignment. At a meeting with an IU committee that included some of his closest friends, he learned they had "decided they were going to hire General Electric. We had a very tough discussion."

He wasn't involved in all of it. "He had to go through one of his Bill Cooks," Steve Ferguson said, which involved leaving the meeting in genuine anger. "Bill goes through the ceiling and says, 'Give me my goddamn money back.' And goes out and slams the door. There's silence in the room. One of them said something like, 'Well, Steve . . . ?' I said, 'I think what you'd better do is what he wants.'" The Musco system was installed.

"I said it must be Musco," Cook said, "because all of the igniters and the things that set the lights off are down below where you can reach them. With General Electric they're right up next to the lights, and if you have a power outage you have to climb to fix it. Down low, you can protect the boxes. Up high, you don't know what weather will do to them, and you have to have somebody go up the pole to reset them. That's one of the reasons there are very few power outages at the stadium, because they can get at those boxes momentarily." That hadn't been IU's conclusion, but the prospect of the check flying away made for a quick "on-second-thought" swing to Musco—with satisfactory results.

Ferguson's recommendation of the strings-attached policy to major gifts had its roots in the 1989 Charles Dotter Institute flap at Oregon. There Cook has now donated more than $18 million to its origin and continuance, but it took another threatened pullout to get it as he wanted it.

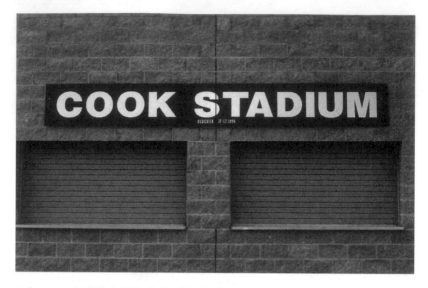

A donation by Bill and Gayle Cook helped Rose-Hulman University build a football and track stadium.

"Those situations were typical of how Bill was making his donations," Ferguson said. "He'd send them $10 million and then expect them to do what he wants. I told him, 'Put that in writing before you give it to them, Bill. Then if they don't want to do it, you don't give it to them.' He's been doing better about that. It's hard, but he's doing better."

The Herman Wells Way

The Bill and Gayle Cook gifts and donations over the years have accumulated to more than $275 million. More will be coming, usually for a stated purpose. "We make it that, No. 1, we have an input into the donation, if we need it," Cook said. "For example, we gave money to the IU School of Music, and on Dean Charles Webb's suggestion we designated it for the School of Music's library. So we had some authority where that money went."

His warm relationship with Indiana University started with the university's longtime president Herman B Wells, whom Cook got to know in a variety of roles: as a member of the Bloomington Public Utilities Board, an IU trustee, and a member of the IU Foundation.

"Everyone was a friend of Herman Wells. I remember where I met Herman—on the sidewalk, at the corner of Third and Hawthorne [at a time when the Cooks were still years away from wealthy]. Gayle, Carl, and I were watching the Homecoming parade, standing over by a fireplug. Here came Herman. He stepped over on the other side of the fireplug, and he started talking to Carl, who was about 4 or 5. They talked together for about twenty minutes—I'll never forget that, how he could carry a child's conversation.

"He was such a gentleman. Even in his nineties, he would come to all the IU Foundation meetings and all the trustee meetings. In trustees' meetings, if he was asked about a proposal that he didn't like, he wouldn't answer—he'd move on to a different subject. That never happened to me, but I did observe it, particularly when I went to a couple of Foundation meetings as a trustee." His negative tactic was different there. "They asked Herman what he thought, and he just looked like he was asleep. Then a few minutes later when we'd talk about something that was of interest to him, he'd brighten right up.

"He went to everything. If you invited Herman Wells, he would be there. One time we were down at the Jones House, before we donated it to the state. We sat down at lunch, about twenty of us at a long, narrow table, very easy to talk across. The food was out of this world—fried chicken and all the things in a down-home farm dinner. I was sitting next to Herman, and when I had finished, I turned to him and said, 'I am so full I think I'm going to die.' He just kept eating and said, 'Bill, what a way to go.'

"Every honor we ever got, every major thing that happened in the company—there was always a note from Herman, always some kind of congratulations, always handwritten.

"During the early stages of our reconstruction at West Baden, he had his driver take him down. He insisted on touring the construction in his wheelchair—and there was snow falling. He had first been there as a student.

"He was getting pretty frail when he came to one of the first shows of Brass Theater. He was in his wheelchair. He said, 'Bill, that was lovely.' And he had tears in his eyes.

"He just never missed a trick. You can see all the twinkle the man had by reading his book. Like saying the best place to do business is at a funeral. Who else would say that?"

"I relied upon Herman several times when I was on the City Utilities Service Board. We were putting a big tank up east of town, near the IU golf course. People opposing it didn't want that water tank where it is because it would spoil the view. That tank was necessary, to protect the high-rise apartments and dormitories out there. I went to Herman and said, 'What do we do?' He said, 'Bill, it's only going to be two months and the students will be gone. I would suggest the tank be built then.' He knew how it would be eventually. Now trees have grown up around it, and you can hardly see that tank. But when they built it, one piece was left out—a large piece of metal. And on the side of the tank, some student painted: 'This is going to leak.' Students are great.

"Another time with CFC we wanted to take a house down that was next-

J property. I went to see Herman to see if he had any objection,
d no, that house really didn't have any value. That didn't mean
t not be city opposition. I said, 'How in the world can we get
: way the city is?' Herman said, 'Bill, I would suggest that any
omes down should come down at night.' That's exactly what

Everything he did was so practical and so appropriate."

Cook also had a close relationship with the longtime president of the Indiana University Foundation, Bill Armstrong, and a strong feeling for John W. Ryan, whose sixteen-year tenure as IU president (1971–87) was the longest and most successful of the six presidents who came after Wells—before inauguration in 2007 of No. 7 in the post-Wells presidential succession line, Michael McRobbie.

"John Ryan was our last giant, one of the really great educators. I think Adam Herbert [McRobbie's immediate predecessor] could have been an excellent long-term president—dynamic—if he hadn't run into health problems [severe diabetes] nobody had any reason to suspect."

His enthusiasm for financial support of IU, which had waned in the twenty years after Ryan, revived only a few weeks into McRobbie's reign. "I'm changing my attitude a lot more favorably toward IU again. They seem to have a real leader. Leadership can take a faculty and, even if they don't have the credentials, demonstrate a way it can become top rank very quickly. This we have not been able to do. IU needs to get its academic standards up and become better at what it's doing.

"Steve [Ferguson, who succeeded Cook on the IU Board of Trustees and in his fourth term is the board's president] has been doing a fantastic job, trying to get priorities reestablished. For so many years they just went along aimlessly. I do believe they are coming along now with a real plan for the future."

Sights Now on High Schools

Cook is looking in a new direction with his educational philanthropy. "I'd really like to concentrate now on the high school level. The high schools have been sacrificed at the expense of higher education. The high schools are just not getting enough money, and the money is not getting put in the right places. They have enough for basketball and football, that kind of thing, but not enough for music. I'd like to see that corrected, even to the extent where kids could receive music lessons if they were talented. I don't know about art. Maybe what we have there now is okay, maybe not.

"I think it's just a shame that so many of these things have gone by the wayside. I can understand why, because the money is critical in high schools today and the legislatures are trying to get academics at the highest level they think they can. But there are other things in high school life. For example, machine shop. How about complex machines? How about electronics? If we trained them properly, a lot of kids leaving high school would never have to worry about a college education, because they would be ready to go into the workforce."

In late summer 2007, Bloomington announced plans to add a new public high school, specializing in high-tech training. The first major outside supporting gift was $150,000 from Cook Inc.

The high school interest likely will carry over into the next Cook company reign as well. Carl Cook already has spearheaded one drive supporting an alternative high school, Harmony, including renovation of the old Elm Heights building where he went to elementary school and Harmony now operates. Carl's personal commitment there was just under $1 million.

"In Indiana, school boards are elected, and it seems to be a popularity contest," Bill Cook said. "I've seen an awful lot of inept decision-making by school boards. How many kids today are coming to school poor? How much would it take to see uniforms on high school kids, if it could be mandated? We have too much structure from the superintendent on down. How in the world did we all get along with one-room schoolhouses, where the parents paid the teacher? Why do we need all that structure? They need a principal, but I don't think they need an 'assistant superintendent of curriculum.'"

19

Rising Stars

A 20-Year, $28 Million Investment in Kids

The first time Carl spent a summer in drum corps I
recognized that it was more than a musical program. That's
why I got started in drum corps. He came back totally different—
more disciplined, more fit, more thoughtful, more respectful.
It changed his life, and it has done the same thing to every
person I've seen—made them a better person. That opened
my eyes that you can alter an environment slightly and get a
completely different and better result. That's what I kept seeing
in almost everyone who was a part of Star of Indiana. It favorably
altered people's attitudes, completely changed people's lives.

—*Bill Cook*

That's the concise Bill Cook explanation of his link to a pastime that for
nearly a decade quite happily consumed him and in many ways defined
him. Because of what he saw in his own son after his first summer of marching in drum corps, and what he continued to see throughout nine years as
an underwriter, Cook considers the $28 million it cost him and Gayle a

worthwhile investment in young people. The period also had a dramatic impact on the drum corps world, which never had a champion quite like the Bill Cook creation, Star of Indiana.

Bill Cook has been out of drum corps longer now than he was in it, but it's going to take a whole lot longer than that before that world will ever forget those names: Star of Indiana and Bill Cook.

Star of Indiana—Fast to Rise

"Drum corps" is not a name of instant recognition throughout America, à la Boy Scouts and Little League. Still, drum corps itself is a little bit unbelievable in lots of ways that start with the passion of its participants and its fans, whose number is big-time.

Drum corps roots are in patriotism. Its name is short for drum and bugle corps, variations of which popped up all across America in the 1920s primarily as veterans' groups (conquering heroes home from World War I) marching with drums and bugles in Fourth of July parades and such. Naturally, the volunteer groups soon figured out ways to compete with each other. And, ultimately, kids got involved.

In winter 1971, Drum Corps International was organized. Rules were drawn up for a formalized, centrally administered youth activity. A nation that has always loved its high school and college marching bands found pockets everywhere of people swept away as drum corps developed into a summertime refinement-advancement-enhancement of those colorful scholastic marching bands. DCI's website says, "Some call it extreme marching band; others compare it to professional marching band; one director even refers to it as a cross between a Broadway musical and a marching band show." The website www.DCI.org offers its own description: "independent youth organizations made up of up to 135 14–22-year-olds who spend the summer rehearsing and performing an eleven-minute show in which they play a variety of horns or percussion instruments, or spin flags, rifles, sabers, and other implements, all while marching around a football field."

Don't skip lightly past that key item: "an eleven-minute show." That is a drum corps summer: 135 performers playing and playing and playing again, marching and drilling over and over and over again, daily, on the same eleven-minute musical show.

Jim Mason is a drum corps lifer—started in it as a performer at 7, played the saxophone in a marching band, jazz band, and concert band while attending the University of Northern Iowa, but came out "really wanting a chance" to be what he became: a drum corps director.

The charm of drum corps to him: "It's all about perfection. It's taking eleven minutes of a show and fine-tuning it, making sure that every hand is in the right place, every foot is in the right place, everything from a timing standpoint, a look standpoint, a sound standpoint is all synchronized and as close to perfection as possible. That's the quest we're on."

Hundreds of groups start out on that quest every summer. And, oh, those groups compete. And entertain. And, oh, they draw crowds. Which go wild.

Nobody loves those glorious, colorful shows more than Bill Cook. Epiphany day came for him at home in late summer 1980 when Carl was watching a telecast of the DCI World Championships out of Birmingham, Alabama. As the competition built toward its climax, Carl wasn't watching alone.

"I got more enjoyment out of it than he did, I think," Bill said. "Man, I wouldn't let him turn the set off or do anything. I just sat there glued."

And hooked. Both of them, actually. Carl had just graduated from Bloomington High School South, where he had played the saxophone in a band directed by Kem Hawkins. That day with his dad, Carl was a few weeks away from leaving for Purdue University to start his college career, but the drum corps germ had taken hold in him. He played his sax in the marching band at Purdue, but as soon as spring classes ended in his sophomore year, he started his first season with the Colts in Dubuque, Iowa. (The Colts were marching in Dubuque long before there was a Colts pro-football team in Indianapolis.)

There are no saxophones in drum corps. "I got an old bugle and taught myself the fingers," Carl said. "I eventually wound up on the flugelhorn, which Chuck Mangione plays. I played flugelhorn and mellophone from then on in drum corps.

"Jim Mason was the Colts' director. They were a Top-20 corps. They played well, they marched terribly, and that was fine with me. I didn't like marching anyway."

Drum corps, at its "junior" and most prominent level, has some pertinent numbers: ages 14 through 22, blending high school and college kids, totaling 135 in a corps. It's not a summer "job." Money goes the other way. Corps members pay to be part of it. And they keep coming back.

That first year, Carl entered the Colts' routine, which he later learned was typical: collegians reported first, joined by the rest as soon as high school classes ended.

"We would practice evenings during May. Memorial Day we would do a bunch of parades—we called it the Memorial Day Death Camp. You practice all day, go do a parade, and come back to practice. In June, the high school kids came in, and we would go to all-day practice. Our first show—at Geneseo or Canton, Illinois, they kind of alternated—was the third weekend in June." That is the Canton where his dad grew up.

"Once those shows started, we'd do one, then the next weekend loop into

Stars of the Star

Iowa, Minnesota, Wisconsin, and back. We called it the 'Cornfield Tour.' On June 25 we would leave on a full-blown tour—in July and August, maybe as far as the East Coast and back.

"It's like a long camping trip. You're riding in old buses, you're sleeping on gym floors, you're practicing all day, and you're doing a show every night or every other night. Wherever we were on the Fourth of July, we'd do about eight parades. My second year marching, we spent the Fourth at Green Bay, Wisconsin, and we played a show at Lambeau Field. I actually got to be on the 'frozen tundra.'"

Lambeau, the most famous of all pro football playing fields, site of the epic "Ice Bowl" game with Dallas for the NFL championship in 1967, darned near was tundra that day, even in July. "We got up on the morning of the Fourth for practice and a bank sign said 47 degrees. You're not prepared for that. When we played the show that night, it was so cold you could see steam coming out of the bells."

Carl turned 22 as a Colt in 1984. In drum corps talk, that's "aging out," the end of the line. His parents were in the stands when Carl marched with the Colts at the world championships in Atlanta, and his career was over.

That's when a whole new show began, launched by surely the most frenetic four days in drum corps history.

Those are the days Bill Cook tucks up nicely: "I talked to Carl a few minutes—the competition was just over—then went over to the bus to see Jim Mason before he could leave, and Jim said, 'Give me a little bit of time and I'll think about it.'"

When Carl heard his father's plans to finance a drum corps, he was surprised but not totally shocked. "He *had* talked about having a corps, and I thought he would do it. He always said he wouldn't do it until after I had aged out. I didn't expect him to wait only fifteen minutes."

Salesman at Work

Bill did forget to mention one thing to Carl in their rushed conversation. "I didn't find out until a few days later that Jim Mason was going to be the director," Carl said. "That was a shock."

Mason still gets a little breathless remembering how many shocks came for him that weekend, beginning with his conversation with Cook at Atlanta.

"Bill was with Bob Lendman. We knew each other. We had been directors in the same district. I had always thought of Bill as just a nice guy in a cardigan sweater who watched practice and seemed to enjoy it. I had heard that Carl was from an affluent background, but I didn't know what that meant.

"So they came over and Bill said he wanted to start a drum corps. I said, 'Okay, to do that you're going to have to buy buses, a place to rehearse, uniforms, gear, and have a staff. It's going to cost about a million dollars.' He said, 'Okay.' Then I tried to explain to Bill what a million dollars is.

"Now, understand that *I* . . . am trying to tell *Bill Cook* . . . what a *million dollars* is."

The attempted turn-off didn't work. "Bill said, 'I'd *really* like to talk to you.'

"I'm thinking, 'He's a very, very nice gentleman, very personable, with lots of enthusiasm, and just doesn't realize what he's getting himself into.' I said, 'Bill, I'm really not interested. Colts are going very well. We're climbing the ladder.' I had taken this traditional drum corps out of the ashes, and now they were climbing the ranks very quickly. I was really enjoying myself, and I loved the people I worked with. I was trying to talk him out of my participation, but I did want to help him find people. He said, 'Great, I'll give you a call when I get back.'

"I drove a van full of kids all night from Atlanta back to Dubuque, arrived early Sunday morning, got out of the van . . . and one of our parents who had said he would take some of our kids an hour and a half to Davenport backed out, said he hadn't been with his kid for several weeks and Davenport—'That's *your* problem.' I didn't have any choice. I drove the kids we had from there down to Davenport, came back, rolled in around 9 AM, said hi to my kids, and said, 'Daddy's going to go to bed and sleep. I'll see you about 1 o'clock.' I was in bed about ten minutes, and all of a sudden my wife is screaming at me, 'What do you *mean* we're moving to Bloomington, Indiana?' She said, 'This guy on the telephone said you're going to move to Bloomington, Indiana, and he wants to talk to you.'

Bill Cook and Bob Lendman, whose advice led Cook to hire Jim Mason
as director of the Star of Indiana drum corps.

"Now, I'm thinking this nice guy in the cardigan sweater is starting to irritate me. He said he was going to call me when I got back. I didn't know he was going to call me the moment I got back. I picked up the phone, kinda surly, and I said, 'I just got home. I had to drive. I'm not in a very good mood.' And he said, 'Oh, that's fine. Why don't you sleep until about noon, and I'll have my plane there to pick you guys up.'

"I said, 'What?'

"'Yeah, Bob Lendman and I will come pick you guys up.'

"I said, 'I haven't seen my family in a month. I really need some family time.'

"He said, 'That's fine. If you want to bring them, we'll set them up with a hotel room. There'll be a pool there. It'll be nice. The kids can play.'

"I'm standing there looking at the phone.

"On the airplane, he said, 'What's the scenario of how we build this thing? What will it take to get you to leave the Colts?'

"Again I said I wasn't interested, but I would try to help line up some people for him. That was a Monday. I went to work on the phone the next morning from an office in his office building, lining up a staff. I knew some very good people whose corps had just folded. They were happy to talk about being part of a new corps. About noon, we went to lunch. Afterward, he said, 'I've got a couple of places I want you to look at.'

"The first one we went to was Brown Elementary School [a vacant school

331

building north of Bloomington, no longer used then but still owned by the county school corporation]. We drove into the school parking lot. I thought school was still in session; there were about twenty cars parked in the lot. We pulled up, and doors opened on all those cars—Cook people, heating and cooling people, electricians, construction people, the realtor who was in charge of selling the building. They gathered in front of the school.

"We all walked through the building with everybody taking notes as Bill would ask me, 'What should be here? And how about over there?' We went room by room by room and on the fly designed the perfect corps hall. We got to the end of the corridor and he said, 'What do you think?' I said, 'Bill, this is amazing. This would work out really well. All you'd have to do is maybe flatten a couple of these hills.' He turned to the excavating guy, who said, 'No problem. We can do it.' I'm just thinking, my gosh!

"He turned to me and said, 'I can buy this building for $150,000—forty acres with it. If you were the director, would you want it?' I said yes." Out came a checkbook and the deal was made in front of Mason's popped eyes.

"I looked at Bill—I hadn't talked to my wife—and I said, 'Mr. Cook, I don't know what's going on, but you just showed commitment, and I want you to know, you have yourself a corps director.'"

Saturday in Atlanta, Sunday a phone call, Monday in Bloomington, Tuesday acceptance. Four days that changed Jim Mason's life and drum corps forever.

Big League from Beginning

Salary hadn't been mentioned. "Bill ended up offering me $2,000 more than I made with the Colts. But it had nothing to do with money. I wanted a new challenge. And I made sure the Colts were okay. I left the entire staff intact. I had named the director to follow me. It was as seamless as that kind of transition could be."

It even included Carl, who had agreed to help coach the Colts the next summer. His dad's hiring of Mason "did kind of strain my friendship with some of the guys in the corps for a while," Carl said. "It blew over. I stayed on staff for two years. I didn't enjoy it." He never was tempted to pitch in with instructing back in Bloomington. "I wasn't at that level. These guys were big league from the beginning."

There was never any question about that, never any need for Mason to persuade Cook to go after top talent. "Bill had said 'We're starting at the top,'" Gayle Cook remembers. "Everybody he asked about starting a drum corps said, 'Don't do it.' That made him want to do it more. He would say, 'I *know* if we do this right, it will work.' Hundreds of corps are started every year, and they fold. They recruit the kids and never have enough money.

He started by hiring the right people and giving them the money to do it right the first year."

The name was in place from the beginning: Star of Indiana. This was in a world where its elite wore names like Cavaliers, Blue Devils, Cadets, Kingsmen, and Phantom Regiment, commonly without a geographic reference in the title at all.

Michael Boo, a corpsman himself (the Chicago-based Cavaliers, seven-time world champions), for years has been one of drum corps' leading columnists and writers. He recalls the first time he learned of this new operation starting to stir in Indiana. "I had heard that this businessman was going to start a corporate-sponsored corps in Bloomington. I was in the DCI office for something, and the person in charge of public relations said, 'We've got the worst name ever created for a corps: Star of Indiana.' We're all used to it now, but at the time 'Star of Indiana' seemed . . . *not very creative*. Now nobody even thinks of that because it's so much in our vernacular."

Jim Mason knew word was getting around, so he flaunted everything—the name, the staff he had put together, even nationally known Indiana University basketball coach Bob Knight, who, as a Bill Cook friend, okayed use of his name in one of Mason's zany trumpetings.

In mid-November 1984, the Bloomington newspaper, the IU campus newspaper, the Indianapolis *Star,* and—straight into the activity's bloodstream—*Drum Corps World* magazine each ran a full-page ad headlined INDIANA HAS THE BEST. Far more flamboyantly than pre-game introduction of a starting lineup at one of Knight's IU games, the ad presented the brand-new Star of Indiana staff—with, of course, stars arrayed across the page each with a face, identified as:

> Dennis DeLucia, percussive arranger, judged to have
> the top DCI percussion line three straight years.

> Michael Cesario, program consultant/uniform designer,
> Broadway costume designer, and program conductor
> for the world champion Garfield Cadets.

> George Zingali, visual arranger, visual designer
> for the Garfield Cadets.

> Larry Kerchner, brass arranger, well known arranger for band
> and drum corps.

> John Simpson, brass educator, taught numerous DCI top horn lines.

The man who drew it up had a star for himself:

Jim Mason, director, past vice president Drum Corps Midwest, former director of Colts.

There was a seventh face in a seventh star in the middle of the galaxy, identified:

> Oh, by the way, the man in the center is Bobby Knight, U.S. gold medal–winning coach and IU's basketball coach.

"I just tried to think of what Bloomington was known for, and Bobby Knight was the name that jumped out to me," Mason said. "I wanted to create controversy right off the bat—call attention to everybody in drum corps what we were doing. I knew the response to that ad would be, 'What is going on?' I was called everything from a nice corps director to the biggest SOB who ever lived."

It was an impressive opening staff. Zingali, DeLucia, and Cesario are all in the DCI Hall of Fame.

Mason sent a mailing to band directors throughout Indiana, notifying them of Star of Indiana's tryout camp over Thanksgiving weekend that year and announcing dates for the first pre-season camp the next summer. "I got an irate call from an Indiana band director: 'Jim, I have sixteen kids coming to your camp. I run a summer program. What are you going to do about it?' I said, 'I don't want your sophomores, juniors, and seniors. I want your graduates.' He couldn't believe it. He became one of our best spokesmen out and around the state. We had about two hundred people at our first camp to pick our corps. We had a good group to choose from. We opened June 18 at Normal, Illinois."

Star of Indiana was in its first show, but not exactly as prime-time performers.

Businessman-Busdriver

A new corps—any first-year drum corps competing in DCI—pays its dues at every event of the summer. It's the first that has to perform, always, while the sun is still bright, while the crowd is still coming in, while rivals are working in practice.

"The show starts at 6 PM, but the good corps aren't on until 9 or 10. You miss three or four hours of practice during the important part of the afternoon every day. Then after you perform you sit around at the show until midnight, then drive all night to the next place, sleep for a few hours, get up. You've got half the practice time of any other corps." But that night at Normal, it was show time.

The ad, the buzz—Star of Indiana wasn't coming in unknown. "Rumors were flying around," Mason said. "Word was out." Star was the new drum corps with a millionaire's silver spoon in its mouth. "The first year it was more of an undercurrent, chuckle-chuckle, having fun with it. But I knew we were going to be controversial. I thought we might be booed right off the field.

"About ten of the really premier groups were there that first night. It was amazing. We finished third place overall and first in brass! We upset the Cavaliers. We upset the Madison Scouts, who were known for their brass. That sent a message around the drum corps world. And it set the tone for the Star of Indiana. That's when we realized we were on the quest to be No. 1. Nothing was going to get in our way.

"From there on out the group went through an amazing season, a storybook season. We finished tenth in the world championships." No other first-year corps has ever done that.

"People think it had to do with Bill's money. Bill's money helped. But Bill's support, Bill's vision, Bill's caring—those were the things that really mattered. You can't fool the public. You either belong in that group or you don't. We kicked the door down. They didn't want to let us in.

"That first year we traveled from Missouri to Corning, New York, one night, because we couldn't get in shows. We got into Corning at 5 AM and the show was at 6 PM. That whole summer we zigzagged across the country. My bus drivers weren't very happy. And Bill was one of them."

That's true. The man who was paying all the bills—the man who drove a truck in his early teens and a Chicago cab in his early twenties—drove a Star of Indiana bus that first year and stayed with it as a full-time regular throughout the corps' lifetime. "I just picked up driving a bus in 1984," he said. "I got my license and passed the written exam with no problem. I had past experience."

It wasn't easy driving, rolling through the night from one performance site to another.

"Usually a drive would start at 11 PM or midnight, right after a show, and we would normally drive until 4 in the morning, up to 8. Gayle and I would have breakfast, then go to bed. We'd get up around 5 PM, dress, and go have supper, then go out to wherever the corps was performing. I'd take the staff to the venue with the bus. We'd see thirty-eight shows a year that way—every night."

The group traveled in a caravan, connected by radio. "We had some fun times," Bill said. "Everett Farley headed up the bus drivers [his full-time role with Cook Inc.]. One time he said something to us on the radio about a turn coming up. I acknowledged that I had heard him by saying, 'You're the boss.' He said, 'Okay, Cook—you're fired.'"

The bus Bill drove carried Star of Indiana staff people, not the marchers. "He laid down rules for the staff and had them printed out, so they took care of the bus properly and behaved properly on the bus," Gayle said. "When you travel with 150 people, unless you have rules, everything can fall apart, especially when you have mostly teenagers. But I know he enjoyed it very much. I was never on his bus. We had three semis, four buses, two vans, and a car. I drove the car.

"Everybody had a job. At first, I was kind of lost. I tried sewing, but they always had other people. I tried cooking. Everybody does something. Then when I started driving, it was much better, because people who drive have to—*must*—sleep during the day. So my day was taken care of, and Bill's, too. It was a good experience. Exhilarating because teenagers are so emotional and excitable and enthusiastic and physically fit. And they did well. That was always rewarding.

"Jim Mason was so organized. He had his rules—in our corps, if you were caught with drugs and it's obvious, there's no hearing, you're out. If you're caught stealing, you're out. Drinking on the bus, I think they give a warning first. Some kids came from other corps where it was ignored."

The Cooks set up disciplinary rules even for themselves.

"Bill and I tried not to have too many personal relationships with the performers," Gayle said, "because they have to answer to the director. We found when we got close to any of them, they would come to us and say, 'My sister's getting married. I need to go to the wedding.' There's no time off in drum corps. You can't have people missing when you're performing. We decided we couldn't be in that position. Everything had to go through Jim Mason."

Bill wasn't always in his bus on Star of Indiana trips. Michael Boo saved an e-mail from brass educator John Simpson, who remembered riding in a car with Bill to a first-year competition site. They were several miles ahead of what Simpson called "the entourage of buses, equipment trailer, etc.," but he knew where it was. "He parked on a side with the car lights aimed at the highway. He was like a little kid, excited to watch the corps soon pass by. . . . Bill was not the only one in the car who felt the thrill of this."

It didn't take long for Bill Cook to become the best-known character of DCI. "I was extremely controversial," he says, reflecting on his DCI years more than a decade later. "I was not liked universally, mainly because Star of Indiana was perceived to be a very moneyed organization, which they were, because we financed them. We put them in buses that actually ran, with drivers who actually were skilled. I consider myself to be one.

"But we did not mess around. We had discipline. Star of Indiana was considered to be quite an organization, because straight out of the box we were successful. I was very proud of that. But we paid the price—notoriety and success.

"So what? We were doing what we wanted to do: teach these young people how to really be musicians and compete. Always compete on the field and leave it on the field. When you did the best you could, get out of there, get on the bus, and start practicing the next day. They started practice at 8 or 9 AM and practiced all day until 6 and then performed at 8 or 9. It's a killer in the summer. Sure wore me out. Gayle, too."

The work schedule was so intense it impressed a man known for driving his own kids hard: "Coach Knight was great. He always supported our kids, came out to our shows, did everything we could ask," Mason said. "The summer before the 1986–87 basketball season, he watched one of our practices and said, 'I'm going to send my team out to see what hard work really is.' So he did. One morning there they all were: Steve Alford, Daryl Thomas, Keith Smart, the team that won the national championship that year. A normal practice day at drum and bugle corps campus has the kids on the field from 9 to noon, 1 to 5, and 6 to 11. I told the basketball guys, 'All I want you to do is take an instrument and follow a person around the field, carrying what he does. After a while, they were panting, doubled over. Keith Smart is a very personable guy, lots of personality. He asked me, 'How much do they get paid?' I said, 'They don't get paid anything. As a matter of fact, they pay to do it.' He said, 'Why do they do that?' I said, 'Well, Keith, the love of their sport.' In '91 when we won the championship, Coach Knight came out to our celebration, and I couldn't resist kidding him: 'Isn't it about time to send your kids out to one of our practices again? You know, you haven't won an NCAA championship since the last time you did that.'"

An Irrepressible Target

Particularly at the world championships, Bill Cook's playfulness knew no bounds. He dressed up in his own uniform, themed by whatever Jim Mason had chosen for Star's show that year. His incentive came that very first year of competition, when the legend of lavish spending manifested in a cynical nastiness in the final-night crowd. Mason's theme choice that introductory year—when his advisers were suggesting something more orthodox and respectful, from, say, Gershwin—was *Salute to Walt Disney.*

"We cheesed it to the max," Mason said. "We even had our kids do some singing. That wasn't done in drum corps at the time."

And that final night of the 1985 competition at Madison, Wisconsin, Michael Boo says, "When they sang the Mickey Mouse song—M-I-C-K-E-Y M-O-U-S-E—you could hear some corps fans singing M-I-C-K-E-Y M-O-N-E-Y. That was the perception. And it never went away."

The urban legend of Latin expressions is *Illegitimas non carborundum*— "Don't let the bastards grind you down." Bill Cook they never, ever did. Instead, his ornery side fed that jealousy. In an interview somewhere along the DCI trail, he laughed and called his creation "the best corps money could

Bill Cook in costume—a regular feature at world championship time

Bloomington lawyer Bill Finch, IU Alumni Association director Jerry Tardy, and IU Foundation president Bill Armstrong congratulate Bill Cook at Dallas, where Star of Indiana at last won the world drum corps championship

buy." Those words echoed from someone, acidly, at every Star performance the rest of the way, for sure at every world championship.

"That was so Bill, just having fun—his lightheartedness being expressed," Mason said. "But the fraternity was looking for anything to jump on, as I knew it would. When Bill made that statement, the money thing *really* began."

Until Bill Cook and Star of Indiana, big-money resentment within drum corps focused on California teams and the financing that their loose bingo laws allowed, Mason said. "Gail Royer [whose Santa Clara, California, Vanguard won the second and third DCI championships in 1973 and 1974 and added four others later] told me we were the best thing that ever happened to California drum and bugle corps. The money stigma came over to us. We represented an entity that nobody else had. As we kept ascending toward the throne, they had to demonize something. And Bill only knew to attack. I spent probably 60 percent of my time doing P.R. cleanup work."

It wasn't hard to spot Bill Cook among the thousands at the world championships each August. When Star's theme in 1990 at Buffalo was *Belshazzar's Feast*, Bill mixed with the crowd and sat in the stands lavishly dressed as King Belshazzar. Another time he was the Joker.

"The kids just loved Bill's dressing up in those costumes," Gayle said. His celebrity extended well past his own drum corps. "He was probably more recognized and better known within the drum corps world than anywhere else. Not everybody in the medical community who had heard of Cook Inc. would know Bill in a room. In drum corps, everybody knew him."

Mason said, "He was really enjoying the whole activity, enjoying the celebrity status. He was being playful with how quirky he could be."

"He is certainly not without a sense of whimsy," Michael Boo said.

One Night in Dallas

There was no stereotyping in Star of Indiana themes. That was Mason's determination from the start. "Drum corps love to pigeonhole. If you play jazz, you play jazz for thirty years. If you play classical music, you're the classical corps. Somebody said to me, 'What style is your drum corps going to be?' I said, 'We're going to be chameleon plaid. As soon as you think we're doing this, we're doing that.' And that worked well for us." So after the opening year with Disney came a variety of themes:

- *Out of This World* in the season that climaxed at Madison in 1986 (around John Williams music and the Conversation scene from *Close Encounters of the Third Kind*);
- *The Greatest Show on Turf* at Madison in 1987 (circus: dancing pink elephants and all);

- *Porgy & Bess* at Kansas City in 1988 (George Gershwin's folk opera employed visually without sets);
- *British Invasions* at Kansas City in 1989 (an exploration of the music of Great Britain, with a drum corps touch).

Then came *Belshazzar's Feast* in 1990, leading—after the heartbreak of near misses—to the breakthrough to the championship with gala George Zingali treatment of *Roman Images* at Dallas in August 1991.

Bill, Gayle, and Carl Cook were there, of course. So was much of Cook Inc. This was Quest Realized. "We won a world championship—in Dallas, at the Cotton Bowl, 30,000 people sitting there," Bill Cook recalls. "We won it all."

"We hugged each other," Mason said. "I think Bill was happy for me and I was happier for him. There was an element of relief, of getting a monkey off our back. But, like most championships, you're happiest of all for the kids."

There were tears, of course. And there were some ugly boos, of course. Gayle heard them and never showed bitterness. "Oh," she said, "it was funny." Not funny-funny. "Strange. It was jealousy. There's not a corps that would turn down money, so they wouldn't have to have bake sales or scrimp on buses. A lot of little corps scrape the money together and get sixty-five kids, and then they fold. It's an extremely expensive endeavor. You need all those buses, and semis, and uniforms, and you feed the kids. A lot of drum corps charge more. In Star we charged only a $250 per-season fee, so we could go after the best musicians and just consider everybody on scholarship. Kids who were good would come to audition.

"But at those shows it was the kids who were performing, and they didn't seem to mind the boos because they were doing well. It was, after all, their work and talent that was winning."

Revenge, by Medea

The championship seemed only to intensify the hate-Star segment of drum corps crowds. Mason went into the off-season seething. "After we won, I knew there was going to be great resentment. That's when the boobirds *really* started.

"I learned something from vaudeville. Whenever a comic is in trouble, a cute little girl comes out, waves the American flag, and everybody goes crazy. I thought, I'm going to do the same thing. I decided to do [in the 1992 season] an entire show of color presentations—an American show, waving the American flag. We played 'America the Beautiful,' we played 'The Star-Spangled Overture,' a Morton Gould thing built around the anthem—

Indiana governor Evan Bayh hosted Star of Indiana after it won the championship at Dallas in 1991. Also pictured: corps director Jim Mason, Teresa Mason, and Bill Cook, along with Mason's sons A.J. and Todd.

we had the Statue of Liberty and fireworks going off." And still they were booed.

In the championships that year at Madison, the defending champions came in third. "I've never been homered so bad in all my life," Mason said. "We were undefeated for the whole year going into the world championship. At quarterfinals, we won and got booed off the field—with our American flags! And we won! The second night, the semifinals, we walked in and the crowd was throwing things at us—throwing money. One of our kids got hit by a coin.

"I wasn't around Bill, but I knew it had to be really embarrassing for him. Bill cares about the kids. He knew the effort they were putting out. The third night, we came in—and now the crowd was in a frenzy. We're waiting to go out onto the field—football stands on each side of us—and people were just pitching things at us, throwing drinks. Now I'm really ticked. This is an activity I've been involved with all my life. I'm embarrassed. Bill had invited a bunch of people in to see the show as his guests."

Mason sought his revenge with the show he and brass arranger Jim Prime put together for 1993, built around one of the most evil women in Greek mythology, Medea. "It's not a happy story," Mason said. "I decided to let our kids take out their frustration. I challenged Jim Prime to not let the audience in the performance at all, from the first note to the last note, not even give them time to applaud—don't let the music stop, don't let the audience breathe, just move through the show so fast and so angrily it's like letting our kids punch the crowd in the face as many times as they wanted to, and then get the hell off the field. It ended in a flurry of musical violence. I wanted to leave nothing on the field. Say it and get off."

Michael Boo, in a copyrighted CD package of the nine Star of Indiana world championship performances, wrote of that one in 1993 at Jackson, Mississippi:

> Like a swift kick to the face, Star's final show took the audience and shook them with all the tenderness of an exploding volcano. Mixed between moments of silence and interpretive movement were the most cataclysmic sounds to ever assault a field. The drill and guard equipment were equally hard-edged. The gasps from the audience have yet to quiet down, and the show is now seen as a classic that was years ahead of its time.

Fourteen years later, Boo said, "This show broke all the molds. It was so cutting-edge, so minimalist, so irritating to people who are still longing for the days of Sousa. So when they were winning all season long, every time they were announced in first, audiences would boo—certainly not the majority but enough to be heard. They didn't understand the show.

"We recently had a poll of what's called Drum Corps Planet—a website of thousands of people who belong to it and chat about drum corps and other things all year long. The poll was to pick the best show in DCI history. That *Medea* show won hands down."

"And we lost!" Mason said.

Carl Cook has no doubt that the boos from the crowd made the difference that year in judging that gave the Cadets victory by the slimmest possible cumulative judging margin, a tenth of a point, 97.4 to 97.3. "I don't think any of those judges had the courage to face that hostile crowd," Carl said. "Anybody would tell you now they were the best, by a point and a half. They had them all beat. The first eight minutes were perfectly executed but didn't get the crowd into it. But people remember the last two minutes as some of the greatest ever done. But there was no way—and we knew it going in—that they were going to let us win that night, because you would have had a riot. It was that hostile.

"The Star disappeared after that, but every corps within two or three years was trying to be the next *Medea*. What you have now is every corps trying to do *Medea*. That's why a lot of people, including myself, are turned off. And that makes *Medea* look even better, because none of those shows have worked. There's never been another one."

Carl Cook hasn't forgotten the meanest of the anti-Star boos. "Alumni of drum corps that have folded tend to be very bitter. They have reunions and sit there and bitch about how the judges screwed them in '72, or if they hadn't been disqualified in '75 they wouldn't have folded. And a lot of these people, even if their corps folded ten years before Star was formed, think somehow Star had something to do with their demise. These people would be sitting in the stands drinking cheap gin and yelling obscenities at Star when they'd take the field. It was not fun, particularly that '93 year because there was so much hostility to that show."

The grand quest had a nine-year lifespan but a longer memory for Bill Cook, the man who first thought of, then set out on, that quest.

Michael Boo says, "All that animosity at the end wasn't there at the start. At first there was a curiosity about Star. People weren't rooting for them to fall on their face until they started beating their favorite corps.

"Bill became real good friends with George Bonfiglio, who was the director of the 27th Lancers of Revere, Mass. They competed, pretty much on the same level, but once when the Lancers' bus broke down, Bill sent a bus to pick them up. In January 2006, DCI had a meeting in Chicago of what were jokingly referred to as 'the dinosaurs'—a handful of people who had been around drum corps from the beginning—to talk about the organization's roots for those who didn't know the story.

"Bonfiglio told all the DCI directors, 'You had a savior. You chased him away.'"

Chased isn't really accurate, Boo concedes, but it's not way off. "Let's just say a lot of people were very happy to see him go. And it had to have been tiring for him to hear the corps get booed."

Still . . .

"Bill can never say he doesn't care about drum corps anymore," Boo said. "When the 2005 finals were in Foxboro, Massachusetts, I got a call on my cell phone. 'I'd like to hear the scores tonight.'" That's how the crowd and the corps learn the champion is revealed—by announcement of judging results over the stadium public address system.

"I let Bill listen to the scores live, as they were being announced. The next year I called and asked him if he'd like to do that again. 'Oh, yeah,' he said. And I put him on again."

A Tony and an
Emmy for *Blast!*

A Tony, an Emmy, a Blast

Bill Cook and Jim Mason "knew the whole three months of that 1993 season it was our last year," Mason says—knew because they had signed a contract guaranteeing it.

Each remembers well when and where two frustrated minds came together and changed Star—July 4, 1992, at Stillwater, Minnesota, a small river town just east of Minneapolis–St. Paul on the Wisconsin border.

"One thing that bothered both Jim and me was that we worked all summer on just eleven minutes of music," Bill said. "That is a killer. You try to play eleven minutes of music, in perfect form, and march to it. Those performances became so repetitive. In Stillwater, we were warming up and on the Fourth of July we couldn't play 'The Star-Spangled Banner.'

"I said to Jim, 'Ain't that the shits.'"

Mason was in his own funk. "I had walked with Bill to the bus, and I'm mad as hell. We had just warmed up for an hour, played a standstill eleven-minute performance, the crowd went crazy—and we were done.

"I said, 'Bill, I feel terrible. Drum corps is the biggest waste of time. If you were spending this amount of money and wanted me to design the best possible musical youth venture, this isn't what I would design.'

"He said, 'What would *you* want to do?'

"I said, 'I'd like to expose these kids to professional musicians, because that's what they are aspiring to be. I'd like to play the major venues in this country. I'd like to play a vast musical repertoire and see what happens.'

"He was bright-eyed, right in step. 'That's really a great idea!'

"It was just an idea then. The idea kept growing in my mind and I kept developing it."

Cook said, "All of that kinda rang the bell that maybe it was time to move on and learn a large repertoire and be with an organization that would make these kids professionals."

Already by then, Mason said, "We had made friends with the Canadian Brass." That's a touring group of five professionals, playing a tuba, a trombone, a horn, and two trumpets, showmen who since their formation in 1970 have performed in black suits and white gym shoes and wowed crowds. They performed at the IU Auditorium in March 1992. Star performed as the warm-up.

After that warm-up act, Mason said, "Chuck Daellenbach, the tuba player, came running backstage and gave me a big hug—I hardly knew the guy—and he said, 'That's the first time I've ever heard a brass symphony.' That struck a nerve in my brain that we had reached a quality and level of sound that somebody of that level would appreciate—that we had some value."

Bloomington has its own tuba legend, Indiana University School of Music professor Harvey Phillips, who every Christmas season puts together a whole red-and-white-clad orchestra of "Tuba Santas." Cook remembers at a party at Phillips's home after the Canadian Brass performance, Daellenbach and his group "were having cocktails, and Chuck walked over to Jim and me and said, 'Would you be interested in traveling with us for the summer?' We told them our problem, that it was against the rules to perform as professionals outside the drum corps. We couldn't do it. Then, before the evening was over, Jim and I decided that maybe this was the opportunity for a lot of kids to have a real experience."

It was an idea that still needed to be developed. "After Bill and I had that talk in Stillwater, we finished that season. I was lying on a beach at St. Petersburg, and I said to my wife, 'I just had a very clear vision of what this might become—in an arena, with lights on the stage, and the show happening, using the kids in a different way.' I could see it.

"I was so excited that I called Chuck Daellenbach, who lives in Tampa. He came over, listened, and said: 'This is a great idea. I get your vision. But why don't you take a year or two traveling with us, back us up, you guys do a number, do a number with us, we'll do one by ourselves—let's create something.'"

Thus was born "Brass Theater." Contracts were signed three months before the 1993 world DCI championships.

Evolution: Of a Show, and a Name

"The first year [1994], it was just 'the Canadian Brass and Star of Indiana join forces,'" Mason said. "The second year, I wanted to get more movement in. We did a tour de force and performed in six major arenas. We played the Hollywood Bowl, Lincoln Center, Tanglewood—the most glorious places—and exposed our kids to wonderful conductors and symphony people.

"We put together about a two-hour program that had a taste of everything. Bill gave me a list of his favorite songs—I still have the list, on a scratchy piece of paper, everything from 'Birth of the Blues' to 'Swing Low, Sweet Chariot,' an eclectic list. I think eventually I got them all in.

"That list is something I will always treasure. It tells me about his musical personality. There was some classical music. It's amazing how well rounded he is." It's the music taste that had its origins in his young piano-playing days, stretched through his choral participation (and direction) at Northwestern, and is indulged now every time he is in his car—the radio set to XM Satellite's "Escape" channel 78 and its mellow blend of hits from the fifties to the eighties. "I've continued to love choral music," Cook said. "All of this from drum corps on came out of that love."

Brass Theater ran three years (1994–96). "The last two years, we got the idea that maybe we were good enough to be a stand-alone," Mason says. "Chuck Daellenbach told me, 'These people are going crazy over you guys. We'll always have our fans. I think it's time for you to try something on your own.'"

Mason booked a theater in Branson, Missouri, for a season. "We offered scholarships to be in the program—not paying kids but offering scholarships. We did a couple of years in Branson, in theater space. I was getting used to the size of stage, the kind of movement we had to do, the vocabulary of the different types of lights, the new environment we were working in. Our biggest fan was Bobby Vinton. He would finish his show, walk across the street to our place, watch our show, then go back."

After Brass Theater's second Branson season, Mason felt it was time to take wing and leave the nest.

"I sent out videotapes to people I didn't know—booking agents. One went to a guy in Europe who came over and loved the show. This guy was slick. He met with Bill, Gayle, and me and said, 'We'll bring this to London, and you guys will be able to make money.' Gayle looked at him and said, 'We know how to make money and how to make money much easier and faster than this. So it's not about money with us.' Totally disarmed the guy.

"At dinner the guy told us, 'I really want to bring this over to London, but I don't want it to be called Brass Theater. Something else.' Bill said, 'That's no problem. Jim, tomorrow morning come in here and tell us the new name of the show.'

"I went to my hotel room, went to bed, thought about it, nothing. I got up, jumped in the shower—and, sure enough, it came to me. I knew I didn't have to sell the guy. I had to sell Bill and Gayle. I told them, 'I want to keep it simple, short, punchy—nothing to do with drum and bugle corps, something we can get on Broadway. Something that would excite people and be catchy. Hard-hitting. The word is 'Blast!'"

He didn't read instant excitement in Bill's face, so he pressed on.

"When I think of blast, I think of a loud sound . . . of a good time . . . of a noise from a trumpet. It has multiple meanings, and I think they're all good for this particular show."

And *Blast!* it was, complete with the exclamation point.

"I found out later that in London *blast* has another meaning, as a swear word." Mason said. "It means *damn!* That works, too."

Autograph, Sir?

The show opened at the Apollo Theater in London on December 14, 1999. The reviews were better than the early ticket sales.

Critic Roger Foss wrote, "It's pure razzle dazzle Americana . . . as if Busby Berkeley and Florenz Ziegfeld had risen from the dead. . . . I was too gobsmacked to join the standing ovation."[1]

But, Mason said, "We were in the London suburbs. You think of Broadway, and off-Broadway, and off-off-Broadway. We were the off-off-off-West End in London, in a place known more as a rock 'n' roll venue. We had 2,500 seats. We were doing a brisk 10 percent of the potential."

Cook said, "We went to London because it was cheaper than New York—and we almost died there. Just when we were about ready to close up, the BBC said, 'We have two segments of shows that we'd like to put you on.' We jumped at it. After the British heard us, it was SRO there. We closed in May, not because we weren't successful."

"Our work visas were up," Mason says.

Gayle has a favorite memory from those days after the show had caught on in London. "We were in the audience one night, waiting to see the show. People all around us kept turning and looking toward Bill." It was heady stuff, but "we just thought it was normal—people who come to the theater anywhere know who the producer is. Then pretty soon people with a program and a pen were coming toward where we were sitting. But they reached their programs out not for Bill to sign but to the ordinary-looking young guy sitting next to him. Bill and I looked at each other. I asked the person on my side, 'Who *is* that?'"

After a shocked look at the American's abysmal ignorance, he said, "Why, Beckham!" The nation's No. 1 soccer hero, David Beckham, was there, having a *Blast!*

"We've laughed about that," Gayle said. "Bill says, 'I thought they knew me even in London!'" (The story took on a currency when, in late 2006, Beckham signed American soccer's first eight-figure contract to play with Los Angeles.)

Reviewing the Reviews

The *Blast!* troupe left London to begin a quick tour of the United States. A PBS special—filmed at a London performance of *Blast!*—aired across America on August 5, 2000, just as the tour was beginning. The limited tour began at the Wang Center in Boston and played Bloomington, then Milwaukee, Detroit, Chicago, and the Kennedy Center in Washington.

The Chicago stop was at the Oriental Theater, and it was given prominent play in the *Chicago Tribune* October 30, 2000. The headline: MARCHING MADNESS: FOR BAND GEEKS, 'BLAST!' IS THE BEST REVENGE OF ALL. Manny Cordova, 17, a drum major and trombone player for St. Rita's high school band, called the show "the best thing I ever saw in my life. It gave me the shivers." Kimberly Bohannon, a sousaphone player from the Northwestern

University band, said she watched the tubas. "I was really impressed with the way the players moved so precisely and rapidly without running into each other onstage with such large instruments."

Blast! played at the Kennedy Center December 19 through January 14. Somewhere in there a gossipy *New York Observer* report said Bill Clinton—in his last days as president, awaiting turnover of the White House to George W. Bush—wasn't just a spectator; he "stood up and gave a big, stinky Razorback hog-yell."

Waiting was a booking at the Broadway Theater in New York—as the first show in there after the historic ten-year run of *Miss Saigon* ended. The show opened April 17, 2001.

The next-biggest thing to opening nights on Broadway is the next morning's reviews in the New York newspapers. On *Blast! Variety* scored it three favorable, five unfavorable, one mixed. The bloodiest cut came from critic Bruce Weber in the *New York Times*: "*Blast* bored me cross-eyed. It was a halftime show that had wandered onto the stage at the Broadway Theater, as if it got lost on the way to the stadium."

Another day later, on its front page, the *Wall Street Journal* started reporter Renae Merle's ridiculing review of the reviews, its target the show's underwriter, under the headline WHAT'S A BILLIONAIRE TO DO WHEN HE TIRES OF STENTS? There was a gleeful air to the way Merle gathered up the barbs. Weber's was first on the list. From Clive Barnes of the *Post*: "I rather resent it taking up valuable theater space." From *Newsday*: It was "an Indiana high school assembly with delusions of Las Vegas." The story described Jim Mason as spending the morning after the opening "combing the pans for a few kind words that could be used as advertising blurbs." Merle's sniping wasn't limited to the show. "Mr. Cook looks more like a retired engineer than a cutting-edge billionaire. He wears beltless trousers, shoes with an orthopedic look, and he is never far from a pack of Kents." And she included from John E. Abele, co-founder of Cook Inc. competitor Boston Scientific, a friendly description of classic Bill Cook decisions: "Against the grain. He'd always do something a little bit outrageous, just to shock you." Abele cited the time the two were at a medical conference, and Cook "boasted to him that the new manager of a Cook unit in Denmark had once been a high school band-leader."

Michael Boo was in New York for the opening. "The first reviews were not favorable," he said. "They didn't get it. They were looking for a connection to cheerleaders. It was just a running theme. A lot of people had no idea what they were trying to do: 'It's something we haven't seen before, so . . .' But the one that really hurt was the *Wall Street Journal* 'review of the reviews.' Talk about laziness!"

The *Journal* story didn't touch all the reviews. The *Daily News* called it "a winning event," and the Clive Barnes line quoted from the *Post* was

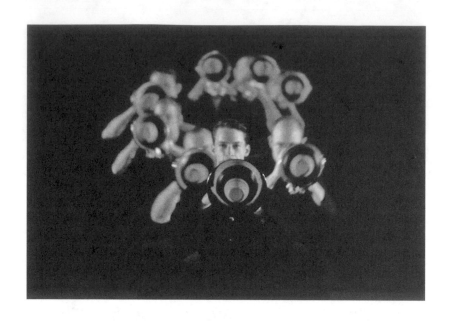

Blast! (*above*) and Brass Theater (*below*)

in a review headlined "*BLAST! REALLY TAKES OFF.*" Other lines in it—"as quaintly beguiling as it is loud . . . a precision the Rockettes might envy . . . all this buckling of swashes, all this circus panache, all this oom-pah music, the glittering brass and perfectly synchronized movements might suggest a Fourth of July translated into a month of Sundays and then squared."

A gathering of all newspaper reviews that came in from that opening night scored it 16–8 in favor of *Blast!*

And in the autobiography of Dance Music Hall of Fame inductee Quincy Jones that came out in 2002, there was a line that superseded all reviews, praising the cast of the Broadway show *Blast!* "whose work moved me to tears."

The Best Special Theatrical Event . . .

Broadway is used to crowds and critics differing radically in what they like, and it happened with *Blast!* What was booked as a twelve-week run was entering its twenty-second week when New York and the world changed. This was 2001. The city's devastation and grief after the September 11 attack on the World Trade Center towers dimmed Broadway's lights as no disaster ever had before. Within two weeks, five of the twenty-one downtown shows had closed, including *Blast!*

It went out with precious hardware. *Blast!* won a Broadway Tony. And the PBS show about it won an Emmy.

Cook shakes his head. "To watch those kids grow as they did into such a success—a Tony and an Emmy, in just one year's time—phenomenal! We had no idea when we went to New York we would win a Tony. We got to Broadway, and our booking agent said, 'You guys are good enough we're going to put you in for a Tony.'" The problem was classification. Musicals had a Tony. *Blast!* wasn't truly a musical, like *Carousel* or *South Pacific*. "They nominated us, and everybody got up in arms. *Forty-second Street* had the inside track that year [with the revival of one of Broadway's all-time hits]. They decided to create a new Tony, just for our type of entertainment—for 'the best special theatrical event.' That seemed to satisfy everyone. That could include things like *Riverdance*."

The Tonys were presented in a telecast Sunday, June 3, 2001, from Radio City Music Hall in Lower Manhattan. "Jim Mason wanted me to go up and make the acceptance speech," Cook said. "We were third on that night. A windbag who thanked everybody, including his bartender, was up first. So when it was our turn the director said, 'Mr. Cook, could you shorten your talk because we're way behind.' I said sure, I said my few words, and it never did get on TV. The windbag was so long they just cut us all out."

"On the TV program," Gayle said, "they show Bill receiving the Tony and speaking, but there's no sound. That is a big event in New York City. We casually walked down the street afterward holding this Tony, and people would gather around. Then we went to a deli, and the waiters were so excited that there was a Tony on the table, *they* were getting out their cameras."

Bill remembers. "There was a huge party afterward. But we went to the deli first and had a sandwich. I wasn't feeling very good, so Gayle and I skipped the party." No TV appearance, no party, just a Tony that sits on display in Bill's office. "It means a lot," he said.

By the time of the sudden closing, Mason said, "We had a contract for a tour—a year-and-a-half tour, every night—different venues, universities, large auditoriums in cities. From there on, the bookings just kept coming." And they haven't stopped. The show has been continuous since 2000.

On April 16, 2001, just before the Broadway run began, a benefit and tribute to actor Dudley Moore at Carnegie Hall brought out some of America's brightest stars and biggest names. Chevy Chase, Bo Derek, Mary Tyler Moore, even Barbara Walters were involved. So was a group from *Blast!*— there to play the opening number of its show: Maurice Ravel's beguilingly repetitive *Bolero,* the theme of the movie *10,* which had starred Moore and Derek.

Before the tribute, Mason said, "Here I am, backstage kibitzing with Barbara Walters and Bo Derek, and somebody taps me on the shoulder. I hear, 'Mr. Mason, I have a note for you from Julie.' I know that voice, everybody knows that voice, but I can't believe what I'm hearing. I turn around and it *is* Lauren Bacall.

"She handed me this note from Julie Andrews. Inside is this touching letter, saying how much she loved *Blast!* She had worn out her CD, and she wondered if I could send her another. And sign it.

"From drum and bugle corps to standing backstage with Lauren Bacall—I just scratch my head sometimes and think, none of this would have happened without Bill Cook. And Gayle—what a wonderful part of it all she has been. I've seen many, many times the beauty of having Bill and Gayle working together on a project. It works in an amazing, caring, and loving way."

With *Blast!* launched, Cook eased out of the music business. "I think Bill wanted to make sure I was taken care of as he was settling up his properties," Mason said. "He basically gave me the *Blast!* company—sold it to me for $100. I created Mason Entertainment Group, and *Blast!* is one of my entities. I always said if Bill ever let me go, I would shake his hand and thank him for the greatest ride I ever had. That's what I was able to do.

"When I was being hired, I rode out to Brown School one night with Steve Ferguson. Steve told me, 'Bill has a lot of interests. He's a busy guy. Things go in and out real quick. If I were you, I wouldn't put down very serious roots here, because it will probably last a year or two and then Bill will move on to something else. I just think it's fair to share that with you.'

"I lasted about eighteen years longer than Steve thought I would."

On the Road with Mellencook

Bill Cook didn't limit his bus driving to Star of Indiana drum corps trips. He also drove three times for one of America's top rock stars, John Mellencamp, who grew up southeast of Bloomington in Seymour, Indiana, but has lived since the 1970s just outside Bloomington. Mellencamp is fearless with his music. For years he has thrived while delivering in his songs a frequent liberal message in mostly midwestern states that, on presidential election night maps, usually wind up Republican red. "It's not like my contemporaries who live in New York or Los Angeles and play to a liberal base. I'm always playing to a conservative base. Sometimes it makes my message kind of confusing and hard to understand, for the liberals *and* the conservatives." Bold fellow.

But John Mellencamp doesn't claim to have been fearless on those trips: "Riding with Cook is taking your life in your own hands. He gets behind the wheel and he's like 15 years old." That was friend-about-friend needling. Rather than being nervous on those trips, Mellencamp recalls that conversation flowed freely between him and his ex–Chicago cabbie bus driver— and still does, over lunch or wherever they get together. "I find Bill pretty talkative. I've never been bored with him."

Twice Cook took Mellencamp and his band to performances at college towns—East Lansing, home of Michigan State, and Columbia, site of the University of Missouri. Each time was the same: Mellencamp's appearance officially unannounced, at what Cook described as "theaters without seats—with balconies." Word-of-mouth produced the crowds. "People walk in, off to the side are the bars, serving beer, and the college kids get tanked up. They were raucous.

"The one at Columbia, the crowd got so drunk on the warm-up band, John played forty-five minutes into his concert and said, 'Let's get the hell out of here.' And we left. Somehow we got out. He just said 'Sayonara,' and that was it. The kids hadn't paid a lot of money to get in. The people running it made their money off beer."

The third trip was to the Rock 'n' Roll Hall of Fame at Cleveland, in conjunction with the Hall's opening in 1995. "We drove up there with him and his family," Cook said. "He sang at a big event at the old Municipal Stadium—he and Willie Nelson, just a whole slew of stars. They packed the place." And, in spring 2008 when Mellencamp was inducted into the Hall, the Cooks were there to cheer and celebrate.

"John traveled with a relatively small group," Cook says of his busing days. "He had three guitarists, one or two playing violin, one percussion, and keyboard players—very, very good instrumentalists. Usually he had sent one or two advance people a couple of days ahead of him, and he had maybe eight trucks for the instruments and set-up. Some of those amplifiers

John Mellencamp entertains Cook employees at the Cook company's
fortieth anniversary celebration in 2003.

were as big as a room. And he had guys who were taking care of the instruments—that's a full-time job. He had a security group. He traveled pretty light, for a rock star. His wife, Elaine, traveled with the band. Sometimes she was the only spouse, but there were times when others were there."

Mellencamp said the relationship started when Cook called to offer his airplanes. "I was flying in and out of Cook Aviation [hangar at the Bloomington airport] back in the 1980s. He said, 'You're using our airport. Why don't you use our airplanes?'" Cook said he made the call after he read a newspaper story about Mellencamp's increasing problems traveling on airlines. "Fans in the airport, that kind of thing. I told him, 'We could help you out periodically, if you need it.' There was no money involved. Every so often he would give a concert for our employees in exchange, which was a pretty good deal for us."

Mellencamp didn't immediately accept the offer. "I kinda got to know Bill. I went to lunch with him. Now, I would consider him a friend, and we've been friends for twenty-some years. I've enjoyed his company for many, many hours and many, many years. I can't remember a time when I didn't laugh at least half a dozen times at things he said. He's just a well informed, entertaining fellow and a very generous man.

"I *wouldn't* want to go into business with him. I'm sure you would be successful, but if you go into business with Bill thinking you're equal partners, you're crazy. Because Bill is the boss. He's always going to be the boss. And it's probably a good thing that he *is* the boss. He's been successful at being the boss."

The Mellencamps, Cook said, are "great people. Elaine is a wonderful person, a very nice addition to that family. John's father, Richard, is a ten, and his mother, Marilyn, is just wonderful. I have some nice art of Marilyn's in our building. She gave me a picture that I thought was very good. It's one of my favorites. She learned to paint after John became enamored with painting. And John became quite an accomplished artist, going to exhibitions and having his own exhibits. They're both very talented.

"Richard was an electrical contractor with a rather large electrical company. His very last job was to assist with the opening of the New Orleans Superdome. He was one of the electrical contractors working down there, and when it was finished, they asked him to help open the Dome. Then he came home to help John with his finances and his career. He does a heck of a job with that because he's a good businessman.

"Richard says he's retired, but he has a motto: 'Find something you want to do every day.' And he does. Plays a lot of golf. He lives in Seymour in a very pretty old house out on Route 11.

"John was never poor."

Unfortunate Thing about Rock . . .

Meanwhile, there's the thought of Bill Cook, easy-listenin' radio music devotee, at rock concerts. "I enjoy rock music, although during the years rock was at the top of the charts I didn't follow it much," he said. "If rock could be played without amplification, it would be wonderful to hear. It's just unfortunate that you have to hear all that slamming and banging going on when you could hear these melodies on guitars backed by other instruments—occasionally a violin or percussion.

"Now, to fans of rock, that amplification is part of the awe. But whatever they're listening to at that sound level, you cannot hear the undertones that are so prevalent with unamplified instrumentation.

"I'd be there every night if it wasn't amplified. But it is so loud and so bad you can get your hearing affected even with earplugs. Gayle thoroughly enjoyed one of their performances, but she wore earplugs and she still was slightly deaf for a couple of days."

Far from offended, Mellencamp agrees with Cook—on hearing damage ("*I* am half-deaf because of rock music") and the loss of distinctive instrumentation ("He's exactly right"). The amplification is a necessity forced by the size of today's rock venues, Mellencamp said. "We're playing for quite a few people, and they have to hear. That's why it became so loud. Part of the battle we fight is for ambience in a great big arena."

The Mellencamp concert audiences are by no means all young, Cook says. "The rockers age with John. There's a lot of gray-haired people out there. The mix of ages is amazing—anywhere from 14 to 75 or 80. You get a good rocker, like John, somebody who has something to say in their songs, they all know the songs, and they stand during the whole performance. Nobody sits down. They stand up, raise their hands, and they sing. They're fun. But they are very hard on the hearing."

Mellencamp says what Cook saw was typical of the crowds he draws. "I'm very fortunate. All across the United States, everywhere we go, we have quite a mixture of people. Hopefully that will continue. I've been making records since 1976. Here it is 2008. I've been very fortunate."

Star 7, on the Ohio River, passes Cincinnati's Great American Ballpark and downtown landmarks.

Star 7

It's one of those eye-catchers, a boat that people just go,
"Wow!" and then go get a camera to take pictures of it. It's
90 feet long, 35 feet high, and it weighs 140,000 pounds
empty. It's just an absolutely beautiful, gorgeous boat.

—Bill Cook

Land-locked Canton, Illinois, became his hometown, but Bill Cook never forgot his two years as a child in Peoria, a river town. Summer days. Other days. Along a river. Watching and wondering. "I always wondered where those barges were from and where they were going up and down the Illinois River. I was fascinated with them. I thought it would be the neatest thing to be able to travel up and down—to see those cities where Mark Twain grew up. But I never owned a boat in my life until . . ."

Until *Star 7*, which was conceived in Alaska, born in Australia, and brought to America as the shiniest toy—by far—in unpretentious billionaire Bill Cook's toybox.

It's an aluminum catamaran, not picked out of a catalog but every inch of it built to Cook's specifications, to match his dreams. "There had never been a catamaran built privately like that—only for passenger or ferry service," he says. "When Gayle and I were on a cruise in Alaska, the captain let me drive a catamaran for just a few minutes on the Yukon River, and I fell in love. I wanted one."

Back home, he went to work on getting one built. It wasn't simple. "I couldn't find a manufacturer in the United States who would give me the time of day. I told them I wanted to build a catamaran of this specific design. I don't know whether they thought I was kidding or what. They never sent me literature. Catamaran builders are a very small group. In America, there's only one guy in Boston and one in Seattle.

"I went on the internet and googled, and I came up with this builder in Fremantle, Australia: Bill Harry. Bill [who owns the company Sabre Catamarans] said, 'Sure, I'll build you a boat.' Three days later he was in the United States. He was serious, and we signed a contract while he was here. Then I got telephone calls from both these American guys—after they found out Harry was going to build me a boat. They had the nerve to call me afterward and try to get in on it."

Hands-On, Long Distance

George Ridgway, the architect responsible for all of the Cooks' recent industrial and restoration construction projects, also has *Star 7* on his proud-achievements list.

"When Bill came back from that Alaskan cruise, he showed me all his boat pictures and said, 'Now, I'm going to build a catamaran. I want you to find me a marine architect.'"

Ridgway didn't have to look far. "I told him I did that kind of work from 1964 to 1966 in Canada. I was 19 when I went up there. We had a hotshot salesman who came in one day and said he had a customer who wanted to turn a lake freighter into a luxury yacht and asked if we could do the drawings to do that. We got out all the books and started working with another marine architect. We did a lot of it.

"Bill said, 'I'm going to put you in contact with this guy in Perth.' That night I went home and told my wife, Jan, 'I'm going to do a boat.' She said, 'You know how to build a boat?' I said, 'Yeah, I know quite a bit about marine architecture. I've probably forgotten most of it.'

"I went up in the attic. I had a marine slide rule that tells you about hull thicknesses and different planes you can put on sides of the bow to get more speed and less fuel consumption. I got all my books. The math doesn't change, but my slide rule did. After all that time in the attic, it wouldn't slide anymore. I called a guy I had worked with and said, 'Do you still have your slide rule?' He said, 'Oh, come on, George, they have computer programs now.' I got my computer program and started with Bill Harry. We were working through the internet and e-mail, samples shipped back and forth from the west coast of Australia. Bill Cook is the kind of guy who knows what he likes, when he can put his hands on it."

But this was not a "hands-on" project. "I was very, very apprehensive," Ridgway said. "We're building a boat twenty-six hours of flying time away, can't put our hands on it, don't know how it feels. We get scale models, we get videos of all the construction, we get 3-D renderings of all the drawings. We tried to get everything so Bill could really know what he was building, knowing full well that if he didn't like it, there would be hell to play. At that time, it wasn't called *Star 7*. Bill had coined a name for it: *Miss Directed*."

Construction took a year—"and that is really busting everything to get it done," Cook said.

In July 2004, word came from Perth that the boat was ready. Ridgway went with Bill, Gayle, and Carl Cook to check it out—stomach-butterflies time for Ridgway. "I thought, 'Okay, if he likes it, this is going to be great. If he doesn't, and the odds are that he won't, I've got twenty days of hell. And I can't get away from it.'

"We walked onto the boat, and I'm living in sheer terror. He walked into the galley, looked around, and he had just a little bit of a tear in his eye. And I thought, 'Yes!'"

Cook remembers that moment, too. "I thought, 'Boy, this is my kind of boat!' It's just wonderful."

That Was Pretty Darned Exciting

Next step was getting it to the United States, not exactly a matter of heading out into the open seas and opening up full throttle. "They sailed her from Fremantle all the way up and over Australia to Brisbane," Cook said. "It was picked up by yacht transport vessel and brought back to the United States, through the Panama Canal. It arrived six weeks late because of hurricanes."

Star 7 was launched for the first time in the United States with the Cooks aboard in April 2005, heading out onto the first of Bill's dream adventures— exploring the rivers of eastern America. "I don't particularly like to travel to someplace like Bermuda, the Bahamas, the British Virgin Islands. So in the summer of 2005 we did most of the rivers and in the summer of 2006 all of the Great Lakes."

The boat takes a crew of two. Captain Aaron Steenbhom came with the boat, and his aide (and as of December 23, 2006, wife) Nicky came on as first mate. "Just beautiful people, both Australians," Cook said.

"It takes a lot of experience to drive it. I can pilot the boat, but piloting and docking the boat are two different things. Putting the boat into the shore, putting it up against hard surfaces, that's something else. I have pulled her away from a hard surface, and several times I took it into locks. That wasn't bad, but I wouldn't want to do it every day because it is a little bit nerve-racking.

"To protect the sides of *Star 7*, we've got great big fat rubber fenders. We call them Fat Alberts. In those locks, they're great. Parking it just using the controls of the engine is tricky. That's why I have a captain."

But he has piloted out on open water and found it the thrill he had always imagined. "I've only had it up to 34 knots [equal to just under 40 mph]. Aaron has had her up to about 40 knots [46 mph]. It's fast! You can overtake most boats. Here's this huge thing coming down on them. If you have nice flat water, it feels like you're going pretty good, but you have to have something next to you to feel the speed. You do feel the speed when you're in waves. Any wave over six feet you get shaken up pretty well."

There are no speed limits on the open sea. "On some rivers, yes," Cook said. And there are matters of practicality and liability, when other boats are around. "The smaller boats have the right-of-way. You've got to be very careful that you don't tip them over. You can get people awfully wet and awfully mad—or even injured. It has a wake, and you 'own' your wake. If that wake gets up against some of those small boats, it can wreck them. I did about $1,000 worth of damage to a houseboat, with just the wake of our boat. I did not see where the boat was when I came out of a lock. I powered up, and the wash went right up into the boat's slip and just demolished all the pins and everything else." Cook apologized, wrote a check to cover the damage, and headed on.

On the river trip, he said, "We came across Florida and went up into Tennessee via the Tombigbee River and channel. It's called the Tenntom, and it runs all the way from Mobile, Alabama, into Kentucky Lake. We stopped overnight. We rarely stopped for lunch. The object was to sightsee. We just kept on going. Tennessee River to Knoxville . . . then the Ohio River to Pittsburgh . . . then the Allegheny and the Monongahela to Morgantown, West Virginia . . . up the Kanawha to Charleston . . . up the Mississippi to Illinois River, all the way up the Illinois to within forty miles of Chicago where a low railroad bridge stopped us. Then back to the Mississippi and all the way up to Minneapolis–St. Paul. That was the end of our 2005 season. Took us all summer to do that. Got back to Florida in September.

"Those rivers are fascinating. We stayed different places every night. I thought that would be the neatest thing, to be able to travel up and down, to see those cities, to go into these little places in Missouri and spend the night, have a great meal at a very old restaurant, going into St. Louis. That was something.

"Far and away the most fabulous river was the Tennessee, just the pure beauty and the depth of it—40 to 50 feet deep, some places 200 feet deep, crystal clear. And huge dams—near Florence, Tennessee, up to 120 feet high. You look up and think, 'We've got to go up there, and we also have to come down.' That was pretty darned exciting.

"Then in 2006 we did all the Great Lakes. On the way up the east coast, we went through the Dismal Swamp. That was fun. Spent a night in Edenton, North Carolina, which in my opinion is one of the most beautiful towns in the United States. And finally we reached the St. Lawrence Seaway. On the way back to Florida in late August, *Star 7* blew an engine in Nova Scotia, but we did every lake, stopped at the various little towns, and just had a great time. Our map from those two years is pretty incredible."

A Home for the Boat

The historian in Gayle magnified her enjoyment of the river travels. "It was pleasant and beautiful, but the early history of our country is along riverways. So the towns are often historic, with some old buildings and charm. I've enjoyed that very much."

She thought for a minute in picking out a favorite experience. "On the Ohio, *in* Ohio," she decided, "where we stopped at Marietta and a few other places where there is a lot of riverboat history and they have capitalized on that. They have docks that allow you to dock right at the center of the old town and just walk up. You don't need a rental car or a taxi. You're right there. Many of them have fixed up their riverfronts so you can get ashore and get right into the town. I especially liked those. And then on the Mississippi—Hannibal, that stretch of the Mississippi has a lot of nice towns. The shame is a lot of those Mississippi River towns don't have a docking place. You see some old town and you can't get there."

Cruising the Ohio did give her a river view of some special places: their own weekend getaway home, Cedar Farm, and the old Karch family farm outside Evansville. "For the first time, I saw the farm where I grew up from the water. That was hard to recognize, because it was just a river bank."

Each year after the cruises, the Cooks head back to Indiana, and the boat and crew return to Florida. The toy begat some other needed toys down there.

"We bought a home at Fort Lauderdale with a dock," Bill said. "We've been there three or four times, that's about it. We didn't need a home down there, but we needed the dock and the canal. Fort Lauderdale is a center of boating where it's very easy to get your boat fixed, very easy to buy parts, and the house is not too far away from the seashore, a half-mile.

"And it does give Aaron and Nicky a place to live."

The Cooks and the boat traveled western U.S. rivers and the Pacific up into Alaska in the summer of 2008, adding to a store of memories and pictures that is almost endless.

Winters are for planning, and there's still a lot of cruising to do.

Restorations

Bill likes the bricks, the mortar, the big things.
I like the research, the history,
the interior. Together . . .

—*Gayle Cook*

Colonel William Jones House

"In 1972, when we first published our *Guide to Southern Indiana,* my father's cousin's wife called to tell me we had left out a very historic building in Spencer County, the Jones House," Gayle Cook recalls. "Her family, the Bullocks, had lived in the house; she, in fact, had inherited a share of it. She wondered if we would want to buy it and restore it.

"Then came Bill's bypass surgery in 1974. He didn't know how active he was going to be. He didn't know yet that he was going to be walking—running—four and a half miles a day. He thought he might have to go into a semiretirement, and this would be a project, plus a place to go to get away." (Yes, says builder Charlie Pritchett, making the house into a weekend getaway home was the original idea. "But it turned out Bill was allergic to that place. Too many hoot owls. He didn't stay down there very much.")

Still, as an aftermath of the father's cousin's wife's call, Gayle says, "We looked into it and decided to buy the house as a project. At the same time we were restoring the Cochran House. It was finished first. Which one we actually got involved in first it's hard to say. On both of them, we learned. We made some mistakes.

"We found at the Jones House the solid brick walls were in such bad shape that the Pritchetts wouldn't put their ladders against them because the walls were in jeopardy of collapsing. The inner brick was soft, which was common. When they fired the brick, the brick that was farthest from the fire was soft, so they put that inside toward the plaster and put the hard brick on the exterior. After all those years, it was all just crumbling.

"We had to take it apart and put the pieces back together. That was the only way to do it. It is the same house, same woodwork, same porch. We had to explain to local people that we could have done one wall, the one that was in the most danger, then, in a few years, do another wall and then another wall. Instead, we just did it all at once. It made sense, but people thought we were tearing it down. We said, 'Oh, no, no.' There was a barn at that time. We just lifted off chunks and put them in the barn: whole windows and the porch and roof parts."

She smiled about her description of how Bill's restoration interests and hers fit together. "You have to think big with his part. 'Okay, let's put a whole new roof on.' I would say, 'Maybe we could save part of it over here.' When you restore buildings, you're guided by history and research. Research on Jones was very difficult because of the name William Jones. There were multiple people named William Jones in the Civil War. I was able to identify his records, however. And he was also in the state legislature—you can find his name there. But in tracing his family, his early life, it was very difficult with the name William Jones."

But there is this part-story, part-legend about the early 1800s:

1. Between the ages of 7 and 21, Abraham Lincoln lived most of his Indiana years in a cabin near the Jones home;
2. The wealthy William Jones befriended the knowledge-hungry Lincoln boy;
3. Some of young Abe's renowned early reading was in the Jones home, with Jones's newspapers and books.
4. In 1844, as an Illinois lawyer-politician campaigning for presidential candidate Henry Clay, Lincoln was said to have come through to visit Jones, spoken to a group there, and stayed overnight in that house.

Gayle wanted to confirm those tales and more, and she thought she was about to do that once. "A woman told us she saw boxes of uncataloged papers that had belonged to a man who did some writing about Spencer County and Lincoln in the nineteenth century. Who knows what was in them, but he had referred to Lincoln and to Jones in his published writings, and I thought I ought to look at those. So I called the Spencer County Library in Rockport, to make sure when they were open, that there would be librarians there when I came, and I picked the date. I got Simone Robbins, a retired IU librarian, to go with me, figuring she would know what to look for and we could separate the papers. We went down there, went into the library, and this embarrassed librarian said, 'I'm sorry, but we did some checking, and we discovered that those boxes had been thrown away.'"

Gayle's voice took on a tone more anguished than angry. "There is so little about Lincoln's life in Indiana that every scrap of paper is preserved, every piece of wood he might have touched. And these people threw away a box!"

Up, redone, and paid for, the Jones House became state property for public showing. "I understand since we gave the house to the state, a historian has found out a lot more about Colonel Jones and the Lincoln connection," Gayle said. Found it outside the box, the missing Spencer County Library box, it can be presumed.

Cedar Farm

The house on Cedar Farm was built in 1837, which dates it almost as far back as the Jones House. It exudes Southern charm—a two-and-a-half-story home, with white cellar-to-attic columns out front and a row of cedar trees between it and the Ohio River. It sits on one of the deepest thrusts south that Indiana makes—thirty-eight miles below the most famous Indiana-Kentucky border town: Louisville, Kentucky. The farm has its own history, with characters not as legendary as Lincoln but in their own way colorful, starting with J. L. Kintner, the Lincoln-opposite who built the home for himself and his bride.

Gayle Cook found and put into print a personal history written by the Kintners' oldest child, Addie Kintner Graham, born in 1843. In her eighties, Addie wrote: "My father, with hired help, of course, . . . cleared the land, made rails of the trees and fenced it, built large storehouses for his grain and to shelter his stock, dug cisterns."[1] And built the house.

The land was lush, producing crops of grain, hay, corn, and potatoes, with fruit trees, vegetable gardens, grapevines, and berry plants. Addie was seventeen when "the dark cloud of civil war cast a gloom over our whole land." Her father was too old to be a soldier, but he wasn't uninvolved:

> Kentucky was a slave state, Indiana a free state, and most people north of
> the Ohio River were Unionists; but most of our friends were in Kentucky
> and slave owners, therefore Southern sympathizers. My father became a

Southern sympathizer, or Rebel as he was called, and was not as careful of his words as he should have been.

Soon it was reported to the authorities at the nearby fort that he had been guilty of making remarks considered rebellious, so at night a band of soldiers came and arrested him, intending to take him to Fort Lafayette, a place where rebel prisoners were confined. Of course the family were greatly troubled over this.

But fortunately when the train on which he was confined passed through Indianapolis, a friend of my father's, a lawyer, heard of his being in trouble and immediately had him released and given a trial in court, where it was decided that he had not done anything deserving of imprisonment, and he was sent home.

The war was still going on.

"His front yard was the Mason-Dixon Line," Gayle noted. Indiana's closest brush with Civil War military activity was a thrust through the southeastern corner of the state led by Confederate general John Hunt Morgan. "Morgan's Raiders came into Indiana at Mauckport, which is about nine miles east [of Cedar Farm, up the Ohio]. Then they headed north. They did not come to Cedar Farm, but the story goes that at Cedar Farm they hid the horses because Morgan's men were stealing and changing horses wherever they came through."

Cedar Farm didn't leave family hands for almost 150 years. "Julia Withers, the last person who lived there, was a granddaughter of J. L. Kintner," Gayle says. "She loved the house. When she was a girl—I think she was born in 1888—she had a boyfriend from across the river in Kentucky. She refused to get married because she wouldn't leave Cedar Farm. Her brothers had been educated in the 1890s, and they had long ago gone off to professional careers, so she was left at the farm. She refused to leave because she wanted to keep the house, and he refused to leave his farm and come to Indiana. The years went by, and finally Fort Knox bought his farm when the government expanded it. That freed him to come to Cedar Farm, so they got married. He was 45, and she was 39. She then had three boys. And it was from those three boys that we bought the farm."

After her husband died, Julia Withers couldn't maintain the farm or the buildings, but she turned away potential buyers. In the early 1960s, one of her sons was a Pioneer Seed Corn salesman in southern Indiana. So was Glenn Karch, Gayle's brother. "Glenn had been there on business, and he told Bill and me, 'You should see the house I saw down on the river.' So we drove down there looking one time in the 1960s. It was covered with vines, the paint had worn off, it had been intruded upon with fences and shacks and farm equipment, rusty stuff sitting around. That was years before we had ever restored anything."

And it was years before they did anything there. Julia Withers' refusal

to sell stayed with her until her death at 92 in 1980. Her three sons weren't so sentimental. "We negotiated to buy the farm in 1983 and closed the sale in 1984," Gayle said.

As with the Cochran House and Jones House, the Cooks looked at the decay of the present and saw the grandeur of the past and the future. It was the first project primarily put in Joe Pritchett's hands. "That was really fun," he said. "I was 30. I wasn't married. I stayed down there in a trailer that we set up on the property. I was the only one from the family down there. They would come down occasionally and help. My dad and Charlie were still very active in the business at times, but they left that one with me."

Its Own Shade of Yellow

On one of Bill Cook's Saturday morning breakfast flights with his buddies, Charlie Pritchett remembers, "We flew down to Cedar Farm. They have a runway down there."

For Cook, it was an in-progress check on the restoration project, which by then was far enough along that the lumber of the house had been painted. "The place was supposed to be white, according to Bill," Charlie says. "But I knew better."

Gayle had seen an 1898 painting by Indianapolis artist William Forsyth, who showed the house to be yellow with white trim and green shutters. She

Bill and Gayle Cook's Cedar Farm, before (*at left*) and after restoration

called down to tell the Pritchetts how it should be painted: "light yellow and white," Richard remembers.

Charlie said when the breakfast group landed and got out of the plane, "Bill threw a fit, stomped and cussed, hit the table. He's got a little temper. Bob Shedd, the dentist, was with us. He said, 'God durn, Bill, it's just a few dollars' worth of paint.' That set him off again.

"We didn't tell him Gayle had called. He got back home, and we found out who the boss really was."

Richard said, "He just came back and said, 'Leave that color on. It's all right.'"

Ever since, Charlie said, the particular light yellow shade has its own name with the Pritchetts. "We call it Cedar Farm yellow."

On June 22, 1985, the only antebellum plantation in Indiana that remains complete—with main house, cookhouse, milkhouse, icehouse, schoolhouse, tenant houses, livestock and tobacco barns, and 2,500 acres of land—went on public display for two days. There was a stunning response both days—almost 15,000 people in all.

Since then, on almost every weekend, it has been a private, quiet, peaceful retreat for Bill and Gayle Cook. "Down there," Bill said, "I don't do much of anything. I watch a lot of television. During the weekend, I'll spend three or four hours out on the trails with either a Jeep or Kawasaki or sometimes a golf cart. I like hiking. I can't hike anymore, but I can get in a Jeep or a Kawasaki and spend hours out there. Gayle sews—she makes quilts, she hems her own dresses—I can't tell you all the things she does. She's a genius with her hands. And she loves to read."

Gayle said at Cedar Farm, "We have a large library. I like biographies and detective stories. We don't really look at it as a place where we need to live like we do here. We're kind of housebound there in the evenings. We watch movies now and then, but not very much, simply because it seems we have enough to do."

Bill said, "Our lifestyles are very similar. She grew up on a farm. She never had a whole lot, even though her parents were fairly well off. I lived in a town, but I did a lot of farm things. We don't have a whole lot of wants for anything."

Gayle said the restoration, "besides making it convenient and homey for us, is sort of like caring for a museum for the future. We're the caretakers, and we do what's necessary for a very historic and significant property. And we're also conserving 2,500 acres—the trees and the land."

Just sitting outside and viewing has its pleasures for both. There's a main-floor porch, sixteen wide steps up from the luscious green lawn, and a second-floor balcony with its own handsome railing. "We also have chairs down at the river," Bill said. "The river's six hundred feet away." And there are all those cedars in between. "Fantastic!"

French Lick and West Baden: The Crown Jewels

I have pictures of my parents standing outside the West
Baden Hotel. I can't even remember when I first saw it. I
remember stopping by when the Jesuits were there. Then
Bill and I saw it several times. Little did we know.

—*Gayle Cook*

On the night of June 23, 2007, the grandest of all the Cooks' restorations
glistened in its considerable glory. *Gala* was the word used for the event
that brought 1,000 people out that night to celebrate the return to life of the
West Baden Springs Hotel. *Gala* fits that event, but understates. "It was the
highlight of my life," said Bill Cook.

That's some highlight. Because Bill Cook has had some life. And so have
the grand old hotels of the Orange County area that blends the communities of French Lick and West Baden into "The Valley"—Springs Valley, the
natives call it.

The name came for the unusually high sulfur content in spring water
around the area, great for what ails you, the pitch of the early 1900s ran.
And for a good while, it worked—oh, did that sales pitch work, a whole lot
better commercially than medicinally. Then came the bad days.

Stars Came Out, and Others

Originally, Bill and Gayle Cook had no Valley thoughts at all. They had seen
the two magnificent though ancient hotels, admired them, and included
them in their 1960s Sunday auto trips with their son, Carl, and their *Guide
to Southern Indiana*.

That was about the extent of what the Cooks could do with the hotels
then. It took a lot of things over the next thirty years to pull them more
deeply into effective involvement, including accumulation of a lot of personal wealth.

Wealth and the Valley have had a peek-a-boo relationship. Look elsewhere around French Lick and West Baden, and there aren't many signs
of opulence except for the two oases of it on the grounds of the two hotels
that sprang up in rivalry.

French Lick was first: a 40 × 100 foot frame building that went up on
the present hotel site in the mid-1840s, before the state of Indiana was 30
years old or the United States was 70. Dr. William Bowles built the hotel
on a site his father had bought in 1833 and deeded over to him. Bowles
went off to fight in the Mexican War as a commissioned officer, and he
engaged Dr. John Lane to run it. Lane made the place boom, and when

Bowles came back from the war and reclaimed command, the irked Lane went barely a mile away and put up the inn that became West Baden Springs Hotel.

Escalation of both the hotel competition and national awareness of the area brought major changes to both just as the 1900s began. Indianapolis mayor Thomas Taggart bought the French Lick building in 1901. He later became National Democratic Party chairman, and his hotel became a state and national political center. It was at the National Governors Conference there in 1931 that New York governor Franklin D. Roosevelt announced he would be a 1932 presidential candidate and highlighted the conference with a Depression era demand that had twenty-first century Hurricane Katrina forebodings: "More and more, those who are the victims of dislocations and defects of our social and economic life are beginning to ask respectfully but insistently of us who are in positions of public responsibility why Government cannot and should not act to protect its citizens from disaster. I believe the question demands an answer and that the ultimate answer is that government, both State and National, must accept the responsibility of doing what it can do . . . along definitely constructive, not passive, lines."[2]

Tom Taggart knew his territory in landing national events. Indiana was no longer a western outpost, more and more accessible and proximal. The 1920 census established the nation's center of population just upstate in Bloomington, and a once-backwoods state had taken on some contemporary political clout. That 1920 census gave Indiana more congressional seats—hence more census-affirmed residents—than California.

Not only politicians found little French Lick, beginning in the 1920s and carrying into the 1940s. So did Bing Crosby, Groucho Marx, Georgie Jessel, Bud Abbott and Lou Costello . . . John Barrymore, Greta Garbo, Lana Turner, and Bob Hope . . . Howard Hughes, Harry Truman, Joe and Rose Kennedy, and Gloria Swanson . . . from music, Louis Armstrong, Duke Ellington, and Hoagy Carmichael . . . singer Tony Bennett, drummer Gene Krupa, and Boston Pops conductor Arthur Fiedler. During World War II, radio comics Abbott and Costello presided at an auction there that produced more than $2 million in war bonds sales.

It wasn't just hospitality or sulfur water—"Pluto Water"—bringing people in. Gambling, though illegal, flourished. Big-time stuff: "Diamond Jim" Brady was a regular, and so was the kingpin of the era's mobsters, Al Capone.

That dried up after World War II, when the winking stopped from state government. The French Lick Hotel stayed huge (six hundred rooms at its peak), but changed ownership repeatedly. The Sheraton chain took over in the 1950s and upgraded it, air-conditioning and all. But at the top, Sheraton Hotels and Resorts Inc. soured on all of the chain's old and out-of-date buildings and unloaded French Lick. By 1997, four other owners—the last a casino chain that couldn't get a gambling approval request through the Indiana legislature—had given the old yellow-brick hotel a try and watched its value and appearance wither.

After a Fire, the Dome

West Baden disappeared from competition long before that.

John Lane had first called his new hotel Mile Lick Inn, but he soon saw the similarity in the region's appeal to that of Germany's most famous "miraculous springs" area at Wiesbaden. Lane Anglicized his building's name into West Baden Springs Hotel, and it has stuck for not just the hotel but also the little community around it. For twenty-eight years, doctors Lane and Bowles played can-you-top-this with their rival hotels.

There was a brief interruption in the personal sparring while Bowles served prison time for being a Civil War–period Southern sympathizer even more outspoken and active than Cedar Farm's J. L. Kintner. After Bowles's death in 1873, the competition raged on under new ownership there. Lane died in 1883, four years before the Monon Railroad came in and gave the hotels a powerful assist, linking the area with Chicago, Indianapolis, and Louisville—high rollers and High Society now just a train ride away.

In 1888, Indiana banker-textile industrialist Lee Wiley Sinclair took possession at West Baden, and a new era in competing began. Sinclair modernized the hotel (heating, lights in every room, the place's own electricity plant) and added a swimming pool, a casino, and then an opera house that drew artists on a circuit shared by Louisville and Chicago. And Sinclair put in a touch no one else matched: a huge wooden, double-decked, roof-topped track with horse-riding on the bottom level and bicycles on the top. The tracks and stands were so big they surrounded an area with tennis courts and a baseball diamond that, in the early 1900s, brought eight major league teams in for spring training periods. Included were all five in close range: the Chicago Cubs and White Sox, the St. Louis Cardinals and Browns, and the Cincinnati Reds.

At about the time that Tom Taggart bought the French Lick hotel, disaster hit Sinclair and West Baden. Just after midnight on June 14, 1901, the huge wooden hotel caught fire and was ashes within an hour.

That day started Sinclair and West Baden toward its dome. Sinclair brought in architect Harrison Albright, whose most noted work up to then was the West Virginia Capitol Annex (with a dome). He shared plans and dreams with Albright and turned him loose with orders to get his job done in two hundred working days or be docked $100 a day until completion. The first brick was laid October 15, 1901, and one year to the day after the fire—on June 14, 1902—Albright had his revolutionary new work far enough along that Lee Sinclair moved into his rooms there. The first guests were received in September, and the building, immodestly touted as the "Eighth Wonder of the World," was formally dedicated on April 16, 1903.[3]

The Valley was the construction capital of Indiana during those feverish days. Albright and his commissioned contractor, Caldwell and Drake of Columbus, Indiana, employed 516 men on sixty-hour weeks, using more than 1,200 railroad cars of building material and 10,000 square feet of glass. And French Lick was a construction center, too. In a countermove made— lore says—as soon as he heard about Sinclair's fire and thought a bold move might push his rival into folding, Taggart announced he was doubling the size of his hotel.

Rather than ending the rivalry, Taggart's poker move heightened it. And when his bet was called and both projects were done, it was West Baden that won the wows.

It might be the only luxury hotel in the world—might have been then, might still be now—where the "rooms with a view" are the ones facing in. It has six floors, and it is round, a corridor separating inside and outside rooms and a person walking that corridor finds a constantly adjusting compass woven into the carpeting. It is the inside rooms that can look out into the atrium, with its 31,416 square feet of floor space and 2.73 million cubic feet of air space. And its dome. Exquisite and stunning then, exquisite and stunning now. In between, it all almost became extinct.

The Crashes of 1929 and 1991

A few years after Sinclair's death in 1916, his heirs sold the West Baden building to Ed Ballard, a freewheeling man who had it during the Roaring Twenties. That decade of national naughtiness was boom time in the Valley. At one time seventeen hotels and thirteen casinos, primarily interspersed along West Baden's brash and brassy one-street business district, divided up the tourist dollars, but that divvying-up was overwhelmingly dominated by the two super-hotels.

The stock market crash of 1929 stopped the area's carousel. The French Lick hotel stayed alive. As a hotel, West Baden didn't. In 1932, Ballard had to close it, and in 1934 he unloaded it, idyllic grounds and all, to the Jesuits for one dollar. For thirty years, it was a seminary, and then from 1967 to 1983 it housed a small college, Northwood Institute. All the while, decay was decomposing "the Eighth Wonder." "For several years," Marsh Davis, executive director of the Historic Landmarks Foundation of Indiana, said, "the condition of this great landmark declined, steadily for decades and precipitously in the early 1990s."

In January 1991, a section of the hotel's exterior collapsed, laying bare— as World War II bombs cleaved open buildings—hotel rooms that hadn't been used for six decades. "A huge section from the sixth floor just pancaked down," Gayle Cook remembers. The grand old structure's death knell was in the air. Davis says even a well-known preservationist said: "Time is up on the building. We should declare it a ruin and let people crawl on it." Instead, Davis said, in last-gasp desperation the Indiana landmarks group "bought the whole place for a quarter of a million dollars, with no exit strategy in sight."[4]

J. Reid Williamson Jr. had Davis's job then, and in trying to raise funds just to keep the building standing, Williamson came to Bloomington and met with Bill and Gayle Cook and Steve Ferguson in a room at Fountain Square.

"He came down looking for a much smaller sum of money, to help them buy the building so they could stabilize it," Gayle said. "Bill surprised him. He said, 'Oh, yeah, we'll do it.' And he shook Reid's hand."

Chuck Franz was working at the time in a room next to where the meeting took place. "I couldn't hear the small talk," he said, but he got the basic dialogue—which, almost twenty years later, he can't relate without laughing. "Bill asked the distinguished-looking man with him [Williamson], 'So what kind of money are you looking for?' He said they needed a million dollars to stabilize the back wall. They talk for about five minutes, and then I hear, bam, Bill's fist bang down on the table, and he says, 'Well, Steve, what the heck? We'll go a million.' I'm sitting there laughing—I can only imagine what the gentleman's face looks like. The conversation goes on for five or ten minutes, and bang, Bill's hand slams down again, and 'Two million, Steve. We can do that.' A little bit later, Steve walks the guy out, and he looks stunned. Then Bill opens the door, comes out, and says to me, 'Did you hear what Ferguson's got me into now?' Gayle said, 'Oh, no, Bill, that was all you.'"

"I think we all surprised ourselves," Gayle says. "We were all saying, 'Oh, let's do it.' We knew it was worth saving. It's a National Historic landmark, not just on the National Register. And it was on the National Trust's list of the eleven most endangered historic properties in the United States." This led to what preservationists nationally call "The Save of the Century." At that point, even the Cooks were just thinking survival. "It was a rescue attempt," architect George Ridgway said.

"When Bill started in 1996, he was just shoring it up and cleaning it up," Joe Pritchett said. "It was supposed to be about an eight- or twelve-month project, and we were there two and a half years. It kept going from there. You just always hoped it would."

Ridgway says, "Once we completed the first phase—$30 million plus—the project was for sale." The sellers found no bidders but lots of suggesters, Gayle says. "People would say, 'Oh, it would make a great religious retreat.'

Or 'a great health retreat.' Or 'a great performing arts center.' There was a feasibility study for a performing arts high school—very elaborate, very bizarre. We saw the plans for it. But there was never any money offered."

Chief Justice Randall T. Shepard of the Indiana Supreme Court, in a tribute to the Cooks at the 2007 gala, said of those days: "All the developers who came to look at the place just shook their heads with sorry expressions. 'It's an awesome place,' they agreed, 'but it's just too big, too deteriorated, too far from an interstate . . . too strange (an acre of expensive-to-heat, unleasable space . . . surrounded by small rooms . . . with curved walls).' Too risky for people who want to make a quick buck—or even a slow one. This was in the 1990s, when the stock market was rewarding investors with double-digit returns."[5]

The Cooks had a $30-million white elephant on their hands. "That building was a wreck," Bill said. "We had stabilized it. And nobody wanted to buy it."

The Night of the G Word

And then one October night in 2000, accepting the year's Outstanding Hoosier Preservationist Award at the French Lick hotel, Bill Cook for the first time personally said the G-word. "Gayle and I have run the gamut of the usage of the West Baden hotel," he said, "and about the only use we can find would be as an adjunct to gambling."

It was a thunderbolt that surprised even Gayle, but only in its timing. Bill had previewed his surprise in conversation with her—"a little bit," he said, "and it was kind of distasteful to her. We never spent any time talking about it. We were both just enamored with making this thing work."

They were doing a lot of public talking about the hotel before various groups around Indiana, Gayle remembers. "We had a slide talk that we gave several places after West Baden was stabilized. We would always talk about the building's classic architecture and the Conrad Schmitt restoration of the art work. Then we would show slides of renderings of what it would look like as a casino—neon lights flashing all over the big dome, a typical Las Vegas style casino. And there would be gasps in the audience, because they were all preservationists." And at those times, under those conditions, Gayle would be one of the gaspers. For her, a moral issue was involved—"in the beginning, yes," she says.

Even that night at French Lick, after dropping the casino bombshell, Bill followed it by saying, "Gayle and I will not be a part of that." That in-character disassociation was included in the news coverage of an event which, except for his surprise gambling comment, wouldn't have been the statewide story it became. But, he says, "Gaming was never a moral issue with me. The moral issue was to save the hotel. It could have been done as a donation or a gift, but I never like to do any kind of building and not have a prospect of making a profit. Just having a living history is not good enough. The building should be alive and doing its thing. You can't make every building a museum."

The two are in harmony on that. "Sometimes preservationists are not practical," Gayle said. "They'll say, 'Oh, do anything to save the building.' But you have to find a use for it. That's a point we always make: finding a use is the key to saving architecture."

That's when his esteemed vision kicked in for Bill Cook at the French Lick banquet. "I could visualize it [getting the hotel not just stable but back to its original splendor], but I couldn't see how to get there, until that Eureka light came on in front of those people that night. Everybody was dumbstruck, because they knew that neither Gayle nor I gambled. It was the best thing I ever said in my life, because it *was* the only thing that could save those hotels. That's the only reason I got in the casino business, not because I like gambling. I know nothing about gambling."

He said he and Gayle had been to Las Vegas and other gambling centers, but only as light participants. "I did a little gambling on baccarat—I remember the cards were all waxed, and they played out of a shuttle. I never found poker particularly fun, nor seeing Twenty-one played. I see many people enjoy gaming. It's a good pastime for them."

Gayle says, "For my personal self, I don't enjoy seeing the money disappear. I enjoy seeing the slot machines and putting in a dollar, or ten dollars, just to see how they work. I accept the fact that I'm different from other people. You look at all those people having so much fun just punching a slot machine. Someone there said, 'I lost $300, but I sure had fun.' There must be something mesmerizing. I'm not talking about an addict. I understand there are those who get in trouble. But there's something that a quite average person gets out of it. I'm not like that, but I accept it."

The Fall and the Rise of the Eighth Wonder

What had flashed into Bill Cook's head that night was, "Hey! There is a way to save that building—and not just that building but a whole lot more. But it all has to fit together, and it starts with gambling."

Starts is a key word. What he saw in that "Eureka" moment was that just gambling wasn't enough, and just an astonishingly beautiful hotel wasn't enough, considering the remote location. A bigger, broader enticement was needed to pull enough people in, somehow making a visit to the Valley a grand and unmatchable experience.

That meant upping his own ante a lot by buying the French Lick hotel, too, and giving it the same expensive, wholesale preservation and luxury update as West Baden—to three-and-a-half- to four-star status for both. That meant making championship-level golf part of the experience to be offered. And first-class restaurants, swimming pools, spas, shops, to go

A giant helicopter maneuvers one of the West Baden Springs
Hotel's four finials into position on October 24, 1998.

with the magnificently groomed and historic gardens and grounds already
at both places. And, of course, a casino, which by Indiana law couldn't be
inside either hotel but had to be—for quaint reasons—floating on water. So
a moat-sized lake had to go in, with a casino in it.

For George Ridgway and the Pritchetts, that's where fun that almost
became a religious experience began. "Oh, man, it was a once-in-a-lifetime
opportunity," Jon Pritchett said. "Just the history, knowing what all happened here. Going back to the shape it was in back in 1996—I was there the
first day with a group of about fifteen, and it was awful. Part of the building
was coming down, trees had overgrown. It was literally falling in. It was a
race to just keep it up. Probably a sixty-foot section came all the way down.
I had heard about it, but when I came to see it, it was incredible. We tore
all those old walls out and then did all the shoring. Then it grew into the
atrium." And then it grew into a multi-package. "To get to do both hotels
was incredible."

West Baden was the one that had been shut down since the 1930s, the one that needed resuscitation, the one where Bill Cook's vision was so exact and exacting that anecdotes were inevitable. "We were about halfway through the project the first time around," Joe Pritchett said, a grin spreading across his face. "Bill and I walked into the atrium [through one of the five wide entrances], and some of the doors were open. I really didn't know it, but I found out real quick they were supposed to be shut. He let me have it. They were shut from then on.

"But my best one was up in the presidential suite." That's the $5,000-a-night showpiece "room" on the ultra-desirable sixth floor. "Bill and George came up there one day [with Pritchett working elsewhere in the suite], went into the bedroom, and Bill called out, 'Joe . . .' I thought he was going to tell me something nice. I walked into the bedroom, and he tied into me on ceiling heights. I started to argue back, and I realized I wasn't going to win. I thought I had a legitimate excuse for what I did. I turned around to see where George was, for a little backup. George was gone. So I stood there and took it. He let me have it."

Ultimately that day Ridgway told Cook, "There are pipes in the way. We can move the pipes. It will cost more money, but we can get the ceiling pipe up where it's supposed to be.' He said, 'Well, by God, get them up.'

"Joe had dropped the ceiling a little lower than anticipated—a couple of inches. At West Baden that's significant because the ceilings are low in the room areas anyway—seven-feet-ten at the most. That's as high as we could get them. There are a couple of places where the building has settled and we had to put more steel in. Those ceilings are seven-two."

Joe said, "After Bill left, I told George, 'Thanks a lot for all your help. I took a lot of grief before you stepped in.' He said, 'I know when it's time to leave.'"

It wasn't a long-lasting storm. "I was sitting down in our meeting room rewriting my notes," Joe said, "and Cook walked into the room, sat down in the chair, and said, 'You all right?' I said, 'Yeah, I'm fine.' I've always thought that was his way of telling me it was over."

The Day of Thrills

The highlight day of the restoration was October 24, 1998, when a giant helicopter airlifted peaked towers onto the building's four corners.

The hotel building, though round at its core, does have squared-off corners. Each in the hotel's heyday was topped by what looked like a cap from ground level but was a tower itself *and* a cap—technically, a finial (dictionary definition: "a usually foliated ornament forming an upper extremity especially in Gothic architecture").

All four of the originals had deteriorated beyond reclamation, but one finial showed up in West Baden as a town citizen's preserved treasure. Ridgway used it and photographs to draw up plans and have new corner towers built, complete with twenty-foot yellow-and-white square bases. Each corner weighed 19,000 pounds. He named them Matthew, Mark, Luke, and John because "we needed all the help we could get."

For Joe Pritchett, the day the towers went on "was the biggest thrill of the whole thing." Jon Pritchett calls it "one of my top five experiences of my life. It was a beautiful sunny day, a great day."

It was some show. *Life* magazine came and gave it a photo spread. Five hundred VIP seats were set up in the close-by sunken gardens and sold out at $50 apiece. Another 1,200 people paid $10 each for standing-room viewing spots—a quick $37,000 for Historic Landmarks Foundation of Indiana.

"I was on the roof for setting a couple of the towers, and so was Cook, who stayed for all four installations," Joe said. "I went out in the garden for the last two and watched with my family. The helicopter [22,000 pounds itself, certified to lift its weight] was so loud, and it gave off 70 mph winds, straight down. They couldn't bring it straight down, the way they could have if they had been setting one down out in the middle of a field. The turbulence off the roof was pushing those towers back and forth. That helicopter pilot was really good." Max Evans had flown Huey helicopters for the army in Vietnam before going to work for the Erickson "air crane" company of Columbus, Ohio.

Jon said, "On the second or third one we were having trouble stabilizing it, so I was holding one of the ropes to help guide. The wind alone would literally lift you up—that was probably my number one experience. There were about twenty people. That was dangerous. Those guys were really brave to do what they did."

The excitement leading up to tower placement day was more of a temptation than the puckish Pritchetts could pass up. "We had taken one of the Erickson company's pictures and one of the dome," Jon said. The day before, after a little photo-blending magic, "We went into a meeting— Mr. Cook was there, too—and we told George Ridgway, 'We hope you don't mind, but we did a practice run.' And we passed the (doctored) picture around. It looked so good. There was a stone-cold look on George's face. Then we told him we didn't actually do it. I'm not sure I've got my payback for that yet, but I'll get it."

The Wow! Factor

On May 23, 2007, more than seven years after the tower-placing, a ribbon was cut in front of the main entrance, and the West Baden Springs Hotel officially opened to its first paid occupants in seventy-five years.

Architect George Ridgway addresses a mostly local audience at
opening day festivities in West Baden, May 23, 2007.

That, too, was a neat occasion. State and local officials were there. Architect George Ridgway, the son of a small southern Indiana community himself, was the speaker who best charmed the audience, with its blend of townsfolk wearing T-shirts and outsiders in suits and ties. The man who designed
and supervised every act of the storied hotel's recovery from the brink of
demolition to its radiance of old was almost a full-time resident on-site
through it all. And his love after all that intimacy showed in his closing line:
"Some people call it 'The Eighth Wonder of the World.' I call it home."

Lieutenant Governor Becky Skillman, from nearby Bedford, headed the
line of ribbon-cutters, which did not include Bill or Gayle Cook. They intentionally arrived about forty-five minutes afterward. "That was a day for
other people to be in the spotlight," said Cook, who was represented in snipping and speaking by aide Steve Ferguson. By their arrival, the crowd had
spilled through the doors to see from inside the reborn "Eighth Wonder."
The Cooks casually blended in with the milling mix of celebrators.

The doorway where the ribbon was cut is the hotel's "main" but not
primary entrance—by design, of Bill Cook and George Ridgway, not Lee
Sinclair and Harrison Albright.

They put the parking lot for overnight guests on the opposite side of the
building. On arrival, guests are directed to an entrance all the way across
from the lobby and the registration desk. At that entrance are greeters, and
a bellman who leads on a long, purposeful walk with welcoming conversation while crossing a moderately lighted circular corridor to enter, as from

outer halls into an arena, the vast atrium, whose boundary beauty pulls the eyes to it—walls and curtained windows never more elegant. The bellman pulls the bag cart onto a carpeted path and chats in tour-guide talk of the floor's tiny, inlaid marble mosaic tiles—millions of them, arranged in intricate design patterns nearly one hundred years ago when each cost a penny and that whole circular floorful represented a pretty penny: $120,000 in 1917 dollars. The tiles and their striking patterns pull the eyes down until, exactly halfway across, the bellman theatrically stops in a round, marked area, where the guests' eyes automatically slide upward until they're looking straight up, and . . .

Way up there, the equivalent of nine or ten or eleven stories up, is a breathtaking sight: the splendidly appointed, historically high freestanding dome.

"Here," the bellman says, "is what we call the wow factor."

Actually, it's the climax of wowing that began a few steps before. Jon Pritchett, of the construction company that did the resurrection work, said, "I've been in this building over a thousand times—I couldn't tell you how many times. And it's still a jaw-dropping experience every time I walk through the doors. I tell friends who haven't been in here yet I want to be in front of them their first time so I can see their jaw when they walk in. Almost without exception, it's unbelievable."

Ridgway says, "The emotion that you see—even in people who have been here time after time—never changes. Like Bill Cook says, 'Every time you walk into this atrium, there's only one word: Wow!'"

It's the Hope diamond on a Wal-Mart shelf, every bit that shocking to first-timers dulled down in expectations by travel on two-lane roads through cornfields and curling small-town streets unacquainted with stoplights, let alone swank.

Suddenly they're in America's Pantheon. For more than 1,600 years, the world's highest freestanding dome *was* the Pantheon, built by the Roman government in AD 128 as a holy place. The diameter of its 43.4-meter dome, more than twice the previous world record, was unmatched until Benedictine monks built one slightly wider (46.0) in St. Blaise, Germany, in 1781. St. Blaise's Abbey remained the world's biggest freestanding dome—and the U.S. Capitol in Washington, with its 39.0-meter dome built in 1864, was America's biggest—until 1902, when both titles were lost to this hotel building in bitsy West Baden in sparse southwestern Indiana.[6]

Sinclair and Albright's 60.0-meter diameter wasn't beaten in America until the Astrodome went up in Houston in 1965—enormously bigger, 216.4 meters, and stereotypically Texan: all size, minimal beauty, built to make baseball and football inside games. The closest thing to a game ever played under the West Baden Springs Hotel dome was when in pre-restoration days local hero Larry Bird put on a basketball clinic in the atrium. Even in Indiana, basketball surely has never been more beautiful.

Today I Turn It over to the World

As the years of the new century passed by, the part of the Sinclair-Albright achievement that took on new impressiveness was its completion in exactly one year, ashes to splendor. Ridgway and the Pritchetts weren't working with a cast of five hundred or lax workday definitions, but they did have computers and a century's worth of engineering and technology advancements. And still it took much longer to get all the pieces completed, all the details worked out to Bill Cook's satisfaction. The jewel being worked with in the end could have no avoidable flaws.

One of those details was restoration of the atrium's multimillion-dollar Rookwood fireplace, with its elaborate ceramic inlays—works of art themselves—and a mouth so big it can handle fourteen-foot logs.

A "detail" even more spectacular is a round chandelier-type light just under the dome. In daylight, it's dazzling. At night, it is bathed by a computer-operated light system that turns it into a show of its own. "Up there are forty-eight light fixtures with three light tubes," Ridgway said. "They all blend together. You can get every color in the spectrum." From those interior rooms, or from anywhere on the floor of the atrium, that centerpiece takes on different hues, blends of gold and blue and green, fading to a glowing-embers red at goodnight-time. "Then on top of each column there are two 400-watt lights on each side," Ridgway said. "Rob Cross with Cross Lighting did all the computerization. One dark night, Rob and I went up on a hill on top of West Baden. We looked down and saw these lights chasing each other—Rob had set them to chase a circle. It looked like the whole dome was ready to lift off. We don't *do* that. They just light up. But they can be set to chase."

The morning of the ribbon-cutting, just before the ceremony, Ridgway sat in the atrium and weighed a question: In the middle of all that splendor, what jumps out to you?

"You walk in through a huge opening—there are five of them, each ten feet wide—but that's small, in terms of scale, once you step inside this ring. It just opens up to where you as a human are almost insignificant. It's a humbling experience. So huge and so elegant. 'What is man, that thou art mindful of him?'" That was the Bible's David asking the question, in the eighth Psalm's fourth verse, and it was George Ridgway feeling a holiness in the humility he says he—a man of spatial appreciations—always feels on entering the West Baden cathedral of Harrison Albright. "The greatest respect I have for Harrison Albright is not his ability to get a job completed but to come up with a unique design," Ridgway said. "He had great sense of scale and proportion."

Ridgway looked around. Wistfully or playfully, he thought of what that day, opening those hotel doors to paying customers, meant to him. "I've spent eleven years of my life waiting for this day, eleven years of being in this building, having a key to everything, able to go any time anyplace, check out anything. Today I turn it over to the world. And my key doesn't go anyplace."

Jon Pritchett understood and felt he had a crew of workers who did, too. "We had a meeting every Monday morning. Two weeks ago, the meeting was winding down. I said, 'The meeting's over.' And nobody moved. They genuinely felt sorry this was ending. That's how much everybody put into this."

Joe Pritchett said, "My wife, Lisa, and I have three kids—Zane, 8, Emily, 12, and Shelby, 14. We stayed down here the Saturday night before the opening. I didn't want them to miss it. The kids were thrilled, they understood what's going on. The girls gave me hugs and told me how proud they are. They know it's a once in a lifetime."

Jon has a family, too, and opening day at the dome was a mini-crisis for him. "My son had eighth-grade graduation. It's not like high school graduation, but it was a big deal to him. But I had to miss it. I told my wife it's like playing in the last game of the World Series and missing the ninth inning. I can't do that. I put in ten years of my life, and I was not going to miss the grand opening."

A Hurdle or Two

The Bill and Gayle Cook money that made the Valley miracle happen did add up. "For the entire project, the cost now is right at $450 million—$272 million in bonds and the rest is us," Cook said.

There were hurdles to clear along the way in getting to the opening. One came early in the project and was both painful and unforeseen. During demolition at West Baden, a conflict with environmental laws gave Cook and the project embarrassment and the threat of legal charges, and brought the first rupture to the warm relationship with the Pritchetts. When his own investigation indicated the offenses weren't unintentional and were timed to get around his on-site visits, he demanded the firing of the responsible employee. The severance came, but not before Cook had assigned the construction contract for his new company headquarters building in Bloomington—a newly $100 million project—to Jack Thompson of Bloomington, not to the Pritchetts.

Yes, Jon Pritchett admits, he thought the relationship that had been the backbone of his company's operations his entire lifetime might have been permanently over back then. "It was that close. It was a tough situation. I honestly still don't know what all was going on and don't know if I want to know." When the decision later was made to expand the project to renovate and restore both hotels, he said, "Bill called Joe and me in and said, 'Here's your shot.' We were still down there working. He still must have trusted in Joe and me. I think Joe and my dad had a lot to do with that."

That was a tempest that blew over quickly compared with the project partnership with Lauth Construction Co. of Indianapolis that turned bitter. That led to a long and acrimonious suit that got the media attention of a Hollywood divorce. The partnership covered both hotels and the casino, but a complaint filed by company president Robert L. Lauth Jr. on June 20, 2006, primarily zeroed in on the casino. It accused Bill Cook of "tortuously interfering with the casino-resort project to which he has no legal relationship [while] Lauth has been powerless to stop Mr. Cook's involvement . . . nor are workers, contractors, subcontractors, or architects willing to stand up to Indiana's richest man. As a result, an individual with absolutely no legal authority, no ownership, and no casino license is literally building a casino in southern Indiana."[7] Cook's lawyers countered that such allegations were "baseless."

In the finding on Lauth's complaint, Orange Circuit Court Judge Larry Blanton "thought he was doing me a favor by saying I could do anything to help the project, but I couldn't slow it down," Cook said. "As a result, there were many instances where the project should have been slowed down, and in some cases stopped, until we could have rectified certain things. By not being able to make these alterations and corrections, it cost us a great deal of money."

When the issue was settled in June 2007, with the Cook-financed Blue Sky Corporation buying full control and with all litigation dropped, the air cleared and Cook said the project never fell off schedule. "The court restrictions were a minor problem for me. But did they cause any undue problems? No. There were several things I would have done differently that, even if we hadn't saved money, we would have had a better result."

Primarily he's talking about the casino, where his voice and preferences were least involved in construction. He's not pleased with the casino as it is now and plans to make major improvements. He's still hot over the Lauth company's free-spending and meddling charge against him. "Every expense that we put into a building we considered an investment. They considered it a cost. That is a huge difference. We said the West Baden Hotel was going to be a three-and-a-half to four star hotel. They didn't understand what it took to have a designation like that. They also didn't understand what a tax credit is . . . that if you receive tax credits for work on a designated National Historic Landmark, you are subject to the regulations of the Department of the Interior." Those regulations demand fidelity to duplicating what is being replaced. The West Baden Springs Hotel project was granted $25 million, the largest tax credit ever authorized by the Department of the Interior,

Ridgway said. Tax-credit laws were set up "because of the inordinate costs that come in restoring" rather than demolition and all-new construction. "Restoration does take money."

Even with the tax credits, Cook says, the West Baden building as it stands now probably could have been built brand-new at a lower net cost. "We have about $75 million in it, and we probably could have got it up for $40 million. But I don't think the charm would have been there. That was what we were after, to make it have a luxurious feel and yet make it in such a way that everyone could enjoy it—not just the rich, or the people who love restoration, but everyone who comes in there and feels they didn't get ripped off when they came in."

There was a practical side to Bill Cook's insistence on aesthetics. "The casino would have not been nearly as successful if we had gone on the cheap with the hotels. There's competition on practically all sides of us. We would not have been able to compete for the Evansville, Louisville, or Cincinnati area markets. Without these magnificent hotels, what would be the reason anyone would come to a little town like French Lick?"

My God, How Could This Ever Be?

The court restrictions from which the settlement unshackled him would have been more inhibiting if the people on-site carrying the project to completion hadn't been people close to Cook who had his full confidence and awareness of what he wanted done—his son Carl, longtime associate Steve Ferguson, architect George Ridgway, and the Pritchett brothers. That's where he spread the credit for the gem that was produced.

"We relied on each other. George Ridgway is probably the most renowned architect in the state. His reputation spreads all over the country. The Pritchetts have demonstrated time and time again over the years just how efficient and proficient they are. What wonderful eyes they have for quality and detail.

"Carl was the one in charge of making the calls that involved expense. There are options. Sometimes the best way to go is the most expensive. Sometimes the best way to go, you won't get quite the results that you would like. An architect with the brilliance of George can give you the options, but you have to make the decisions. They're tough to make, particularly when there's a lot of them. There might be 500 decisions a day to make in building something of that magnitude. Because of the immense size of these hotels and the building of the casino, this is the largest historic preservation project ever attempted in this country, including Grand Central Station.

"I think that everybody, once they get there, from anyplace in the country, will be impressed. They'll look at those hotels and think, 'My God, how could this ever be? How could this ever happen in this little part of the world that nobody knows anything about?' People will be coming from all over the world to see this. There's usually one great hotel somewhere. But two? And golf courses—I don't know anyplace like this. There still are a hundred different things that need to be done. All of them take an immense amount of money."

Bill Cook will always remember that night of the gala and the words Chief Justice Shepard showered on him, Gayle, and Carl while announcing them as first recipients of an award to be given by the Indiana Historic Landmarks Association—"The Cook Cup for Outstanding Restoration":

> When the legislature approved a casino for the Valley, the Cooks had both hope and concern—hope that the casino would attract people to fill the West Baden Springs Hotel, and concern that gambling might overshadow this landmark and overshadow the French Lick Springs Hotel, its companion one mile away. Bill and Gayle and Carl Cook had a vision of meticulously restored and thriving historic hotels, with a casino that offered one reason to visit, but not the only reason. Professional gaming companies tended to look at the situation through a narrower set of lenses.
>
> . . . They bought the thread-worn French Lick Springs Hotel, built in 1901. They restored the 443-room French Lick hotel—top to bottom, inside and out. And then they came to complete the rescue they started here at West Baden in 1996. They created a 246-room luxury hotel in a place that had been legitimately called a ruin.
>
> Whether you visit the casino or not, I think you'd be safe in betting on the success of these landmarks under Cook stewardship, safe in betting that they'll realize their aspiration of a heritage tourism destination that will rival if not eclipse the Homestead, the Greenbrier, the Grand Hotel—a destination that will represent one of the greatest saves in the whole history of the historic preservation movement in this country.
>
> Well, a skeptic might ask, won't one of Indiana's wealthiest families get wealthier from this endeavor? Historic Landmarks Foundation's response is: "We very much hope so. That would mean that the enterprise is a rousing success—one that proves preservation is good business." But getting richer is not Bill and Gayle and Carl Cook's motivation. Once the restoration expenses are paid off, nearly half the profits from the Cooks' operation of the two hotels and the casino will go directly to a foundation they created that will make grants for preservation and education in Indiana.[8]

"I've gotten honorary degrees, and Sagamore of the Wabash [the Indiana governor's top honorary citizen citation] five times," Bill Cook said, "but nothing compares to that night."

A Golf Course to Dye For

With all that was completed by the ribbon-cutting and the gala, there was still a delicacy to come, a year or so out.

The "valley" towns, French Lick and West Baden, are united by the Springs Valley High School, which produced Larry Bird, but geographically they are separate, a long drive apart.

A long golf drive, not auto.

And golf is pertinent down in the Valley—always has been, since the most noted golf architect of his era, Donald Ross, came to French Lick and built for Tom Taggart such a gorgeous, challenging course that, in its fifth year of use, the 1924 PGA tournament was played there, and the Tiger Woods of the era, Walter Hagen, won. About the same time, Thomas Bendelow—American golf's Johnny Appleseed, credited with building more than seven hundred courses in spreading the sport into communities throughout (and even outside) the United States—built a handsome second course close by.

Both courses still thrive, meticulously and lovingly and expensively renewed as part of the Cooks' commitment to the area, but they are about to be upstaged. Taking shape for probable unveiling sometime in late summer 2009 is The Pete Dye Golf Course at French Lick, a creation of today's leading golf course architect.

Dye, an Ohio native who has spent most of his eighty-plus years in Indiana, has dotted America with creations that show up repeatedly at tournament sites on the Professional Golf Association tour and frequently get the ultimate in golf-course recognition as sites for the U.S. Open or PGA. In his longtime hometown of Indianapolis, he built Crooked Stick (where the 1991 PGA tournament first spotlighted pro golf's winningest flake, John Daly) and Brickyard Crossing (outside and inside the city's most famous landmark, the 500-Mile Racetrack, from which he utilized a dismantled outer retaining wall). In Florida he built Sawgrass, the touring professionals' tournament home (with its "world's most terrifying hole," the island seventeenth green) and lavish courses at Hilton Head (Harbour Town) and Kiawah Island in South Carolina, the Dunes and Mountain courses at La Quinta, California—dozens of America's best.

And still, Pete Dye's eyes well up when he talks about the land he is working with in shaping what will be the artist's signature course. Besides its valleys, the verdant, tree-enhanced acreage includes the second-highest point in Indiana.

"Pete says it's the most beautiful course he has ever done," Bill Cook said. "It gives him the most vistas. He spends so much time walking—every time he comes upon a hole, he's looking out over a huge, expansive valley with a gorgeous view of southern Indiana."

Jon Pritchett, the construction engineer for the entire West Baden–French Lick project, said Dye "grabbed me by the arm on the course one time, turned me around, and said, 'Look at that! Now, turn around *here* and look! Where else in the world can you get that? There's nothing like it!' It just gives you cold chills to know where his vision is on that land."

Previous page: West Baden Springs Hotel

Above: French Lick Springs Hotel

The French Lick casino boat at night, as it debuted

The atrium at West Baden Springs Hotel

The West Baden Sinclair's dining room in 1994 (*above*) and in 2008, fully restored

Genuine gold adds luster to the interior of the restored French Lick Springs Hotel

Gayle and Bill Cook at Cedar Farm

Dye's challenge on this course is a rare one in his field, not to create ups and downs but to make it manageable for golfers walking the course. "He is leveling it off some," Cook says. "The hilarious thing—we knew that Pete liked to alter land and landscape. We had no idea he liked to take down hills. A few more feet and we could mine coal."

Pritchett said, "Although it's on a hillside, he has it so you can walk it without feeling like you're dropping in elevation. I don't know exactly the elevation change now, but Pete made the comment that it's not as bad as Augusta [site of the Masters, and widely considered the most beautiful course in America]."

Steve Ferguson, an ardent golfer, has supervised the golf work around the hotels, first in sprucing up the Donald Ross course, then in converting the Bendelow course to nine holes with an improved driving range and other complementary touches, then with the new construction. Cook said, "Steve has become very close to Pete Dye and Pete's idiosyncrasies, and Pete's got a lot of them because he is a master golf designer. He knows exactly what the needs are for a golf course, and he makes absolutely certain everything is in place. There is no compromising with Pete."

It's all coming without a contract—with a handshake agreement, and no budget: classic Bill Cook *and* Pete Dye, word-is-bond old warriors untamed by a litigious society.

The highest point on the course is where the house sits that ultimately will be the clubhouse. There Taggart built a mansion atop Mount Airie. Jerry and Carolyn Fuhs were its owners, and they lived there until the elaborate course construction necessitated a friendly buy-out. They built a new home nearby.

"That will be another neat restoration," Jon Pritchett said of the stately two-story house/clubhouse-to-be. "Right now they're leaning toward a small restaurant on the first floor, some guest rooms on the second floor, and use of the carriage shop as the pro shop. It depends on where their vision ends up."

Vision as Pritchett used the word there is spelled with a lot of dollar signs. He laughed as he recalled, "We were at lunch one time with Bill and some other guys, and a newspaper guy asked how financially he came up with what to do on something. Bill started to explain, then just said, 'You either have the money or you don't.'"

Bill Cook, who does have it, was asked when this whole project had begun, when the West Baden hotel that triggered it all was in its worst shape, did even he look at that wreckage and see such a total return? He thought, and mused—about what he saw then, how he felt along the way.

"Aw," he said, "if you throw enough money at anything, you can make it work."

Chief Justice Randall T. Shepard honors Carl, Gayle, and Bill Cook at the 2007 gala formally dedicating the renewed West Baden Springs Hotel.

The Pete Dye Golf Course, shown here under construction, is slated to open in 2009.

21

A Good Time in Our Lives

Oh, my. I think this is a good time in our life to be able to do
some of the things that we're doing. We love these preservation
projects and feel they're doing good. Our actual lifestyle
hasn't changed much. We're still in the house that we bought
for $36,750 and moved into in 1967. We're right in town,
where we always wanted to stay.

— Gayle Cook

A thriving company, its eventual ownership transfer to son Carl assured;
at last a garage on their comfortable, longtime home; the historic hotels
they rescued and resurrected now resort palaces in pastoral environs; away-
from-it-all weekends at Cedar Farm, long stretches of summers (or whatever time they wish) on their *Star 7* boat—life is pretty close to idyllic for
Bill and Gayle Cook these days.

Idyllic, not idle.

Once a week—Mondays, when it's closed—Gayle goes to the Monroe
County Historical Museum in work clothes and works alongside others—
outside, trimming bushes and the like, or inside, tackling clean-up projects
or preparing collections or exhibits for display in the museum. Twice a
year—at a February auction of donated objects (which usually brings in
about $5,000) and a late-spring super garage sale ($16,000 net in 2007)—

she is involved in set-up, the daylong sale, and eventual clean-up. "There wouldn't be a museum without her," another key museum volunteer, Mary Lee Deckard, said. Without her *and* Bill—the Cooks' checkbook also is involved. Annually facing a financing problem that the two sales and solicited contributions and membership fees struggled to meet, the museum—like the COPS organization—got a surprise sustaining boost a couple of years ago: a $3 million endowment, with about 5 percent in interest available for use every year while keeping the endowment intact. That's a $150,000-a-year stabilizer in perpetuity.

I think this is a good time in our life to be able to do some of the things that we're doing.

Life today also includes one simple pleasure for Bill, even an occasional tingle, in just going to work each morning.

Daniel's Way is a new, artfully curving street that brings visitors off Third Street to the handsome headquarters of Cook Inc. The street straightens out in time to give an approaching driver a city block or so with a dead-ahead, straight-on, windshield-wide look as this twenty-first-century building comes into its full and impressive view. It's long and low, a skyscraper built horizontally, stretching too wide for peripheral vision to take in as one approaches. It's Sto (a synthetic stucco), a very light beige with dark green rounded-glass corners. And it all sits behind a stone rectangle out front that announces COOK in silver letters, in front of a fountain centered by a round pavilion with eight Grecian-style white stone columns.

Even to Bill Cook, "It's rather . . . imposing. But, yeah, I get a kind of aw–gee whiz! Now, I don't get that big kick *every* time I come to work." But he did the first time, and the first several times, and even in anticipation when it was just a dream taking shape on a drawing board: "There's enormous excitement when you see something that is going to be a part of your life. It was very easy to visualize what it would look like. We had the scale model and some very good renderings. But you can't get an idea of the scope, how big it really is, until you actually see the panoramic view."

"I get a kind of *aw–gee whiz!*"

A Couple of Alterations

The building is a masterwork of company architect George Ridgway, who until completion of the West Baden Springs Hotel project counted it—"Park 48" by name, for its plat number—as his favorite of all his Cook designs.

Ridgway has stories about both the rounded corners on the windows and the pavilion.

(1) **"The rounded glass corners**—radius glass," he calls them—weren't his idea, he says. "It was The Man Upstairs—The Man *way* upstairs."

Sketch of Park 48, the world headquarters of Cook Group Incorporated, in Bloomington, Indiana

Ridgway has his own architectural firm with its office in Vincennes, about sixty miles from Bloomington. He and a staff had put together a scale model of what he was proposing for construction to Cook and other company executives when they wanted to relocate from their outgrown Curry Pike complex. "One of our guys was working on the model. He left it in the office overnight, and that night we had a water leak in the office ceiling. It dripped right on top of that model. The next morning I was supposed to pick it up and take it to Bloomington to show to Bill for the first time. I walked in that morning, and my guys were sick. Every one of those corners had sucked up the water and warped. A couple of guys were trying to fix it. I said, 'Wait. Just dry it. That's what we want, right there. That's what it takes to smooth out this building—that radius glass.' We had the glass coming together in the corners. When it warped, it rounded it off.

"I showed up with this model that was wet and stained and set it down on the table. Bill looked at it like, 'My God, what a piece of crap.' I said, 'Now just glaze your eyes over. Get them out of focus. And look at this thing.' That was easy for Bill. All he had to do was take his glasses off. He said, 'You're right. The radius glass works. That's what we'll do. How did you come up with that?' I told him. "The ceiling leaked."

(2) The pavilion. "*That* could be better," Ridgway says, pain in his words.

This was the one Ridgway-designed Cook building that Pritchett Bros. didn't put up. "Jack Thompson built it. I was up here on a Sunday. They had the foundations and the base stones in, the first block. That pavilion was supposed to be rotated fifteen more degrees."

The effect to the straight-on approaching driver would have been a view through the columns framing the front entrance of the building and the COOK logo. "What you see now is a column, straight on," he said. "Most people don't know, but I do. You're supposed to look *through* those columns."

The day he saw that first block wrongly started, he pointed out the difference. "Jack didn't want to move it. I got up there again Tuesday morning and now they had the columns up. I said, 'Jack, that's not right! You've got to take it back down and rotate it.' He talked to Bill, and Bill said, 'Oh, I think it'll be fine. Let's leave it alone.'

"Jack and I are good friends, and to this day, whenever we talk about the building, I'll mention something about that, and he'll say, 'How long are you going to be pissed off about that pavilion?' And I'll say, 'How long is it going to be wrong?'"

The rounded radius windows at the entrance to the Cook Inc. headquarters building (*below*) and the pavilion in front of it at night (*right*)

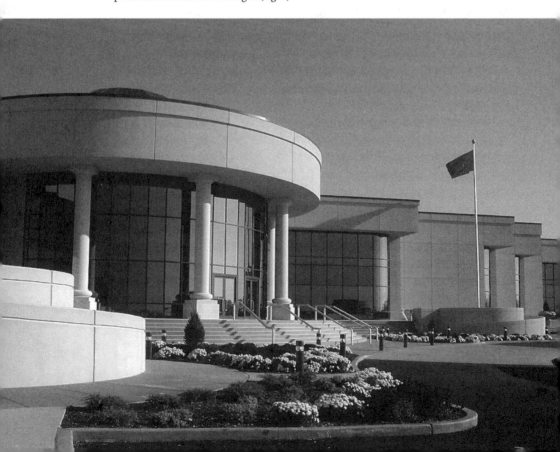

Looking Down the Road

Park 48 may be the last main corporate home Bill will build. It may not be the company's last, big as it is. "Whether or not it's sufficient, I'll leave that up to the future. The technology is changing so quickly. This building already has eight-year-old technology. In another ten years, we'll probably be ready for something else. And we don't know how much we'll be in devices and how much we'll be in drugs by then. I'd like to be around in ten years to see what *is* going to happen."

Just up Daniel's Way, about halfway between Third Street and Park 48, is another new complex with burgeoning needs. Ivy Tech is Bloomington's No. 2 university, one of a state-backed network of community vocational schools as new in the IU-dominated town as its gleaming buildings. Every year its Bloomington campus enrollment multiplies as it answers training needs in a variety of fields, including nursing. It's also a potential buyer if Park 48 ever becomes insufficient for Cook Inc. and goes on the market.

"If we outgrow this one I just hope that we—they—are ready to move on to another building when Ivy Tech needs one," Cook says. "This would be ideal for an education building. Fabulous!"

As for that $36,750 home they bought in 1967: whatever slim chance there might ever have been for a move from it probably vanished with completion of a three-car garage in October 2007.

Like virtually all Cook construction, the garage was designed by Ridgway and built by the Pritchetts. It came sooner than Gayle expected. She asked Ridgway to do the job when the West Baden work was completed and nothing else in the Cook domain was pressing—which might have meant a long, long wait. Ridgway remembers: "I said, 'Gayle, I will make time. Don't you worry.'"

The bridging link between garage and house did add some room. Gayle said, "We told George what we wanted, and he's good. For our old age we wanted an accessible master bedroom. We have no bedroom on the first floor of the house." The new master bedroom is on the second floor, but the addition includes a small personal elevator. "A lot of condos are putting those in," Gayle said. "I guess they're a lot cheaper now than they used to be. We thought we would build something we can stay in forever."

That's true for their cars, too, at last with their own garage. "I've been told it doesn't take long before the garage is full and there's no place for the cars," she said. "That is *not* going to happen."

acknowledgments

Everything in this area starts, as the book itself did, with Bill Cook. The two of us were not close acquaintances when, in September 2006, we took a ride in his car to the West Baden–French Lick hotel renovation and preservation projects then under way. Doing a biography of Bill Cook had been an ultimate ambition for me in some vague, out-there-somewhere day, but it was not in my mind when I got in the car.

We hadn't reached the southern limits of Bloomington before he came out of the blue with a question: "How would you like to do my book?"

I thought long and hard, maybe a full second. Then I said, "I'd *like* to do that." It isn't recommended driving procedure, but he kept the car going, controlled the wheel with his left hand, reached his right across, and said, "Fine. Let's do it." That quickly I shared one of those legendary Bill Cook handshakes. An ultimate commitment.

Of course, as a writer, the potentially troublesome word in his initial eight words was "my." I have done two autobiographies, in which I wrote in the voice of, first, a career baseball scout named Jim Russo, who was from my home town of Huntington, Indiana, and then—much more acclaimed, and bought, four weeks in the Top 5 on the *New York Times* bestseller list—of the other Bloomington personage whom I had always thought of as ideal book material, Indiana University basketball coach Bob Knight.

Autobiographies, I later learned, most commonly are done with little real connection between writer and subject. A professional writer, of a personal intimacy that might or might not be great, acquires a familiarity through some interviews and clippings and takes off with "I did" and "I thought" in the subject's voice and gets the job done in a few efficient months (which explains why, occasionally, there is a baffling cry after a "self-written" book that "I was misquoted").

That quicky style of autobiography wasn't the way I did it with either Russo or Knight. I operated primarily with tape recordings of conversations between us, although with Knight there were hundreds of mutually shared experiences and memories that fed into the database as well. The thoughts definitely were theirs, and so, to an overwhelming extent, were the specific words. Where bridges were needed to tie together quotes, I felt able to do it because I knew the voice so well, hence the phrasings. And, in each case, because it was their book and not mine, I felt it essential to run finished products by them to make sure what was said in the book truly was what they thought and wanted to say. That most exactingly was true with Knight, who more than once caught me in (I admit with some professional embarrassment) even grammatical slips. Not many, but a few, each of which he treasured.

I didn't want to do that kind of book with Bill Cook, whom I didn't know nearly so well. On that auto trip, I outlined how I would like to do a book. He agreed fully, and he never went back on his end of the commitment in any way. Almost daily in the early weeks, he sat down with me for taped interviews. When the number of those sessions topped twenty I lost count; most lasted more than an hour. He answered every question candidly, without an "I don't want to go into that" or the one familiar in congressional hearings when a probe reaches sticky territory, "I don't recall." Bill Cook's recall is remarkable, but he did have a few times when his memory on something wasn't precise, and on such occasions he always suggested asking someone who would remember: Phyllis McCullough, his longtime associate who rose from secretary to company president, or Steve Ferguson, the Bloomington lawyer who had the same length of association and rise within the company after an acquaintance that started at their wives' sorority party. There were some other "Ask So-and-So" directions for confirmation or answers, none more frequent or more reliable than the ones that brought, "Ask Gayle."

Gayle Cook also was generous and gracious with her taped interview time, and her availability later as a clearing-up source for a dozen quick questions that came up. She was forthright with answers even on subjects that couldn't have been comfortable for her. She had never given an interview about her twenty-six-hour kidnapping, but she knew its importance and could not have been more forthcoming or cooperative—on that nadir of all the experiences that she and her husband shared—and on all the rest, triumphal and trying.

That was vital. This is a Bill Cook biography, but so much of what is he, is they. In years to come, there's a question whether the Cook name will be better known for the international medical-products company that Bill's vision built or for the philanthropic joint projects of Bill and Gayle, the crown jewels of which were brought into full fruition with the opening of the spectacular West Baden Springs Hotel in 2007, a scant two miles from its twin in southern Indiana splendor, the French Lick Springs Hotel, renovated to its own old-time luxury in 2006.

Interviews with those two were the hub of this book, but there were many spokes that fleshed it out of hagiographic status. Carl Cook, Bill and Gayle's son, played his own key role in the hotel project, and in interviews, as his father's designated successor, he was particularly helpful in discussing the company's future. Teresa Steinsberger, Aimee Hawkins-Mungle, and Jim Heckman of the Cook Inc. corporate "family" were invaluable in many ways and always gracious. Cook Inc. artist Linda Wysong was of patient and valuable help. Taped, conversational, e-mail, or telephone interview contributions came from Phyllis McCullough (who was of immense and frequent help) and four men who in a corporate sense were there earliest, longest, and most integrally: Steve Ferguson, Miles Kanne, Tom Osborne, and Ross Jennings. Valuable insights also came from interviews with Jerry Arthur, Brian Bates, Michael Boo, Bill Carper, Ellie Carper, Roy Church, Mary Lee Deckard, Gene DeVane, Thad Drost, Chuck Franz, Kris Gebhardt, Dr. Dan Grossman, Bob Harbstreit, Phil Hathaway, Amanda Hawkins-Vogel, Kem Hawkins, Bob Heppenstall, Dr. Tom Hollingsworth, Joe Horn, Francie Hurst, John Kamstra, Len Kuchan, Chris Leininger, Jim Mason, John Mellencamp, John Mutz, John Myers, Charlie and Joe and Jon and Richard Pritchett, Gloria Saurbaugh Pschirrer, Sister Rose Mary Rexing, George Ridgway, Steve Riggins, Dr. Larry Rink, Sharon Rogers, Chief Justice Randall Shepard, Rick Snapp, Dan Sterner, Linda Stines, Gene Taylor, Dennis Troy, Jim Van Sickle, Sue Ellen Wasick, Pete Yonkman, and Charlotte Zietlow. Particularly helpful were Troy's detailed security files.

Photographers whose work was used include Doug Dreisbach, Adam Frangione, Kris Gebhardt, Amy Drake, Ed Plimpton, Chris Smith, Ian Vaughn, and Nile Young.

Help in vital ways came from many others, starting with remarkable tolerance and understanding by my wife of fifty years, Julie, whose only "reward" for surrendering priority status was sneaking a peek or two at chapters brought home in folders to satisfy some of her curiosity about two people she had long admired, and about what really was taking shape. Two great personal friends two generations apart, retired distinguished history professor George Juergens and brilliant young novelist Michael Koryta, were volunteer editors whose separate piece-by-piece readings and recommendations helped immeasurably along the way. Tom Schumaker, a career journalist of exceptional skills and a friend of fifty years, gave the completed manuscript a check-out and improved it with suggestions—editing is one of those skills. Greg Dawson, another extraordinary journalist and wonderful writer, is a forty-year friend who also improved the writing and encouraged the writer.

Director Janet Rabinowitch, marketing and sales director Pat Hoefling, and all at Indiana University Press who took this from manuscript to book form, and Robert Meitus, of invaluable help at the end, also deserve acknowledgment and thanks.

sources and notes

More than fifty face-to-face interviews—nearly half with Bill Cook, the rest with Gayle Cook, more than a dozen Cook Inc. employees, law enforcement officers, and some early-age Bill Cook friends in Canton, Illinois—provided most of the information and quotes used in this book. Exceptions are attributed or covered here.

Kidnapping

1. Bloomington *Herald-Times,* December 22, 1999.
2. Spencer *Evening World,* June 3, 1999.
3. Bloomington *Herald-Times,* November 22, 2001.
4. Rick Coates, *Northern Express,* November 30, 2006.
5. Jeff McKinney and Joe Gerrety, Lafayette *Journal & Courier,* March 18, 1989.
6. Associated Press, March 24, 1989.
7. Bloomington Police report, March 8, 1989 (Cook Inc. security files).
8. From court transcripts and police records.
9. From signed statement entered into Monroe Circuit Court records at 1993 appeal.
10. Recorded by Kenny Rogers 1977; composed by Hal Bynum and Roger Bowling.
11. From signed statement entered into Monroe Circuit Court records at 1993 appeal.
12. Police report, Cook Inc. security files.
13. Police report, Cook Inc. security files.
14. Court testimony FBI Special Agent William Baird.

1. Playing in Peoria

The sources for almost everything in this chapter are newspaper clippings from Cook family scrapbooks and my interviews with Bill and Gayle.

1. Election advertisement, Evansville newspaper.
2. Convention ticket, in family scrapbook.

3. A Wide Gold Band

1. Works manager William B. Gates, Joliet Arsenal, to Cook, July 16, 1953.

4. Road to Bloomington

1. Speech at Jasper Chamber of Commerce luncheon, October 10, 2006.

5. Bedroom Beginning

1. Sven-Ivar Seldinger, "A Leaf out of the History of Angiography," in *Radiology: Faculty Proceedings of the VI European Congress of Radiology, Lisbon, Portugal, 31 May–6 June 1987*, ed. M. E. Silvestre, F. Abecasis, and J. A. Veiga-Pires (New York: Elsevier Science, 1987).
2. Bloomington *Courier-Tribune*, April 17, 1973.
3. Speech at Jasper Chamber of Commerce luncheon, October 10, 2006.

6. Moving Up

1. All annual sales figures from "Cook Group Incorporated Sales History," company treasurer John Kamstra.

8. Foothold in Europe

1. Information in this chapter comes from Cook Inc. files, unless otherwise noted.
2. Brian Werth, Bloomington *Herald-Telephone*, April 19, 1978.

9. Doctors

1. L. A. Geddes and L. E. Geddes, *The Catheter Introducers* (Chicago: Mobium Press, 1993).
2. Josef Rösch, Frederick S. Keller, and John A. Kaufman, "The Birth, Early Years, and Future of Interventional Radiology," *Journal of Interventional Radiology* 14 (2003): 841–53.
3. Jan Greene and Otha Linton, *The History of the Dotter Interventional Institute, 1990–2005* (Portland: Oregon Health and Science University, Dotter Interventional Institute, 2005).

10. Stents and Suits

1. Brian Werth, Bloomington *Herald-Times*, January 3, 2003.

12. The Guidant Fiasco

1. *Indianapolis Star*, August 14, 2002.
2. Bloomington *Herald-Times*, January 3, 2002.

14. Religion

1. Speech at Jasper Chamber of Commerce luncheon, October 10, 2006.

15. Politics

1. Mike Leonard, Bloomington *Herald-Telephone*, May 25, 1982.
2. Kurt Van der Dussen, Bloomington *Herald-Telephone*, December 3, 1982.
3. Kurt Van der Dussen, Bloomington *Herald-Telephone*, November 17, 1982.
4. Kurt Van der Dussen, Bloomington *Herald-Telephone*, December 3, 1982.
5. Jackie Sheckler, Bloomington *Herald-Times*, April 22, 1994.
6. Editorial, Bloomington *Herald-Times*, April 22, 1994.

Kidnapping Redux

Prior to March 19, 1989, and the recovery of Gayle Cook with the arrest of Arthur Curry, there were two primary sources of information: Gayle Cook's comments (in personal interviews with the author and on the witness stand) and the files of Cook Inc. security chief Dennis Troy. After the arrest, newspaper coverage was exhaustive, primarily through reporters' work in the Bloomington *Herald-Times, Indiana Daily Student, Indianapolis Star, Louisville Courier-Journal,* and *Lafayette Journal & Courier,* as well as the Associated Press. Those same sources were primary in coverage when the case went to trial, as well as transcripts of court records. Statements not identified as court testimony came in interviews with the author, most of them taped. Reports by Rick Coates in the Michigan weekly newspaper *Northern Express* and by Roy Church in the *Wabash Plain Dealer* also were sources for post-trial information on Arthur Curry. Other news sources are attributed.

1. Laura Lane, Bloomington *Herald-Telephone,* March 18, 1989.

2. Taken from newspaper accounts of Arthur Curry's arrest and trial.

3. Letters from Judge James Dixon's file, Monroe County Circuit Court.

4. Steven Higgs, Bloomington *Herald-Times,* and Bruce Smith, *Indianapolis Star,* April 4, 1990.

5. Steven Higgs, Bloomington *Herald-Times,* April 4, 1990.

6. Letter from Judge James Dixon's file, Monroe County Circuit Court.

7. Dave Bancroft, Lafayette *Journal and Courier,* January 25, 1991.

8. Linda Thomas, Bloomington *Herald-Times,* April 16, 1990.

9. Dave Bancroft, Lafayette *Journal and Courier,* April 13, 1990.

10. Ibid.

11. From Cook Inc. files, Dennis Troy.

12. Ibid.

13. Bruce Gray, *Indiana Daily Student,* March 4, 1993.

14. Court records, trial, appeal.

15. Pete Winton, *Indiana Daily Student,* April 3, 1990.

16. Brett Corbin, Marion *Chronicle-Tribune,* June 13, 2003.

17. Roy Church, *Wabash Plain Dealer,* March 7, 2006.

18. Brett Corbin, Marion *Chronicle-Tribune,* June 13, 2003.

19. Rick Coates, *Northern Express,* December 7, 2006.

20. James Boyd, Bloomington *Herald-Times,* March 3, 2006, and news release, Susan W. Brooks, U.S. attorney for the Southern District of Indiana.

21. Roy Church, *Wabash Plain Dealer,* September 21, 2006.

22. Roy Church, in interview with the author, 2007.

23. Indiana State Police records (internet).

17. The Future

1. Sunny Schubert, Bloomington Sunday *Herald-Times,* May 22, 1977.

18. Power and Opportunity

1. Review, "What's On in London" (see www.visitlondon.com), December 22, 1999.

19. Restorations

1. All excerpts from Mary Ruth Willis, *A Graham Chronicle: Records of the Craig and Graham Families of Graham, and including Kintners of Indiana, Hunts of Kentucky* (Dallas: privately published, 1977).

2. National Governors Association records, 1931.

3. Chris Bundy, *French Lick Springs Resort: America's Grande Dame* (self-published, 2006); Chris Bundy, *West Baden Springs: Legacy of Dreams* (self-published, 2007).

4. Marsh Davis, speech, West Baden Springs Hotel reopening, May 23, 2007.

5. Randall P. Shepard, speech, West Baden Springs Hotel dedication banquet, June 23, 2007.

6. Wikipedia, "List of World's Largest Domes."

7. Laura Lane, Bloomington *Herald-Times,* August 1, 2006.

8. Shepard address.

index

BOB HAMMEL served as a sports editor and columnist on Indiana newspapers for fifty-two years, starting at age 17. From 1966 until his retirement in 1996, he was sports editor for the Bloomington *Herald-Times,* then a Sunday op-ed columnist for the newspaper until 2006. He was named Indiana Sportswriter of the Year seventeen times by the National Sportscasters and Sportswriters Association. In 1995 he received the Curt Gowdy Award from the National Basketball Hall of Fame, and in 1996 he was awarded the Indiana Basketball Hall of Fame's silver medal for distinguished service. In 1996 he received the Bert McGrane Award of the Football Writers Association of America, the Jake Wade Award of the College Sports Information Directors Association, and the Fred Russell Award of the All-American Football Foundation. He was inducted into the U.S. Basketball Writers Association Hall of Fame in 1990, the Indiana Journalism Hall of Fame in 1997, and the Indiana Sportswriters and Broadcasters Association Hall of Fame in 1998. He is the author of eight books, including *Beyond the Brink with Indiana* (1987) and *A Banner Year at Indiana* (1993), both published by Indiana University Press. With Bob Knight, he authored *Knight: My Story.*

SPONSORING EDITOR
Janet Rabinowitch

MANAGING EDITOR
Miki Bird

PRODUCTION DIRECTOR
Bernadette Zoss

BOOK AND JACKET DESIGN
Pamela Rude

COMPOSITION
Tony Brewer